THE LIFE OF JESUS CHRIST

and

BIBLICAL REVELATIONS

Volume II

Blessed Anne Catherine Emmerich
1774-1824
Mystic, Stigmatist, Visionary and Prophet

THE LIFE OF JESUS CHRIST

AND

BIBLICAL REVELATIONS

From the Visions of the

Blessed Anne Catherine Emmerich

as recorded in the journals of Clemens Brentano

Arranged and edited by the Very Reverend
Carl E. Schmöger, C.SS.R.

Translated by an American Nun

Volume II

"But they that are learned shall shine as the brightness of the firmament; and they that instruct many in justice, as stars for all eternity."
—Daniel 12:3

TAN Books
Charlotte, North Carolina

Nihil Obstat: Em. De Jaegher
                  Can. lib. cens.
                  Brugis, 14 Februarii 1914

Imprimatur: A. C. De Schrevel
                  Vicar General
                  Brugis, 14 Februarii 1914

This English translation published in 1914 by Desclée De Brouwer
& Co. of Lille, Paris, and Bruges, in conjunction with The Sentinel
Press of New York. Reprinted by Academy Library Guild in 1954,
and later by Apostolate of Christian Action, both of Fresno, Cali-
fornia. Reprinted in 1979 by TAN Books. Retypeset and repub-
lished again in 1986 by TAN Books; full-size edition (same content
with enlarged type) published in 2004 by TAN Books.

ISBN: Vol. 1 978-0-89555-787-2
ISBN: Vol. 2 978-0-89555-788-9
ISBN: Vol. 3 978-0-89555-789-6
ISBN: Vol. 4 978-0-89555-790-2
ISBN: Set 978-0-89555-791-9

Cover picture, *Christ Expelling the Money-Changers from the Temple*, by Carl
Bloch (1834-1890), Copyright © Frederiksborg Slot–Hope Gallery, Inc., Provo,
Utah.

Printed and bound in the United States of America.

TAN Books
Charlotte, North Carolina
www.TANBooks.com

2011

"But there are also many other things which Jesus did; which, if they were written every one, the world itself, I think, would not be able to contain the books that should be written."

—St. John the Evangelist
(John 21:25)

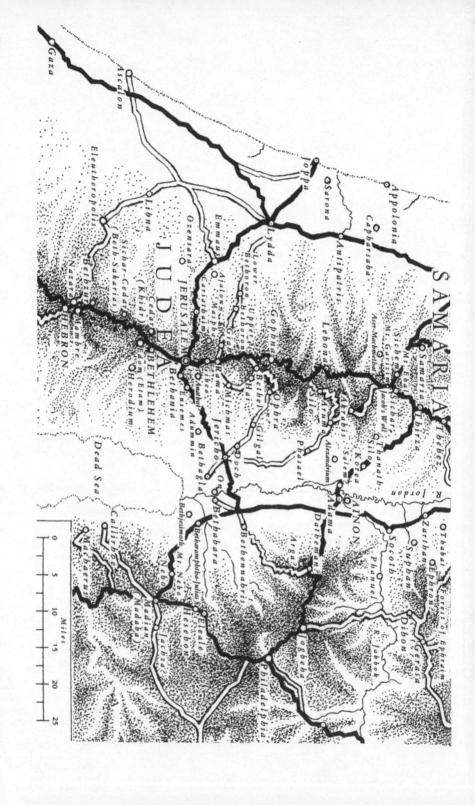

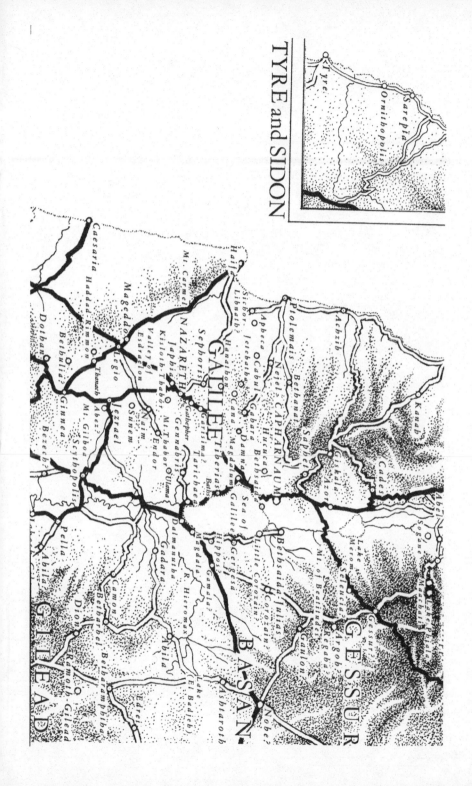

TYRE and SIDON

Sarepta
Ornithopolis
Tyre

Caesaria
Haddad-Rimmon
Dotha?
Bethulia?
Ginnea
Bezech?
Thanath
Megiddo
Mt. Gilboa
Scythopolis
Legio
Jezrael
Pella
Abila
Mt. Carmel
Sichor-libnath?
NAZARETH
Valley of
Esdraelon
Abez?
Sunem
Endor
Naim
Ulama
Mt. Tabor
Thabor
Kisloth-
Iaphia
Gabathon?
Sepphoris
Libnath?
Haifa
Hanabon
Apheca
Ocheni
Cabra
Danna
Magdalum
Bethsaida
Huncao
Netel
Bethana
Ptolemais
Achzib
Sabet
Kanab?
Cades
Azo
Cineroth
Giskala
CAPHARNAUM
Tiberias
Bethsaida-Julias
Corozain?
Little Corozain
Gergesa
Hippos?
Sea of
Galilee
Gamala?
Magdala
R. Hieromax
Lake
(El Badjeb)
Abila
Gadara
Dalmanutha
Camon
Betharbel
Dion
Ramoth Gilead
Edrei
Mt. of Beatitudes
Mt. Seleucia
Argob
Regaba
Gaulon?
Lake Merom
Sogane
Nobe?
Marabala
Sbtaroth
GAULANITIS
GESSUR
BASAN
GILEAD
GALILEE

Anne Catherine Emmerich

Anne Catherine Emmerich was born on September 8th, 1774, at Flamske, near Koesfeld, Westphalia, in West Germany, and became a nun of the Augustinian Order on November 13th, 1803, in the Convent of Agnetenberg at Dülmen (also in Westphalia). She died on February 9th, 1824. Although of simple education, she had perfect consciousness of her earliest days and could understand the liturgical Latin from her first time at Mass.

During most of her later years she would vomit up even the simplest food or drink, subsisting for long periods almost entirely on water and the Holy Eucharist. She was told in a mystic vision that her gift of seeing past, present and future was greater than that possessed by anyone else in history.

From the year 1812 until her death, she bore the stigmata of Our Lord, including a cross over her heart and wounds from the crown of thorns. Though Anne Catherine Emmerich was an invalid confined to bed during her later years, her funeral was nevertheless attended by a greater concourse of mourners than any other remembered by the oldest inhabitants of Dülmen.

Her mission in life seems to have been to suffer in expiation for the godlessness that darkened the "Age of Enlightenment" and the era of the Napoleonic wars, a time during which she saw her convent closed and her order suppressed by Napoleon.

During the last five years of her life the day-by-day transcription of her visions and mystical experiences was recorded by Clemens Brentano, poet, literary leader, friend of Goethe and Görres, who, from the time he met her, abandoned his distinguished career and devoted the rest of his life to this work.

The immense mass of notes preserved in his journals forms one of the most extensive case histories
of a mystic ever kept and provides the source for the
material found in this book, plus much of what is
found in her two-volume definitive biography written by V. Rev. Carl E. Schmöger, C.SS.R.

Preface

This book is the first and only English version of the combined Biblical visions of the Blessed Servant of God, Anne Catherine Emmerich. The original was published in 1914 by Desclée, de Brouwer (Bruges, Belgium) as *The Lowly Life and Bitter Passion of Our Lord and Saviour Jesus Christ and His Blessed Mother, together with the Mysteries of the Old Testament.*

The text is that of the 4th German edition of the 1881 version of the Very Rev. Carl E. Schmöger, C.SS.R., a compilation of the three classic works: *The Life of Our Lord and Saviour Jesus Christ, The Bitter Passion of Our Lord Jesus Christ,* and *The Life of Mary.* The translation was made by an American nun, since deceased, who wished to remain anonymous.

The first edition was issued with the approval and warm recommendation of the following members of the American hierarchy: Cardinal Gibbons, Archbishops Gross, Feehan and Elder, and Bishop Toebbe. It also included testimonials from Michael Wittman, Bishop of Ratisbon, Dean Overberg, Sister Emmerich's spiritual director, Count Leopold von Stolberg, J. J. Goerres, Dom Prosper Guéranger and several others less well known in our day. To this list might be added the names of Claudel, the Maritains, Huysmans, Father Gerard Manley Hopkins, Leon Bloy . . . to name but a few who have written in glowing terms of the saintly "Bride of the Passion" who was privileged to bear the wounds of Him whose life she beheld in the prophetic eye of her spirit.

The publishers, in reprinting these volumes, do so in complete and willing conformity to the decrees of Pope Urban VIII respecting private revelations, persons not as yet canonized, and the prudence with

which all alleged supernatural phenomena not attested
to by the Church must properly be regarded. The final
decision in all such matters rests with the See of
Rome, to which the publishers humbly submit.

Like other private revelations, Sister Emmerich's
accounts of the life of Our Lord, His Blessed Mother,
and other biblical personages should be treated with
that respect and that degree of faith which they seem
to merit when compared with the holy dogmas of our
Faith as derived from Scripture and Tradition, as
well as when compared with our knowledge of history, geography, and science. These revelations are
not, of course, guaranteed free from all error, as are
the Sacred Scriptures. The *Imprimatur* which these
books bear simply means they have been judged by
ecclesiastical authority to be free of error in matters
of faith and morals. Nevertheless, these revelations
show a remarkable harmony with what is known
about the history, geography, and customs of the
ancient world.

The visions of Anne Catherine Emmerich provide
a wealth of information not found in the Bible. In
these times of disbelief, when the Sacred Scriptures
are so often regarded as symbolical narratives with
little historical value, the visions of this privileged
soul providentially confirm the Christian's faith in
the rock-solid reality of the life of Our Lord Jesus
Christ, of His words, His deeds, and His miracles.

In addition, Sister Emmerich's visions show how
our sacred religious heritage goes back in an unbroken line all the way to the time of Adam, to the very
beginning of the world—a line which no other religion but the Roman Catholic can claim. These revelations show how the Roman Catholic Church
faithfully follows the teachings, and administers the
Sacraments, of Jesus Christ Himself—which teachings and Sacraments are in turn the perfect fulfillment of the Old Testament religion.

This crucial fact, which has been almost totally

forgotten in our day, is nevertheless all-important in proving which is the one true religion established by Almighty God. The unbroken line of the Roman Catholic Church becomes obvious to all who read these accounts of the marvelous events which Anne Catherine Emmerich was privileged to behold. For this reason alone, they are priceless—a gift of Divine Providence to an unbelieving world.

May God guide these revelations into the hands of those who need them most. May they do immense good for souls, both in time and for eternity.

—The Publishers
January 31, 1986
Feast of St. John Bosco

Contents of Volume II

JESUS IN THE DESERT. MARRIAGE FEAST OF CANA.
JESUS CELEBRATES THE PASCH IN JERUSALEM
FOR THE FIRST TIME

FROM THE CLOSE OF THE FIRST PASCH
TO THE CONVERSION OF THE
SAMARITAN WOMAN AT JACOB'S WELL

JESUS' TEACHING MISSION IN THE
COUNTRY OF GENESARETH AND ON THE
BANKS OF THE JORDAN

FROM THE SECOND FEAST OF TABERNACLES TO
THE FIRST CONVERSION OF MAGDALEN

THE LIFE OF
JESUS CHRIST

and

BIBLICAL REVELATIONS

Volume II

JESUS IN THE DESERT. MARRIAGE FEAST OF CANA. JESUS CELEBRATES THE PASCH IN JERUSALEM FOR THE FIRST TIME

1. The Forty Days' Fast of Jesus

Accompanied by Lazarus, Jesus went to the inn belonging to the latter situated near the desert. It was just before the hour at which the Sabbath began. Lazarus was the only one whom Jesus had told that after forty days, He would return. From this inn He began His journey into the desert alone and barefoot. He went at first, not toward Jericho, but southward toward Bethlehem, as if He wished to pass between the residence of Anne's relatives and that of Joseph's near Maspha. But He turned off toward the Jordan, shunned the different cities and villages by taking the footpaths around them, and passed that place near which the Ark had once stood and at which John had celebrated the feast.

About one hour's distance from Jericho, He ascended the mountain and entered a spacious grotto. This mountain rises to the southeast of Jericho, and faces Madian across the Jordan.

Jesus began His fast here near Jericho, continued it in different parts of the desert on the other side of the Jordan, and after the devil had borne Him to the top of the mountain, concluded it where it had been commenced. From the summit of this mountain, which is in some parts covered with low brushwood, in others barren and desolate, the view is very extended. Properly speaking, it is not so high as

1

Jerusalem, because it lies on a lower level; but rising abruptly from low surroundings, its solitary grandeur is the more striking. The height that commands the whole plateau upon which stand the Holy City and its environs is the Mount of Calvary, the loftiest point of which is almost on a level with the highest parts of the Temple. On the south side, the nearest to Bethlehem, Jerusalem is flanked by rocks dangerously steep. There was no gate on this side, the whole being taken up by palaces.

It was night when Jesus climbed that steep, wild mountain in the desert now called Mount Quarantania. Three spurs, each containing a grotto, rise one above another. Jesus climbed to the topmost of all, from the back of which one could gaze down into the steep, gloomy abyss below. The whole mountain was full of frightfully dangerous chasms. Four hundred years before, a Prophet, whose name I forget, had sojourned in that same cave. Elias, also, had dwelt there secretly for a long time and had enlarged it. Sometimes, without anyone's knowing whence he came, he used to go down among the inhabitants of the surrounding district to prophesy and restore peace. About twenty-five Essenians one hundred and fifty years ago dwelt on this mountain. It was at its foot that the camp of the Israelites was pitched when, with the Ark of the Covenant, they marched around Jericho to the sound of trumpets. The fountain whose water Eliseus rendered sweet was not far off. St. Helena caused these grottoes to be transformed into chapels. In one of them, I once saw on the wall a picture of the Temptation. At a later period a convent arose on the summit of the mountain. I wondered how the workmen could get up there. Helena erected churches on numerous sacred spots. It was she who built the church over Mother Anne's birthplace two hours from Sephoris. In Sephoris itself Anne's parents owned a house. How sad that most of these holy places have gone to ruin, some even

lost to memory! When as a young girl I used to go
before the day through the snows of winter to Coes-
feld to church, I used to see all those holy places so
plainly. And I often saw how good men, to save them
from destruction, would cast themselves flat in the
road before the destroying soldiers.

The words of Scripture: "He was led by the Spirit
into the desert," mean that the Holy Spirit, who
descended upon Jesus at the moment of His baptism
when He allowed His Humanity to be, in some measure, visibly penetrated by the Divinity, impelled Him
to go into the desert to prepare as Man in close communication with His Heavenly Father for His vocation to suffering.

Jesus, kneeling in the grotto with outstretched
arms, prayed to His Heavenly Father for strength
and courage in all the sufferings that awaited Him.
He saw all in advance, and begged for the grace necessary for each. All His afflictions, all His pains passed
before me in vision, and I saw Him receiving consolation and merit for every one. A cloud of white light,
large like a church, descended and hovered over Him.
At the end of each prayer spirits approached Him.
When close to Him, they assumed a human form,
offered Him homage, and presented to Him consolation and promises from On High. I saw then that
Jesus here in the desert acquired for us all our consolation, all our strength, our help, our victory in
temptation; purchased for us merit in struggle and
conquest; gave value to our fasting and mortifica-
tions; and offered to God the Father all His future
labors and sufferings, in order to give worth to the
prayers and spiritual works of all His faithful followers in the ages to come. I saw the treasure that
He thereby laid up for the Church, and which she,
in the forty days' fast, opens to her children. During this prayer, Jesus sweat Blood.

From this mountain Jesus went down again toward
the Jordan to the country between Gilgal and John's

place of baptism, about an hour further on to the
south. He crossed that narrow but deep part of the
river on a beam, and journeyed on leaving Bethabara
to the right. Crossing several highroads that led to
the Jordan, He took the rugged mountain paths from
the southeast through the wilderness. Proceeding
through the valley leading to Callirrhoe, He crossed
a small stream and climbed a mountain spur a little to the north where Jachza lies in a valley opposite. The Children of Israel defeated Sihon, king of
the Amorrhites, here in a battle in which the Israelites
were only three against sixteen. But God wrought a
miracle in behalf of His people. A frightful noise
swept over the Amorrhites and terrified them.

Jesus was now upon a very wild mountain range
about nine hours from the Jordan, and far more savage and desolate than the one near Jericho, almost
opposite to which it lies.

The Divinity of Jesus, as well as His mission, was
hidden from Satan. The words: "This is My beloved
Son in whom I am well pleased," were understood
by Satan as spoken of a mere human being, a
Prophet. Jesus had already been frequently and in
many ways interiorly afflicted. The first temptation
that He experienced was: "This nation is so corrupt.
Shall I suffer all this and yet not perfect the work
for which I came upon earth?" But with infinite love
and mercy, He conquered the temptation in the face
of all His torments.

Jesus prayed in the grotto sometimes prostrate,
again kneeling, or standing. He wore His customary
dress, but ungirded, loose and flowing, His feet bare.
His mantle, a pair of wallets, and the girdle lay on
the ground nearby. Daily was His labor of prayer different; daily did He acquire for us new graces, those
of today unlike those of the preceding eve. Were it
not for this labor of His, our resistance against temptation would never have been meritorious.

Jesus neither ate nor drank, but I saw Him

strengthened by angels. He was not emaciated by His long fast, though He became perfectly pale and white.

The grotto was not quite on the summit of the mountain. In it was an aperture through which the wind blew chill and raw, for at that season it was cold and foggy. The rocky walls of the grotto were streaked with colored veins; had they been polished, one would have thought them painted. There was space enough in it to afford room for Jesus, whether kneeling or prostrate, without His being directly under the aperture. The rock outside was overgrown by straggling briars.

One day I saw Jesus prostrate on His face. His unsandaled feet were red, wounded by the rugged roads, for He had come to the wilderness barefoot. At times He arose, and again prayed lying prostrate. He was surrounded by light. Suddenly a sound from Heaven was heard, light streamed into the grotto, and myriads of angels appeared bearing with them all kinds of things. I was so afflicted, so overcome, that I felt as if pressed into the rocky wall of the grotto; and, filled with the sensation of one falling, I began to cry out: "I shall fall! I shall fall next to my Jesus!"

And now I beheld the angelic band bending low before Jesus, offering Him their homage, and begging leave to unfold to Him their mission. They questioned Him as to whether it was still His will to suffer as man for the human race, as it had been His will to leave the bosom of His Heavenly Father, to become incarnate in the Virgin's womb. When Jesus answered in the affirmative, accepting His sufferings anew, the angels put together before Him a high cross, the parts of which they had brought with them. It was in shape such as I always see it, of four pieces, as I always see the winepress of the cross. The upper part of the trunk, that is the part that arose between two inserted arms, was likewise separate.

Five angels bore the lower portion; three, the upper; three, the left and three, the right arm; three, the ledge whereon His feet rested; and three carried a ladder. Another had a basket full of ropes, cords, and tools, while others bore the spear, the reed, the rods, the scourges, the crown of thorns, the nails, the robes of derision—in a word, all that figured in His Passion.

The cross appeared to be hollow. It could be opened like a cupboard, and then it displayed the innumerable instruments of torture with which it was filled. In the central part, where Jesus' Heart was broken, were entwined all possible emblems of pain in all kinds of frightful instruments, and the color of the cross itself was heartrending, the color of blood.

The various parts presented different tints symbolical of the pain there to be endured, but all, like so many streams, converged to the heart. The different instruments were likewise symbolical of future pains.

In the cross were also vessels of vinegar and gall, as well as ointment, myrrh, and something like herbs, prefiguring perhaps to Jesus His death and burial.

There were also numbers of open scrolls like billets of about a hand in width. They were of various colors, and on them were written pains and labors to be realized by sufferings of innumerable kinds. The colors were significant of the several degrees and species of darkness which were to be enlightened and dissipated by that suffering. What was utterly lost was typified by black; aridity, dryness, agitation, confusion, negligence were symbolized by brown; red was significant of all that was heavy, earthly, sensual; while yellow betokened effeminacy and horror of suffering. Some of the scrolls were half yellow and half red; they had to be bleached entirely white. There were others white like currents of milk, and the writing on them shone and glittered. They signified the won, the finished.

These colored bands of writing were like the summing up of all the pains that Jesus would have to endure in His mortal life, all His labors, all that the Apostles and others would cause Him to suffer.

Then there appeared before Him, as in a procession, all those men through whom were to come the most keenly felt sufferings He would have to endure, the malice of the Pharisees, the treason of Judas, the insults of the Jews at His bitter and ignominious death.

The angels arranged all, unfolded all before the Saviour, doing all with unspeakable reverence, like priests performing the holiest functions. While thus the entire Passion was unfolded and passed in detail before His gaze, I saw Jesus and the angels weeping.

On another occasion, I saw the angels placing before Jesus the ingratitude of men, the skepticism, the scorn, the mockery, the treachery, the denial of friends and of enemies up to the moment of His death and after it. All passed before Him in pictures, as also those sufferings and labors of His that would bear no fruit. But for His consolation, they showed Him likewise all that would be gained by them. As these pictures floated past, the angels pointed them out with a motion of the hand.

In all these visions of Jesus' Passion, I always saw His cross composed of five kinds of wood, the arms set in with a wedge under each, and a block upon which the feet were to rest. The piece above the head, on which was the inscription, I saw put on separately, for the trunk of the cross was too low to admit of the writing over the head. It fitted on like the cover on a needle case.

Jesus Tempted in Many Ways by Satan

Satan knew not of the Divinity of Christ. He took Him for a Prophet. He had noted His holiness from early youth, as also that of His Mother. But Mary

took no notice whatever of Satan. She never listened
to a temptation. There was nothing in her upon which
Satan could fasten. Though the fairest of women, the
fairest of virgins, she never thought of a suitor excepting at the holy lottery, at the flowering of the rods
in the Temple, when there was question of her marriage. That Jesus was wanting in a certain pharisaical severity toward His disciples in nonessential
points, puzzled the wicked fiend. He took Him for a
man, because the pretended irregularities of His disciples scandalized the Jews.

As Satan had often seen Jesus fired with zeal, he
thought at one time to irritate Him by assuming the
appearance of one of the disciples who had followed
Him thither; and as he had also seen examples of
His tenderness of heart, he tried at another time,
under the form of a decrepit old man, to excite His
compassion; and again as an Essenian, to dispute
with Him. I saw him therefore at the entrance of the
grotto under the form of the son of one of the three
widows, a youth especially loved by Jesus. He made
a noise to attract attention, thinking that Jesus would
be displeased at His disciple's following Him against
His prohibition. Jesus did not look toward him even
once. Then Satan put his head in and began to talk,
first of one thing, then of another, and at last of John
the Baptist who, he said, was very indignant at Jesus
for encroaching upon his rights, by allowing His disciples to baptize from time to time.

Foiled in this first ruse, Satan tried another. He
sent seven, eight, or nine apparitions of the disciples
into the grotto. In they came one after another, saying to Jesus that Eustachius had informed them that
He was there, and that they had sought Him with so
much anxiety. They begged Him not to expose His
life in that wild abode, not to abandon them. The
whole world was talking about Him, they continued,
and He should not allow such and such things to be
said. But Jesus' only reply was: "Withdraw, Satan! It

is not yet time," and the phantoms disappeared.

Again Satan drew near under the form of a feeble old man, a venerable Essenian, toiling painfully up the steep mountain. The ascent seemed so difficult for him that, really, I pitied him. Approaching the grotto, with a loud groan he fell fainting from exhaustion at its entrance. But Jesus took no notice of him, not even by a glance. Then the old man arose with an effort, and introduced himself as an Essenian from Mount Carmel. He had, he said, heard of Jesus and, though almost worn out by the effort, had followed Him thither in order to sit with Him a little while and converse on holy things. He too knew what it was to fast and to pray, and when two joined their prayers to God, edification became greater. Jesus uttered a few words only, such as: "Retire, Satan! It is not yet time." Then I discovered that it was Satan, for as he turned away and vanished, I saw him becoming dark and horrible to behold. I felt like laughing when I thought of his throwing himself on the ground and of having to pick himself up again.

When Satan next came to tempt Jesus, he assumed the appearance of old Eliud. Satan must have known that His Cross and Passion had been shown to Jesus by the angels, for he said that he had had a revelation of the heavy trials in store for Him, and that he felt He would not be able to resist them. For a forty days' fast, he continued, Jesus was not in a state; therefore, urged by love for Him, he had come to see Him once more, to beg to be allowed to share His wild abode and assume part of His vow. Jesus noticed not the tempter, but raising His hands to Heaven, He said: "My Father, take this temptation from Me!" whereupon Satan vanished in a horrible form.

Jesus was kneeling in prayer when, after a time, I saw three youths approaching. They were those who, on His first departure from Nazareth, were with

Him and who subsequently abandoned Him. They
appeared to approach timidly. They cast themselves
on the ground before Him, complaining that they
could find no rest until He pardoned them. They
begged Him to have mercy on them, to receive them
again to favor, and allow them to share His fast as
a penance for their defection, and they promised
thenceforth to be His most faithful disciples. They
had ventured into the grotto, and they surrounded
Jesus with tears and loud lamentation. Jesus rose
from His knees, raised His hands to God, and the
apparitions vanished.

On another day as He knelt in the grotto praying, I beheld Satan in a glittering robe borne, as it
were, through the air up the steepest and highest
side of the rock. This precipitous, inaccessible side
faced to the east; in it were some apertures opening into the grotto. Jesus glanced not toward Satan,
who was now intent on passing himself off for an
angel. But he was a poor imitation, for the light that
enveloped him was far from transparent. It looked
as if it had been smeared on, and his robe was stiff
and harsh, while those of the angels are soft and
light and transparent. Hovering at the entrance of
the grotto, Satan spoke: "I have been sent by Thy
Father to console Thee." Jesus turned not toward
him. Then Satan flew around to the steep, inaccessible side of the grotto and, peering in through one
of the apertures, called to Jesus to witness a proof
of his angelic nature, since he could hover there
without support. But Jesus noticed him not. Seeing
himself foiled in every attempt, Satan became quite
horrible, and made as if he would seize Jesus in his
claws through the aperture. His figure grew still
more frightful and he vanished. Jesus looked not
after him.

Satan came next under the appearance of an aged
solitary from Mount Sinai. He was quite wild, almost
savage-looking, with his long beard and scanty cov-

ering, a rough skin being his only garment. But there
was something false and cunning in his countenance
as he climbed painfully up the mountain. Entering
the grotto, he addressed Jesus, saying that an Essenian from Mount Carmel had visited him and told
him of the baptism, also of the wisdom, the miracles, and the present rigorous fasting of Jesus. Hearing which, notwithstanding his great age, he had
come all the way to see Him, to converse with Him,
for he himself had long experience in the practice of
mortification. He told Jesus that He should now desist
from further fasting, that he would free Him from
what remained, and he went on with much more talk
in the same strain. Jesus, looking aside, said: "Depart
from Me, Satan!" At these words, the evil one grew
dark and, like a huge, black ball, rolled with a crash
down the mountain.

Then I asked myself how it was that Christ's Divinity remained so concealed from Satan. And I received
the following instruction: I understood clearly that
it was the most incomprehensible advantage for men
that neither they nor Satan knew of Christ's Divinity, and that they were thereby to learn how to exercise faith. The Lord said one word to me that I still
remember. *"Man,"* said He, *"knew not that the serpent tempting him was Satan; in like manner, Satan
was not to know that He who redeemed man was
God."* I saw too that the Divinity of Christ was not
made known to Satan until the moment in which He
freed the souls from Limbo.

On one of the subsequent days, I saw Satan under
the form of a distinguished man of Jerusalem. He
approached the cave in which Jesus was praying and
told Him that sympathy had urged him to come to
Him, for he felt assured that He was called to give
freedom to the Jewish nation. Then he related all
the reports, all the discussions rife in Jerusalem on
His account, and told Him that he had come to offer
his support in the good cause. He was one of Herod's

officers, he said. Jesus might unhesitatingly accompany him back to Jerusalem, might even take up His abode in Herod's palace, where He could lie concealed, gather His followers around Him, and set His undertaking on foot. And he urged Him to return with him at once. The pretended officer laid his proposal before Jesus in a multiplicity of words. Jesus looked not toward him, but continued earnestly to pray. Then I saw Satan retreating, his form becoming frightful, fire and smoke bursting from his nostrils, until at last he vanished.

When Jesus began to hunger, and especially to thirst, Satan appeared in the form of a pious hermit and exclaimed: "I am so hungry! I pray Thee give me of the fruits growing here on the mountain outside Thy grotto. I would pluck none of it without asking the owner" (pretending that he took Jesus for the owner), "then let us sit together and talk of good things." Not at the entrance of the grotto, but on the opposite side, that is, toward the east, and at a little distance, grew figs and berries, and another kind of fruit something like nuts, though with soft shells like those of the medlar. Jesus answered the false hermit: "Depart from Me! Thou art from the very beginning *the* liar. Harm not the fruit!" Then I saw Satan as a little somber figure hurrying off, a black vapor exhaling from him.

But he returned again in the form of a traveller, and asked Jesus for permission to eat of the fine grapes growing nearby, because they were so good for thirst. But Jesus gave him no answer, did not even look at him.

On the following day, Satan tempted Jesus again on the same head, only this time it was with a spring instead of fruit.

Satan Tempts Jesus by Magical Arts

Satan appeared to Jesus in the grotto as a magician and philosopher. He told Him that he had come to Him as to a wise man, and that he would show Him that he, too, could exhibit marvels. Then he showed Him hanging on his hand a piece of apparatus like a globe, or perhaps still more like a bird cage. Jesus would not look at the tempter, much less into the globe as Satan desired, but turning His back on him, He left the grotto. I saw that a look into Satan's raree-show disclosed the most magnificent scenes from nature, lovely pleasure gardens full of shady groves, cool fountains, richly laden fruit trees, luscious grapes, etc. All seemed to be within one's reach, and all was constantly dissolving into ever more beautiful, more enticing scenes. Jesus turned His back on Satan, and he vanished.

This was another temptation to interrupt the fast of Jesus, who now began to thirst and to experience the pangs of hunger. Satan did not yet know what to think of Him. He was aware, it is true, of the Prophecies relating to Him and he felt that He exercised power over himself, but he did not yet know that Jesus was God. He did not know even that He was the Messiah whose advent he so dreaded, since he beheld Him fasting, hungering, enduring temptation; since he saw Him so poor, suffering in so many ways; in a word, since he saw Him in all things so like an ordinary man. In this Satan was as blind as the Pharisees. He looked upon Jesus as a holy man whom temptation might lead to a fall.

Satan Tempts Jesus
To Turn Stones into Bread

Jesus was now suffering from hunger and thirst. I saw Him several times at the entrance of the grotto. Toward evening one day, Satan in the form of a large, powerful man ascended the mountain. He had furnished himself below with two stones as long as little rolls, but square at the ends, which as he mounted he molded into the perfect appearance of bread. There was something more horrible than usual about him when he stepped into the grotto to Jesus. In each hand he held one of the stones, and his words were to this effect: "Thou art right not to eat of the fruit, for it only excites an appetite. But if Thou art the beloved Son of God over whom the Spirit came at baptism—behold! I have made these stones look like unto bread. Do Thou change them into bread." Jesus glanced not toward him, but I heard Him utter these words only: "Man lives not by bread!" These were the only words that I caught distinctly. Then Satan became perfectly horrible. He stretched out his talons as if to seize Jesus (at which action I saw the stones resting on his arms), and fled. I had to laugh at his having to take his stones off with him.

Satan Carries Jesus to the Pinnacle of the Temple, and then to Mount Quarantania. Angels Minister Unto Jesus

Toward evening of the following day, I saw Satan in the form of a majestic angel sweeping down toward Jesus with a noise like the rushing wind. He was clad in a sort of military dress such as I have seen St. Michael wear. But in the midst of his greatest splendor, one might detect something sinister and horrible. He addressed boasting words to Jesus, something in this strain: "I will show Thee who I am, and what I can do, and how the angels bear me up in their hands. Look yonder, there is Jerusalem! Behold the Temple! I shall place Thee upon its highest pinnacle. Then do Thou show what Thou canst do, and see whether the angels will carry Thee down." While Satan thus spoke and pointed out Jerusalem and the Temple, I seemed to see them both quite near, just

in front of the mountain. But I think that it was
only an illusion. Jesus made no reply, and Satan
seized Him by the shoulders and bore Him through
the air. He flew low toward Jerusalem, and placed
Jesus upon the highest point of one of the four towers that rose from the four corners of the Temple,
and which I had not before noticed. The tower to
which Satan bore Jesus was on the west side toward
Zion and opposite the citadel Antonia. The mount
upon which the Temple stood was very steep on that
side. The towers were like prisons, and in one of
them were kept the costly garments of the High Priest.
The roofs of these towers were flat, so that one could
walk on them; but from the center rose a hollow, con-
ical turret capped by a large sphere, upon which
there was standing room for two. From that position, one could view the whole Temple below.

It was on the loftiest point of the tower that Satan
placed Jesus, who uttered no word. Then Satan flew
to the ground, and cried up to Him: "If Thou art the
Son of God, show Thy power and come down also,
for it is written: 'He has given His angels charge
over thee, and in their hands shall they bear thee
up, lest perhaps thou dash thy foot against a stone.'"
Jesus replied: "It is written again: 'Thou shalt not
tempt the Lord, thy God.'" Satan, in a fury, returned
to Jesus, who said: "Make use of the power that hath
been given thee!"

Then Satan seized Him fiercely by the shoulders,
and flew with Him over the desert toward Jericho.
While standing on the tower, I noticed twilight in
the western sky. This second flight appeared to me
longer than the first. Satan was filled with rage and
fury. He flew with Jesus now high, now low, reeling
like one who would vent his rage if he could. He bore
Him to the same mountain, seven hours from Jerusalem, upon which He had commenced His fast.

I saw that Satan carried Jesus low over an old
pine tree on the way. It was a large and still vigor-

ous tree that had stood long ago in the garden of
one of the ancient Essenians. Elias had once lived a
short time in its vicinity. The tree was back of the
grotto and not far from the rugged precipice. Such
trees used to be pierced three times in one season,
and each time they yielded a little turpentine.

Satan flew with the Lord to the highest peak of
the mountain, and set Him upon an overhanging,
inaccessible crag much higher than the grotto. It
was night, but while Satan pointed around, it grew
bright, revealing the most wonderful regions in all
parts of the world. The devil addressed Jesus in
words something like these: "I know that Thou art
a great Teacher, that Thou art now about to gather
disciples around Thee and promulgate Thy doctrines.
Behold, all these magnificent countries, these mighty
nations! Compare with them poor, little Judea lying
yonder! Go rather to these. I will deliver them over
to Thee, if kneeling down Thou wilt adore me!" By
adoration the devil meant that obeisance common
among the Jews, and especially among the Pharisees, when supplicating favors from kings and great
personages. This temptation of Satan was similar to
that other one in which, under the guise of one of
Herod's officers, he had sought to lure Jesus to take
up His abode in the castle of Jerusalem, and had
offered to assist Him in His undertaking. It was
similar in kind, though more extended in degree. As
Satan pointed around, one saw first vast countries
and seas, with their different cities into which kings
in regal pomp and magnificence and followed by
myriads of warriors were triumphantly entering. As
one gazed, these scenes became more and more distinct until, at last, they seemed to be in the immediate vicinity. One looked down upon all their details,
every scene, every nation differing in customs and
manners, in splendor and magnificence.

Satan pointed out in each the features of special
attraction. He dwelt particularly upon those of a

country whose inhabitants were unusually tall and magnificent-looking. They were almost like giants. I think it was Persia. Satan advised Jesus to go there above all to teach. He showed Him Palestine, but as a poor, little, insignificant place. This was a most wonderful vision, so extended, so clear, so grand, and magnificent!

The only words uttered by Jesus were: "The Lord thy God shalt thou adore and Him only shalt thou serve! Depart from Me, Satan!" Then I saw Satan in an inexpressibly horrible form rise from the rock, cast himself into the abyss, and vanish as if the earth had swallowed him.

At the same moment I beheld myriads of angels draw near to Jesus, bend low before Him, take Him up as if in their hands, float down gently with Him to the rock, and into the grotto in which the forty days' fast had been begun. There were twelve angelic spirits who appeared to be the leaders, and a definite number of assistants. I cannot now remember distinctly, but I think it was seventy-two, and I feel that the whole vision was symbolical of the Apostles and the disciples. And now was held in the grotto a grand celebration, one of triumph and thanksgiving, and a banquet was made ready. The interior of the grotto was adorned by the angels with garlands of vine leaves from which depended a victor's crown, likewise of leaves, over the head of Jesus. The preparations were made rapidly, though with marvelous order and magnificence. All was resplendent, all was symbolical. Whatever was needed appeared instantly at hand and in its proper place.

Next came the angels bearing a table, small at first but which quickly increased in size, laden with celestial viands. The food and vessels were such as I have always seen on the heavenly tables, and I saw Jesus, the twelve chief spirits, and also the others partaking of refreshment. But there was no eating by the mouth, though still a real participation, a passing of the essence of the fruits into the partakers. All was spiritual. It was as if the interior signification of the aliments entered into the participants, bearing with it refreshment and strength. But it is inexpressible.

At one end of the table stood a large, shining chalice with little cups around it, the whole similar to that which I have always seen in my visions of the institution of the Blessed Sacrament. But this that I now saw was immaterial, was larger. There was also a plate with thin disks of bread. I saw Jesus pouring something from the large chalice into the cups and dipping morsels of bread into it, which morsels and cups the angels took and carried away. With this the vision ended and Jesus, going out from the grotto, went down toward the Jordan.

The angels that ministered unto Jesus appeared under different forms and seemed to belong to different hierarchies. Those that, at the close of the banquet, bore away the cups of wine and morsels of bread, were clothed in priestly raiment. I saw at the instant of their disappearance, all kinds of supernatural consolation descending upon the friends of Jesus, those of His own time and those of after ages. I saw Jesus appearing in vision to the Blessed Virgin then at Cana, to comfort and strengthen her. I saw Lazarus and Martha wonderfully touched, while their hearts grew warm with the love of Jesus. I saw Mary the Silent actually fed with the gifts from the table of the Lord. The angel stood by her while she, like a child, received the food. She had been a witness of all the temptations and sufferings of Jesus. Her whole life was one of vision and suffering through compassion, therefore such supernatural favors caused her no astonishment. Magdalen, too, was wonderfully agitated. She was at the time busied with finery for some amusement. Suddenly anxiety about her life seized upon her, and a longing rose in her soul to be freed from the chains that bound her. She cast the finery from her hands, but

was laughed at by those around her. I saw many of
the future Apostles consoled, their hearts filled with
heavenly desires. I saw Nathanael in his home thinking of all that he had heard of Jesus, of the deep
impression He had made upon him, and of how he
had cast it out of his mind. Peter, Andrew, and all
the others were, as I saw, strengthened and consoled. This was a most wonderful vision.

During Jesus' fast, Mary resided in the house near
Capharnaum, and had to listen to all kinds of
speeches about her Divine Son. They said that He
went wandering about, no one knew where; that He
neglected her; that after the death of Joseph it was
His duty to undertake some business for His Mother's
support, etc. Throughout the whole country the talk
about Jesus was rife at this time, for the wonders
attendant on His baptism, the testimony rendered
by John, and the accounts of His scattered disciples
had been everywhere noised abroad. Only once after
this, and that was before His Passion, at the resurrection of Lazarus, were reports of Jesus so wide-
spread and active. The Blessed Virgin was grave and
recollected, for she was never without the internal
vision of Jesus, whose actions she contemplated and
whose sufferings she shared.

Toward the close of the forty days, Mary went to
Cana, in Galilee, and stopped with the parents of
the bride of Cana, people of distinction who appeared
to be of the first rank. Their beautiful mansion stood
in the heart of the clean and well-built city. A street
ran through the middle of it, I think a continuation
of the highroad from Ptolomais; one could see it
descending toward Cana from a higher level. This
city was not so irregularly and unevenly built as
many others of Palestine. The bridegroom was almost
of the same age as Jesus and he managed his
mother's household with the cleverness of an old
married man. The parents of the young people consulted the Blessed Virgin upon all the affairs of

their children and showed her everything.

John was at this time constantly occupied in administering baptism. Herod did his best to procure a visit from him, and he likewise sent messengers to draw him out on the subject of Jesus. But John paid very little attention to him, and went on repeating his old testimony of Jesus. From Jerusalem also, messengers were again sent to call him to account concerning Jesus and himself. John answered as usual that he had never laid eyes on Him when he began his own career, but that he had been sent to prepare for Him the way.

Since Jesus' baptism, John taught that through that baptism and the descent of the Holy Spirit upon Him, water had been sanctified and out of it much evil had been cast. Jesus' baptism had been like an exorcism of the water. Jesus had suffered Himself to be baptized in order to sanctify water. John's baptism had in consequence become purer and holier. It was for this end that Jesus was baptized in a separate basin. The water sanctified by contact with His Divine Person had then been conducted to the Jordan and into the public pool of baptism, and of it also Jesus and His disciples had taken some for Baptism in distant towns and villages.

2. Jesus Goes to the Jordan, and Orders Baptism to be Administered

At break of day Jesus went over the Jordan at the same narrow place which He had crossed forty days before. Some logs lay there to facilitate a passage. This was not the usual crossing place, the terminus of the public road, but a neighboring one. Jesus proceeded along the east bank of the river up to a point directly opposite John's place of baptism. John at that moment was busy teaching and baptizing. Pointing straight across the river, he exclaimed: "Behold, the Lamb of God who taketh away the sins of the world." (*John* 1:36). Jesus then turned away from the shore and returned to Bethabara.

Andrew and Saturnin, who had been standing near John, hurried over the river by the same way that Jesus had passed. They were followed by one of the cousins of Joseph of Arimathea, and two others of John's disciples. They ran after Jesus, who, turning, came to meet them, asking what they wanted. Andrew, overjoyed at having found Him once more, asked Him where He dwelt. Jesus answered by bidding them follow Him, and He led them to an inn near the water and outside of Bethabara. There they entered and sat down. Jesus stayed all this day with the five disciples in Bethabara, and took a meal with them. He talked of His teaching mission about to begin and of His intention to choose His disciples. Andrew mentioned to Him many of his own acquaintances whom he recommended as suitable for the work, among others Peter, Philip, and Nathanael. Then Jesus spoke of baptizing here at the Jordan, and commissioned some of them to do so. Whereupon they objected that there was no convenient place around those parts. The only suitable locality was where John was baptizing, and it would never do to interfere with him. But Jesus spoke of John's vocation and mission, remarking that his work was well nigh its completion, and confirming all that John had said of himself and of the Messiah.

Jesus alluded also to His own preparation in the desert for the mission of teaching that was before Him, and of the preparation necessary before undertaking any important work. Jesus was cordial and confidential toward the disciples, but they were humble and somewhat shy.

Next morning Jesus went with the disciples from Bethabara to a group of houses that stood near the river ferry. Here He taught in presence of a small audience. After that He crossed the river and taught in a little village of about twenty houses, distant

perhaps one hour from Jericho. Crowds of neophytes
and John's disciples kept coming and going, to hear
His words and report them to the Baptist. It was
near midday when Jesus taught here.

After the Sabbath Jesus commissioned several of
the disciples to cross the Jordan and go up the river
to the distance of about one hour from Bethabara,
there to prepare a pool for Baptism. The site chosen by Jesus was that upon which John, when going
down from Ainon, had baptized before he had crossed
to the west bank of the river opposite Bethabara.

The people of this place wanted to give Jesus an
entertainment, but He would not stay. He crossed
the Jordan and returned to Bethabara where He celebrated the Sabbath and taught in the synagogue.
He ate with the principal of the school and slept in
his house.

The baptismal pool which John had used just
before he removed near Jericho was soon put in
order again by the disciples. It was not quite so large
as that just mentioned. It had an elevated margin
and a projecting tongue of land on which the baptizer could stand. A small canal surrounded it, and
from this the water could be turned into the basin.

There were now as many as three pools for Baptism: that above Bethabara, that of Jesus on the
lately formed island in the Jordan, and that in use
by John.

On Jesus' arrival, He poured into the baptismal
pool some of the water from the well on the island
where He Himself had been baptized, and blessed
it. Andrew had brought the water with him in a
flask. The neophytes became unusually touched and
agitated. Andrew and Saturnin administered Baptism, but not by complete immersion. The neophytes
stood in the water near the edge of the pool, the
sponsors' hands upon their shoulders, while the baptizers, dipping the water up in the hollow of their
hand, poured it thrice over them, baptizing in the

name of the Father and of the Son and of the Holy
Ghost. John baptized somewhat differently. He used
a three-channeled shell for dipping up the water.
Crowds were baptized at this time, most of them
from Peraea.

Jesus, standing on a little green hill nearby,
instructed the people on penance, baptism and the
Holy Ghost. He said: "When I was baptized, my Father
sent down the Holy Ghost and uttered the words,
'This is My beloved Son in whom I am well pleased.'
These words are addressed to everyone that loves
his Heavenly Father and is sorry for his sins. Upon
all that will be baptized in the name of the Father
and of the Son and of the Holy Ghost, He sends His
Holy Spirit. They then become His sons in whom
He is well pleased, for He is the Father of all that
receive His Baptism and to Him by the same are
born again."

It is always a subject of astonishment to me that
the Gospel narratives of the facts in Jesus' life are
so short; for instance, it records the meeting of Jesus
with Peter as happening close upon Andrew's following Jesus after the testimony of John; while in
reality, Peter was at the time not in that part of the
country, but in Galilee. But still more wonderful is
it to read of the Last Supper and the Passion's following so closely the triumphal entrance of Jesus
into Jerusalem, celebrated by us on Palm Sunday,
since I always see so many days, and hear Jesus
delivering so many instructions between the two
events. So I think that Jesus remained here fourteen days before going to Galilee.

Andrew had not as yet been formally received as
a disciple; indeed, Jesus had not even called him.
He had come of himself, had offered himself, for he
would gladly be near Jesus. He was more eager to
serve, more ready to offer service than Peter. Peter
was ever ready to quiet himself with the thought:
"Oh, I am too weak for that! That is beyond my

strength," and so went about his own affairs. Saturnin and the two nephews of Joseph of Arimathea, Aram and Themeni, had, like Andrew, followed Jesus of their own accord.

John's place of baptism was daily becoming less frequented, and many more of his disciples would have gone over to Jesus, had they not been prevented by some others, pertinacious characters, who took it hard that so many of his disciples abandoned John. They complained to him about it, saying that Jesus had no right to baptize in those parts, that He was encroaching upon John's privilege, etc. John had some difficulty in convincing them to the contrary. He told them that they should call to mind his words and how he had always foretold what was now happening. He repeated that his duty was only to prepare the way, which done, he was to desist entirely from the work, and that that would be soon, since the way was almost prepared. But his disciples were greatly attached to him and they would not understand his words. Jesus' baptismal place was already so crowded that He told His disciples they should on the morrow move further down the river.

With about twenty companions, among them Andrew, Saturnin, Aram, and Themeni, Jesus left Bethabara and went over the Jordan at the usual crossing place where the passage was easy. Leaving Gilgal on the right, He went to a very densely settled place called Ophra, situated in a narrow mountain valley. Hither flocked the merchants from the regions beyond Sodom and Gomorrha. With their camels laden with merchandise they passed to the east side of the Jordan, where they were baptized by John. There was at this place a byway leading from Judea to the Jordan. Ophra was in many respects quite forgotten. It was between three and four hours from John's place of baptism, not quite so far from Jericho, and from Jerusalem about seven hours. It was not exposed to the influence of the sun; consequently, though well built, it was cold. The inhabitants were made up of merchants, publicans, and smugglers. They were not exactly wicked, but they were indifferent, and as is often the case among traders and innkeepers, they cleared great profits. It seemed as if they made something off everyone that passed through their city. As yet they had paid little attention to John's baptism; they hungered not after salvation. Things went on here as in places of which it is said: Business thrives there.

When they approached Ophra, Jesus sent the nephews of Joseph of Arimathea on ahead, in order to get the key of the synagogue and to call the people to the instruction. Jesus always entrusted such messages to these youths, for they were very clever and amiable. At the entrance of the city, the possessed and lunatics ran around Jesus, crying out: "Here comes the Prophet, the Son of God, Jesus Christ, our enemy! He will drive us out!" Jesus commanded them to be silent and to cease their frantic gestures. All became quiet and followed Him into the synagogue, to which He had to go from almost one end of the city to the other. There He taught till evening, going out only once to take some refreshment. His theme was, as usual, the nearness of the Kingdom of God and the necessity of Baptism. In vigorous words He warned the inhabitants to awake from their indifference and fancied security, lest judgement should come upon them. He spoke in strong terms against their usury, their smuggling, and such sins as are common to publicans and merchants. His hearers did not contradict Him, though they were not very well disposed. They were captives to their gains. Still some of them were really touched and very much changed by His teaching. That evening several of the most important men of the city, as well as some of the humblest class, called upon Jesus at the inn. They had resolved

to receive baptism, and on the following day they
went to John.

Next morning Jesus and His disciples left Ophra
and returned to Bethabara. On the way they separated, Andrew and the greater number being sent
on ahead by the same route by which they had come;
while Jesus with Saturnin and Joseph of Arimathea's
nephew went on toward John's place of baptism, He
took the same road as at the time upon which John
rendered to Him the first public testimony after His
baptism. On the way He entered some of the houses,
taught their occupants, and exhorted them to Baptism. They reached Bethabara in the afternoon, where
Jesus again delivered an instruction at the place of
Baptism. Andrew and Saturnin baptized the crowds
that succeeded one another. Jesus' teaching was generally the same; viz., that to all that did penance
and were baptized His Heavenly Father had said:
"This is My beloved Son," and that, in truth, all then
became God's children.

Most of those who now received Baptism were under
the jurisdiction of the Tetrarch Philip, who was a good
man. His people were tolerably happy, and therefore
had thought little about receiving Baptism.

From Bethabara Jesus, with three disciples, went
up through the valley to Dibon, where He had lately
been for the Feast of Tabernacles. He taught in some
houses, also in the synagogue, which was somewhat
distant from the city on the road running through
the valley. Jesus did not enter Dibon itself. He stayed
overnight at a poor, retired inn which indeed was
little more than a shed where the field laborers from
the country around obtained food and lodging. It
was now seed time on the sunny side of the valley,
the crops of which were to ripen about the Pasch.
They had to dig the ground here, for it was made
up of soil, sand, and stone. They could not use the
implement generally employed in breaking up the
ground. Part of the standing-out harvest was now

gathered in for the first time. The inhabitants of
this valley, which was about three hours in length,
were good people, of simple habits, and well inclined
toward Jesus.

In the synagogue, as also among the field laborers, Jesus related and explained the parable of the
sower. He did not always explain His parables. He
often related them to the Pharisees without an explanation.

Andrew and Saturnin with some other disciples went
afterward to Ophra, to confirm in their good resolutions those that Jesus had roused by His teaching.

When Jesus left the inn near Dibon, He started
southward for Eleale about four hours distant, taking a road two hours farther to the southeast of the
Jordan than that by which He had come thither
from Bethabara. He arrived with about seven disciples, and put up with one of the Elders of the synagogue. When the Sabbath began, He taught in the
synagogue taking for His subject a parable upon the
waving branches of a tree scattering around their
blossoms and bearing no fruit. By this parable Jesus
intended to rebuke the inhabitants who for the most
part had not become better after having received
John's baptism. They allowed the blossoms of penance
to be scattered by every wind without bearing fruit.
Such were they here. Jesus chose this similitude
because these people found their support chiefly in
the cultivation of fruit. They had to carry it far away
for sale, as no highroad passed near their isolated
city. They were also largely engaged in coarse embroidery and the manufacture of covers.

Up to the present Jesus had met no contradiction. The people of Dibon and the country around
loved Him, and said that never before had they heard
such a teacher. The old men always likened Him to
the Prophets of whose teaching they had heard from
their forefathers.

After the Sabbath Jesus went about three hours

westward to Bethjesimoth on the east side of a mountain, the sunny side, about one hour from the Jordan. Andrew and Saturnin with some others of John's
disciples met Him on the way. Jesus spoke to them
of the Children of Israel who had formerly encamped
here, and of Josue and Moses who had instructed
them, applying it to the present time and to His
own teaching. Bethjesimoth was not a large place,
but it was very fruitful, especially in wine.

Just as Jesus arrived, some demoniacs, who had
been confined together in a house, were led out into
the open air. All at once they began to rage and to
cry: "There He comes, the Prophet! He will drive us
out!" Jesus turned, enjoined silence upon them, commanded their fetters to fall, and that they should
follow Him into the synagogue. Their chains fell
miraculously and the poor creatures became quite
calm. They cast themselves down before Jesus,
thanked Him, and followed Him into the synagogue.
There He taught in parables of the culture of the
vine and its fruitfulness, after which He visited and
cured many sick in their homes. Bethjesimoth did
not lie on any highroad. The people had to carry
their fruit to market themselves.

Jesus healed here for the first time since His return
from the desert. On account of the cures wrought
among them, the people were instant in their prayers
for Him to remain. But He departed. With Andrew,
Saturnin, Joseph of Arimathea's nephews, and others, about twelve in all, He went in an oblique line
toward the north until He reached the public ferry
leading to the highroad of Dibon, over which He had
crossed in going from Gilgal to Dibon at the Feast
of Tabernacles. It takes tolerably long to cross the
river at this point, because the steep bank directly
opposite does not afford a landing place. From here
Jesus and His little company journeyed on for about
an hour over the base of a mountain in the direction of Samaria, until they arrived at a small place

consisting of only one row of houses and which had no school.

It was occupied entirely by shepherds and kind-hearted people, who were habited in almost the same style as the shepherds I saw at the Crib. Jesus taught in the open air on a little elevation whereon a teacher's chair of stone was erected. The people here had received John's baptism.

3. Jesus in Silo, Kibzaim, and Thebez

I next saw Jesus in Silo, a city built around a high, steep rock with an extended plateau on a gently rising mountain range. On this plateau, the highest elevation of the mountain range, in early times after the departure from Egypt and during the journey through the desert, the Tabernacle with the Ark of the Covenant had rested. There was a large space surrounded by a wall partly in ruins, and in it might still be seen the remains of the little building that had been erected over the Tabernacle. On the spot whereon the Ark had stood, under a roof which rested upon open arches, was a pillar similar to the one in Gilgal, and under it a kind of vault excavated in the rocky foundation. Not far from the spot occupied by the Ark was a place for offering sacrifice and a covered pit for the reception of the refuse of the slaughter, for they were permitted to offer sacrifice here three or four times in the year. The synagogue also was built on this enclosed space of the plateau, from which was presented a widely extended view. From it one could see the plateau of Jerusalem, the Sea of Galilee, and far over many mountains.

Silo itself was a somewhat dilapidated and not very populous city. It possessed two schools, one belonging to the Pharisees, the other to the Sadducees. But the people were not good; they were arrogant, full of self-conceit and false assurance. At some distance from the city gate with its dilapidated

towers, stood an Essenian cloister now fallen to ruin,
and nearer to the city was the house wherein the
Benjaminites had confined the virgins whom, at the
Feast of Tabernacles, they had brought captive to
Silo. (*Judges* 21:19-24).

Jesus with His twelve companions put up at a
house at which travelling teachers and prophets were
privileged. It was adjoining the schools and dwellings
of the Pharisees and Scribes, who had a kind of sem-
inary here. About twenty of these Scribes in their
long robes and girdles, with long, rough tufts hanging from their sleeves, gathered around Jesus. They
feigned not to know Him, and spoke of Jesus as of
a third person using all kinds of cutting speeches,
such as: "Now, how will it be? There are two bap-
tisms, that of John and that of Jesus, the carpenter's son of Galilee. Which, now, will be the right
baptism?" They went on to say that they had heard
also that women attached themselves to the mother
of this carpenter's son; for instance, a widow with
her two sons. These latter, at the instigation of their
mother, joined the followers of Jesus, while she herself went with His Mother, and so they travelled
about. But as for themselves, they needed not such
novelties. They had the Promise and the Law. All
this they did not express bluntly and rudely, but with
a semblance of mock friendship for Jesus. He
answered their pointed speeches by saying that He
was the One of whom they were speaking. And when
they referred to the voice heard at His baptism, He
informed them that it was the voice of His Heavenly
Father, who was the Father of everyone who would
repent of his sins and be regenerated by Baptism.

Then, affecting to consider it a very sacred place,
they expressed unwillingness to allow Jesus and
His disciples to enter the enclosure where formerly
the Ark of the Covenant had stood. But Jesus, heed-
less of their opposition, entered. He reproached them
with having, on account of their wickedness, lost

the Ark of the Covenant; that now, preserving only the remembrance of it, they were still just as bad; that they had always violated the Law in the past, as well as in the present; and that, as the Ark had been withdrawn from the keeping of their ancestors, so now would the fulfillment of the Law be taken from themselves. As these men showed a desire to dispute with Him on some points of the Law, He stood them out, two by two, and interrogated them like children, proposing to them many deep questions in the Law. They were unable to answer; so, confused and angry, muttering and nudging one another with the elbow, they began to slink away. Then Jesus led them to the covered pit in which had been thrown the refuse of the sacrifice. He ordered them to uncover it and told them in a similitude that they were like unto that pit, inwardly full of ordure and rottenness and unfit for sacrifice, though outwardly clean, their unsightliness covered over by a fine exterior. He reminded them that from this very spot, as punishment of the sins of their forefathers, the Holy Ark had been taken away. They all left the place in anger.

When Jesus taught in the synagogue, He insisted especially upon the reverence due the aged and love toward parents. He spoke warmly on these points, for the people of Silo had long been in the wicked habit of slighting, despising, and disowning their aged parents.

A road led to Silo from Bethel on the south. Lebona was not far distant, and to Samaria from Bethel, it may have been from eight to nine hours. The Prophet Jonas lies buried at Silo.

When Jesus left Silo from the opposite side of the city, the northwest, Andrew, Saturnin, and Joseph of Arimathea's nephews separated from Him, and proceeded on ahead to Galilee. Jesus with some disciples of John, then in His company, directed His steps to Kibzaim, where He arrived before the Sabbath.

Kibzaim lay in a valley between two branches of a
mountain range that extended through the middle
of the country, and assumed in this place almost the
exact shape of a wolf's claw. The people were good,
hospitable souls, and well-inclined to Jesus, whose
coming they were expecting. Kibzaim was a Levitical city. Jesus put up near the school with one of the
head men.

There arrived also to salute Jesus, Lazarus, Martha,
Johanna Chusa, the son of Simeon (who was employed
at the Temple), and the old servant of the first named.
They were on their way to the wedding at Cana, and
had been informed by messengers that they would
here meet Jesus. Jesus, from the very first, always
treated Lazarus with distinction and as a very dear
friend. And yet I never heard Him ask: How is such
or such a one of thy relatives or acquaintances?

Kibzaim was a solitary place hidden away in a
corner of the mountain. The inhabitants subsisted
chiefly by the cultivation of fruits. The manufacture
of tents and carpets was also carried on, and many
were engaged in sandal-making. Jesus spent the Sabbath here, and cured several sick persons by a word
of command. Some were dropsical and others simpletons. They were brought on litters to Jesus and
set down in front of the school. Jesus took a repast
at the house of a distinguished Levite. After the Sabbath He went again to Sichar, where He arrived late,
and passed the night at an inn appointed for Him.
Lazarus and his party went from Kibzaim straight
to Galilee.

Early next morning, Jesus went from Sichar northeastwardly toward Thebez. In Sichar, or Sichem, He
could not teach. There were no Jews there. The inhabitants were made up of Samaritans and some others who had settled there either after the Babylonian
Captivity, or in consequence of a war. They used to
go up to the Temple at Jerusalem, though they did
not join in the Jewish sacrifices. Near Sichem is that

beautiful field which Jacob bought for his son Joseph.
A part of it already belonged to Herod of Galilee. A
boundary consisting of stakes, a rampart of earth,
and a path ran through the valley.

Thebez was quite an important city, traversed by
a highway and possessed of considerable trade. Heavily laden camels, their burdens rising high upon their
backs, came and went. It was something wonderful
to see those animals with their packs like so many
little towers, climbing slowly over the mountain, their
head at the end of the long neck moving from side
to side before their lofty burden. Raw silk formed a
chief staple of trade. The people of Thebez were not
bad, nor were they prejudiced against Jesus, but they
were neither simple nor childlike. They were indifferent, as well-to-do tradespeople often are. The
priests and Scribes were content with themselves
and indifferent to others. As Jesus entered the city,
the possessed and the lunatics raised their cry: "There
comes the Prophet of Galilee! He has power over us!
He will drive us away!" Jesus commanded them
silence, and instantly they became quiet. Jesus put
up near the synagogue whither the crowds followed
Him, bringing with them their sick, of whom He
healed many. That evening He taught in the school
and celebrated the Feast of Dedication, which then
began. In the school and in all the houses seven
lights were lit, also outdoors in the fields and on the
roads near the shepherds' huts were little burning
tufts of something on the ends of stakes. Thebez was
admirably situated on the mountain. At some distance, one could see the mountain road running
through it and the laden camels climbing up; but
near the city the view was hidden.

Andrew, Saturnin, and Joseph's nephews had
already left Silo and gone to Galilee. Andrew had
been up among his relatives at Bethsaida. He had
informed Peter that he had again found the Messiah, who was taken on His way up to Galilee, and

that he would take him (Peter) to Him. All went now
to Arbela, called also Betharbel, to see Nathanael
Chased, who was there on business, and to induce
him to go with them to celebrate the feast at Gennabris. Chased resided at that time in Gennabris in
a high house that, with several others, stood by itself
outside the city. The disciples spoke much to him of
Jesus. Andrew had purposely taken them there for
the feast because he, as well as they, counted upon
Nathanael. They were eager to hear his opinion, but
Nathanael appeared rather indifferent to the whole
affair.

Lazarus had brought Martha and Johanna Chusa
to Mary then at Capharnaum, whither she had come
from Cana. They set off again for Tiberias where
they hoped to meet Jesus. Simeon's son was one of
the escorts, and the bridegroom of Cana went also
to meet the Lord. This bridegroom was the son of
the daughter of Sobe, the sister of Anne. His name
was Nathanael. He did not belong to Cana, though
he was married there. Gennabris was a populous city.
A highway ran through it, and there was much business and traffic carried on, especially in silk. It was
in the country, a couple of hours from Tiberias, from
which it was separated by mountains. To reach it,
one had to go somewhat southward between Emmaus
and Tiberias, and then turn to the latter. Arbela was
between Sephoris and Tiberias.

4. First Formal Call of
Peter, Philip, and Nathanael

Jesus departed before daybreak from Thebez. He
and His disciples proceeded at first eastward, and
then turning to the north, journeyed along the base
of the mountain and through the valley of the Jordan toward Tiberias. He passed through Abelmahula,
a beautiful city, where the mountain extends more
to the north. It was the birthplace of Eliseus. The

city is built on a spur of the mountain, and I noticed the great difference between the fruitfulness of its sunny side and its northern one. The inhabitants were tolerably good. They had heard of the miracles wrought by Jesus at Kibzaim and Thebez, so they stayed with Him on the way, begging Him to tarry with them and heal their sick. The excitement became almost tumultuous, but Jesus did not stay with them long. This city was about four hours from Thebez. Jesus passed near Scythopolis and on to the Jordan.

As He was journeying from Abelmahula, He met near a little city about six hours from Tiberias, Andrew, Peter, and John. Leaving the other friends in Gennabris, these three had come on to meet Jesus. Peter and John were in this part of the country upon some business connected with their fishery. They intended to proceed direct to Gennabris, but Andrew persuaded them to go first to meet the Lord. Andrew presented his brother to Jesus, who among other words said to him: *"Thou art Simon, the son of Jonas; thou shalt be called Cephas."* This was said at the first salutation. To John, Jesus addressed some words relative to their next meeting. Then Peter and John went out to Gennabris, while Andrew accompanied Jesus into the environs of Tarichaea.

John the Baptist had by this time abandoned his place of baptism on this side of the Jordan. He had crossed the river and was now baptizing about one hour to the north of Bethabara, at the place whereon Jesus had lately allowed the disciples to baptize and where John himself had baptized at an earlier period. John had made this change to suit the convenience of the people from the region under Philip the Tetrarch. Philip was a good-natured man. Many of his people desired baptism, but were unwilling to cross the Jordan to receive it. Among them were many of the heathens. The last visit that Jesus made to this part of the country had roused in numbers the desire after baptism. Another reason also influenced John to baptize where Jesus' disciples had lately been similarly engaged, and that was to show that there was no disunion between him and Jesus.

When Jesus with Andrew reached the neighborhood of Tarichaea, He put up near the lake at a house belonging to Peter's fishery. Andrew had previously given orders for preparations to be made for Jesus' reception. Jesus did not go into the city. There was something dark and repulsive about the inhabitants, who were deeply engaged in usury and thought only of gain. Simon, who here had some employment, had with Thaddeus and James the Less, his brothers, gone for the feast to Gennabris, where James the Greater and John were. Lazarus, Saturnin, and Simeon's son came here to meet Jesus, as also the bridegroom of Cana. The last named invited Jesus and all His company to his marriage.

The principal motive that led Jesus to pass a couple of days in the vicinity of Tarichaea was that He desired to give the future Apostles and disciples time to communicate to one another the reports circulated about Himself, and especially what Andrew and Saturnin had to relate. He desired also that, by more frequent intercourse, they should better understand one another. While Jesus traversed the country around Tarichaea, I saw Andrew remaining in the house. He was busy writing letters with a reed upon strips of parchment. The writings could be rolled into a little hollow, wooden cylinder and unrolled at pleasure. I saw men and youths frequently entering the house, and seeking employment. Andrew engaged them as couriers to convey to Philip and his half-brother Jonathan, also to Peter and the others at Gennabris, letters notifying them that Jesus would go to Capharnaum for the Sabbath and engaging them to meet Him there.

Meanwhile a messenger arrived from Capharnaum begging Andrew to solicit Jesus to go thither right

away, for a messenger from Cades had been there
awaiting Him for the past few days. This man wanted
to ask Jesus for help.

Accordingly, with Andrew, Saturnin, Obed, and
some of John's disciples, Jesus set out from the fisher-
house near Tarichaea to Capharnaum. This last
named city was not close to the lake, but on the
plateau and southern slope of a mountain. On the
western side of the lake, the mountain formed a valley through which the Jordan flowed into the lake.
Jesus and His companions went separately, Andrew
with his half-brother Jonathan, and Philip—both of
whom had come in answer to his notification—walked
together. Jonathan and Philip had not yet met Jesus.
Andrew spoke enthusiastically to them. He told them
all that he had seen of Jesus, and protested that He
was indeed the Messiah. If they desired to follow
Him, he added, there was no need of their presenting to Him a formal petition to that effect; all they
had to do was to regard Him attentively, and He,
seeing their earnest wish, would give them a hint,
a word to join His followers.

Mary and the holy women were not in Capharnaum itself, but at Mary's house in the valley outside the city and nearer to the lake. It was there
that they celebrated the feast. The sons of Mary
Cleophas, Peter, James the Greater, and his brother
John had already arrived from Gennabris with
others of the future disciples. Chased (Nathanael),
Thomas, Bartholomew, and Matthew, however, were
not present. But there were many other relatives
and friends of the Holy Family who had been invited
to Cana for the wedding, celebrating the Sabbath
here, because they had been notified that Jesus was
expected.

Jesus along with Andrew, Saturnin, some of John's
disciples, Lazarus, and Obed, stopped at a house
belonging to the bridegroom Nathanael. Nathanael's
parents were dead. They had left a large patrimony

to their son.

The future disciples, just come from Gennabris, experienced a certain shyness in Jesus' company. They were actuated in this by the influence Nathanael Chased's opinion had over them and then again, by the thought of the wonderful things they had heard of Jesus from Andrew and some others of John's disciples. They were restrained also by their own natural bashfulness and likewise by the remembrance of what Andrew had told them; viz., that they were not to make advances themselves, but merely pay attention to the teaching of Jesus, for that would be sufficient to make them decide to follow Him.

For two whole days had the messenger from Cades been waiting here for Jesus. Now he approached Him, cast himself at His feet, and informed Him that he was the servant of a man of Cades. His master, he said, entreated Jesus to return with him and cure his little son who was afflicted with leprosy and a dumb devil. This man was a most faithful servant; he placed his master's trouble before Jesus in very pathetic words. Jesus replied that He could not return with him, but still the child should receive assistance, for he was an innocent boy. Then He directed the servant to tell his master to stretch himself with extended arms over his son, to recite certain prayers, and the leprosy would disappear. After which, he, the servant himself, should lie upon the boy and breathe into his mouth. A blue vapor would then escape from the boy and he would be freed from dumbness. I had a glimpse of the father and servant curing the boy, as Jesus had directed.

There were certain mysterious reasons for the command that the father and the servant should stretch themselves alternately upon the boy. The servant himself was the true father of the child, of which fact, however, the master was ignorant. But Jesus knew it. Both had therefore to be instrumental in freeing the child from the penalty of sin.

Cades was about six hours from Capharnaum, on the boundary toward Tyre and west of Paneas. It was once the capital of the Canaanites, but was now a free city whither the prosecuted might flee from justice. It bordered on a region called Kabul, which had been presented by Solomon to the king of Phoenicia. I saw this region ever dark, gloomy, dismal. Jesus always shunned it when going to Tyre and Sidon. I think robbery and murder were freely carried on in it.

When on the Sabbath Jesus taught in the synagogue, an unusually large crowd was assembled to hear Him, and among His audience were all His friends and relatives. His teaching was entirely novel to these people, and quite transporting in its eloquence. He spoke of the nearness of the Kingdom of God, of the light that should not be hidden under a bushel, of sowing, and of faith like unto a mustard seed. He taught, not in naked parables, but with explanations. The parables were short examples and similitudes, which He used to explain His doctrine more clearly. I have indeed heard Him in His teaching making use of a great many more parables than are related in the Gospel. Those there recorded are such as He most frequently used with explanations more or less varied to suit the occasion.

After the close of the Sabbath, Jesus went with His disciples into a little vale near the synagogue. It seemed intended for a promenade or a place of seclusion. There were trees in front of the entrance, as well as in the vale. The sons of Mary Cleophas, of Zebedee, and some others of the disciples were with Him. But Philip, who was backward and humble, hung behind, not certain as to whether he should or should not follow. Jesus, who was going on before, turned His head and, addressing Philip, said: "Follow Me!" at which words Philip went on joyously with the others. There were about twelve in the little band.

Jesus taught here under a tree, His subject being

"Vocation and Correspondence." Andrew, who was full
of zeal for his Master's interests, rejoiced at the happy
impression made upon the disciples by the teaching
of Jesus on the preceding Sabbath. He saw them convinced that Jesus was the Messiah, and his own heart
was so full that he lost no opportunity to recount to
them again and again all that he had seen at Jesus'
baptism, also the miracles He had wrought.

I heard Jesus calling Heaven to witness that they
should behold still greater things, and He spoke of
His mission from His Heavenly Father.

He alluded also to their own vocation, telling them
to hold themselves in readiness. They would, He continued, have to forsake all when He called them. He
would provide for them, they should suffer no want.
They might still continue their customary occupations, because as the Passover was now approaching
He would have to discharge other affairs. But when
He should call them, they should follow Him immediately. The disciples questioned Him unrestrainedly
as to how they should manage with regard to their
families. Peter, for instance, said that just at present
he could not leave his old stepfather, who was also
Philip's uncle. But Jesus relieved his anxiety by His
answer, that He would not begin before the Paschal
feast; that only insofar as the heart was concerned,
should they detach themselves from their occupations; that exteriorly they should continue them until
He called them. In the meantime, however, they
should take the necessary steps toward freeing themselves from their different avocations. Jesus then left
the vale by the opposite end, and went to His Mother's
house, one of a row that stood between Capharnaum
and Bethsaida. His nearest relatives accompanied
Him, for their mothers also were with Mary.

Very early the next morning, Jesus with His relatives and disciples started for Cana. Mary and the
other women went by themselves, taking the more
direct and shorter route. It was only a narrow foot-

path running for the most part over a mountain. The women chose it as being the more private. It was besides wide enough for them, as they usually walked single file. A guide went on ahead, and a servant followed at some distance. Their journey was to the southwest of Capharnaum, almost seven hours.

Jesus and His companions took a more circuitous route through Gennabris. The road was broader and better suited to conversation. Jesus taught along the way. He often halted, gave utterance to some truth, and then explained it. This road was more to the south than that which Mary took. It was almost six hours by it from Capharnaum to Gennabris, at which place it turned southward, and three hours more took the traveller to Cana.

Gennabris was a beautiful city. It had a school and a synagogue. There was also a school of rhetoric, and the trade carried on was extensive. Nathanael had his office outside the city in a high house that stood by itself, though there were others at some distance around it. In spite of the invitation received from the disciples to that effect, he did not go into the city to meet Jesus.

Jesus taught in the synagogue and, with some of the disciples, took a luncheon at the house of a rich Pharisee. The rest of the disciples had already continued their journey to Cana. Jesus had commissioned Philip to go to Nathanael and bring him to meet Him on the way.

Jesus was very honorably treated at Gennabris, and the inhabitants were eager to keep Him with them longer. They brought forward as a reason for His doing so that He was one of their own countrymen, and also that He should have compassion on their sick. But Jesus soon left them and proceeded to Cana.

Meantime Philip had gone to Nathanael's office, in which he found several clerks, Nathanael being in a room upstairs. Philip had never before spoken of Jesus to Nathanael, since he, Nathanael, had not accompanied his friends to Gennabris. They were, however, well acquainted with each other, and Philip, full of joy, was enthusiastic when speaking of Jesus. "He is," he said, "the Messiah of whom the Prophets have spoken. We have found Him, Jesus of Nazareth, the Son of Joseph."

Nathanael was of a bright, lively disposition, energetic and self-reliant, consequently frank and sincere. In reply to Philip's remarks, Nathanael said: "Can anything very good come from Nazareth?" He knew the reputation of the Nazareans, that they were of a contradictory spirit and were not distinguished for the wisdom of their schools. He thought that a man who had been educated there might indeed shine in the eyes of his credulous and simpleminded friends, but that he could never satisfy his own pretentious claims to learning. But Philip bade him come and see for himself, for Jesus would soon pass that way to Cana. Nathanael accordingly accompanied Philip down by the short road to that house which stood a little off the highway to Cana. Jesus, with some of His disciples, was standing where the road branched off into the highway. Philip, since Jesus' injunction to follow Him, had been as joyous and unrestrained as before he had been timid. Addressing Jesus in a loud voice as they approached, he said: "Rabbi! I bring you here one who has asked: 'What good can come from Nazareth?'" But Jesus, turning to the disciples who were standing around Him, said as Nathanael came forward: "Behold! A true Israelite, in whom there is no guile!" Jesus uttered the words in a kind, affectionate manner. Nathanael responded: "How dost Thou know me?" meaning to say: How knowest Thou that I am true and without guile, since we have never before spoken to each other? Jesus answered: "Before Philip called thee, I saw thee when thou wast standing under the fig tree." These words Jesus accompanied by a significant look at Nathanael intended to recall something to him.

This glance of Jesus instantly awoke in Nathanael the remembrance of a certain passerby whose warning look had endued him with wonderful strength at a moment in which he was struggling with temptation. He had indeed been standing at the time under a fig tree on the pleasure grounds around the warm baths, gazing upon some beautiful women who, on the other side of the meadow, were playing for fruit. The powerful impression produced by that glance, and the victory which Jesus had then enabled him to gain, were fixed in his memory, though perhaps the form of the Man to whom he owed both the one and the other had faded from his mind. Or he may indeed have recognized Jesus without being aware that the warning glance had been designedly given. But now that Jesus reminded him of it and repeated the significant glance, Nathanael became greatly agitated and impressed. He felt that Jesus in passing had read his thoughts, and had been to him a guardian angel. Nathanael was so pure of heart that a thought contrary to the holy virtue had power to trouble his soul. He recognized, therefore, in Jesus his Saviour and Deliverer. This knowledge of his thoughts was enough for his upright, impetuous, and grateful heart, enough to make him, on the instant, joyfully acknowledge Jesus before all the disciples. Humbling himself before Him as he uttered those significant words, Nathanael exclaimed: "Rabbi! Thou art the Son of God! Thou art Israel's King!" Jesus responded: "Thou believest now because I have said that I saw thee under the fig tree. Verily, thou shalt greater wonders see!" And then turning to all, He said: "Verily! Ye shall see the heavens open and the angels of God ascending and descending over the Son of Man!" The other disciples, however, did not understand the real import of Jesus' words concerning the fig tree, nor did they know why Nathanael Chased had so quickly declared for Jesus. It was like a matter of

conscience hidden from all excepting John, to whom
Nathanael himself intrusted it at the marriage feast
of Cana. Nathanael asked Jesus whether he should
at once leave all things and follow Him, for that he
had a brother, to whom he could make over his employment. Jesus answered him as He had the others on
the preceding evening, and invited him to Cana for
the marriage feast.

Then Jesus and His disciples proceeded on their
way to Cana, Nathanael Chased meanwhile returning home to prepare for the wedding, for which he
set out on the following morning.

5. The Wedding at Cana

Cana, situated on the west side of a hill, was a
clean, pleasant place, not so large as Capharnaum.
It had a synagogue to which were attached three
priests. Near it was the public house at which the
wedding was to be held. It had a forecourt planted
with trees and shrubs. From this house to the synagogue, the street was adorned with leafy festoons
and arches from which hung garlands and fruits. The
festal hall extended from the entrance of the house
back to and beyond the fireplace, a high wall with
ledges in it, which was now adorned like an altar
with vases and flowers and gifts for the bride. Almost
a third of this spacious hall was behind the fireplace,
and there the women sat at the wedding banquet.
The beams supporting the upper story were likewise
hung with garlands, and there were means of ascent
in order to light the lamps fastened to them.

When Jesus with His disciples arrived near Cana,
He was most deferentially received by Mary, the
bride's parents, the bridegroom, and others that had
come out to meet Him. Jesus with His familiar disciples, among them the future Apostles, took up His
abode in an isolated house belonging to the maternal aunt of the bridegroom. This aunt also was a

daughter of Anne's sister Sobe. She held the mother's place to the bridegroom during the wedding ceremonies. The bride's father was named Israel and was a descendant of Ruth of Bethlehem. He was an opulent merchant, who carried on a large freighting business. He owned warehouses and great inns and storing places along the highroads for supplying caravans with fodder. His employees were numerous, for most of the inhabitants of Cana earned their living by working for him; in fact, all business transactions were wholly in the hands of himself and a few others. The bride's mother was a little lame; she limped on one side and had to be led.

All the relatives of St. Anne and Joachim had come from around Galilee to Cana, in all over one hundred guests. Mary Marcus, John Marcus, Obed, and Veronica had come from Jerusalem. Jesus Himself brought about twenty-five of His disciples with Him.

Long ago had Jesus, in His twelfth year at the children's feast held in the house of St. Anne upon His return from the Temple, addressed to the bridegroom words full of mysterious significance on the subject of bread and wine. He had told him that at some future day He would be present at his marriage. Jesus' participation in this marriage, like every other action of His earthly career, had, besides its high, mysterious signification, its exterior, apparent, and ordinary motives. More than once had Mary sent messengers to Jesus begging Him to be present at it. The friends and relatives of the Holy Family, judging from a human view, were making such speeches as these: "Mary, the Mother of Jesus, is a lone widow. Jesus is roaming the country, caring little for her or His relatives, etc., etc." It was on this account, therefore, that Mary was anxious that her Son should honor His friends by His presence at the marriage. Jesus entered into Mary's views and looked upon the present as a fitting opportunity to disabuse them of their erroneous ideas. He undertook also to supply

one course of the feast, and so Mary went to Cana
before the other guests and helped in the various
preparations. Jesus had engaged to supply all the
wine for the feast, wherefore it was that Mary so
anxiously reminded Him that the wine failed. Jesus
had also invited Lazarus and Martha to Cana. Martha
assisted with Mary in the preparations, and it was
Lazarus who defrayed (a circumstance known only
to Jesus and Mary) all the expenses assumed by
Jesus at the feast. Jesus had great confidence in
Lazarus, and willingly received everything from him,
while Lazarus was only too happy to give to Jesus.
He was up to the last like the treasurer of the Community. During the whole feast, he was treated by
the bride's father as a person of special distinction,
and he even personally busied himself in his service.
Lazarus was very refined in his manners, his whole
demeanor earnest, quiet, and marked by a dignified
affability; he spoke little, and his bearing toward
Jesus was full of loving devotedness.

Besides the wine, Jesus had also engaged to supply one course of the banquet, which course consisted
of the principal viands, such as birds of all kinds,
fruits, and vegetables. For all these provision had
been made. Veronica had brought with her from
Jerusalem a basket of the choicest flowers and the
most skillfully made confections. Jesus was like the
Master of the feast. He conducted all the amuse-
ments, which He seasoned with His own instructions.
He it was, too, who arranged the whole order of the
wedding ceremonies. He directed that all guests
should amuse themselves on those days according to
the customs usual on such occasions, but at the same
time draw some lesson of wisdom from their various
enjoyments. Among other things, He ordered that
twice in the day the guests should leave the house,
to amuse themselves in the open air.

Then I saw the wedding guests in a garden, the
men and women separate, amusing themselves with

conversation and games. The men reclined in circles
on the ground. In the center were all kinds of fruit
which, according to certain rules, they threw at one
another. The thrower aimed at making it fall into
certain holes or circles, while the others sought to
prevent its doing so. I saw Jesus with cheerful gravity taking part in the game. Frequently He smilingly
uttered a word of wisdom that made His hearers
wonder. Deeply impressed, they received it in silence,
the less quick to perceive its meaning asking for an
explanation from their neighbor. Jesus had the inner
circle and decided the prizes, which He awarded with
beautiful and sometimes quite astonishing remarks.
The younger of the guests amused themselves by
running and leaping over leafy festoons and heaps
of fruit. The women sat apart and played also for
fruit, the bride's seat being always between Mary
and the bridegroom's aunt.

There was also performed a kind of dance. Children played on musical instruments and sang cho-
ruses at intervals. The dancers, both the men and
the maidens, held scarfs with which they touched
one another when dancing in rows or in rings. Without those scarfs they never touched one another. Those
of the bride and bridegroom were black, the others
were yellow. At first, the bride and bridegroom danced
alone, then all danced together. The maidens wore
veils, but partly raised over the face; their dresses
were long in the back, but a little raised in front by
means of laces. There was no leaping nor springing
in the dance, as is customary amongst us. It was
more a moving in all kinds of figures, accompanied
by frequent swaying of the person and keeping time
to the music with the hands, the head, and the whole
body. Though perfectly modest and graceful, it
reminded me of that swaying of the Pharisaical Jews
at prayer. None of the future Apostles took part in
the dance; but Nathanael Chased, Obed, Jonathan,
and some others of the disciples entered into it. The

female dancers were the maidens only. The order
observed was quite extraordinary, and a spirit of tranquil joyousness prevailed among the guests.

During those days of rejoicing, Jesus had frequent
private interviews with those disciples that were later
on to become His Apostles. But the others were not
neglected. Jesus often walked with them and with
all the other guests in the country around and
instructed them. The future Apostles often explained
Jesus' teachings to their companions. This going
abroad of the guests facilitated the preparations for
the feast indoors. Several of the disciples, however,
and even Jesus Himself at times, were present at
the preparations going on in the house, helping to
arrange this or that, and besides, several of them
had a part in the bridal procession.

Jesus intended to manifest Himself at this feast
to all His friends and relatives. He wished also that
all whom He had chosen up to the present, should
become known to one another and to His own relatives. This could be done with greater freedom on
such an occasion as this marriage festival.

Jesus taught likewise in the synagogue before the
assembled guests. He spoke of the enjoyment of lawful pleasures, of the motives through which they might
be indulged, and of the moderation and prudent
reserve that ought to accompany them. Then He spoke
of marriage, of husband and wife, of continence, of
chastity, and of spiritual unions. At the close of the
instruction, the bridal pair stepped out in front of
Jesus, and He addressed each separately.

The Nuptial Ceremony
The Women's Game. The Men's Lottery

On the third day after Jesus' arrival, at about nine
o'clock in the morning, the marriage ceremony was
performed. The bride had been adorned by her bridemaids. Her dress was something like that worn by

the Mother of God at her espousals. Her crown, too, was similar, though more richly ornamented. But her hair was not netted in strands so fine as was that of Mary, the braids were fewer and thicker. When fully attired, she was presented to the Blessed Virgin and the other women.

The bride and bridegroom were conducted processionally from the house of festivity to the synagogue and back again. Six little boys and as many little girls with garlands and wreaths headed the procession. Then came six larger boys and six larger girls with flutes and other musical instruments. On their shoulders stood out some kind of stiff material like wings. Twelve young maidens accompanied the bride as bridemaids, and the same number of youths the bridegroom. Among the latter were Obed, Veronica's son, Joseph of Arimathea's nephews, Nathanael Chased, and some of John's disciples, but none of the future Apostles.

The nuptial ceremony was performed by the priest in front of the synagogue. The rings exchanged by the young pair had been presented to the bridegroom by Mary after Jesus had blessed them for her. I remarked something at this marriage that had escaped me at the nuptials of Joseph and Mary; viz., the priest pierced the left ring finger of both bridegroom and bride with a sharp instrument, just at the place where the ring was to be worn. Then he caught in a glass of wine two drops of blood from the bridegroom and one from the bride. The contents of the glass the young couple then drank in common, and afterward gave away the glass. After this many other articles, such as scarfs and other pieces of clothing, were bestowed upon the poor gathered around. When the bridal pair were reconducted to the festal house, Jesus Himself received them.

Before the wedding banquet I saw all the guests again assembled in the garden. The women and maidens sat on a carpet in an arbor and played for fruit.

They passed from one to another a little, triangular
tablet on the edge of which were inscribed certain
letters, and which was provided also with an index.
The tablet was rested on the lap, the index twirled,
and the point over which it paused determined the
prizes.

But for the amusement of the men, I beheld a wonderful game, contrived by Jesus Himself in the sum-
merhouse. In the center of the house stood a round
table with as many portions of flowers, leaves, and
fruits placed around the edge as there were players.
Jesus had, beforehand and alone, arranged these portions, each with reference to some mysterious signification. Above the surface of the table was a movable
disk with a slot in it. The portion of fruit or flowers
over which the slot rested when the disk was revolved,
became the prize of him who had turned it. In the
center of the table, a vine branch laden with grapes
rose out of a bundle of ears of wheat. The longer the
disk was turned, the higher rose the grapes and
wheat. Neither the future Apostles nor Lazarus took
part in the game. I was told at the time that whoever had received a call to teach or who was to be
favored with greater knowledge than his companions, should not engage in the game: he should watch
the results and be ready to season them with instructive applications. Thus would gravity and hilarity
mutually temper each other.

In this game arranged by Jesus, there was something very wonderful and more than fortuitous, for
the prize that fell to the players severally was significant of his own individual inclinations, faults,
and virtues. This Jesus explained to each as the
prize he had won was assigned him. Each prize was,
as it were, a parable, a similitude upon the winner
himself, and I felt that with the fruit he actually
received something interiorly. All were touched and
animated by the words of Jesus, perhaps also by the
partaking of the fruit whose significant properties

were now producing their effect. What Jesus said about each prize was quite unintelligible to all that it did not concern. It was received by the bystanders as only a pleasant, pointed remark. But each felt that the Lord had cast a deeply penetrating glance into his own interior. The same thing happened here as at Jesus' words to Nathanael relative to that gazing under the fig tree. They had sunk deep into Nathanael's soul, while from the others their meaning remained hidden.

I remember even yet that mignonette was one among the flowers, and that Jesus, when awarding his prize to Nathanael Chased, said to him: "Now canst thou understand that I was right in saying to thee: Thou art a true Israelite in whom there is no guile."

I saw one of the prizes producing most wonderful effects. Nathanael, the bridegroom, won a remarkable piece of fruit. There were two pieces on a single stem: one was like a fig, the other, which was hollow, more like a ribbed apple. They were of a reddish color, the inside white and streaked with red. I have seen similar in Paradise.

I perceived that the bystanders were very much surprised when the bridegroom won that fruit, and that Jesus spoke of marriage and of chastity, and dwelt upon the hundredfold fruit of the latter. And yet in all that Jesus said on these subjects, there was nothing that could shock the Jewish ideas on the score of marriage. Some of the Essenian disciples, James the Less for instance, comprehended better than the others the deep significance of His words.

I saw that the guests wondered more over that prize than over any other, and I heard Jesus saying that those fruits could produce effects far greater than was the remarkable signification attached to them. After the bridegroom and bride had eaten the fruit they had won, I saw the former become very much agitated. He grew pale, and a dark vapor escaped from him, after which he looked to me much brighter and purer, yes, even transparent when compared with what he had been before. The bride, too, who at a distance was sitting among the women, became after eating her piece of fruit quite faint. A dark shadow appeared to go out from her. The fruit that the bridal pair ate bore some reference to chastity.

There were certain penances connected with the different prizes. I remember seeing both the bride and bridegroom bringing something away from the synagogue, and performing certain devotions. Nathanael Chased's prize was a little bunch of sorrel.

In each of the other disciples, there awoke after eating their prizes his predominant passion. It struggled a little for the mastery, and then either departed, or the possessor became by the combat strengthened against its assaults. The vegetable kingdom before the Fall was endowed with certain supernatural virtues, but since the taint of sin the power of plants remains for man a secret. The form, the taste, the effects of the various herbs and fruits, are now but simple vestiges of the virtues they possessed before sin touched them. In my visions, I have seen upon the celestial tables fruits such as they were before the Fall. But their peculiar attributes were not always quite clear to me. Such things appear confused to our darkened understanding rendered even more obtuse by the customs of ordinary life.

When the bride fainted, her attendants relieved her of some of her heaviest ornaments. From her fingers they drew several of her numerous rings. Among them was a gold funnel-shaped shield worn like a thimble on the middle finger. They removed also the bracelets and chains from her arms and breast. The only ornament she retained beside the marriage ring, which the Blessed Virgin had given, was a gold pendant from the neck. It was in shape something like an oblong arch on the plain of which was inlaid some-

thing in brown, like that of the wedding ring of Mary
and Joseph. On that brown ground reclined a figure
attentively considering a flowerbud which it held in
its hand.

The game in the garden was followed by the nuptial banquet. That part of the spacious hall of the
festal house on this side of the adorned fireplace,
was divided into three spaces by two movable screens
so low that the guests reclining at the different tables
could see one another. In each of these compartments
was a long, narrow table. Jesus reclined at the head
of the middle one, His feet toward the fireplace. At
the same table sat Israel, the bride's father, Lazarus,
the male relatives of Jesus, and those of the bride.
The other wedding guests, along with the disciples,
sat at the two side tables. The women sat in the
space back of the fireplace, but where they could
hear all that Jesus said. The bridegroom served at
table, assisted by the steward, who wore an apron,
and by several servants. The women were waited
upon by the bride and some maid servants.

When the viands were brought in, a roasted lamb,
the feet bound crosswise, was set before Jesus. When
the bridegroom brought to Jesus the little case in
which lay the carving knife, Jesus bade him recall
that children's entertainment after the Paschal feast,
at which He had related the parable of a marriage,
and had foretold to him that He would be present
at his (the bridegroom's) marriage. These words were
intended for Nathanael alone. On hearing them, he
became very thoughtful, for he had quite forgotten
the circumstance. Jesus was at the banquet as He
had been during the whole celebration, very cheerful and always ready with a word of instruction. He
accompanied every action with an explanation of its
spiritual signification, and spoke of hilarity and the
enjoyment of the feast. He remarked that the bow
must not always be bent, that the field must sometimes be refreshed by rain, and upon each He uttered

a parable. As He carved the lamb, most wonderful
words fell from His lips. He spoke of separating the
lambs from the flocks, not for the greater advantage
of the little animals thus chosen, but that they should
die. Then He alluded to the process of roasting in
which the meat was divested of its rawness by the
fire of purification. The carving of each member signified, as He said, the manner in which they who
would follow the Lamb should separate from their
nearest relatives according to the flesh. When to each
one He had reached a piece and all were partaking
of it, He said that the lamb had been separated from
its companions and cut into pieces, that it might
become in them a nourishment of mutual union, so
too must he that would follow the Lamb renounce
his own field of pasture, put his passions to death,
and separate from the members of his family. Then
would he become, as it were, a nourishment, a food,
to unite by means of the Lamb his fellow men to the
Heavenly Father. Before every guest was a plate or
a little wheaten cake. Jesus set a dark brown plate
with a yellow rim before Himself, and it was afterward handed around. I saw Him at times holding up
a little bunch of herbs in His hand, and giving some
instruction upon it.

Jesus had engaged to supply the second course of
the banquet as well as the wine, and for all this His
Mother and Martha provided. This second course consisted of birds, fish, honey confections, fruits, and a
kind of pastry which Veronica had brought with her.
When it was all carried in and set on a side table,
Jesus arose, gave the first cut to each dish, and then
resumed His place at table. The dishes were served,
but the wine failed. Jesus meanwhile was busy teaching. Now when the Blessed Virgin, who had provided
for this part of the entertainment, saw that the wine
failed, she went to Jesus and reminded Him that He
had told her that He would see to the wine. Jesus,
who was teaching of His Heavenly Father, replied:

"Woman, be not solicitous! Trouble not thyself and Me! My hour is not yet come." These words were not uttered in harshness to the Blessed Virgin. Jesus addressed her as "Woman," and not as "Mother," because, at this moment as the Messiah, as the Son of God, He was present in divine power and was about to perform in presence of all His disciples and relatives an action full of mystery.

On all occasions when He acted as the Incarnate Word, He ennobled those that participated in the same by giving them the title that best responded to the part assigned them. Thus did the holiness of the divine action shed, as it were, some rays upon them and communicate to them a special dignity. Mary was the "Woman" who had brought forth Him whom now, as her Creator, she invokes on the occasion of the wine's failing. As the Creator, He will now give a proof of His high dignity. He will here show that He is the Son of God and not the Son of Mary. Later on, when dying upon the Cross, He again addressed His weeping Mother by the appellation of Woman, "Woman, behold thy son!" thereby designating John.

Jesus had promised His Mother that He would provide the wine. And here we see Mary beginning the role of *mediatrix* that she has ever since continued. She places before Him the failure of the wine. But the wine that He was about to provide was more than ordinary wine; it was symbolical of that mystery by which He would one day change wine into His own Blood. The reply: "My hour is not yet come," contained three significations: first, the hour for supplying the promised wine; secondly, the hour for changing water into wine, thirdly, the hour for changing wine into His own Blood.

But Mary's anxiety for the wedding guests was now entirely relieved. She had mentioned the matter to her Son, therefore she says confidently to the servants: "Do all that He shall tell you."

In like manner does the Church, the Bride of Jesus, say to Him: "Lord, Thy children have no wine." And Jesus replies: "Church" (not *Bride),* "be not troubled, be not disquieted! My hour is not yet come." Then says the Church to her priests: "Hearken to His words, obey all His commands, for He will always help you!"

Mary told the servants to await the commands of Jesus and fulfill them. After a little while Jesus directed them to bring Him the empty jugs and turn them upside down. The jugs were brought, three water jugs and three wine jugs, and that they were empty was proved by inverting them over a basin. Then Jesus ordered each to be filled with water. The servants took them off to the well which was in a vault in the cellar, and which consisted of a stone cistern provided with a pump. The jugs were earthen, large and so heavy that when full it took two men to carry them, one at each handle. They were pierced at intervals from top to bottom by tubes closed by faucets. When the contents to a certain depth were exhausted, the next lower faucet opened to pour out. They were only tipped up on their high feet.

Mary's words to Jesus had been uttered in a low tone, but Jesus' reply, as well as His command to draw water, was given in a loud voice. When the jugs filled with water had been placed, six in number, on the side table, Jesus went and blessed them. As He retook His place at table, He called to a servant: "Draw off now, and bring a drink to the steward!" When this latter had tasted the wine, he approached the bridegroom and said: "Every man at first setteth forth good wine, and when men have well drunk, then that which is worse. But thou hast kept the good wine until now." He did not know that the wine was provided by Jesus as was also this whole course of the feast. That was a secret between the Holy Family and the family of the bridal pair. Then the bridegroom and the bride's father drank of the wine, and great was their astonishment. The servants protested that they had drawn only water, and that the drinking vessels and glasses on the table had been filled with the same. And now the whole company drank. The miracle gave rise to no alarm or excitement; on the contrary, a spirit of silent awe and reverence fell upon them. Jesus taught much upon this miracle. Among other things, He said that the world presents the strong wine first, and then deceives the partially intoxicated with bad drinks; but it was not so in the Kingdom that His Heavenly Father had given Him. There pure water was changed to costly wine, as lukewarmness should give place to ardor and intrepid zeal. He alluded also to that banquet at which in His twelfth year, after His return from teaching in the Temple, He had been present with many of the guests now assembled, and who were then mere boys. He reminded them that He had on that occasion spoken of bread and wine, and had related the parable of a marriage at which the water of tepidity would be changed into the wine of enthusiasm. This, He said, was now fulfilled. He told them that they should witness greater miracles than this; that He would celebrate several Paschs, and at the last would change wine into Blood and bread into Flesh, and that He would remain with them till the end to strengthen and console. After that meal they should see happen to Him things that they could not now understand, even were He to explain them. Jesus did not say all this in plain terms. He hid it under parables, which I have forgotten, though I have given their sense. His listeners were filled with fear and wonder, and the wine produced a change in all. I saw that, not by the miracle alone, but also by the drinking of that wine, each one had received strength, true and interior, each had become changed. This change was similar to that wrought in them at an earlier stage of the entertainment by the eating of the fruit. His disciples, His relatives, in a word, all present were now convinced of Jesus' power and dignity, as well as of His mission. All believed in Him. Faith at once took possession of every heart. All became better, more united, more interior. This same effect was produced in all that had drunk of the wine, *Jesus at this wedding feast was, as it were, in the midst of His community for the first time. There it was that He wrought that first miracle in their favor and for the confirmation of their faith. It is on that account that this miracle, the changing of water into wine is recorded as the first in His history; as that of the Last Supper, when His Apostles were staunch in the Faith, was the last.*

At the close of the banquet, the bridegroom went to Jesus and spoke to Him very humbly in private. He told Him that he now felt himself dead to all carnal desires and that, if his bride would consent, he would embrace a life of continence. The bride also, having sought Jesus alone and expressed her wish to the same effect, Jesus called them both before Him. He spoke to them of marriage, of chastity so pleasing in the sight of God, and of the hundredfold fruit of the spirit. He referred to many of the Prophets and other holy persons who had lived in chastity, offering their bodies as a holocaust to the Heavenly Father. They had thus reclaimed many wandering souls, had won them to themselves as so many spiritual children, and had acquired a numerous and holy posterity. Jesus spoke all this in parables of sowing and reaping. The young couple took a vow of continence, by which they bound themselves to live as brother and sister for the space of three years. Then they knelt before Jesus, and He blessed them.

On the evening of the fourth day of the marriage, the bride and bridegroom were conducted to their home in festal procession. Lights arranged so as to form a letter were carried. Children went before carrying on strips of cloth two wreaths of flowers, an open one and a closed one, which they tore to pieces and scattered around in front of the house of the newly-married couple. Jesus had gone on ahead. He received them at the house and blessed them. The priests also were present. Since the miracle wrought by Jesus at the banquet, they had become very humble, and gave Him precedence everywhere.

On the Sabbath spent at Cana, Jesus taught twice in the synagogue. He alluded to the wedding feast and to the obedience and pious sentiments of the bridal couple. On leaving the synagogue, He was accosted by the people, who threw themselves at His feet and implored Him to cure their sick.

Jesus performed here two wonderful cures. A man had fallen from a high tower. He was taken up dead, all his limbs broken. Jesus went to him, placed the limbs in position, touched the fractures, and then commanded the man to rise and go to his home. The man arose, thanked Jesus, and went home. He had a wife and children. Jesus was next conducted to a man possessed by the devil, and whom He found chained to a great stone. Jesus freed him. He was next led to a woman, a sinner, who was afflicted by a bloody flux. He cured her, as also some others sick of the dropsy. He healed seven in all. The people had not dared to crowd around Him during the marriage festivities; but now that it was rumored that He was going away after the Sabbath, they could no longer be restrained. Since the miracle of the marriage feast, the priests did not interfere with Jesus. They allowed Him to do all that He wished. The miracles, the cures just related happened in their presence alone, for the disciples were not there.

6. Jesus in Capharnaum and at the Lake of Genesareth

The Sabbath over, Jesus went that night with His disciples to Capharnaum, the bridegroom, his father, and several others accompanying Him a part of the way. The poor had been bountifully supplied at the marriage feast, for nothing appeared a second time on the table; whatever was left was immediately given away.

For two fasting days that occurred immediately after the Sabbath, I saw the cooking done in advance.

All the fires were covered, and the windows not absolutely necessary were closed. In the homes of the rich, there were little receptacles on the hearth in which, covered with hot ashes, the food kept warm. Jesus kept these fasts in Capharnaum where, too, He taught in the synagogue. Twice a day, the sick were brought to Him, and He cured them. The disciples from Bethsaida went home, but some of them afterward returned. Jesus traversed the country around teaching, but in the hours of rest He stayed with Mary.

Andrew, Saturnin, Aram, Themeni, and Eustachius were sent by Jesus to the great baptismal place on the Jordan this side of Jericho. It had been abandoned by John, and the disciples were now to baptize there. Jesus went with them a part of the way, and then turned off to Bethulia where He cured the sick and taught. From there He walked back between seven and eight hours toward Hanathon, northwest of Capharnaum, in whose vicinity there was a mountain formerly used by the Prophets for teaching. It had a gentle elevation of about an hour, and on it was a space arranged in olden times for teaching. It consisted of a high stone seat surrounded by stakes, over which a tent could be stretched as a protection against sun and rain. The space thus enclosed could accommodate a large audience. The tent was removed at the end of the instructions. From the mountain-ridge arose three hills, one of which was the Mount of Beatitudes. From the place where Jesus taught was a widely extended view: the Sea of Galilee lay below the observer, and he could see far around toward Nazareth. Some parts of the mountain were fertile and inhabited, but not so where Jesus taught. It was surrounded by the foundations of a ruined wall, upon which might still be seen the remains of several towers. Around the mountain lay Hanathon, Bethanat, and Nejel. Their proximity leaves the impression that they were formerly but one large city.

Jesus had with Him three disciples: one the son of the widowed aunt of the bridegroom of Cana; the second the son of the other widow; and the third Peter's half-brother Jonathan. The people were summoned by them to Jesus' instruction on the mountain. Jesus taught here of the diverse spirits in men of different places, yea, even of the same family, and of the spirit that they should receive through Baptism. By this last spirit, they should all become one; one in penance, satisfaction, and expiation, as well as one with the Heavenly Father. Then He gave them some signs by which they might be able to recognize in what degree they had received the Holy Spirit in Baptism. He taught also on prayer and individual petitions. I was astonished to hear Him explaining several petitions of the Lord's Prayer, although as a whole He had not yet repeated it. This instruction lasted from noon till evening, when He went down to Bethanat and stayed there overnight. The preceding night He had spent in Hanathon.

On the following day Jesus went from Bethanat toward the lake. Five more of John's disciples had come to Jesus in Bethanat. They were from Apheca, the native city of St. Thomas, situated in a region to the north on the Mediterranean. They had long been with John; but now they followed Jesus.

Toward noon I saw Jesus and His disciples on a little hill about one half-hour from the lake, between Bethsaida and the spot where the Jordan flows into it. They commanded a view of it upon which they saw Peter, John, and James in their boats. Peter owned a large ship, and on it were his servants; but he was at the time in a small one which he was

steering himself. John and James, in company with
their father, owned a large ship and several small
ones. I saw Andrew's little boat near those of Zebedee,
but he himself was at the Jordan. When the disciples remarked their friends on the lake, they wanted
to go down to call them. But Jesus would not allow
it. I heard the disciples asking: "How can those men
down there still go around fishing after seeing what
Thou hast done and hearing Thy teaching?" But Jesus
answered: "I have not yet called them. They, and
especially Peter, carry on a large business upon which
many depend for subsistence. I have told them to
continue it, and in the meantime hold themselves in
readiness for My call. Until then I have many things
to do. I have also to go to Jerusalem for the Pasch."

About six and twenty dwellings were on the west
side of the hill, occupied principally by peasants and
the families of the fishermen. As Jesus approached
these houses, a possessed person cried after Him:
"There He goes! Here He comes! The Prophet before
whom we must flee!" and soon He was surrounded
by a crowd of such creatures, clamoring and raving,
who were followed by their keepers. Jesus commanded them to be at peace and to follow Him. Then
He went up on the hill and taught. There were about
one hundred people, including the possessed, around
Him. He spoke of evil spirits, of how to resist them,
and of reformation of life. The possessed were freed
from the spirits that held them. They became perfectly calm, they wept, they thanked, and declared
that they could now recall nothing of what had happened to them during the time of their possession.
Among these poor creatures were some who had
been brought chained together from different parts
of the country around, their friends having heard
that there was on His way thither a Prophet as holy
as Moses. After all their trouble, they would have
missed Jesus had not one broken loose and cried
after Him.

From this place Jesus went to join His Mother between Capharnaum and Bethsaida, the former of which was a little to the north and not far from the hill mentioned above. That evening when the Sabbath began, Jesus taught in the synagogue of Capharnaum. A feast was being celebrated. It had some reference to Tobias, who had frequented this part of the country and had done much good. He had also bequeathed property to the schools and synagogues. Jesus gave an instruction on gratitude.

After the Sabbath, Jesus returned to His Mother with whom He conversed alone far into the night. He spoke of His future movements: He would first go to the Jordan, then celebrate the Pasch at Jerusalem, afterward call His Apostles, and make His public appearance. He predicted the persecution He should endure at Nazareth, alluded to His career after that, and explained in what way she and the other women should bear a part in it. There was at that time in Mary's house, a woman already far advanced in years. She was the same poor widowed relative whom Anne had sent to Mary, to take the place of a servant to her in the Crib Cave. She was now so old that Mary rather served her than she Mary.

With eight disciples, Jesus set out before break of day on His journey to the place of baptism on the Jordan. Their way ran to the east of the lake and over the hill whence they had seen the boats of the Apostles. The Jordan here flows through a deep bed. About one half-hour before its discharge into the lake, the river is spanned by a bridge high and steep. This the Lord and His disciples crossed. On the other side, in a retired corner near the lake, lay a little fishery surrounded by numerous outstretched nets. It was called Little Corozain. Not quite an hour northward from the lake was Bethsaida-Julias. Great Corozain was a couple of hours east of the lake, and there dwelt Matthew the Publican.

Jesus travelled down the eastern shore of the lake and remained overnight in Hippos. Next morning He went on to Gadara in whose neighborhood He cured a man possessed. The unfortunate creature was being led after Him bound, but he freed himself and set up the cry: "Jesus, Thou Son of David! Jesus! Whither goest Thou? Thou wilt drive us away!" Jesus stood still, commanded the devil to be silent and to depart from the man, indicating at the same time whither he should go.

A couple of hours from Gadara, Jesus again crossed the Jordan, and went on toward the southwest, leaving Scythopolis to the left. He crossed Mount Moreh to Jezrael, a city on the west side of the plain Esdrelon. Jesus cured numbers there openly before the synagogue. But He stayed a few hours only in Jezrael, so that Magdalen who, at the earnest entreaty of Martha, had come with her to see Jesus, did not find Him on her arrival. She heard only of His miracles from the lips of those whom He had cured. The sisters here separated, and Magdalen retraced her steps to Magdalum.

The next place in which I saw Jesus was Hai, not far from Bethel, and about nine hours distant from the place of baptism. Hai had in ancient times been destroyed, and later partly restored. It was a retired little place. Jesus cured and taught there.

Among the Pharisees of Hai were some that had been present in the Temple at the teaching of Jesus in His twelfth year. They now referred to it as to a piece of consummate hypocrisy. He had, they said, in the synagogue of learned men taken His place on the ground among the scholars, disputed with them, and then, as if demanding information on the words of His opponents, had called upon the teachers with such questions as these: "What think you? Tell us, when will the Messiah come?" Having drawn them thus into the manifestation of their opinion, He ended by a show of His own superior knowledge. They now put to Jesus the plain question whether He was not that Child.

7. Jesus Permits Baptism to Be Given At the Jordan

From Hai Jesus departed for John's former baptismal place, on the Jordan three hours from Jericho. Andrew and many of the disciples had come about an hour's distance to meet Him. Several of John's disciples, some also from Nazareth, were here. Some of them went on ahead to the little village of Ono, about an hour's distance from the place of baptism, and gave notice that Jesus would there celebrate the Sabbath and cure the sick. They told the people that Jesus was continuing John's work and teaching, and that openly and effectively He perfected that for which John had laid the foundation. Outside of Ono and about one half-hour from the baptismal place there was a private inn for Jesus' accommodation. Lazarus had purchased it for Him and had placed there a man to see to the cooking, though Jesus usually took His meals cold. This inn served Him as a stopping place when in that part of the country, and from it He went around to the neighboring villages teaching and baptizing. When He reached Ono for the Sabbath, He taught in the synagogue and cured many sick persons who had been brought thither, among them a poor, emaciated woman suffering from a bloody flux.

In these last days, Herod frequently went to John, but the latter always treated him with contempt as an adulterer. Herod interiorly acknowledged that John was right, but his wife was furious against John. John baptized no more, and Jesus was now the whole subject of his preaching. All the candidates for Baptism, he sent across the Jordan to Him.

At the place of Baptism, many changes had been made by the disciples sent thither from Cana, and

all in accordance with Jesus' orders. It now presented a festal appearance, and things were better
arranged than when John was there. On account of
the crowds desirous of crossing, the ferry was
removed to a lower point of the river, at a greater
distance from that large circular enclosure which
John had arranged in the open air around the baptismal pool. The spot upon which Andrew, Saturnin,
and the other disciples baptized in turn upon Jesus'
command, was the little island upon which He Himself had been baptized. It was now covered by a
large awning. While the disciples baptized, Jesus
taught and prepared the aspirants for Baptism. The
pool in which Jesus had been baptized was now
very much changed. The five canals leading from
the Jordan into the pool, and which had at first
been covered, were now uncovered, and the four
stones from the center, as well as the large, three-
cornered, red-veined one at the edge upon which
Jesus was standing when the Holy Spirit came upon
Him, had all been removed. They had been taken
to the new place of Baptism.

That the spot upon which Jesus had been baptized was the same as that upon which the Ark of
the Covenant had stood, that the stones in the Baptism pool were those upon which it had rested in
the bed of the Jordan, were facts known only to
Jesus and John, and of which neither had spoken.
So, too, the Lord was the only one who knew that
these stones now formed the foundation of the baptismal basin. The Jews had long forgotten the resting place of these stones, and it was not made known
to the disciples. Andrew had hewn a circular basin
in the three-cornered stone which rested on the four
others in a cavity filled with water which surrounded
the stones like a canal. This water, as also that in
the basin of the three-cornered stones, had been
brought from the baptismal pool of Jesus, and Jesus
had blessed it. When the aspirants stood in the

canal around the triangular basin, the water reached
up to their breast.

Near the place of Baptism was a kind of altar
upon which lay the baptismal garments. Two of the
disciples imposed hands upon the shoulders of the
neophytes while Andrew or Saturnin, sometimes
another, dipped the hollow hand three times into
the basin and poured the water over their head baptizing them in the name of the Father and of the
Son and of the Holy Ghost. The baptizers, as well
as those that imposed hands, wore long white robes
girdled, and from their shoulders hung long white
strips like broad stoles. John was accustomed to
baptize from a triple-channeled shell from which
the water flowed in three streams, and the words
he used were of Jehovah and of Him that had been
sent, somewhat different from those now uttered by
the disciples at Baptism. None of those that had
been baptized by John were here rebaptized; but I
think that after the descent of the Holy Ghost, at
the Baptism administered at the Pool of Bethsaida,
they were again baptized. Nor were there here any
women as yet baptized. The Baptism with triple
immersions I saw for the first time at the Pool of
Bethsaida.

There was an opening in the awning just above
the basin of Baptism. The neophytes stood at the
side, the baptizer and sponsors on the corner of the
stone.

Jesus taught from an elevated teacher's stand in
the open air. During the heat of the day, a tent or
awning was stretched over it. The subjects of Jesus'
discourse were Baptism, penance, the approach of
the Kingdom of God, and of the Messiah, whom they
should seek not among the distinguished of this
world, but among the poor and lowly. He designated
this Baptism a cleansing, a washing away, while
John's baptism was one of penance. He spoke also
of a Baptism of fire, a Baptism of the Spirit, which

was yet to come.

The bushes and trees that John had planted in the form of an arbor around the baptismal pool rose above them all. On the pointed top I saw a figure like a little child. It appeared to be rising out of the trunk of a vine, its little arms outstretched in the act of scattering yellow apples with one hand, and roses with the other. It was a remnant of the adornments of the festival that celebrated the commencement of Jesus' baptizing mission.

Jesus was now gone with several of His disciples southward from the place of Baptism and toward the west of the Dead Sea. He had entered the region in which Melchisedech sojourned when he measured off the Jordan and the mountains. Long before Abraham, he had conducted the Patriarch's forefathers thither. But the city that they built had been destroyed with Sodom and Gomorrha. I saw at that time, at about half an hour's distance inland from the Dead Sea, in the midst of a desolate region where immense caves and black, jagged rocks met the gaze, the dilapidated walls and towers in the ruined city Hazezon Thamar. Where now appears the Dead Sea, was before the submersion of those godless cities, only the river Jordan. It was here about a quarter of an hour broad. The people, who dwelt in caves and ruined buildings of all kinds at some distance from the sea, were not real Jews. They were slaves belonging to wandering tribes that had settled in those parts, and for whom they were obliged to perform all the field labor. They were poor and humble and very greatly neglected. They looked upon Jesus' arrival among them as an inconceivable favor, and gave Him a very loving reception. He cured many of them.

At the present day that region is not so desolate as it was in the time of Jesus, but in very early ages it was indescribably fruitful and lovely. It was in Abraham's time changed by the formation of the Dead

Sea from one of the most magnificent regions into a dreary desert. The shores of the Jordan were then walled in with freestone and on them once stood a great number of cities and towns, beautiful mountains and hills rising up between them. The whole region was covered with groves of date palms, vineyards, orchards, and fields of grain. Its fruitfulness surpassed description. Previously to the formation of the Dead Sea, the Jordan had, just below its greatest depth, divided into two branches between the cities that were afterward submerged. One of these branches flowed eastward, receiving in its course the waters of many smaller streams; the other watered the desert through which the Holy Family fled into Egypt, as far as the region of Mara, where Moses had rendered the bitter waters sweet, and where Anne's ancestors had sojourned. There were salt mines in the neighborhood of those cities, but they exercised no deleterious influence upon the waters of the numerous springs around. The tribes dwelling at a considerable distance in this region that afterward became so desolate, used the water of the Jordan and found it excellent.

The remote ancestors of Abraham, who had been settled in Hazezon by Melchisedech, had become very degenerate, and Abraham was, by a second exercise of God's mercy, led to the Promised Land. Melchisedech had been in these parts long before the Jordan existed. He had measured off and determined everything. He often came and went, and sometimes he was accompanied by a couple of men, who appeared to be slaves.

Jesus went afterward with His disciples in a direction leading to Bethlehem. After His Baptism He crossed the valley of the shepherds. The people depended upon the caravans that passed through for their principal support. It is about four hours from Bethania and on the boundary between Judah and Benjamin.

There were in Betharaba many possessed. They ran about outside the city crying out that Jesus was coming. Jesus commanded them to cover themselves, and in a few moments they had made aprons of leaves. Jesus delivered them from the evil spirits and, on entering the city, sent back to them messengers with clothes. There were some among them whose body used suddenly to swell to a great size.

Andrew and five other disciples had left the place of Baptism and preceded the Lord to Betharaba in order to announce His coming and to give notice that He would there celebrate the Sabbath.

Jesus and His disciples put up at a private inn, one of those free inns, such as in those times were always found in the different cities for the accommodation of travelling teachers and rabbis. Lazarus, Joseph of Arimathea, and others from Jerusalem had come hither to meet Jesus.

Jesus taught in the synagogue, also from a stone seat that stood in a public place intended for such use, and on all the streets and corners, for the crowds were too great for the school to accommodate. He healed numerous sick of different kinds whom the disciples brought to Him, making a way for them through the crowd. Lazarus and Joseph of Arimathea stood in the distance.

At the close of the Sabbath, the Lord returned to Ono with His disciples. They passed through the little town of Bethagla, one of the stopping places of the Children of Israel after they had crossed the Jordan, for they did not all cross at one and the same place. They went over in bands at different points of the dry bed of the river. When arrived at Bethagla, they arranged their clothing and girded themselves. Jesus passed the stone of the Ark of the Covenant where John had celebrated the feast.

Lazarus and Joseph of Arimathea returned to Jerusalem. Nicodemus had not come. He was more reserved, on account of the office that he held, but he served Jesus in secret, and to the end notified the little Community of any danger that threatened.

The next day was the first feast of the new moon, and I saw that the serving class and civil functionaries in Jerusalem had a holiday. It was kept as a festival of joy, a day of rest, consequently there was no baptizing on it.

The flags for the Feast of the New Moon were waving from long flagstaffs on the roof of the synagogue. Large knots were made at intervals on the staves between which the folds of the streamers opened in the breeze. The number of knots signified to those at a distance what month had just begun. Such flags were unfurled also as signals of victory or of danger.

The whole day Jesus was busy preparing for Baptism the people who had gathered there on the eve and encamped around; but there was no baptizing, because a feast was being celebrated in commemoration of the death of a wicked King (Alexander Jannaeus). The place of Baptism had been very beautifully arranged and adorned. Andrew and the other disciples began very early on the following day the Baptism of those that Jesus had prepared the day before.

The preceding evening Lazarus had returned with Obed, Simeon's son, and with them Jesus started very early the next morning for the neighborhood of Bethlehem, passing between Bethagla and Ophra, which was more to the west. Jesus took this journey with Lazarus in order to hear what reports were circulating about Himself at Jerusalem, also to give him some instructions, which he was to transmit to the little Community, as to how they should conduct themselves under certain circumstances. They took the road once trodden by Joseph and Mary when going to Bethlehem, and in about three hours reached a row of poor, isolated dwellings belonging to shepherds. Lazarus told Jesus all that was being said

about Him at Jerusalem, and that they spoke of Him
in a manner partly derisive, and partly inquisitive.
They said that they would see whether He would
come to Jerusalem for the Pasch and, if He did,
whether He would as daringly perform His miracles
in a great city as among the credulous people of
Galilee. He told Jesus also of the spying of the Pharisees and of what they reported of Him in different
places. Jesus relieved Lazarus' anxiety on these
points, and drew his attention to various passages
in the Prophets wherein all this had been foretold.
He said that He would be about eight days longer
at the Jordan, would then return to Galilee, then
go to Jerusalem for the Pasch, and after that call
His disciples. Jesus consoled Lazarus on the subject
of Magdalen, of whom He said that already there
had fallen upon her soul a spark of salvation, which
would entirely consume her.

They spent the greater part of the day among the
shepherd dwellings, at which they were entertained
with bread, honey, and fruit. There dwelt here only
about twenty-one women of the shepherd class, all
widows. Some had grown sons, who supported them
in their old age. Their dwellings were merely cells
separated from one another by hedges of living brushwood. Some of these women had visited the Crib
Cave at the birth of Christ and offered gifts. Jesus
taught here. He entered some of the cells and cured
the sick inmates. One was very old and emaciated,
and lay upon a couch made of leaves. Jesus led her
forth by the hand. The women had a refectory and
dormitory in common.

Lazarus and Obed went back to Jerusalem, while
Jesus continued visiting and curing the sick. Toward
three in the afternoon, I saw Him again at the place
of Baptism.

8. Jesus in Adummin and Nebo

Jesus, with most of His disciples, passed through
Bethagla to Adummin, a place hidden away in a
frightfully wild, mountainous region, broken by innumerable ravines. The road running along by the
rocks was in some places so narrow that even an
ass could scarcely tread it. It was about three hours
from Jericho, in a district so retired on the boundary between Benjamin and Juda that I never before
noticed it. It was wonderfully steep. It was a refugial city for murderers and other malefactors, who
found here protection from capital punishment.
They were either kept in custody until they reformed
or employed in the quarries and in the most painful
field labors. The place received on this account the
appellation "The Path of the Red, the Bloody." This
city of refuge was in existence even before David's
time. During the first persecution of the Community after Jesus' death, it came to an end. Later on,
a convent was built there to serve as a stronghold,
or fortress, for the first religious guardians of the
Holy Sepulcher.[1] The people subsisted by the culture of the vine and other fruits. It was a frightful
wilderness, consisting chiefly of naked rocks, which
sometimes toppled from their base, carrying down
with them the clinging vines.

The road proper from Jericho to Jerusalem did not
run through Adummin, but westward of it, on which
side there was no access to the city. But that from
Bethagla to Adummin was intersected by another
running from the shepherd valley to Jericho, and at
about one half-hour's distance from Adummin. Near
this crossroad was a very narrow and dangerous pass,
designated by a stone as the spot where long before
had really happened the fact upon which Jesus based
the parable of the good Samaritan and the man that

1. Sister Emmerich refers to those early religious congregations founded
   by the first Bishops of Jerusalem for the protection of the Holy Sepulcher.

had fallen among robbers. As Jesus was approaching Adummin, He turned a little out of the
way with His disciples, to give an instruction on that
memorable spot. Seated on the stone chair and surrounded by the disciples and the people of the immediate neighborhood, He taught, taking for His text
the incident just quoted. He celebrated the Sabbath
in Adummin and taught in the synagogue, relating
a parable that referred to the advantages offered to
malefactors by the refugial city, all which He applied
to the grace of doing penance on this earth. He also
cured several persons, most of them dropsical. The
Sabbath over, Jesus and the disciples returned to the
place of Baptism.

Next evening Jesus went with His disciples to the
city of Nebo, situated on the opposite side of the
Jordan at the foot of Mount Nebo, whose height is
such that several hours are necessary to reach the
summit. Messengers had previously been sent to
implore Him to enter the city and teach. The population was a mixed one, Egyptians, Moabites, and
Israelites that had in former times defiled themselves with idolatry. They had been aroused by John's
preaching, but had not had the courage to go over
to Jesus' place of Baptism. I think they dared not.
On account of some crime of their forefathers (of
what kind I no longer remember), they were held
by the Jews in great contempt. They dared not go
about freely, but to certain places only. They now
came to Jesus humbly begging Him to baptize among
them. The disciples had brought from the baptismal
pool, water in leathern bottles, which they had left
under the care of some guards.

Nebo was about one half-hour from the Jordan,
from which it was separated by a mountain, and
between five and six hours from Macharus. The country around was not fertile. To reach Nebo, one must,
after crossing the river, climb the mountain and then
descend on the other side. Just opposite the place

of Baptism stands the mountain, affording no place
for a landing, and behind was the city Nebo. It was
tolerably large, the foundation hilly, and separated
by a valley from the mount of the same name. There
was still here a heathen temple, but it was closed
and something built around it.

Jesus, from a teacher's chair and out in the open
air, prepared the people for Baptism, which the disciples administered. The baptismal basin was placed
over a cistern into which the neophytes stepped, and
which was filled with water to a certain height. The
disciples had brought with them the baptismal robes,
rolled up and wrapped around their person, which
were put on the neophytes during the ceremony.
They floated around them on the water. After the
Baptism a kind of little mantle was placed on their
shoulders. At John's baptism, it was something like
a stole and as wide as a hand-towel, but at the Baptism of Jesus, it was more like a real little mantle
on which was fastened a stole like a lappet trimmed
with fringe. Among the newly baptized were mostly
tender youths and very old men, for many of the
middle-aged were postponed until they should become
less unworthy. Jesus healed many sick of fevers and
many dropsical who had been carried thither on litters. The possessed among the heathens were not
so numerous as among the Jews.

Jesus blessed also the drinking water, which was
not good here. It was muddy and brackish. It was
collected among the rocks whence it was brought in
bottles and poured into a reservoir. Jesus blessed it
crosswise, and rested His hand upon several different points of the surface.

On their return journey to the inn outside Ono,
Jesus and the disciples spent the greater part of
the day on the road, only one hour long, from Nebo
to the Jordan ferry. Jesus taught the whole way.
The road was bordered by huts and tents in which
the people from Nebo sold to travellers fruit and

distilled wine. It was these vendors that Jesus instructed. Before evening He returned with the disciples to His inn at the place of Baptism.

Jesus went afterward through the surrounding district, instructing the peasants singly and in crowds. Among them were many good souls, who during the time that John was baptizing here supplied the crowds with food. Jesus appeared to be seeking out everyone, even those in the most remote corners, for He was soon to leave these parts and go on to Galilee.

He stopped for a while at the house of a rich peasant whose fields covered a whole mountain. On one side the harvest was ripe, when on the other they were just about to sow. Jesus taught in a parable of sowing and harvesting.

There was here an old, dilapidated teacher's chair formerly used by the Prophets. The peasants had restored it very handsomely, and from it Jesus delivered His instructions.

Several such places for teaching had been restored since John had here baptized. He had ordered it, for that, too, was a part of *his preparing the way.* These teaching chairs had here, as with us the pictures of the Stations, quite gone to ruin since the times of the Prophets. Elias and Eliseus had frequented this part of the country. Jesus celebrated in Ono the morning of the Sabbath, which was followed by a feast that must have had some connection with fruit. I saw whole basketfuls carried during those days into the synagogue and town halls.

The arrangements at the place of Baptism had already been taken apart and stowed away by the disciples. Near the spot upon which the stone of the Ark of the Covenant lay, there were now scattered around about twenty dwellings. Bethabara was not close to the shore, but about one half-hour from the ferry; one could see it however. From the ferry to John's present place of baptism beyond Betharaba was a good hour and a half's distance.

I saw Jesus going from house to house at Ono. At first I knew not for what reason, but later I heard that it was on account of the tithes, to the paying of which He was urging the people. He reminded them also of the alms which it was customary to give on the feast of fruit trees now beginning. That evening He celebrated the Sabbath in the synagogue where He taught. After that began the preparations for the new year's fruit festival. It was a threefold feast: first, it commemorated the rising of the sap in the trees; secondly, because today tithes of all the fruits were offered; and lastly, it was a feast of thanksgiving for the fertility of the soil. Jesus gave an instruction upon all these points. They ate much fruit, and gave to the poor whole figures of fruit that were built up on the tables. About twenty new disciples had, up to the present, come to Jesus.

9. Jesus Cures in Phasael the Daughter of Jairus the Essenian. Magdalen's First Call to Conversion

At the close of the feast, Jesus left Ono with twenty-one disciples and journeyed to Galilee. His way led through the region in which Jacob had owned a field, and among those shepherd houses, from one of which Joseph and Mary had been so harshly turned away on their journey to Bethlehem. He visited the occupants of the inn that had extended hospitality to the holy travellers, and instructed them; with those of the inhospitable one, He stayed overnight and admonished them to be converted. The woman of the house was still alive, though on a sickbed. Jesus cured her. Then He passed through Aruma where He had before been. Jairus, a descendant of the Essenian Chariot, dwelt in the neighboring and somewhat despised place, Phasael. He had some time previously begged Jesus to cure his sick daughter, and Jesus had promised to

do so, though not just then. Although his daughter
was dead, Jairus now dispatched a messenger to meet
Him and remind Him of His promise. Jesus sent His
disciples on ahead after appointing a certain place
where they should again meet Him, and He Himself
accompanied Jairus' messenger back to Phasael.

When He entered the house of Jairus, the daughter lay wrapped in the winding-sheet ready for burial, her weeping friends around her. Jesus ordered
the neighbors to be called in, and the winding-sheet
and linens to be loosened. Then taking the dead girl
by the hand, He commanded her to arise. She did
so, and stood before Him. She was about sixteen
years old and not good. She had no love for her
father, although he prized her above all things. He
was charitable and pious, and shrank not from communication with the poor and despised. That was a
source of vexation to his daughter. Jesus roused her
from death both of soul and body. She reformed, and
some time after joined the holy women. Jesus warned
those present not to speak of the miracle they had
witnessed. It was through the same desire of secrecy
that He had not allowed the disciples to accompany
Him. This was not the Jairus of Capharnaum whose
daughter also was, at a later period, raised from the
dead by Jesus.

On leaving Phasael, Jesus turned His steps to
the Jordan which He crossed, and continued His
journey northward through Peraea as far as Socoth,
where He recrossed to the west side of the river
and went on to Jezrael.

Jesus taught in Jezrael and performed many
miracles before a great concourse of people. All
the disciples from Galilee were here assembled
to meet Him. Nathanael Chased, Nathanael the
bride-groom, Peter, James, John, the sons of Mary
Cleophas, all were there. Lazarus, Martha, Seraphia,[1]

1. Veronica.

Cana. The disciples were gathered here. Jesus preached all the next day and till the close of the Sabbath.

Numbers of sick and possessed were brought to Him from the country around. He cured them openly before all His disciples, and drove the devils out in presence of an ever-increasing crowd. Messengers came from Sidon begging Him to go back with them, but He put them off kindly until a future day. The crowd became so great that at the close of the Sabbath Jesus left Capharnaum with some of His disciples, and escaped into a mountainous district about an hour to the north of the city. It was situated between the lake and the mouth of the Jordan, and was full of ravines. Into one of these He retired alone to pray. This is the same mountain range from one of whose spurs, when returning lately from the mount of Bethanat with His disciples, they had seen the ships of Peter and Zebedee on the lake.

The disciples that accompanied Him went down to the dwellings of the fishermen near the lake in order to apprise them of Jesus' coming. Andrew had stayed behind in Capharnaum, teaching and explaining to the assembled multitude.

In the evening Jesus went to His Mother's house between Bethsaida and Capharnaum, whither had come Lazarus with Martha and the other women from Jerusalem. They were on their way from Magdalum and had called to take leave of Mary before returning to Jerusalem. He said that Martha was too anxious, that Magdalen had been very deeply affected, yet she would, notwithstanding, relapse once more into her old ways. She had not yet laid aside her fine attire, for, as she declared, one in her position could not dress so plainly as the other women, etc. As there now began in the city a fast of thanksgiving for the death of a man who, in violation of the Law, had caused certain images to be set up in the Temple, Jesus taught again in Capharnaum.

and Johanna Chusa, who had come before
Jerusalem, had visited Magdalen at her castl
Magdalum to persuade her to go with them to Jez
in order to see, if not to hear, the wise, the admir:
the most eloquent, and most beautiful Jesus, of w
the whole country was full. Magdalen had yie
to the persuasions of the women and, surrou
by much vain display, accompanied them thithe
she stood at the window of an inn gazing down
the street, Jesus and His disciples came walkin
He looked at her gravely as He passed with a gl
that pierced her soul. An unusual feeling of
fusion came over her. Violently agitated, she ru
from the inn and, impelled by an overpowering s
of her own misery, hid in a house wherein le
and women afflicted with bloody flux found a re
It was a kind of hospital under the superintenc
of a Pharisee. The people of the inn from which
dalen had fled, knowing the life she was lea
cried out: "That's the right place for her, among
ers and people tormented with bloody flux!"

But Magdalen had fled to the house of the
rous through that feeling of intense humili
roused in her soul by the glance of Jesus, fo:
had made her way into that respectable pos
among the other women through a motive of p
not wishing to stand in the crowd of poor, con
people. Accompanied by Lazarus, she return
Magdalum with Martha and the other women
next Sabbath was there celebrated by them, for
dalum could boast a synagogue.

10. Jesus in Capharnaum, Gennabris, and Chisloth-Thabor

Toward evening Jesus went for the Sabba
Capharnaum, though not till after He had v:
His Mother. He taught there, and again took u
abode in the house belonging to the bridegro(

Again were brought to Him the sick, of whom He cured many, and again did messengers come to invite Him to other places. There were at this time some very ill-disposed Pharisees around Him and they contradicted Him on several points. They asked Him what would come of all that excitement, for the whole country was in commotion on His account, since He was teaching publicly and daily swelling the numbers of His followers. Jesus rebuked them severely, and told them that He was about to teach and act still more openly.

On that evening began a fast in commemoration of the great victory gained by the other tribes over that of Benjamin, on account of some shameful transgression. I saw that in the country of Phasael, where Jesus had lately raised to life the daughter of Jairus, as also in Aruma, Givea, etc., this day was kept with special strictness, since they had been the theater of those events. I saw that the women in those places made a certain offering and took a prominent part in the fast of atonement.

That night Jesus, with Andrew, Peter, the sons of Mary Cleophas and of Zebedee, was conducted by Nathanael Chased to Gennabris, his own dwelling place. Nathanael had established there an inn for Jesus. He did not enter Nathanael's house which, however, He passed on the way to the city. Nathanael the bridegroom and his wife also visited Capharnaum and Jezrael at this time.

The place of Baptism near Ono was guarded in turn by the inhabitants. Jesus taught in Gennabris and cured some raging possessed. A road for traffic ran through the city. The inhabitants were not so docile as those nearer the lake. Although they did not openly contradict Jesus, yet many received His teaching coldly.

Besides the future Apostles, Jonathan, Peter's half-brother, was also in Gennabris. The other Apostles had scattered around Capharnaum and Bethsaida relating all that they had seen and heard of Jesus.

From Gennabris Jesus went with the future Apostles to Bethulia, about three hours distant, five from Tiberias, and not far from Jezrael. It lay on a height so steep that one might fancy it was ready to topple down at any moment. The fragments of its walls were so broad that a wagon could be driven on them. The road from here to Nazareth passed Mount Thabor, from which it was only a couple of hours to the south.

Nathanael Chased had at this time given over his office in Gennabris to his brother, or cousin. He was, for the future, to follow Jesus.

When Jesus entered Bethulia, the possessed began to cry after Him on the street. On arriving at the marketplace, He stood still near a teacher's chair and sent some of His disciples with directions to the superior of the synagogue to have the doors on all sides of the school opened. Others were sent from house to house to call the occupants to the instruction. The synagogue was surrounded by doors between the columns, and it was customary to throw them open when the crowd was exceptionally great. Jesus taught here of the tiny grain of wheat that must be cast into the earth. During His stay He abode in an inn that had been prepared for Him. The Pharisees here did not indeed openly contradict, but they murmured, and Jesus knew that they did so, because they feared He would celebrate the Sabbath among them. He told His disciples this, and that He would keep it about a couple of hours further on, at a place to the northwest toward Thabor. I cannot now recall the name of that place, but the inhabitants were engaged in dyeing silk for fringes and tassels.

Jesus also cured the sick there. All the disciples that had remained behind met here again.

As Jesus, on account of the murmuring of the Pharisees, left Bethulia, He taught outside of the city at

the distance of about a quarter of an hour where
there was a teacher's chair of stone. Ruined walls
lay around, and the place looked as if it might once
have belonged to the city proper. At about three in
the afternoon, Jesus arrived at Chisloth, which was
almost three hours distant, at the foot of Mount Thabor. Andrew and the others had preceded Him in
order to arrange the inn. A great multitude from the
whole country around had gathered at Chisloth,
among them numbers of shepherds with their crooks
and merchants on their way from Sidon and Tyre.
Jesus' miracles and preaching were already noised
throughout the land. All crowded to the places where
He taught; and when it became known that He purposed celebrating the Sabbath at Chisloth, they
flocked thither to hear Him.

Wherever Jesus now appeared great excitement
prevailed. They called after Him, cast themselves
down before Him, and pressed around Him in order
to be able to touch Him; consequently He came and
went suddenly and unexpectedly, thus to escape the
crowd. Frequently He separated from His disciples
on the road, sent them by another route, and went
on Himself alone. In the towns and villages, they
often had to open a way for Him through the crowd.
Nevertheless He permitted many to draw near and
touch Him, and many a one was thereby interiorly
aroused, converted, or cured.

In the evening Jesus retired to the inn prepared
for Him by the disciples outside of Chisloth-Thabor,
where He had already been twice before. Chisloth
was perhaps seven hours from Nazareth, though in
a direct line about five. As the roads of this country
are so winding, running as they do through the valleys, and as the inhabitants determine distances
sometimes by the length of the roads between two
places, and sometimes by what it might appear to
one gazing down from the mountains, their statis-
tics on that point seldom agree. Galilee was thickly

dotted with cities and towns, but from no elevated
point could more than a few be seen.

Chisloth-Thabor was chiefly a commercial mart
in which were some rich merchants and a great
number of poor people. Many of them were dyers
of raw silk which was afterward manufactured into
fringes and tassels for sacred vestments. These dyers
in earlier times were found principally at Tyre on
the sea, but later many of them removed here. The
rich merchants employed the poor in their facto-
ries. I saw here likewise some people who appeared
to be slaves.

The disciples, with thick ropes run through stakes,
had cut off a space in front of the inn in order to
keep back the crowd. It was from that space that
Jesus preached. As among His audience there were
many of the rich merchants from the city, He taught
upon riches and the danger attending the love of
gain. Their position, He told them, was more per-
ilous than that of the publicans, who more easily
than they would reform. Saying these words, Jesus
pointed to the ropes that separated Him from the
crowd, and uttered the words: "A rope like one of
those would go more easily into the eye of a needle than a rich man into the Kingdom of Heaven."
The ropes were camel's hair, as thick as one's arm,
and drawn four times through the stakes around
the enclosure. The rich people defended themselves
by saying that they gave alms out of all their profits. But Jesus replied that alms that have been
expressed from the sweat of the poor bring down
no blessing. This instruction was not pleasing to
His hearers.

Chisloth was a Levitical city made over by the
tribe of Zabulon to the Levites of the race of Mer-
ari. The most celebrated school of the whole country was here. It was very large and all its exercises
were conducted with solemnity. When on the Sabbath Jesus taught in the synagogue, the priests

assisted at the discourse. They handed Him the rolls
of Scripture or read the passages that He indicated,
upon which He questioned and explained. There was
also singing, but not of the Pharisaical kind. I heard
the voice of Jesus sweetly sounding among all the
others, but I do not remember having heard Him
singing alone.

Next morning Jesus taught in the school of Chisloth. Andrew instructed the children in an adjacent
hall, and recounted to the strangers crowding in all
that he had seen and heard of Jesus. Jesus took for
His subject vanity and presumption. He performed
no cures that day because, as He said, they thought
themselves better than others, and attributed to their
own merit His coming to teach in their city; whereas
He would have them know that He had been led
thereto by His knowledge of their misery and His
desire to humble and convert them.

The preaching ended, Jesus went out into the court
in front of the synagogue, in which there were little
cells belonging to it. They were like sentry boxes in
a courtyard. Here, He cured of convulsions and other
ills numerous children brought to Him by their mothers. He cured them because they were innocent. He
cured several women also who humbled themselves
before Him, saying: "Lord, hearken to my fault, my
transgression!" They cast themselves down in the
hall before Him and bewailed their sins. Among them
were some afflicted with a bloody flux, and others
tormented by evil inclinations from which they
implored to be freed.

That evening Jesus celebrated the Sabbath in the
school and afterward ate at the inn. His future Apostles and intimate friends were with Him at the same
table, and the disciples not engaged in serving were
in adjoining apartments. The next day He celebrated
the Sabbath in the synagogue, and in front of it
healed many sick. He also visited and cured in their
homes many that could not be carried to Him. The

disciples assisted Jesus in this, bringing the sick,
leading them to Him, raising them up, and making
room for them. They executed His commissions and
delivered His messages.

All the travelling expenses, as well as the alms,
were up to the present furnished by Lazarus, and
Simeon's son Obed kept the accounts.

The little cells before the synagogue that looked
like sentry boxes were in the courtyard where,
through a grating, the women spoke in private to
Jesus. It was the custom for female sinners, penitents, or women that had contracted legal impurity
to receive in these cells consolation from the priests.

There was no city upon Mount Thabor, but there
were bulwarks, walls, and something like a vacant
fortress, whither at times the troops retired. On the
evening after the Sabbath, Jesus and His most intimate disciples, the future Apostles, were entertained
by a Pharisee who had been touched and converted
by the teaching of Jesus. Next day Jesus, with His
disciples, was present at a great banquet, given in
His honor in the public feast hall by the most distinguished men of the place. Jesus taught here also,
and on the same evening left the city for Jezrael,
which was not much more than three hours' distance
from Chisloth-Thabor.

In Jezrael, Jesus' relatives and the disciples from
Bethsaida, including Andrew and Nathanael, took
leave of Him in order to visit their homes. He indicated to them where they should again meet. About
fifteen of the younger disciples still remained with
Him while He taught here and performed some cures.
There were all kinds of religious and secular schools
in Jezrael, for it was a large city. Jesus took Naboth's
vineyard for the subject of one of His discourses.

From Jezrael Jesus went one hour and a half
southward to a field in a valley, two hours long and
as many broad, wherein were numerous orchards
surrounded by low hedges. It was an uncommonly

productive and charming fruit region. There were numerous tents here standing in couples at different intervals, and occupied by people from Sichar who guarded and gathered in the fruit. I think it was a kind of service that they were obliged to take turns in rendering. About four occupied one tent. The women dwelt together apart from the men, for whom they did the cooking. Jesus instructed these people under a tent. There were here most beautiful springs and abundant streams, which flowed into the Jordan. The principal source came from Jezrael. It formed in the valley a charming spring, over which a kind of chapel was built. From this spring house the stream divided into several others throughout the vale, united with other waters, and at last emptied into the Jordan. There were about thirty custodians whom Jesus instructed, the women remaining at some distance. He taught of the slavery of sin, from which they should free themselves. They were inexpressibly rejoiced and touched that He had come to them. He was so loving and condescending to these poor people that I had to shed tears myself over it. They set before Jesus and the disciples fruit, of which they ate. In some parts of the valley the fruit was already ripe, in others the trees were only in blossom. There were some brown fruits like figs, but growing in clusters like grapes, also yellow plants from which they prepared a kind of pap.[1] In this valley rises Mount Gilboa, and here also was Saul slain in battle against the Philistines.

---

1. From the description, we may presume that the plant to which Sister Emmerich alludes was a species of maize; and the *brown fruits* were, very probably, the fruit of the date palm. She mentioned likewise *durrha* and several plants used as salads. The whole region south of Gezrael she describes as teeming with fruitfulness.

11. Jesus in Sunem, Ulama, and Capharnaum

In the evening Jesus went through Jezrael and about three hours further to Sunem, an open place on a hill. Some of the disciples had gone on before, in order to make arrangements with the landlord of the inn at the entrance of the city. The fertile valley through which Jesus had just passed lay to the south of Jezrael. He went through a part of Jezrael without attracting notice, and then turned northward toward Sunem. Near this city, that is at a distance of one to two hours, are two others, one of which Jesus had passed on His way from Chisloth-Thabor to Jezrael.

The inhabitants of Sunem depended upon weaving for their livelihood. They wove narrow edging of twisted silk, plain or interspersed with flowers. Sunem did not lie in the vale of Esdrelon, but rather where the mountains took their rise.

The multitude that here pressed around Jesus was simply astonishing, and it was ever on the increase. The people surrounded Him everywhere, cast themselves down before Him, crying and shouting that a new Prophet had arisen, One sent by God! Many were sincere in their acclamations, but others followed through curiosity and shouted merely to swell the noise. The crowd was so dense that it was almost like an insurrection, and because here in Galilee the excitement was daily increasing, Jesus resolved soon to leave it. Sunem was the native city of the beautiful Abisag who had served David in his old age. Eliseus also had had an inn here at which he frequently stopped and in which he had recalled the dead son of his hostess to life. A vision of the same was vouchsafed me, that I might know the place. This city possessed also a free inn for certain travellers. It had been founded as a memorial of Eliseus. I know not, however, whether it was the house that the Prophet once occupied, or whether it was another built upon the same site. Jesus taught on this day in the synagogue and visited many of the houses to console and cure the sick. Sunem was built rather irregularly around a hill whose summit overlooked the city. A road led up the hill. The houses upon it decreased in size with the ascent, the highest being mere huts. The top of the hill was crowned by an open space upon which stood a teacher's seat. It was surrounded by palings over which an awning could be stretched for protection from the sun.

When Jesus, on the morning of the following day, started with His disciples for the teacher's chair, the whole place was alive with excitement. They had brought numbers of sick in litters, and had placed them all along the road leading up the hill. Jesus ascended through the clamoring multitude, healing as He went. The people had mounted to the roofs, the better to see and hear all that He would do and say. From the teacher's chair on the top of the hill the view was magnificent, stretching off toward Thabor. Jesus inveighed against the pride and presumption of the Sunemites who, instead of being converted, doing penance, and keeping the Commandments of God, broke forth into vain shouts over the Prophet that had come among them, the Sent from God, for they attributed His coming as an honor due their own merit, whereas He had come in order to convince them of their sins.

About three in the afternoon Jesus left Sunem. Taking a northerly direction, He reached, in about three hours, a large and closely built city with a less ancient appearance than Sunem. It was enclosed by walls so broad that trees flourished upon them. This city was called Ulama and was about five hours southeast of Thabor. Arbela was about two hours to the north. The rough roads of the surrounding mountains were covered with sharp, white pebbles, on which account there were made in Ulama numbers

of soles to bind as a protection under the feet. The
city was built on a mountain, surrounded by other
mountains, and in an altogether impassable region.
Vines covered those mountains from base to summit. I have seen upon them plants as high as a tree,
their tangled branches as thick as one's arm. They
produce large, pyriform fruits like gourds, and from
them flasks are made.[1] Ulama did not appear so old
as other cities; indeed, there was something about
it that even made it look unfinished. The inhabitants did not bear the stamp of old Jewish simplicity, they appeared to be aiming at greater culture
and refinement. It was as if the Romans or some
other nation had formerly sojourned among them.
Here as elsewhere, the concourse of people was very
great, for they knew that Jesus was about to celebrate the Sabbath in Ulama. Several of the disciples had rejoined Jesus, among them Peter's
half-brother Jonathan and the sons of the widows.
They numbered, in all, twenty. Peter, Andrew, John,
James the Less, Nathanael Chased, and Nathanael
the bridegroom had also come. Jesus had directed
them to do so that they might hear His instructions
and assist Him in His ministrations to the sick, rendered difficult by the turbulence of the multitude.
The people had found out the way by which Jesus
was to come, and they went forth to welcome Him,
carrying green branches and strewing leaves. They
had stretched across the road long strips of stuff
which they lowered for Him to step over, while shouts
of joy proclaimed the advent of the Prophet. The
chief officers of the place maintained order and formally saluted Jesus in the name of the city. There
were in Ulama many possessed, who clamored violently after Jesus and shouted His name. But He
commanded them to be silent. Even at the inn they

---

1. Probably a large species of bottle gourd, the Calabash, not known to
Sister Emmerich. Our supposition is confirmed by her words: "It forms
no real wood."

allowed Him no rest. They ran about raging and screaming, until He again ordered them to be silent and had them removed.

Ulama had three schools: one of jurisprudence; another for youths; and the third, the synagogue. Jesus entered different houses, to cure and to console. Then He taught in the school, speaking especially upon simplicity and of the respect due to parents; for in both of these particulars the people of this place were wanting. He rebuked them severely also for their pride. Vain at the thought of a Prophet's coming among them, they were by their presumption depriving themselves of the benefits attached to these days of penance and instruction.

The Sabbath over, the distinguished men of the place gave Jesus an entertainment in the grand public hall. The Apostles and disciples that had gone home limited themselves to a mere visit to their relatives. They had then called upon Mary, with whom the holy women were becoming more and more intimate.

The Baptist was still in the same place, his followers constantly diminishing. Herod had several times been to see him and had frequently sent his officers for the same purpose.

At nine o'clock on the morning after the Sabbath, Jesus went with His disciples to a mountain along which was a pleasure garden or bathing place, about a quarter of an hour from the city. The garden was almost as large as the cemetery of Dülmen.[2] It had pavilions and little summer houses, a beautiful fountain, and a place for instruction. Jesus had directed the sick, of whom there were numbers, to be transported thither from the city, for He could not, on account of the crowd, cure in the latter place. The disciples busied themselves in the maintenance of order, and the sick on their litters were placed around

2. Dülmen, the little town in which Sister Emmerich's last years were spent.

under tents and in the pavilions. The crowds that
followed from the city were so great that many could
not even reach the garden. The magistrates and
priests also kept order. Jesus passed from litter to
litter curing many. When I say *many,* I generally
mean about thirty. When I say *a few* or *several, I*
mean about ten. Jesus taught and alluded to the
death of Moses, whose anniversary would soon be
celebrated by a fast day, when their food already
cooked would be placed under the ashes, and when
they would eat, as was usual on such days, a particular kind of bread. He also referred to the Promised
Land and its fertility, which was to be understood
not only of the material sustenance of the body, but
also of the spiritual nourishment of the soul; for it
was also fruitful in Prophets and oracles from God,
the fruit of which would be penance and the salvation promised to all that would embrace it.

   This instruction ended, I saw Jesus going into a
building nearby wherein the possessed had been
assembled. He entered to find them raging and shouting. They were for the most part young people, some
of them only children. Jesus caused them to be placed
in a row, commanded silence, and with one word freed
them from the evil spirit. Some of them fell fainting. Their parents and friends were present, and to
all Jesus addressed some words of exhortation and
instruction.

   After Jesus had taught in the synagogue, He left
the city unnoticed, the disciples having gone before
Him. He knew how to manage that. Without entering any of the cities on the way, they proceeded
toward Capharnaum. Jesus was about to leave
Galilee on account of the great excitement there prevailing. He travelled with the disciples the livelong
night, and arrived at His Mother's in the morning.
Peter's wife and sister were there, also the bride of
Cana and other women. The house that Mary occupied here was for the most part like its neighbors

and very roomy. She was never alone. The widows
lived nearby and the women from Bethsaida and
Capharnaum, between which these houses were,
gathered around her as also one or other of the disciples. I saw them keeping the fast with signs of
mourning, the women being veiled. Jesus taught in
the synagogue of Capharnaum, the disciples and holy
women being present.

Capharnaum was situated, measuring in a straight
line over the mountain, about one hour from the Sea
of Galilee, but two hours if one went through the
valley and through Bethsaida on the south. About
a good half-hour on the road from Capharnaum to
Bethsaida were the houses, in one of which Mary
dwelt. A beautiful stream flows from Capharnaum
to the lake. Near Bethsaida it branched off into several arms, rendering the land very fruitful. Mary
conducted no household, she owned neither cattle
nor fields. She lived as a widow upon the gifts of
her friends, engaged in spinning, sewing, knitting
with little wooden needles, praying, consoling, and
instructing the other women.

Jesus, on the day of His arrival, had a private
interview with His Mother. She wept over the great
danger threatening Him on account of the excitement everywhere produced by His teachings and
miracles, for she had been informed of all the murmurs and calumnies uttered against Him by those
that would not presume to say them to His face.
But Jesus told her that His time was come, that He
would soon leave those parts and go down to Judea
where, after the Pasch, still greater vexation would
arise on His account.

That evening there began in Capharnaum a feast
of thanksgiving for rain. The synagogue and other
public buildings were gaily ornamented with young
green trees and pyramids of foliage, while from the
galleries on the roof of the synagogue and other large
edifices, a wonderful, many-toned instrument was

sounded. The servants of the synagogue, people like
our sextons, played on it. It looked like a bag about
four feet in length in which were several pipes and
trumpet mouthpieces. When the bag was not dis-
tended with wind, these pipes and tubes lay together,
one upon another. But when it was inflated by the
breath of a man blowing into one of the mouthpieces,
two other men raised it up and (either by blowing
the breath, or by means of a bellows) introduced air
into it. Then by opening and closing the different
valves of the pipes, which arose in several directions,
a shrill-sounding, many-voiced tone was produced.
Those standing at the side of the instrument blew
into it at certain intervals.

Jesus delivered in the synagogue an extremely
touching discourse upon rain and drought. In it He
told of Elias, who prayed on Mt. Carmel for rain and
six times questioned his servant as to what he saw.
The seventh time, the servant replied that he saw a
little cloud rising out of the sea. It became larger
and larger until at last it bore rain to the whole
country. Then Elias journeyed through the whole land.
Jesus applied those seven questionings of Elias to
the space of time before the fulfillment of the Promise.
The cloud He explained as a symbol of the present
and the rain as an image of the coming of the Messiah, whose teaching should spread everywhere and
bear new life to all. Whoever thirsted should now
drink, and whoever had prepared his field should
now receive rain. This was said so touchingly, so
impressively that all His hearers, as well as Mary
and the other holy women, wept.

The people of Capharnaum were at that time very
well disposed. There were three priests attached to
the synagogue and near it was the house in which
they dwelt. Jesus and His intimate disciples often
took their meals with them, for a certain degree of
hospitality was always extended to the teacher who
had taught in the synagogue.

That evening and early the next morning, I heard them playing again on that wonderful instrument. The feast was celebrated all the next day, but only by the children and young people, who enjoyed themselves heartily. The evening of the feast, Jesus took leave of the disciples related to Him, as also those from Bethsaida, because early the next day He was to depart from Capharnaum and go down into Judea. He took with Him only about twelve, those from Nazareth, those from Jerusalem, and those that had come from John.

12. Jesus in Dothain and Sephoris. From a Distance, He Helps the Shipwrecked

After the Feast of Thanksgiving Jesus, with about twelve disciples, travelled in a southeasterly direction from Capharnaum, as if between Cana and Sephoris. Mary and eight of the holy women, among them Mary Cleophas, the three widows, the bride of Cana, and Peter's sister, accompanied Him to a little city where they took a meal together and then parted from Him. In the neighborhood of this place was the pit into which Joseph was cast by his brethren. The place was called Dothain. But there was another and a much larger Dothain in the vale of Esdrelon, about four hours to the north of Samaria. This Dothain was a little place, and the people lived chiefly by providing for the wants of the merchants travelling through their city. It lay at the end of a little valley large enough to afford pasturage for about eighty head of cattle. At the other side stood that great building in which Jesus had once calmed the possessed; this time He did not enter. Dothain is an hour and a half northeast of Sephoris and between four and five hours from Mt. Thabor.

The disciples had gone on before, to prepare the inn. About eight men, some of them priests, came

out to meet Jesus and the holy women, and escort
them to the public hall of entertainment. No one
lived in it, but already everything was prepared for
a repast. Before the entrance there was spread in
honor of Jesus a carpet upon which He had to walk.
They washed His feet. The women ate apart, back
of the fireplace. Jesus and the disciples reclined at
table and partook of only cold viands, such as little
rolls and honey, green salad steeped in sauce, and
fruits. Their drink was water mixed with balsam.
Little flasks of the same were presented to Jesus
and the women to take away with them. The priests
from the city remained standing during the repast
and served the guests with uncommon love and humility, while Jesus spoke of Joseph, who had here been
sold. It was an indescribably touching scene. I could
not restrain my tears. It appeared to me so strange
that I should behold it so near to me, and yet could
not enter as I so longed to do. I wanted to do this
and that, but I could not. Immediately after the repast,
the holy women departed for Capharnaum.

Jesus took leave of His Mother in private, and
then bade goodbye to the others. I have remarked
that when alone Jesus always embraced His Mother
on His arrival or departure, but before others He
merely extended His hand or inclined His head. Mary
wept. She was still very youthful looking, tall and
delicately built. Her forehead was very high, her nose
rather long, her eyes very large and mildly down-
cast, her lips of a beautiful red, her complexion rather
dark, but beautiful, and her cheeks lightly tinged
with the color of the rose.

Jesus tarried a while longer teaching in the inn,
and the men, who would accept no remuneration for
the repast, accompanied Him on His departure as
far as Joseph's Well, which was at that time not such
as it was when Joseph was let down into it. Then it
was only an empty pit, its mouth surrounded by
green bushes and vines, but now it was a spacious,

four-cornered reservoir, like a little pool, under a roof
supported by pillars. It was full of water and in it
was kept an abundance of fish. I saw some that lifted
their heads up so curiously, not pointed like those
we see. But they were not so large as similar ones
in the Sea of Galilee. There was no visible supply of
water to the well. There was a fence around it, and
it was guarded by people living near. Jesus entered
the springhouse with His companions. The whole way
He had taught of Joseph and his brethren, and He
continued the same discourse at the well, which I
saw Him blessing as He left. His escort now returned
to Dothain, while He and His disciples went on for
about a good hour to Sephoris, where He stopped
with the sons of Anne's sister.

Sephoris was built on a mountain in the midst of
mountains. It was larger than Capharnaum, and there
were many separate residences standing around in
the environs. Jesus was not very well received by
the Doctors of the synagogue, and I heard wicked
people, of whom there were many in this city, calum-
niating Him, saying that He was wandering about
instead of staying with His Mother. Jesus performed
no cures here, and held Himself very much aloof;
still, on the Sabbath He preached in the synagogue
and went to an inn nearby for His meals. He visited
many private individuals and families, principally
Essenians, however, whom He exhorted and consoled,
for many of the wicked inhabitants ridiculed and
slandered them, on account of their affection for Him.
Jesus told several of those that lived in the environs, as also some of His own relatives, not to follow Him just then, but to remain His friends in
secret, and to continue their good works until the
end of His career. His relatives did much good here
and contributed also to the support of the Blessed
Virgin, to whom they sent all kinds of necessaries.
I saw Jesus conversing with these different families
in so affectionate and intimate a way that I have no

words to describe it. His deportment, so full of love,
touched me to tears.

That night I saw something else that appeared to
me surprising and inexpressibly affecting. There happened on that night a great windstorm in the Holy
Land, and I saw Jesus with many others in prayer.
He prayed with outstretched hands that danger
might be averted. Then I had a glance at the Sea of
Galilee, which was lashed by the tempest, the ships
of Peter, Andrew, and Zebedee being in distress. The
Apostles were, as I saw, asleep in Bethania, their
servants alone being on the ships. And lo! As Jesus
stood praying, I saw an apparition of Him there upon
the ships, now on one, now on the other, and then
again upon the raging billows. It was as if He were
laboring among them, holding back the vessels, ward-
ing off the danger. He was not there in person, for
I did not see Him going, but He stood above the sufferers, He hovered on the waves. The sailors did not
see Him, for it was His spirit assisting them in prayer.
Nobody knew anything about His being there, though
He was really helping them. Perhaps the sailors
believed in Him and called on Him for help.

13. Jesus in Nazareth. The Three Youths. The Feast of Purim.

From Sephoris Jesus took a byway around some
country houses to Nazareth about two hours distant,
teaching and consoling as He went. Among the
disciples now with Him were two or three youths,
sons of Essenian widows. Arrived at Nazareth, He
put up with some acquaintances, and without being
remarked visited several good people. The Pharisees,
with an outward show of respect but inwardly full
of malice, called upon Jesus to ask Him what He
now purposed doing and why He did not stay with
His Mother, which questions He answered gravely
and sharply. Preparations were going on all around

for the fast day observed in remembrance of Esther, also for that of the Feast of Purim immediately to follow. Jesus taught very zealously in the synagogue.

That night I again saw Jesus praying with outstretched arms, and again appearing on the Sea of Galilee to bear help in a storm. This time the distress was much greater, and many more vessels were in danger. I saw Jesus laying His hand on the helm without the helmsman's seeing Him. The three rich youths of Nazareth who had once before vainly proferred their petition to Him to be received as disciples came to Him again, reiterating their request. They almost knelt to Him, but He sent them away after pointing out certain conditions that had to be fulfilled before He would allow them to join His disciples. Jesus knew well that their views were wholly terrestrial, and that they could not understand Him. They wanted to follow Him because they saw in Him a philosopher, a learned Rabbi. After a time spent in His school, they could, as they thought, shine with a more brilliant reputation and do honor to their city Nazareth. They were besides somewhat vexed at seeing Him giving the preference to the poor sons of Nazareth rather than to themselves.

Until far into the night I saw Jesus with the old Essenian, Eliud of Nazareth. The holy man looked as if he would soon die of old age. He was no longer able for much, indeed he was almost bedridden. Jesus leaned on His arm at the bedside and talked with him. Eliud was entirely absorbed in God.

At the commencement of the Feast of Purim, a musical instrument, which stood on three feet, was again played on the roof of the synagogue. It was hollow with pipes running through it, the ends extending both above and below. By pushing the pipes in and out, the music was produced. Children also were playing on harps and flutes. Today in commemoration of Esther, the women and young maidens enjoyed certain rights and privileges in the synagogue. They

were not separated from the men, they could even
approach where the priests were. There was a procession in the synagogue of children dressed fanci-
fully, some in white, others in red. Then a maiden
entered wearing around her neck an ornament somewhat frightful looking. It was a blood-red circle
around her throat, as if she had been beheaded, and
from it hung on her white garments, numerous knots
of blood-red threads like so many streaks of blood
from the wounded neck. She wore a magnificent mantle borne by train-bearers, and appeared to be enact-
ing the principal part in some drama. Children and
maidens followed her. She wore a high, pointed ornament on the forepart of her head and a long veil. In
her hand she carried something, whether a sword or
a scepter, I do not know. She was tall, and a maiden
of great beauty. I do not know for certain what distinguished character she represented. It might, I
think, have been Esther, or again, Judith, though not
that Judith who slew Holofernes, for there was with
her a maiden, who carried a beautiful basket containing presents for the chief priest. She presented
to him many precious little shields, such as the priests
wore sometimes on the forehead or the breast. In
one corner of the synagogue, concealed by a curtain,
lay upon a bed of state the effigy of a man, whose
head the maiden struck off and took to the chief
priest. Then, making use of the privilege granted to
females on that day, she rebuked the priests for the
principal faults they had committed during the year.
That done, she withdrew. This privilege to rebuke
the priests belonged to the women on certain other
feasts also.

In the synagogue they read in turn from separate
rolls the Book of Esther, Jesus also taking His turn
to read. The Jews, especially the children, had little
wooden tablets with hammers. When they pulled a
string, the hammer struck a name inscribed on the
tablet, while at the same time holders uttered some

words. They did this as often as the name of Aman was pronounced.

There were also great banquets. Jesus was present at that given to the priests in the grand public hall. The adornments of this feast were similar to those of the Feast of Tabernacles. There were numbers of wreaths, roses as large as one's head, pyramids made up entirely of flowers, and quantities of fruit. A whole lamb was on the table, and I gazed in wonder at the magnificence of the plates, glasses, and dishes. There was one kind of dish many-colored and transparent, like precious stones. They looked as if formed of interwoven threads of colored glass. There was today a great exchange of gifts, consisting principally of jewels and handsome articles of apparel, such as robes, maniples, veils for the head, and sashes trimmed with tassels. Jesus, too, was presented with a holiday robe trimmed in like manner. But He would not keep it; He passed it to another. Many others likewise bestowed their presents on the poor, who were very bountifully remembered that day.

After the banquet, Jesus and His disciples walked with the priests to the pleasure gardens, and the beautifully adorned teaching places near Nazareth. They had with them three rolls of writings, and I saw again the Book of Esther, out of which they read in turn. Crowds of youths and maidens followed them, but the latter listened to the discourse only at a distance. I saw also on that day men going around and taking up a tax.

From Nazareth Jesus and His disciples went to Apheca about four hours distant, but returned to Nazareth for the following Sabbath and visited the dying Eliud. The priests of Nazareth could not comprehend where Jesus, in so short an absence, had come by so much knowledge. They could find nothing reprehensible in His teaching, though many were secretly envious of Him. They escorted Him part of the way when He left Nazareth with His disciples.

14. Jesus at Lazarus' Estate Near Thirza and at His Home in Bethania

Jesus, taking the road travelled by the Holy Family on the occasion of their flight into Egypt, arrived with His disciples at the little place not far from Legio where the Holy Family had put up and where lived a set of despised people like slaves. Jesus bought some bread here, and as He divided it, it was multiplied in His hands; but the miracle created no excitement, since He did not tarry long and performed it, as it were, in passing.

Proceeding on His journey, He was met by Lazarus, John Marc, and Obed, who had come for that purpose. With them Jesus went on to Lazarus' villa near Thirza, about five hours distant. They arrived unnoticed and by night, and found all things ready for their reception. The villa was on a mountain toward Samaria, not far from Jacob's field. A very old Jew, who went barefoot and girt, was the steward, an office he had held even when Mary and Joseph stopped here on their journey to Bethlehem. It was at this same villa that Martha and Magdalen, in Jesus' last year when He was teaching in Samaria, showed Him hospitality and implored Him to come to their brother Lazarus who was sick.

Near that estate of Lazarus was the then small city of Thirza, situated in a lovely region about seven hours' journey from Samaria. The morning sun, to which Thirza was exposed, rendered it extremely fruitful in grain, wine, and orchard fruits. The inhabitants were engaged chiefly in agriculture, the products of which they carried to a distance for sale. The city was once large and handsome and the residence of kings, but the palace had been consumed by fire and the city ruined by war. One king, Amri, had made that property of Lazarus his home until the building of Samaria, whither he then removed. The people of Thirza were in Jesus' time very pious and lived

very retired in their little, isolated city. I think there
are some remains of it even in our own day. The
inhabitants were very reserved in their intercourse
with the Samaritans. (*3 Kgs.* 16:24). Jesus taught in
the synagogue of Thirza, but performed no cures.

On the Sabbath began the Feast of the Dedication
of the Temple of Zorobabel. It was not so solemn as
the dedication feast of the Machabees, though in the
houses, in the streets, out in the fields among the
shepherds, and in the synagogue there were numbers of lights and fires. Jesus spent the greater part
of the day in the synagogue with all the disciples.
His meals were taken at Lazarus', but He ate sparingly. The greatest portion of the food was distributed to the poor of Thirza, of whom there were large
numbers. Such distributions were constantly made
during His stay. The city still possessed, in ancient
walls and towers, some remains of its former greatness. It is probable that the house of Lazarus, which
was now fifteen minutes from the city, was formerly
comprised within its limits, for the gardens were
interspersed with all kinds of ruined walls and foundations. Lazarus inherited this property from his
father. Here as elsewhere, he was held in great honor
and esteem as a very wealthy and pious, yes, a very
enlightened man. His deportment rendered him very
distinguished from other men. He was remarkably
grave and spoke very little, but that little with great
mildness and to the point.

When the feast was over, Jesus left Thirza with
Lazarus and the disciples, and proceeded on His journey to Judea. The direction was that taken by Mary
and Joseph when going to Bethlehem, though the
road was not exactly the same, but it ran through
the same region, through the mountains near
Samaria. I saw them climbing a high mountain on
a night that was lovely, mild and clear, a beneficent
dew bathing the whole region. There were about eighteen companions with Jesus, and they walked two

and two, some before Him, some behind Him, and
some at His side. When the breadth of the road permitted, Jesus often stood still to instruct them and
to pray. A great part of the night was spent on this
journey. Toward morning they rested and took a light
repast, after which carefully shunning the cities and
towns, they continued their way over a mountain on
which the air blew keen and cold.

Not far from Samaria, I saw Jesus going along
with about six of His disciples. A young man from
the city cast himself down on the road before Him,
saying: "Saviour of men, Thou that art to free Judea
and restore to her her former glory," etc. Thinking
that Christ was about to found an earthly kingdom,
he begged to be received into the number of His followers in the hope of being appointed to some post
of distinction. He was an orphan, but had inherited
large possessions from his father, and he held some
kind of an office in Samaria. Jesus treated him very
graciously. He told him that on his return He would
say whether He would receive him or not, that He
was pleased with his good will and humility, and
that He had nothing to say against what he alleged,
etc. But I saw that Jesus knew how greatly the young
man was attached to his riches and that, wishing to
give him a lesson, He would not vouchsafe him an
answer until after He had chosen the Apostles. The
young man came once more to Jesus and that second visit is recorded in the Gospel.

In the evening before the Sabbath began, I saw
them arrive at the shepherd inn between the two
deserts, about four or five hours from Bethania. Mary
and the holy women stayed there overnight when
they went to Bethania, to see Jesus before the Baptism. The shepherds from the country around gathered together bringing gifts and other necessaries.
The inn was transformed into an oratory, a lamp was
lighted, and there they remained. Jesus taught here
and celebrated the Sabbath. While travelling on this

mountainous and lonely road, He stopped likewise at the place where Mary on her journey to Bethlehem had suffered so from the cold and where afterward she had been miraculously warmed.

Jesus and His disciples spent the whole of the Sabbath among these shepherds, who were so happy to have Him and so deeply moved by His presence. Even Jesus Himself appeared brighter among these simple, innocent people. After the Sabbath He went on to Bethania four hours distant.

15. Jesus' First Paschal Celebration In Jerusalem

While at Bethania, Jesus occupied the same room at Lazarus' as formerly. It was the family oratory and was fitted up like a synagogue. In the center stood the usual desk with the prayer rolls and Scriptures. Jesus' sleeping chamber was a little room adjoining.

The morning after His arrival, Martha went to Jerusalem to notify Mary Marcus and the other women that Jesus was coming with her brother to the house of the former. Jesus and Lazarus arrived toward midday. There were present at the dinner besides Veronica, Johanna Chusa, and Susanna, the disciples of Jesus and of John belonging to Jerusalem, John Marc, Simeon's sons, Veronica's son, and Joseph of Arimathea's nephews, about nine men in all. Nicodemus and Joseph were not there. Jesus spoke of the nearness of the Kingdom of God, of His disciples' call, of their following Him, and even hinted at His own Passion.

John Marc's house was beyond the city, on the eastern side and opposite the Mount of Olives. Jesus did not have to enter the city in order to reach it. That evening He returned with Lazarus to Bethania. Here and there in Jerusalem it was noised about that the new Prophet of Nazareth was in Bethania, and many rejoiced at the news, though there were others whom it displeased. In the gardens and on the roads of the Mount of Olives there were loitering here and there people, among them some Pharisees, to see Jesus as He passed. They may have heard accidentally or found out in Bethania that He was to return to the city. But no one accosted Him. Some hid timidly behind the hedges and peeped out after Him. They said to one another: "There is the Prophet of Nazareth, Joseph the carpenter's Son!"

On account of the approaching feast, numbers were at work in the gardens and on the hedges. All was being arranged and ornamented, the paths cleared, the hedges clipped and tied up. From all sides poor Jews and laboring people with asses laden with baggage were wending their way to Jerusalem. During the feast they hired by the day in the city and gardens. Simon, who later on was forced to help Jesus carry His Cross, was one of these people.

The next day Jesus was again in Jerusalem. He was at a house near the Temple, that of Obed, the son of Simeon, also at another opposite the Temple, one in which old Simeon's family had once dwelt. There He partook of a repast that had been prepared and sent by Martha and the other women. The disciples belonging to Jerusalem, about nine in number, and some other devout men were present, but not Nicodemus and Joseph of Arimathea. Jesus spoke very lovingly and earnestly of the near coming of the Kingdom of God. He had not yet gone to the Temple.

He went fearlessly about the city, clad in a long, white robe of woven material such as Prophets usually wore. Sometimes there was nothing remarkable in His appearance, and He passed along without attracting attention, but at others He looked quite extraordinary, His countenance shining with a supernatural light. When in the evening He returned to Bethania, some of John's disciples came to Him,

among them Saturnin. They saluted Him and told
Him on the part of John that very few now came to
him for baptism, but that Herod still continued to
harass him. That same evening Nicodemus went to
Bethania and heard at Lazarus' the instruction given
by Jesus.

On the following morning Jesus went to Simon the
Pharisee's, an inn or public house in Bethania. He
gave an entertainment at which Nicodemus, Lazarus,
John's disciples, and the disciples from Jerusalem
met. Martha also and the women of Jerusalem were
present. Nicodemus scarcely said a word in Jesus'
presence. He behaved with reserve and listened in
astonishment to His words. But Joseph of Arimathea
was more open-hearted, and sometimes even put questions to Jesus. Simon the Pharisee was not a bad
man, though as yet very wavering. He held to Jesus'
party on account of his friendship for Lazarus, but
at the same time he desired to stand well with the
Pharisees.

During the meal Jesus made many allusions to
the Prophets and the fulfilling of their Prophecies.
He spoke of the wonders attending the conception of
John the Baptist, of God's protecting him from Herod's
massacre of the children, and of his now being
engaged preparing the ways. He drew their attention to man's indifference respecting the completion
of the time marked by the Prophets. "It was fulfilled
thirty years ago, and yet who thinks of it excepting
a few devout, simple-minded people? Who now recalls
the fact that three Kings, like an army from the
East, followed a star with childlike faith seeking a
newborn King of the Jews, whom they found in a
poor child of poor parents? Three days did they spend
with these poor people! Had their coming been to
the child of a distinguished prince, it would not have
been so easily forgotten!" Jesus, however, did not say
that He Himself was that Child.

Accompanied by Lazarus and Saturnin, He visited

the homes of several poor, pious sick people of the
working class in Bethania, and cured about six of
them. Some were lame, some dropsical, and others
afflicted with melancholy. Jesus commanded those
that He cured to go outdoors and sit in the sun. Up
to this time there was very little excitement about
Jesus in Bethania, and even these cures produced
none. The presence of Lazarus, for whom they felt
great reverence, kept the enthusiasm of the people
in check.

That evening, upon which began the first day of
the month Nisan, there was a feast celebrated in the
synagogue. It appeared to be the Feast of the New
Moon, for there was a kind of illumination in the
synagogue. There was a disc like the moon which,
during the recitation of prayers, shone with ever-
increasing brilliancy, owing to the lights lit one after
another by a man behind it.

The next day Jesus was present at divine service
in the Temple with Lazarus, Saturnin, Obed, and
other disciples. A ram was sacrificed. The appearance of Jesus in the Temple produced a peculiar excitement among the Jews. The strangest part of it was
that each concealed the impression made upon him;
no one mentioned to his neighbor the wonderful effect
of Jesus' presence upon him. This was a divine dis-
pensation, in order to allow the Saviour to fulfill His
mission. Had they imparted their thoughts to one
another, it would have given rise to open anger; but
as it was, hatred and rage struggled with gentler
emotions in the hearts of many, while others felt
within them an almost imperceptible desire to know
Jesus better, and took steps to do so through the
mediation of others. This was a fast day in memory
of the death of Aaron's children.

The disciples and many other devout persons were
gathered together at Lazarus'. Jesus taught in a
large hall in which was a teacher's chair. He continued the discourse begun in the house of Simon

the Pharisee in which He had spoken of the Three
Kings, and He drew the attention of His hearers to
other facts of the past. He said: "It is now about
eighteen years ago since a little *bachir*" (by which
Jesus must have meant a young scholar) "argued
most wonderfully with the Doctors of the Law who,
in consequence, were filled with wrath against the
Child." And then He related to them the teachings
of the little *bachir*.

Jesus with Obed, who served in the Temple, and
the other disciples of Jerusalem, went again to the
Temple for the celebration of the Sabbath. They
stood two by two among the young Israelites. Jesus
wore a white, woven robe with a girdle, and a white
mantle like those used by the Essenians, but there
was something very distinguished about Him. His
clothing looked remarkably fresh and elegant, probably because *He* wore it. He chanted and prayed
from the parchment rolls in turn with the others.
There were some prayer leaders present. The people were again struck at the sight of Jesus. They
were astonished, they wondered at Him, though
without having said a word to Him. Even among
themselves they did not speak openly of Him, but
I saw the wonderful impression made on many. There
were three instructions or discourses delivered: one
on the children of Israel, another on their departure from Egypt, and a third on the Paschal lamb.
On one of the altars was a sacrifice of incense. The
priest could not be seen, though the fumes and the
fire were visible. The fire could be seen through a
kind of grating upon which there was something
like a Paschal lamb surrounded by rays and ornaments through which sparkled the fire. This altar
stood near the Holy of Holies, its horns apparently
entering it. I saw Pharisees praying, some of them
wearing wrapped around one arm a long, narrow
band that had perhaps once been used as a veil.

About two in the afternoon, Jesus went with His

companions into an apartment in the court of Israel,
where a repast of fruit and rolls had been prepared.
The rolls were twisted like cues, or plaited hair. A
steward had been engaged to see to everything. All
necessaries could be bought or ordered in the precincts
of the Temple itself, and strangers had the right to
avail themselves of the privilege. The Temple was so
large that it seemed like a little city, and in it one
could procure everything. During this repast, Jesus
gave an instruction. When the men had finished, the
women took some refreshment.

I learned on that day what before I had not known;
viz., that Lazarus held a position in the Temple, as
amongst us a burgomaster may also be a church war-
den. He went around with a box and took up a collection. Jesus and His followers remained the whole
afternoon in the Temple. I did not see Him back in
Bethania before about nine o'clock that night. There
were innumerable lamps and lights in the Temple
on this Sabbath.

Mary and the other holy women had now left
Capharnaum to go to Jerusalem. Their route lay
toward Nazareth and passed Thabor, from which district other women came to join them, and then off
through Samaria. They were preceded by the disciples from Galilee and followed by servants with the
baggage. Among the disciples were Peter, Andrew,
and their half-brother Jonathan, the sons of Zebedee,
the sons of Mary Cleophas, Nathanael Chased, and
Nathanael the bridegroom.

On the fourth of Nisan, Jesus spent the whole
morning in the Temple with about twenty disciples,
after which He taught at Mary Marcus' and took a
luncheon. He afterward returned to Bethania and
went with Lazarus to Simon the Pharisee's. Already
many of the lambs brought to the Temple had been
rejected by the priests.

Jesus was again in the Temple and in the afternoon taught at Joseph of Arimathea's not far from

the home of John Marcus, and near a stonecutter's yard. It was a retired quarter of the city and little frequented by Pharisees. At this period no one feared to be seen in company with Jesus, for hatred against Him had not yet been manifested.

Jesus continued to show Himself still more freely and boldly throughout Jerusalem and in the Temple. He went in with Obed even to the place between the altar of sacrifice and the Temple, where an instruction was being delivered to the priests relative to the Pasch and its ceremonies. The disciples remained back in the court of Israel. The Pharisees were greatly annoyed at seeing Him present at that instruction. Jesus also addressed the people on the streets.

The crowds flowing into Jerusalem kept continually increasing, especially workmen, day laborers, servants, and dealers in the necessaries of life. Around the city and on the open places, crowds of huts and tents had been erected for the accommodation of the multitudes flocking for the Pasch. Many lambs and other cattle had been brought into the city, from the former of which selections had already begun. Numbers of heathens also came to Jerusalem for the feast.

Jesus taught and cured openly in Bethania, even sick strangers were brought to Him. Some relatives of Zachary from the country of Hebron came to invite Him to thither.

He went up again to the Temple. When the priests left after the services, on the place where He was standing among His disciples, Jesus taught them and other good people upon the nearness of the Kingdom of God, the Paschal solemnity, the approaching fulfillment of all the Prophecies and symbols, yes, even of the Paschal lamb itself. His words were earnest and severe, and several priests who were still going here and there in the Temple, were troubled at His discourse and secretly annoyed. Jesus then went back to Bethania, and that night, accompanied by some

of the disciples, left with the envoys for Hebron, about
four hours to the south.

Preparations for the feast were actively going on
in the Temple, and many changes were being made
in the interior. Halls and corridors were opened,
stands and partitions were removed. The altar could
now be approached from many sides, and everything
presented quite a different appearance.

Jesus, with the disciples and Zachary's relatives,
proceeded to Hebron by the route running between
Jerusalem and Bethlehem. It was at most a journey
of five hours. Passing through Juttah, Jesus entered
the neighboring city, Hebron, where He taught and
quietly cured many sick. He returned to Bethania
for the Sabbath. His way led high over mountains,
whose exposure to the sun made it very hot. The disciples that had come from John to Jesus in Bethania, now went back to the former.

Jesus went to the Temple on the Sabbath and with
Obed penetrated into the court containing the
teacher's chair, from which later on He also taught.
Priests and Levites were sitting on the circular seats
around the chair, from which a discourse on the
Paschal festival was being delivered. The entrance
of Jesus threw the assembly into consternation, especially when He started objections and asked questions to which not one of them could answer. Among
other things, He told them that the time was
approaching when the symbolical Paschal lamb would
give place to the reality, then would the Temple and
its services come to an end. The language of Jesus
was figurative, and yet so clear that my thoughts
instantly reverted to the words of the *Pange lingua,*
"et antiquum documentum novo cedat ritui." When
they questioned Him as to how He knew that, He
answered that His Father had told Him, but He did
not say who that Father was.

The Pharisees were highly displeased, though at
the same time full of astonishment. They did not

venture to contradict Him. Access to that part of the Temple was not permitted to all, but Jesus had entered in quality of Prophet. In His last year He even taught therein.

After the Sabbath, Jesus went to Bethania. I had not as yet seen Him conversing with Mary the Silent. Her end, I think, was near, for she appeared greatly changed. She was lying on the ground on a gray carpet, supported in the arms of her maids, and she was in a kind of swoon. She appeared to me to have drawn nearer to this world of ours, as if she had ever been absent in spirit, but now she appeared to have been brought back again to life. She was now to know that this Jesus here in Bethania, who lived in her own time and in her own vicinity, was He who had to suffer so cruelly. She was still alive in order to experience through compassion, in her own person, the sufferings of Jesus, after which she was soon to die.

On the night of Saturday, Jesus visited her and conversed long with her. Part of the time she sat up on her couch, and part of the time walked around her chamber. She had now the perfect use of her senses. She distinguished between the present and the future, she recognized in Jesus the Saviour and the Paschal Lamb, and she knew that He was to suffer frightfully. All this made her inexpressibly sorrowful. The world appeared to her gloomy and an insupportable weight. But most of all was she grieved at man's ingratitude, which she foresaw. Jesus spoke long with her of the approach of the Kingdom of God and His own Passion, after which He gave her His blessing and left her. She was soon to die. She was tall and extraordinarily beautiful, white as snow and shining with light. Her hands were like ivory, her fingers long and tapering.

Next morning, Jesus cured openly in Bethania many that had been brought to Him, among them some strangers that had come up for the feast. Some

were lame, some were blind. There came to Him also
several men connected with the Temple who called
Him to account for His actions and conduct. Who,
they asked, had authorized Him on the preceding
day to take part in the conference held in the Temple? Jesus answered them very gravely, and again
spoke of His Father. The Pharisees dared not enter
the lists against Him. They felt a certain terror in
His presence; they did not know what to make of
Him. But next day, Jesus taught again in the Temple. All the Galilean disciples that had been at the
marriage feast in Cana had now come to Jesus. Mary
and the holy women were stopping with Mary Marcus. Lazarus bought many of the lambs that had
been rejected as not fit for the feast and had them
slaughtered and divided among the poor day laborers and other workmen.

16. Jesus Turns the Vendors Out of
the Courts of the Temple.
The Paschal Supper.
Death of Mary the Silent.

When Jesus, with all His disciples, went to the
Temple, He found there, ranged around the court of
the suppliants, dealers in green herbs, birds, and all
kinds of eatables. In a kindly and friendly manner,
He accosted them and bade them retire with their
goods to the court of the Gentiles. He admonished
them gently of the impropriety of taking up a position where the bleating of the lambs, and the noise
of the other cattle would disturb the recollection of
the worshippers. With the help of the disciples, He
assisted the dealers to remove their tables to the
places that He pointed out to them.

On this day, Jesus cured many sick strangers in
Jerusalem, chiefly poor, lame working people who
dwelt in the neighborhood of the Cenacle on Mount
Zion. There was an astonishingly great multitude

gathered in Jerusalem. The city was surrounded by
a perfect encampment of huts and tents. On the large,
open places ran building after building, forming long
streets wherein all things could be had in large quantities, such as tents, everything necessary for their
erection, and whatever was needed for the eating of
the Paschal lamb. There were other stores, also, in
which such things could be bought or hired. Crowds
of day laborers and poor people from all parts of
Israel were busied carrying the above mentioned articles here and there, and putting them up. These people had been at work a long time in Jerusalem,
clearing away whatever might block up the streets,
clipping the hedges, opening the roads, leveling and
measuring off the grounds for encampments, and
putting up booths and stalls. In the same way for
weeks before, the roads and bad crossing places in
the country around were being repaired and made
ready for travel. All these preparations referred to
the Paschal lamb, just as the Baptist's *preparing of
the ways* referred to the true Lamb of God.

When Jesus again went up to the Temple with His
disciples, He admonished the dealers a second time
to withdraw. Since all the passages were open on
account of the immolation of the Paschal lamb soon
to take place, many had again crowded up to the
court of the suppliants. Jesus bade them withdraw,
and shoved their tables away. He acted with more
vehemence than on the last occasion. The disciples
opened a way for Him through the crowd. Some of
the dealers became furious. With violent gesticula-
tions of head and hands they resisted Him, and then
it was that Jesus, stretching out His hand, pushed
back one of the tables. They were powerless against
Him, the place was soon emptied, and all things carried to the exterior court. Then Jesus addressed to
them words of warning. He said that twice He had
admonished them to remove their goods, and that if
He found them there again, He would treat them

still more severely. The most insolent insulted Him
with: "What will the Galilean, the Scholar of Nazareth,
dare to do? We are not afraid of Him." These taunts
began at the moment of their removal. Many were
standing around looking at Jesus in amazement. The
devout Jews approved His action and praised Him
in His absence. They also cried out: "The Prophet of
Nazareth!" The Pharisees, who were ashamed and
angry at what had occurred, had for days past privately warned the people to refrain from attaching
themselves to the stranger during the feast, not to
run after Him, nor even to speak much about Him.
But the people had become more and more interested in Jesus, for there were already many among
them who had heard His teaching or had been cured
by Him.

As Jesus left the Temple, He passed a cripple in
one of the courts. The man cried after Him. Jesus
cured him, and he who had been lame going into the
Temple joyfully proclaimed Jesus as his benefactor.
Upon this, great excitement arose.

John the Baptist did not come to the feast. He was
not a Jew under the Law, nor was he at all like other
men. He was, as it were, a *voice* clothed with flesh.
He had at this time a fresh concourse of aspirants
to baptism on account of the multitudes going to
Jerusalem.

All was very quiet in Jerusalem that evening. The
people were busy in their own homes with cleansing
out the leaven and preparing the unleavened bread.
All the cooking utensils were covered and hung away.
This was done also at Lazarus' on Mount Sion, where
Jesus and His followers were to eat the Paschal lamb.
Jesus Himself was present at these preparations, He
gave instructions upon them, and all was done by
His direction; but the minutiae were not so punctil-
iously observed as among the other Jews. Jesus
explained of what it all was a figure, and how it
should be practiced, showing them at the same time

what the Pharisees, through want of understanding, had added.

Jesus did not appear in the Temple the next day. He remained in Bethania. I thought, as so many vendors had again crowded into the Temple, something would surely have happened to them had He been there. That afternoon the Paschal lambs were slaughtered in the Temple, and that with indescribable order and celerity. Everyone brought his Paschal lamb on his shoulder, and took his place in order, for there was room enough for all. There were three courts around the altar in which they could stand, but the space between it and the Temple was not open to the people. They that did the slaughtering were behind railings, a table with all that was necessary for their work before them; but they were placed so close to one another that the blood of one lamb sprinkled the neighboring butcher. Their clothes were full of blood. The priests were ranged in several rows up to the altar, passing basins from hand to hand, some full of blood, others empty. Before disemboweling a lamb, the Israelites pressed and kneaded it in a certain way. Then the butcher standing next in order held the animal, while his neighbor with a light grasp easily tore out the intestines.

The flaying was done very expeditiously. They loosened a little piece of skin and fastened it to a round stick provided for the purpose. Then they hung the lamb around their neck, with both hands twisted the stick around, and the skin rolled up on it. Toward evening the slaughter was over. The evening sky was blood-red.

Lazarus, Obed, and Saturnin slaughtered the three lambs that Jesus and His friends were to eat. The meal was taken at Lazarus' on Mount Sion. It was a large building with two wings. The oven for roasting was in the dining hall, but it was very different from the hearth in the cenacle. It was higher, like the fireplace in Anna and Mary's house, also like

that at Cana. In the thick, perpendicular wall that
formed it, were holes wherein the lamb was fastened.
It was stretched out and pinned in place with wooden
skewers, just as if crucified. The hall was beautifully
ornamented and the table, at which they ate in three
groups, was exactly like a horizontal cross. At the
upper and shorter end of the cross, upon which were
many dishes of bitter herbs, Lazarus sat. The Paschal
lambs were placed one on each of the arms of the
cruciform table and one toward the middle of the
lower beam. Jesus, Peter, Saturnin, and Obed sat as
follows: Jesus and Peter opposite each other at the
left arm of the table, Obed at the right arm, and Saturnin at the lower beam. Around Jesus stood His
relatives and the disciples from Galilee, around Obed
and Lazarus those from Jerusalem, while John's disciples gathered around Saturnin. There were present, in all, over thirty.

The Paschal supper was very different from Jesus'
last Paschal supper, more strictly Judaical. Each here
held a staff in his hand, was girded as for a journey, and all ate in haste. Jesus had two staves placed
crosswise before Him. They chanted Psalms and,
standing, quickly consumed the Paschal lambs. Later
on they placed themselves at table in a recumbent
position. This supper was different also from that
customary among the other Jews at this feast. Jesus
explained all to the guests, but omitted the ceremonies that had been added by the Pharisees. He
carved the three lambs Himself and served at table,
saying that He did it as their servant. They remained
together far into the night, singing and praying.

Jerusalem was so still and solemn during that
whole day. The Jews not engaged in the slaughtering of the lambs remained shut up in their houses,
which were ornamented with dark green foliage. The
immense multitude of people were, after the slaughtering, so busy in the interior of their homes, and
all was so still that it produced upon me quite a

melancholy impression.

I saw on that day also where all the Paschal lambs for the numerous strangers, of whom many were encamped before the gates, were roasted. Both outside and inside the city, there were built on certain places long, low walls, but so broad that one could walk on them. In these walls were furnace after furnace, and at certain distances lived men who attended to them, and received a small remuneration for their services. At these furnaces, travellers and strangers could, at the different feasts, or at any other time, roast their meat and cook any kind of food. The consuming of the fat of the Paschal lambs went on in the Temple far into the night. After the first watch, the altar was purified, and the doors thrown open at a very early hour the next morning.

Jesus and His disciples spent the night in prayer and with but little sleep at Lazarus' on Mount Sion. The disciples from Galilee slept in the wings of the building. At daybreak they went up to the Temple, which was lighted by numerous lamps, and to which the people were already flocking from all parts with their offerings. Jesus took His stand in one of the courts with His disciples, and there taught. A crowd of vendors had again pressed into the court of the suppliants and even into that of the women. They were scarcely two steps from the worshippers. As they still came crowding in, Jesus bade the newcomers to keep back, and those that had already taken their position to withdraw. But they resisted, and called upon the guard nearby for help. The latter, not venturing to act of themselves, reported what was taking place to the Sanhedrim. Jesus, meantime, persisted in His command to the vendors to withdraw. When they boldly refused, He drew from the folds of His robe a cord of twisted reeds or slender willow branches and pushed up the ring that held the ends confined, whereupon one half of it opened out into numerous threads like a discipline. With this He rushed upon the vendors, overthrew their tables, and drove back those that resisted, while the disciples, pressing on right and left, shoved His opponents away. And now came a crowd of priests from the Sanhedrim and summoned Jesus to say who had authorized Him to behave so in that place. Jesus answered that, although the Holy Mystery had been taken away from the Temple, yet it had not ceased to be a sacred place and one to which the prayer of so many just was directed. It was not a place for usury, fraud, and for low and noisy traffic. Jesus having alleged the commands of His Father, they asked Him who was His Father. He answered that He had no time then to explain that point to men and even if He did they would not understand, saying which He turned away from them and continued His chase of the vendors.

Two companies of soldiers now arrived on the spot, but the priests did not dare to take action against Jesus. They themselves were ashamed of having tolerated such an abuse. The crowd gathered around declared Jesus in the right, and the soldiers even lent a hand to remove the vendors' stands and to clear away the overturned tables and wares. Jesus and the disciples drove the vendors to the exterior court, but those that were modestly selling doves, little rolls, and other needful refreshments in the recesses of the wall around the inner court, He did not molest. After that He and His followers went to the court of Israel. It may have been between seven and eight in the morning when all this took place.

On the evening of this day, a kind of procession went out along the valley of Cedron, to cut the first fruits of the harvest.

Jesus on one of the succeeding days cured in the court of the Temple about ten persons, some lame, some mute, and it gave rise to great excitement, for the cured filled the whole place with their acclamations of joy. Again He was summoned to answer for

His conduct, which He did in severe words. The people were enthusiastic in His favor. After the divine service, Jesus and the disciples attended the instruction given in a hall of the Temple. The text was from one of the Books of Moses. Jesus offered some objections, for it was a kind of conference in which questions might be raised. He silenced His opponents, and gave an explanation of the disputed points very different from what had before been given.

During all these days Jesus hardly saw His Mother. She was staying with Mary Marcus, passing the livelong day in anxiety, tears, and prayer on account of the excitement roused by the appearance of her Son. Jesus kept the Sabbath at Lazarus', in Bethania, whither He had retired after the tumult occasioned by the cures wrought in the Temple. After the Sabbath, the Pharisees went to the house of Mary Marcus in Jerusalem, thinking to find Jesus there and to take Him into custody. They were, however, disappointed. They did not find Him, but only His Mother and the other holy women whom, as the followers of Jesus, they commanded with harsh words to leave the city. The Mother of Jesus and the other women became greatly troubled at hearing this, and in tears hurried to Martha in Bethania. Mary, weeping, entered the room wherein Martha was with her sick sister, Mary the Silent. The latter was again quite rapt in ecstasy. All that she had hitherto seen in spirit, she now beheld about to be fulfilled. She could no longer endure the pain it caused her, and she died in the presence of Mary, Mary Cleophas, Martha, and the other women.

Nicodemus, in spite of the open persecution directed against Jesus, visited Him during these days by invitation of Lazarus. I saw Jesus during the night reclining beside him on the ground and instructing him. Before daybreak both started for Jerusalem, where they went to Lazarus' on Sion. Here came Joseph of Arimathea also to see Jesus. He conversed with them.

122   *Life of Jesus Christ*

They humbled themselves before Him, telling Him
that they did indeed discern that He was more than
human, and they pledged Him lasting fidelity. Jesus
commanded them secrecy, and they begged Him to
remember them kindly.

After that all the other disciples who had eaten
the Pasch with Him came to Jesus. He gave them
His commands and instructions for the near future.
Extending to Him their hands, they wept, making
use of the narrow scarf they wore around the neck
or wound around the head to dry their tears.

FROM THE CLOSE OF THE FIRST PASCH TO THE CONVERSION OF THE SAMARITAN WOMAN AT JACOB'S WELL

1. The Letter of King Abgarus

From Bethania, where Jesus had for some time remained in concealment, He went to the place of Baptism near Ono. The arrangements were still in good order, owing to the care of its custodians. The disciples gathered around Jesus, and crowds of people came streaming in. As Jesus was teaching before the multitude, part of whom were standing, others sitting on wooden platforms in a circle around Him, a stranger approached mounted on a camel. He was followed by six attendants, who rode on mules. They halted at the tents, some distance from the place of instruction. It was an embassy from King Abgarus, who was sick, and who had sent presents to Jesus with a letter in which he implored Him to come to Edessa to cure him. He had had an eruption that had settled in his feet and rendered him lame. Travellers returning to their homes had told him about Jesus and His miracles, of the testimony of John, and the wrath of the Jews at the last Paschal solemnity, all which had excited in him a great longing to be cured by Jesus.

The young man commissioned to bear the king's letter to Jesus was an artist, and he had received commands to bring back Jesus' portrait if He would not come Himself. I saw him vainly trying to reach Jesus. He pressed sometimes here, sometimes there

through the crowd, both to hear the instruction and
to paint Jesus' likeness. Then Jesus bade one of the
disciples to make room for the man that was going
around people unable to push his way to the front,
and He pointed out a platform nearby to which he
should be conducted. The disciple brought the envoy
forward, and placed him and his attendants where
they could see and hear. They had with them gifts of
woven stuffs, thin plates of gold, and very beautiful
lambs.

The envoy, overjoyed at being able at last to see
Jesus, at once produced his drawing materials, rested
his tablet on his knee, regarded Jesus with great
admiration and attention, and set to work. The tablet
before him was white as if made of wax. He began
by sketching with a pencil the outlines of Jesus' head
and beard. Then it looked as if he spread over his
work a layer of wax in which to receive the impression of the sketch. After that he resumed his sketching, touched again and again with his pencil, again
took the impression, and so continued, but without
ever perfecting his work. As often as he glanced at
Jesus, he seemed lost in amazement at the countenance he beheld, and was forced to begin anew. Luke
did not paint in exactly this way. He used a brush
also. The picture this man was producing appeared
to me to be somewhat in relief; one could trace it by
the touch.

Jesus continued His discourse a while longer, and
then sent the disciple to say to the envoy that he
might now approach and deliver his message. The
envoy came down from the platform whereon he was
sitting, followed by his attendants with the presents
and lambs. His doublet was short, almost like those
of the Three Kings, and he wore no mantle. The picture at which he had been working was hanging by
a strap on his left arm. It was like a shield in the
form of a heart. In the right hand he held the king's
letter. Casting himself on his knees before Jesus, he

bowed low, as did also his attendants, and said: "Thy
slave is the servant of Abgarus, King of Edessa. He
is sick. He sends Thee this letter, and prays Thee to
accept these gifts from him." Then the slaves
approached with the presents. Jesus replied to the
envoy that the good intentions of his master were
pleasing to Him, and He commanded the disciples
to take the gifts and distribute them among the poorest of the assembled crowd. Then He unfolded the
letter and read it. I do not remember all that was
in it, but only that the king referred to Jesus' power
to raise the dead, and begged Him to come and cure
him. The part of the letter containing the writing
was stiff; the envelope pliable, as if of some kind of
stuff, either leather or silk. I saw, too, that it was
bound by a string.

When Jesus had read the letter, He turned the
other side of the stiff part and, drawing from His
robe a coarse pencil out of which He pushed something, He wrote several words in tolerably large characters, and then folded it again. After that He called
for some water, bathed His face, pressed the soft
stuff in which the letter had been folded to His
sacred countenance, and returned it to the envoy.
The latter applied it to the picture he had vainly
tried to perfect, when behold! The likeness instantly became a facsimile of the original. The artist was
filled with delight. He turned the picture, which was
hanging by a strap, toward the spectators, cast himself at Jesus' feet, arose, and took leave immediately. But some of his servants remained behind and
followed Jesus who, after this instruction, crossed
the Jordan to the second place of Baptism which
John had abandoned. There these new followers were
baptized.

I saw the envoy on his way home passing a night
outside a city near which were long stone buildings
like brick kilns. Very early the next morning some
of the workmen hurried to the spot, because they

had seen there a bright light like a fire. Something remarkable then took place in connection with the picture, and a great crowd of people gathered on the spot. The artist exhibited to them his picture, as well as the cloth with which Jesus had dried His face, and which, too, had received the imprint of His features. Abgarus came some distance through his gardens to meet his envoy. He was indescribably touched at Jesus' letter and the sight of His picture. He immediately amended his life and dismissed the numerous concubines with whom he had sinned.

I saw again that, after the death of Abgarus' son, in the reign of a wicked successor, the portrait of Jesus, which had been publicly exposed, was concealed by a pious Bishop. He placed it in a niche, a burning lamp before it, and walled up the aperture. After a long time, the picture was discovered, and then it was found that the stone that concealed it from sight also bore its imprint.

2. Jesus on the Confines of Sidon and Tyre

Jesus went from Ono with the disciples to the middle place of Baptism, that above Bethabara and opposite Gilgal. There He permitted Andrew, Saturnin, Peter, and James to baptize. Immense crowds were coming and going, rousing in consequence fresh excitement among the Pharisees. They dispatched letters to the Elders of all the synagogues throughout the country, directing them to deliver over Jesus wheresoever He might be found, to take the disciples into custody, to inquire into their teachings, and inflict punishment upon them. But Jesus, accompanied by only a few disciples, left the place of Baptism, and journeyed through Samaria and Galilee on the confines of Tyre. The rest of the disciples separated and returned to their homes. About the same time, Herod ordered his soldiers to bring John to

Callirrhoe, where he kept him confined for about six weeks in a vault of his castle. Then he set him free.

While Jesus, with a few of His disciples, was crossing the valley Esdrelon on His way through Samaria, Bartholomew passed. Returning home to Debbaseth from the baptism of John, he fell in with some of the disciples, and Andrew spoke to him enthusiastically of the Lord. Bartholomew listened with delight and reverence, and Andrew, whose joy it was to add intelligent men to the number of the disciples, went forward to Jesus and spoke to Him of Bartholomew, who was desirous of following Him. Just at this moment, Bartholomew passed. Andrew pointed him out to Jesus who, glancing toward Bartholomew, said to Andrew: "I know him; he will follow Me. I see good in him, and I shall call him in time." Bartholomew dwelt in Debbaseth not far from Ptolomais. He was a writer. I saw that he met Thomas soon after, to whom in turn he spoke of Jesus and whom he inclined in His favor.

Jesus had to endure great privations on this hurried journey. Saturnin, or some other one of the disciples, had charge of a basket of bread. Several times I saw Jesus steeping the hard crust in water, in order to be able to eat it. In Tyre He put up at an inn near the gate on the land side of the city. He had come over a high mountain ridge. Tyre was a very large city. To one approaching from a distant height, it looked as if hanging from a mountain and momentarily in danger of being detached. Jesus did not enter the city. He kept along the wall on the land side where there were not so many people. The wall was very thick. In it was built the inn, and on top of it ran a road. Jesus wore a brownish robe and a white woolen mantle. He went here and there, but only to the houses of the poor built in the wall. Saturnin and one other disciple had come with Jesus to Tyre. Peter, Andrew, James the Less, Thaddeus, Nathanael Chased, and all the disciples that had been with Him at the marriage feast of Cana followed. They travelled in separate bands, and met Jesus in the Jewish meeting house, situated in another quarter of Tyre, to which led a broad canal bordered with trees. To this house, with which the school was connected, belonged a large bathing garden, which ran down even to the water that cut off this quarter of the city from the mainland. The bathing garden was surrounded by a wall, inside of which was a quickset hedge of bushes cut in figures. In the middle of the garden was an open portico containing numerous passages and little apartments, and around it was the spacious bathing cistern full of flowing water. There was in the middle of it a pillar with steps and hand supports, by means of which one could descend into the water to any depth. This place was inhabited by aged Jews, who were despised on account of their religion or origin, although they were good, pious men.

It was touching to see Jesus saluting the disciples on their arrival. He passed among them giving His hands first to one, then to another. They were full of respectful confidence, for they regarded Him as an extraordinary, supernatural Being. They were indescribably joyous at seeing Him again. He delivered to them a long instruction, after which they told Him all that had happened to them. They took a meal together consisting of bread, fruit, honey, and fish which the disciples had brought with them.

The disciples, some in Jerusalem, some in Gennabris, were called to account by the Pharisees before large assemblies on the subject of Jesus, His doctrine and designs, and their own intercourse with Him. They were molested in many ways. Once I saw Peter, Andrew, and John with their hands bound, but a slight effort burst their bonds asunder, as if by a miracle. They were then allowed to return to their homes in peace.

Jesus exhorted them to constancy and told them

to begin to free themselves more and more from their avocations, and to spread, as far as they could, His doctrine among the people of their district. He added that He would soon be with them again, and that He would resume His public teaching when He should have rejoined them in Galilee.

After the departure of the disciples, Jesus held in the school of the bathing garden an instruction and exhortation before a numerous assembly of men, women, and children. He spoke of Moses, of the Prophets, and of the near coming of the Messiah. He interpreted to them the meaning of the drought that had fallen upon the country in the time of Elias, the Prophet's prayer for rain, the uprising clouds, and the showers that fell, and He showed how all this was soon to be realized. He spoke also of water and of purification, healed many of the sick, and directed them to receive the baptism of John. He cured many boys who had been brought to Him on beds. He plunged several of them, holding them by the arms, into the water, Saturnin having poured into it from a bottle some other water that Jesus had blessed. The two disciples baptized these children. There were other boys approaching manhood, who went down into the cistern and, holding to the column, plunged themselves under the water, and in this way were baptized. I noticed here several circumstances unlike what I had generally seen on such occasions. Many of the adults had to remain standing at a distance. The ceremony went on until night closed in.

3. Jesus in Sichor Libnath

When Jesus left Tyre, He proceeded alone on His way. He had sent both the disciples with orders to Capharnaum, also to John the Baptist. He went from ten to eleven hours south of Tyre to the city Sichor Libnath, through which He had already passed on His journey hither. The Waters of Merom, with the

two cities Adama and Seleucia, lay to the east on His
left. Sichor Libnath, called also Amichores, or "City
built upon the Waters," was a couple of hours inland
from Ptolomais on a small, muddy lake, one side of
which was rendered inaccessible by high mountains.
From this lake arose the little, sandy stream Belus,
which empties into the sea near Ptolomais. The city
was so large that I cannot conceive why so little is
known of it. The Jewish city Misael was not far off.
This is the country that Solomon bestowed upon King
Hiram. Sichor was free, though with some little dependence on Tyre. There was much cattle raising going
on in these parts. I saw numbers of large sheep with
fine wool. They could swim over the water. Beautiful
woolen goods were woven here and dyed in Tyre. I
saw no tilling of fields, but only the cultivation of
orchards. There grew in the water a kind of grain
with very large stalks. Bread was made of the grain.
I think they were not obliged to sow seed for this
plant, it sprang up wild. A road led from Sichor to
Syria and Arabia, but there was no highway to
Galilee. Jesus had come to Tyre by an indirect route.

There were two great bridges outside of Sichor:
the one, high and long to enable the inhabitants to
cross when the whole country was inundated; the
other lower, affording a convenient passage under
the arches formed by the upper one. The houses were
built high and so constructed that, when the city was
submerged, the people could take refuge on the roofs
under tents. Most of the inhabitants were heathens.
I saw little flags waving from several buildings with
pointed towers, which I took for pagan temples. I
was astonished to see here so many Jews, although
held in contempt by their neighbors, occupying handsome houses. I think they were exiles.

The house in which Jesus put up was outside the
city and on the side by which He had come. He had,
however, to cross water to reach it. There was a synagogue nearby. It seemed as if Jesus, on His journey

to Tyre, had announced His return by this route, for
the people of the house at which He stopped appeared
to be expecting Him. They came out to meet Him
and received Him with marks of reverence. They were
Jews, the father an aged man, and the family large.
They occupied a very beautiful house which, like a
palace, had many wings, and smaller buildings around
it. Through respect for Jesus, the master of the family conducted Him not into his own house, but into
one of the neighboring dwellings, where he washed
His feet and showed Him hospitality.

I saw a great procession of all kinds of laboring
people, men, women, and lads, a mixed crowd of heathens, some brown, some black (very likely slaves
of this man) coming from their work. They filed into
a large open place and took their food. They had
with them all kinds of shovels and carts, and carried on their shoulders little, light boats like troughs.
These last were provided with a seat and rudder,
and contained fishing tackle. These laborers were
employed in building and repairing bridges and
banks. They received food in earthen vessels, also
vegetables and birds; the flesh of the latter some of
them ate raw. Jesus had them brought before Him.
He spoke to them kindly, and they were delighted
to see such a Man.

Two old Jews came to Jesus with some rolls of the
Scriptures. They took a repast with Him, and He explained to them many things that they were very
desirous to know. They were instructors of youth.

The rich Jew and master of the house at which
Jesus stopped was named Simeon, and was from the
region of Samaria. Either he or his forefathers had
interested themselves in the temple on Mount
Garizim, and had associated with the Samaritans,
and were on that account driven from their country.
They had settled here.

Jesus taught a whole day at the house of His host
in an open court surrounded by columns, over which

an awning was stretched. The master of the house came and went. There were gathered in the court very many Jews, men and women of all ages. I did not see Jesus performing any cures; indeed, there were no sick nor cripples. The people here were lank and lean, but very tall. Jesus gave an instruction on Baptism, and promised to send some of His disciples hither to baptize. Accompanied by the master of the house, He went out on the road by which the slaves had returned from their work. He spoke to them, encouraged them, and explained to them a parable. There were many good people, who were very much touched. They again received food and wages. It reminded me of the parable that speaks of the lord of the vineyard paying the day laborers. The slaves dwelt in a row of huts about a quarter of an hour from Simeon's. It was some kind of serfdom that they were discharging by their labor for Simeon.

On one of the following days, after Jesus had been preaching from early morn and the Jews had gone away, about twenty pagans came to Him. For several days they had been asking to be allowed to do so. Simeon's was about half an hour from the city, and the heathens dared not approach beyond a certain tower or arch. But Simeon himself brought these newcomers to Jesus, whom they saluted reverently and begged Him to instruct them. He spoke for a long time with them in a hall, so long indeed that the lamps were lighted before He finished. He consoled them, told them in a parable of the holy Three Kings, and said that light would one day shine upon the heathens.

When the two disciples whom Jesus had sent to Capharnaum returned to Him at Sichor, they told Him that the four disciples whom He had summoned were coming. Jesus went a journey of from three to four hours over a mountain to meet them, and came up with them at an inn on Galilean territory. There were, besides those that He had called, seven others

and among them John. Some women also had come
with them, of whom I recognized Mary Marcus of
Jerusalem and the maternal aunt of the bridegroom
Nathanael. Those called were Peter, Andrew, James
the Less, and Nathanael Chased. Although it was
already dark, Jesus walked with the four and the two
other disciples back to Sichor, but the seven that had
not been called returned to Galilee. It was an exceedingly delightful night—the sky was clear and a
delicious fragrance embalmed the air. They walked
sometimes all together, sometimes before or after
Jesus, who then went on alone. Once they rested in
the midst of a very fertile region under trees laden
with fruit, and in the neighborhood of green meadows and running brooks. As they started again, there
rose up from the meadow a flock of birds and accompanied them on their way. They were almost as large
as hens, had red beaks and long pointed wings like
those with which angels are painted, and as they
flew, they kept up the funniest twittering. The birds
followed them even into the city, and there lighted
among the reeds in the water. They could run on the
water like waterfowl. It was a touching sight—the
beautiful night, Jesus pausing from time to time to
pray or to teach, and the birds settling around the
little party of travellers. Thus did they climb the mountain and descend on the other side. Simeon came forward to meet them, washed the feet of all, presented
them a cup to drink and a morsel to eat in the
vestibule, and then conducted them into his house.
The birds, or waterfowl, belonged to Simeon; they flew
around like pigeons. Jesus taught here during the
whole day, and in the evening they celebrated the
Sabbath in Simeon's house, which was very high.
Besides Jesus and the disciples, there were present
about twenty Jews. The synagogue was in a subterranean vault, and arranged in perfect order. A flight
of steps led down to it. A leader sang and read in the
synagogue, after which Jesus delivered a discourse.

The disciples slept in the same house with Jesus.

Their sleep was only a few hours long, for the gray dawn found them again on their way. They journeyed through crooked mountain passes to a little Jewish city in the land of Chabul, where dwelt some other Jewish exiles who had frequently implored to be allowed to return to their country, but the Pharisees would not permit it. Long had they sighed for a visit from Jesus, though they deemed themselves unworthy of it, and for that reason had refrained from sending for Him. But now Jesus went of His own accord. The winding mountainous roads made it a journey of from five to six hours.

When they neared the little Jewish city, two of the disciples went on ahead to notify the Ruler of the synagogue of Jesus' coming. Although it was the Sabbath, Jesus had undertaken this journey, for here in the country, when necessity intervened, He did not strictly observe this law. He went to the Rulers of the synagogue, who received Him with great humility. They washed His feet, also those of the disciples, and offered them a luncheon. Then Jesus had Himself taken around to all the sick, about twenty of whom He cured. Among them were people quite deformed and lame, women afflicted with a flux of blood, others blind, dropsical, and leprous, also many children.

As He went along the street, several possessed cried out after Him and He freed them from the evil spirit. Order and silence reigned throughout the city. The disciples helped their Master. Some assisted the cured to rise, some instructed the crowd that followed Jesus and gathered around the doors of the houses into which He had entered. Before curing some of the sick, Jesus exhorted them to faith and amendment of life; others who already believed, He cured at once. Raising His eyes to Heaven, He prayed over them; some He touched, over others He passed His hand. I saw, too, that He blessed water and sprinkled the people with it, directing the disciples to do

the same to the house. In one of the houses He and
the disciples accepted a little wine and a morsel of
bread. Many of the cured, rising up, cast themselves
at His feet, and then followed Him joyously, as we
here follow the Blessed Sacrament, though always
reverently and at a distance. But to others again,
Jesus gave a command to remain in their homes.

He directed some of the cured to bathe in the water
that He had blessed; these were the children and
the leprous. Jesus went to a well near the synagogue
and blessed it, casting in at the same time salt that
He had previously blessed. This well was very deep;
a flight of steps led down to it. He taught on this
occasion of Eliseus, who with salt had rectified the
water near Jericho; then He explained the signification of salt. He furthermore commanded that the
people, when sick, should use the water of the well
for bathing purposes. He always blessed in the form
of a cross. While He was thus engaged, the disciples
held His mantle, which He sometimes laid off, and
handed Him the salt that He threw into the water.
He performed all these ceremonies with great gravity and recollection.

During this vision, I saw interiorly that a similar
power to heal is given to priests. Some of the sick
were brought to Jesus on beds, and He cured them.
He delivered a discourse in the synagogue, but He
took no repast, for the whole day was spent in teaching and healing. On the evening after the Sabbath,
He left the place with His disciples. On taking leave
of the inhabitants, who were distressed to see Him
go, He ordered them not to follow Him, and they
obeyed humbly. He had blessed and purified the water
for them, because it was bad and full of snakes and
animals with thick heads and long tails. About two
hours from this place Jesus and His disciples put up
at a large inn among the mountains where they ate
and slept. On their journey to the Jewish city, they
had passed this inn at some distance.

The next day, crowds of people bringing their sick gathered in the mountain inn, for they knew that Jesus was come. They were people that lived in huts and caves on opposite sides of the mountain. On the west side, toward Tyre, dwelt the heathens, who also had come; and on the east side, poor Jews. Jesus gave an instruction in which He spoke of purification, of ablutions, and of penance, and cured about thirty persons.

The heathens remained at a distance, and Jesus did not teach them until the others had retired. He addressed to them a consoling instruction that lasted till after midday. These poor people had little gardens and plantations around their caves. Their principal nourishment was sheep's milk, which they made into cheese and ate like bread. The fruits of their gardens, as also those that they gathered growing wild, they carried around the country for sale. Many of them likewise furnished the dwellers, in the little city where Jesus had on the preceding day blessed the water, with good water which they carried thither in leathern bottles. Some other places were provided by them in like manner. There were many lepers among these people, for whom Jesus blessed water in which they might bathe.

Toward evening Jesus returned to Sichor Libnath, where he again taught and announced that on the following day He would baptize. In the court of the large mansion belonging to Simeon, there was a round, shallow basin from which the water overflowed into a surrounding trench. Here, too, the water was not good; it had a bad taste. Jesus blessed it, casting into it at the same time salt in lumps like stones. In this region there was a whole mountain formed of salt.

In that basin, which had previously been drained and cleansed, the Baptism of about thirty persons took place. The master of the house with all the males of his household, some other Jews of the place, many of the heathens that had lately been with Jesus, and some of the slaves from the huts, were baptized. These last Jesus had on several different occasions instructed when returned from their work. The pagans were the last to be baptized. They had to prepare themselves for the ceremony by certain purifications. Jesus poured from a flask into the baptismal basin some of the Jordan water, which the disciples always carried with them, and then He blessed it. The trench around the basin was filled high enough for the neophytes to stand in it up to the knees in water.

Before administering Baptism, Jesus prepared the aspirants by a long instruction. These latter wore long, gray mantles with hoods over the head, something like the mantles worn in prayer. When about to step into the trench around the basin, they laid aside the mantle. Their loins were covered, as also the back and breast, while from the shoulders fell a little open mantle like a scapular. A disciple laid one hand upon the shoulder of the neophyte, the other upon his head. The baptizer, in the name of the Most High, poured over his head several times from a flat shell water dipped from the basin. First Andrew baptized, then Peter, who was afterward relieved by Saturnin. The heathens were baptized last. The ceremony, including the preparations, continued until near evening.[1]

When the people had retired, Jesus and the disciples left the place separately. They met again on the road and went eastward toward Adama on Lake Merom, resting by night in the beautiful high grass under the trees.

4. Jesus in Adama. Miraculous Conversion of an Obstinate Jew

Although Adama did not appear very distant, still Jesus and the disciples had to journey some hours

---

1. Upon the signification of pagan baptism, see p. 335.

up a river before reaching a crossing place. There
was no ferryman, but only a raft of beams, something like a gridiron, which lay on the shore for the
accommodation of travellers. Toward noon the little
troop reached Adama, which was hemmed in on all
sides by water. On the eastern side of the city lay
Lake Merom. The city was surrounded by a stream,
which was at five different points crossed by bridges.
At the bathing gardens, the stream again united with
the lake. The steep shores of the low lake were covered with thick reeds and undergrowth, and its waters
were muddy except in the middle where those of the
Jordan flowed. The country around was infested by
wild beasts.

As Jesus, with the disciples, approached the bathing
garden near the city, several distinguished men of
the place came forward to meet Him. They had been
awaiting His coming in the garden. They conducted
Him into the city and to a large open square, in the
center of which stood the governor's palace. It had
a spacious forecourt, on both sides of which and in
the rear ran rows of low buildings. The court was
cut off from the street by a railing of shining metal
made into various colored plates. Here they washed
the feet both of Jesus and the disciples, brushed and
shook their mantles, and presented them with a luncheon of small fruits and herbs. It was an old custom of the people of Adama to conduct all that visited
their city to this castle, where they interrogated them.
If they were pleased with them, they treated them
hospitably in the hope of attracting blessings upon
themselves; but if they were not favorably impressed
by their guests, they did not hesitate to cast them
into prison. Adama, with about twenty little districts,
belonged to a province under the jurisdiction of one
of the Herods. The inhabitants of the city were Samaritan Jews who, in consequence of their schism, had
embraced sundry perverse notions. Still, there was
no idolatry practiced among them, and heathens liv-

ing here had to carry on their idol worship in secret. After that, Jesus was conducted by the men that had received Him outside the city to the synagogue, a building of three stories. There He found a great part of the Jews assembled, the women in the background. First they prayed and chanted canticles to God, that to His honor they might understand all that Jesus was about to say to them. Then Jesus began His discourse. He spoke of the Divine Promises, of their mutual dependence and their realization, and of grace which, He said, was never allowed to go to waste. If he to whom, on account of the merit of his ancestors, some grace was given, would not receive it, it was passed on to the next most deserving. He told them also of a good action performed by their ancestors in this city so long before that it was to them almost unknown, but the happy results of which they were still experiencing. Their forefathers had once harbored some strangers and exiles.

Jesus and the disciples put up at a large inn near the gate by which they had entered the city.

In the neighborhood of the bathing garden outside, though more to the south, was a place for teaching. It consisted of a green hill in the center of a large, open space in which were trees planted in rows five deep, whose dense shade afforded protection from the sun. On the hill and overshadowed by a tree, was a teacher's chair beautifully hewn out of stone. It was a very delightful place and was known as the "Place of Grace," because the people believed that here a great favor had once upon a time been accorded them. To the north of the city was another place of which there was a popular saying expressive of some great calamity that had come upon them.

The disciples went into the houses throughout the city, inviting the people to the "Place of Grace," where Jesus was about to deliver a great discourse. On the evening before, a banquet was given in the public hall of the Governor's court. About fifty citizens were

present and five tables were spread. Jesus was at
that of the most distinguished, and the disciples were
scattered among the guests at the other tables. I
think Jesus and the disciples also contributed something to the entertainment. Plants like little trees
in pots adorned the table, Jesus taught during the
meal, going from table to table and speaking to all
the guests. When the tables were cleared of all but
their ornamental foliage, and grace said, all present
ranged in a half-circle before Jesus, who delivered
an instruction and invited them to come next morning to the "Place of Grace," where He would discourse
to them more at length.

Next day toward nine in the morning, Jesus set
out with the disciples for the place of instruction,
where over one hundred distinguished men were gathered under the shade of the trees. In the outer circle were some women also. On the way thither, Jesus
and the disciples arrived at the palace of the Governor who, in magnificent robes and attended by his
officers, was just about setting out for the same place.
But Jesus commanded him not to go in such array,
but to make his appearance like the other men in a
long mantle and penitential garb. The mantle was
of dyed wool. They wore also a scapular of one piece
in the back but open on the breast, the two held in
place over the shoulders by a narrow strap. The two
pieces, front and back, were black with the names
of the seven capital sins wrought into them in different colors. The women were veiled. When Jesus
stepped up on the teacher's chair, the people bowed
reverently. The Governor and the most distinguished
men of the city stood close to the chair.

The disciples, standing in the outer circles, had
each around him a group of men and women receiving instructions. Jesus first raised His eyes to Heaven
and prayed aloud to His Father, from whom all graces
flow, that His teaching might fall upon hearts repentant and sincere. He directed the people to repeat

His words after Him, which they did. His discourse lasted without interruption from nine in the morning till about four in the afternoon. Once only there was a pause, during which they brought Him a little refreshment, a glass of wine and a morsel of bread. The listeners came and went, according as their business in the city demanded. Jesus taught of penance and Baptism, of which He here spoke principally as of a spiritual purification and cleansing. No women were baptized before Pentecost, though among the children admitted to Baptism were little girls of from five to eight years old, but no grown girls. The mysterious signification connected with this, I no longer remember. Jesus spoke also of Moses, of the broken tables of the Law, of the golden calf, and of the thunder and lightning on Sinai.

When he had made an end of speaking and the instruction was quite finished, many of the people including the Governor having returned to the city, a tall, prepossessing old Jew with a long beard stepped boldly up to the teacher's chair and thus addressed Jesus: "Allow me now to speak with Thee. Thou hast enumerated twenty-three truths when, in reality, there are twenty-four," and he proceeded to name them one after another and to argue with Jesus on the point. But Jesus replied: "Desiring thy conversion, I have suffered thee here. I might have sent thee away before the whole crowd, since thou didst come hither uninvited. Thou sayest that there are twenty-four truths, and that I have taught only twenty-three. But thou hast already added three to my number, for I taught twenty only." And then Jesus counted up twenty truths according to the letters of the Hebrew alphabet, although it was by the same manner of reckoning that His opponent had proved that there were twenty-four. He then descanted upon the sin and punishment of those that add something to the truth. But the old Jew would by no means acknowledge his error, and he was supported by some present who were glad to hear Jesus contradicted. But Jesus said to him: "Thou hast a beautiful garden. Bring Me some of the best and soundest of its fruits. They will rot away as a sign that thou art in the wrong! Thou hast an erect, robust body. Thou shalt grow crooked if thou art wrong, that thou mayest see how the noblest gifts are ruined and deformed as soon as additions are made to the truth! But if thou canst show forth some such prodigy, we shall admit that there are twenty-four truths."

Thereupon the old Jew hurried with his associates to the garden but a short way off. In it was to be found all that was rare and costly in the shape of fruits, plants, and flowers. All kinds of choice animals and birds were there in cages, and in the center was a large basin in which were kept rare fish for the delight of the beholder. The old man, with the help of his friends, quickly gathered the most magnificent fruits, yellow apples, and bunches of ripe grapes, which they put into two little baskets; the small fruits they put into a cut-glass dish that looked as if made of threads of colored glass intersecting one another. Besides that, he took with him in latticed baskets various birds and rare animals of the size of a hare, or a little kitten.

All this time Jesus continued to speak of the evil of obstinacy and of the ruinous consequences attendant upon arbitrary additions to the truth.

When now the old Jew and his companions placed around Jesus' chair the rare flowers and animals in the baskets and cages, intense excitement prevailed in the crowd. But when he proudly and obstinately maintained his first assertion, the words of Jesus were fulfilled in all that he had brought. The fruit began to stir and from all sides broke forth horrible maggots and worms that soon devoured it, so that of a magnificent apple, nothing more could be seen than a tiny piece of peel on the head of a squirming maggot. The beautiful birds and other rare ani-

mals began to grow faint and exude matter from
which were formed worms that turned and gnawed
their flesh, now become red and raw. The sight was
so disgusting that the crowd, which had pressed forward through curiosity, began to turn away with
expressions of horror, and this all the more as the
old Jew, turning pale and perfectly yellow, became
shrunken on one side.

At this miracle the people set up a frightful noise
and clamor, and the old Jew bewailing himself
acknowledged his error and implored Jesus for mercy.
There was so great a tumult that the Governor of
the city, who had returned home, had to be called to
quell the disturbance. As for the old Jew, he loudly
proclaimed his fault and confessed that he had indeed
tampered with the truth.

In consideration of the man's vehement sorrow and
his entreaties to all present to pray for him that he
might be cured, Jesus blessed the fruits and animals
that had been brought to Him. All were immediately
restored to their first state, including the man himself, who cast himself in tears at Jesus' feet, giving
thanks.

He was so truly converted that he became one of
the most faithful of Jesus' followers and the instrument of many other conversions. In a spirit of
penance, he shared with the poor a great part of the
magnificent fruits of his garden. This miracle made
a deep impression upon all that had now returned
from the city, whither they had gone to take something to eat. And indeed such a miracle was necessary here; for these people, as is often the case among
nations of mixed origin, were obstinate in main-
taining opinions that had been proved to them to
be erroneous. They sprang from Samaritans who had
entered into mixed marriages with heathens, and
who had, in consequence, been banished from
Samaria. They were fasting today not on account of
the destruction of the Temple of Jerusalem, but on

account of their own expulsion from Samaria. They, indeed, acknowledged and lamented their having fallen into error, but at the same time they cared not to abandon it.

They had given Jesus an extraordinarily gracious reception, because many signs contained in an old tradition received by them from the heathens had been fulfilled, and in accordance with the same, they were now expecting some great favor from God to befall them.

This promise had been made at the place afterward named the "Place of Grace." I know only this, that these heathens had once in great affliction prayed on that spot with hands raised to Heaven, and that it had been foretold to them that when new streams should flow into the lake and another into the bathing spring, when the city should have extended as far as the spring, then should the favor be received. And now all these signs had been fulfilled. There flowed at this time, I think, five new streams either all into the lake, or some into it and some into the Jordan nearby. Another sign was fulfilled in the taking place of some change in an arm of the Jordan, and a new stream of good water had begun to flow into the well at the "Place of Grace."

It was at this place that Jesus was about to baptize and it was, very probably, to this that all the prophecies concerning the water referred. The water here, too, was bad. The city had also extended entirely on this side. The northern side lay low and black, full of exhalations arising from its marshes; only some poor heathen outcasts dwelt there in little huts. But toward the southeast of the city were many new houses, gardens, and buildings all the way to the "Place of Grace." The place was low and the country around level. By a change in the river banks and the sudden elevation of a mountain, an arm of the Jordan had bent its course westwardly as far as the garden, where it united with a little stream, and then flowed back into its bed. This bend covered a considerable area. The waters of the Jordan flowing hither constituted one of the aforementioned signs.

As Jesus on the following day was again teaching in the synagogue, in the center of which stood a magnificent chest containing the rolls of the Law, the Jews entered barefoot. Ablutions were prohibited on that day, therefore after the instruction of the preceding eve, they had washed and bathed. Above the clothes of the day before, they wore in the synagogue a long, black mantle with a hood and train. It was open at the sides and fastened with cords. On the right arm hung two rough, black maniples, and on the left arm one. They prayed and chanted in a mournful tone, enveloped themselves for awhile in sacks, open in front, and prostrated face downward in the galleries around the synagogue. The women practiced similar penances in their homes.

The fires had been covered the day before. Not till evening did I see any meal taken, and then it was at an uncovered table in the inn where Jesus ate with His disciples alone. The others took theirs in the large hall of the court. The meal consisted entirely of cold viands brought from the Governor's house. Jesus spoke words of instruction on the subject of eating. Many people, among them the lame and crippled, came in turn to the table upon which were some shallow dishes filled with ashes. The old Jew who had been converted gave many of the best of his magnificent fruits to the poor.

On the next day also, the Sabbath, Jesus again taught in the synagogue and after the instruction walked with His disciples and about ten Jews to the mountain north of the city. The country in that direction was wild and savage. The little party tarried awhile under the trees in front of a house and partook of some food and drink offered them by its inmates.

Jesus gave His companions all kinds of rules for

their direction for, as He said, He would soon leave
them to return but once again. Among other things,
He exhorted them not to make so many motions when
at prayer, a custom here carried to excess; and above
all, not to be so severe toward sinners and heathens,
to be more lenient to them. Thereupon He related
the parable of the unjust steward, proposing it to
them in the form of an enigma. They wondered at
it, and He asked them why the conduct of the steward should be praised. It appeared to me that Jesus
symbolized the synagogue by the unjust steward and
the other debtors by the heathens and the various
sects. The synagogue should reduce the debt of the
sects and heathens while she is furnished with power
and grace; viz., while she undeservedly and unjustly
possesses opulence in order that, when she is herself about to be ejected, she may flee to the mediation of the kindly treated debtors.

5. The Parable of the Unjust Steward

Even as a child, I saw this and the other parables
passing like living scenes before my eyes, and I used
to think that, here and there, I recognized occasional
figures from them in the life around me. And so it
happened also with this steward whom I have always
seen as a hunchback with a reddish beard, a receiver
of revenues. I used to see him running very briskly
and rapidly among the under-tenants, making them
sign their contracts with a pen. I saw the unjust
steward living in a tent castle, in the desert of Arabia, not far from the place where the Children of
Israel murmured. His lord, who dwelt far away across
Mount Libanus, owned here on the frontiers of Palestine a corn and olive plantation. On either side of
the field lived two peasants to whom it was rented.
The steward was a diminutive, humpbacked fellow,
very cunning and full of expedients. He thought: "The
lord will not come yet awhile," and so he feasted

freely and let things go as they would. The two peasants were pretty much of the same stamp, and spent their time in carousing. All on a sudden, I saw the lord coming. Far over a high mountain range, I saw a magnificent city and palace from which a most beautiful road led straight to the plantation. Then I saw the king and his whole court coming down with a great caravan of camels and little, low chariots drawn by asses. I saw all this very much as I see paths coming down from the heavenly Jerusalem. The king was a heavenly king who owned a wheat and olive field on this earth. But he came in the manner of the patriarchal kings, attended by a great retinue. I saw him coming down from on high, for that little fellow, the steward, had been accused to him of dissipating his revenues.

The lord's debtors were two persons in long coats buttoned all the way down. The steward wore a little cap. The castle of the latter was nearer the desert than the wheat and olive plantation, on either side of which the peasants lived. That was more toward the land of Canaan, and formed a triangle with the castle. And now came the lord down over the cornfield. The two debtors had squandered the fruits of the field with the steward, although toward their dependents they were hard and exacting. They were two bad parish priests, and the steward a bishop far from good; or again, it was like a worldling putting his affairs in order. The steward, having espied the coming of his lord while yet he was a long way off, fell into the greatest anxiety. He prepared a grand feast, and became very active and servile. When the lord arrived, he thus addressed the steward: "Why, what is this that I hear of thee, that thou dost squander my property! Render an account, for thou shalt no longer be my steward!" Then I saw the steward hurriedly summoning the two peasants. They presented themselves carrying rolls, which they opened. He questioned them as to the amount of

their indebtedness, for of that he was utterly ignorant, and they showed it to him. With the crooked
reed that he held in his hand, he made them quickly
change the sum to a lesser amount, for he thought:
"When I shall be discharged, I shall find shelter with
them and have whereon to live, for I cannot work."

I saw now the peasants sending their servants to
the lord with camels and asses laden with sacks of
corn and baskets of olives. They that had charge of
the olives carried money also, little metal bars done
up in packages, larger or smaller according to their
sum, and fastened together with rings. But the lord,
glancing at the packages, saw by what he had before
received that these were far too small, and from the
false account rendered, he understood the design of
the steward. Turning to his courtiers, he said with
a laugh: "See, the man is shrewd and cunning. He
intends to make friends of those under him. The children of the world are wiser in their doings than the
children of light, who rarely do for good what the
former do for evil, who rarely take as much trouble
for a reward as this man has done for punishment."
Then I saw that the hunchbacked knave was discharged from his office and banished into the desert.
The soil there was metallic (yellow, hard, unfruitful
ferruginous sand, ocher), its only vegetation the alder
tree. He was at first quite confounded and troubled,
but I saw that he afterward set to work to chop wood
and to build. The two peasants also were sent away,
though to them somewhat better places amidst the
sand of the desert were allotted. But the poor under-
servants, formerly the victims of cruel extortion, were
now entrusted with the care of the field.

6. Jesus and the Disciples Invited to
Teach and Baptize in Seleucia

Jesus and the disciples separated and went in different directions throughout the whole city of Adama.

Jesus took the central portions for Himself, while the disciples went to the most distant quarters even as far as the homes of the heathens. They stopped at almost every house inviting the people, who were already prepared, to go on the following day to the Baptism, and on the day after to the great instruction that Jesus was to deliver in a larger grassy enclosure, on the other side of the lake near Seleucia. The invitations were accompanied by words of instruction. The disciples were thus occupied until dusk, when they left the city and proceeded along the western side of the lake to where some fishing vessels were lying. They went on board, and instructed the fishermen who were fishing by torchlight on the broad side of the lake below the spot where the Jordan flowed into it. The glare of the torches allured the fish, which were then taken with hooks and darts. The disciples told the fishermen to bring their fish over to the green square near Seleucia, where the instruction was to be held, and they should be well rewarded. The green square, of which they made mention, was a kind of zoological garden surrounded by a wall and a hedge. Wild animals taken alive were confined there, consequently it was provided with all kinds of dens and cages for that purpose. The place belonged to Adama and was about one hour and a half from Seleucia.

When morning dawned, Jesus joined the disciples, and they went back to the city together by a roundabout way on which were several huts. Invitations and instructions were given at these huts as at the other houses. Arrived at the city, Jesus and the disciples went to the residence of the Governor, which stood in an open square, and there took some refreshment. The repast consisted of little rolls joined in pairs, and small fish with upright heads. These last were served in a many-colored, shining glass dish formed like a ship. Jesus laid one of the fishes on a roll before each of the disciples. All around the edge

of the table were cavities hollowed out like plates,
and into them the portions were put.

After the repast, Jesus gave an instruction in the
hall opening on the court in presence of the Governor and his household, all of whom were to be baptized. After that He went to the place of instruction
outside the city where He found many already waiting for Him, and there, too, He taught in preparation for Baptism. The people in bands came and went
by turns, proceeding from this place to the synagogue
where they prayed, sprinkled their head with ashes,
and did penance. They repaired afterward to the
bathing garden near the "Place of Grace," where two
by two they performed their ablutions in a bathhouse
separated from each other by a curtain.

When the last band had left the place of instruction, Jesus and His disciples followed. The baptismal
well was that into which the water from the arm of
the Jordan flowed. The basin here, as in other places,
was surrounded by a canal so broad as to afford a
passage for two, and from it five conduits connected
with the basin. These conduits could be opened or
closed at pleasure, and at the side of each ran a path
over the little canal. In the center of the basin rose
a stake which, by a crosspiece that reached to the
bank, could be made to open and close the basin.

This reservoir with its five canals had not been
especially constructed for the Baptism. The number
five was a frequent recurrence in Palestine, and the
five aqueducts leading to the Pool of Bethsaida, to
John's fountain in the desert, to the baptismal well
of Jesus, bore reference no doubt to the five Sacred
Wounds, or to some other mystery of religion.

Jesus here gave instructions as an immediate preparation for Baptism. The neophytes were clothed
in long mantles which they laid aside at the moment
of stepping into the canal, retaining only the covering for the loins and the little scapular on the
breast. Water from the basin had been let into the

canal. On the pathways over it stood the baptizers and the sponsors. The water was thrice poured from a shallow dish over the head in the name of Jehovah and Him whom He had sent. Four disciples baptized at the same time, two others imposing hands as sponsors. This ceremony, with the instructions of Jesus in preparation for it, lasted until evening. Many of the aspirants to Baptism were not admitted to its reception.

At daybreak next morning, the disciples embarked for Seleucia and the appointed place nearby. The lake at some distance from Adama took the figure of a violin, narrowing off to about fifteen minutes in breadth. Seleucia, a city of only moderate importance, was, however, a well-fortified place, being surrounded by two walls and an intervening rampart. On the northern side, especially, it was so steep as to be wholly inaccessible; in that quarter the pagan soldiers dwelt. The women lived to themselves in a separate part of the city in long rows of buildings, each occupying a private apartment. The few Jews here residing were very greatly oppressed. They lived in miserable holes in the walls, and had to perform the lowest and most painful labors on the canals and marshes.

I saw no synagogue here but only a round temple, which stood on a circle of pillars upon which were enormous figures in the attitude of supporting the building. In the center was an immense column, in which were the steps that led up into the edifice. Underneath were subterranean vaults, wherein the urns containing the ashes of the dead were deposited. Nearby was a somber-looking place in which they were accustomed to consume the bodies of their dead. In the temple were idols of serpents with human faces, human figures surmounted by dogs' heads, and one holding the moon and a fish.

The soil around these parts was not very productive, though the inhabitants were remarkably industrious. They made all kinds of cordage for the harness of horses as well as various kinds of armor, everything necessary for military equipments.

The disciples went around in Seleucia inviting the people to the instruction and to partake of the repast prepared at the appointed place. Meanwhile, Jesus went for the same purpose through the pagan quarters at Adama. Then the disciples repaired to the grassy enclosure of the zoological garden, which was beautifully sodded and filled with flowers and bushes, and there, with the fishermen who kept their fish in a cistern, prepared the meal. The tables were broad beams about two feet wide, that had been drawn up out of the lake. Back of the garden were furnaces in which the fish were roasted. It appeared as if meals were often prepared here, for in the caves around were kept a number of flat stone plates, which looked as if formed by nature, and upon which the viands were served up. There were at this repast bread, fish, herbs, and fruit.

When all had been prepared and about a hundred of the pagan men were assembled, Jesus came over the lake. He was followed by about twelve Jews, the Governor, and several heathens from Adama. He taught on a hill. The Governor and the other Jews took part in the management of the repast, and served at table with the disciples. Jesus taught of man's twofold composition, body and soul, and of the nourishment of both the one and the other. The people were free either to listen to His instruction or to partake of the meal. Jesus granted that permission to try them. Some went straight to the table and others soon followed, so that about a third only remained to hear. Jesus taught of the vocation of the heathens and told about the Three Kings, whose history was not unknown to these people.

When the meal and instruction were over, Jesus went toward evening with the disciples and Jews to Seleucia, an hour and a half to the south and at some distance from the lake. The people had already returned thither. Here Jesus and His party were received by the most distinguished men of the city, and a luncheon was served for their refreshment. After that they were conducted into the city and Jesus saluted and instructed the heathen women, who had assembled in a square not far from the gate in order to see Him. They were clothed as Jewesses, though not so modestly veiled. Like most of the people of this region, they were not tall, but stout and robust.

Jesus entered a large public hall wherein a banquet had been prepared in His honor. There was a great deal of feasting going on in these parts. Jesus, the disciples, and the Jews sat by themselves at one of the tables. At first, the Jews were unwilling to partake of the entertainment. But Jesus told them that what entered the mouth did not sully the man, and added that they who would not eat with Him, would not follow His doctrine. He taught unweariedly during the whole of the entertainment.

The heathens used tables higher than those of the Jews and also small single ones. They sat crosslegged on cushions, like the people in the land of the Three Kings. The viands consisted of fish, herbs, honey, fruit, also flesh meat roasted brown.

Jesus so impressed them by His teaching that they were very much grieved when He had to leave. They begged Him so earnestly to remain with them that He allowed Andrew and Nathanael to do so. The heathens were very curious when there was question of novelty. It was already dusk when He left them.

The houses in which the women dwelt faced on a broad street, though their rear was built in the wall or the rampart of the fortification. Some of them were very beautiful, separated at intervals by gardens and squares in which the women carried on their domestic affairs and did their washing. Jesus addressed them in their usual meeting place.

In Seleucia, also, Jesus spoke of the Baptism as of a purification; and when they wished to detain Him longer, He told them that they were at present incapable of understanding more.

From Seleucia Jesus returned to Adama. In the synagogue a feast of thanksgiving was celebrated by the newly baptized who occupied the places of honor and chanted canticles of praise. Numbers of others were baptized when Andrew and Nathanael returned from Seleucia. The converted Jew exhibited naught but humility and a desire to render assistance to Jesus, delighted to act as servant and messenger on all occasions.

A great number of sick had been unable to attend Jesus' instructions and the Baptism; consequently, with Saturnin and the disciple who was related to Him, He went to hunt them up in their homes. The other disciples started for the cities Azor, Cades, Berotha, and Thisbe, all from two to three hours north of Adama, in order to invite the inhabitants to the instruction which Jesus was going to deliver on a gently rising mountain on the road from Cades to Berotha. On the top of that mountain, which was covered with vegetation, and in an open space surrounded by a wall stood a chair used from remote times for teaching. In some places the disciples went to the chief magistrates and called upon them to invite the people to the instruction that the Prophet from Galilee would deliver on the mountain the day after the Sabbath, while in others, they themselves went to the houses and invited the occupants to the instruction.

Meanwhile, Jesus was going around in Adama among the rich and the poor, Jews and heathens, healing the dropsical, the lame, the blind, and those afflicted with a bloody flux. I was especially surprised at the sight of ten possessed men and women, all of them pure Jews. I never saw so many possessed among the heathens. Some of these ten were of distinguished families. They were confined in grated chambers in their own houses, either in the house or the forecourt. As Jesus was coming toward them, they began crying and raging in a frightful manner, but on a nearer approach, they became quiet and stared at Him perplexedly. I saw Him, by His glance alone, driving all the devils from them. They left them under a visible form, a vapor which afterward assumed the shadow of an abominable human figure, and then disappeared. The bystanders were amazed at the sight; the former possessed turned pale and sank down unconscious. Jesus addressed some words to them, took them by the hand, and commanded them to rise. Then, as if coming out of a dream, they sank on their knees giving thanks, and rose up changed men. Jesus then exhorted them and mentioned the faults they should correct.

When the disciples returned to Adama, they took a meal with Jesus at the chief magistrate's. They had purchased fish and bread at the places they had visited, and ordered them to be delivered at the mount of instruction. The food was intended for the audience. Jesus received presents from many people and various places. I saw little bars of gold that looked like twigs. These gifts were devoted to the purchase of food for the multitude. Jesus had not broken His fast since the last meal taken at Seleucia.

On the Sabbath He taught in the synagogue of Adama. There was here also a party formed against Jesus. They sent two Pharisees to where John was teaching in order to hear what he had to say about Jesus, and thence to Bethabara and Capharnaum to inform some of their friends that He was now going around among them baptizing and making disciples. When these messengers returned, they spoke against Jesus and spread the calumnies they had heard, but their efforts gained no adherents to their own party.

Once the magistrates of Adama interrogated Jesus as to what He thought of the Essenians. They wanted

to tempt Him, because they pretended to have
remarked in His sentiments some similarity to those
of that sect, and also because James the Less, His
relative and who was then with Him, was an Essenian. They brought all kinds of accusations against
them, condemning chiefly their retired life and their
celibacy. Jesus answered in very general terms: One
could, He said, find nothing to reproach in those people; if they were called to such a life, they deserved
great praise. Everyone has his own vocation; were a
cripple to aim at walking upright, he would hardly
succeed. When the magistrate objected that so few
families were raised up by them, Jesus enumerated
a great many Essenian families and spoke of their
well-bred children. He alluded to the married state,
first of the good, then of the bad. He neither took
part with the Essenians, nor did He accuse them.
The people did not comprehend Him, though they
saw that He had family connections among the Essenians and kept up intercourse with them.

7. Jesus Preaching on the Mountain
Near Berotha

Before daybreak of the night between the Sabbath and Sunday, Jesus left Adama. He had taken
leave of the people after the exercises of the Sabbath, though without saying that He was not to
return, and He now went with His disciples and several of the Jews to the mountain appointed for the
instruction. He left Adama by the gate through which
He had entered, and that was over a bridge. Had
they gone by another, they would have had to ferry
over the river that ran from Azor to Cades, and
which near Adama flowed into the Jordan. They left
Cades to the right, and proceeded westward over
gently rising mountain terraces. This region had high
mountain ridges that formed great plateaus. There
were fewer ravines and isolated peaks than in south-

ern Palestine. Thisbe was to the left of the little troop on very high ground. Tobias once lived in Thisbe and had there given in marriage his wife's brother, or brother-in-law. He had also been in Amichores, the water city. He might have taken up his abode there permanently, were it not that he preferred to go into captivity, in order to be useful to his people. Elias, too, had been in Thisbe, and Jesus had once before journeyed through it.

The multitude was already gathered upon the mountain. On the preceding evening, people had gone thither after the Sabbath and put the place in order. On the summit was an enclosed space in which stood a teacher's chair. The people living on the sides of the mountain had been busied preparing for the tents, and already the stakes and cords were at hand. They had carried them up and stretched the awnings over the teacher's chair and other available spots around. The place was one of historic interest, for Joshua had here celebrated a feast of thanksgiving after his successful siege of the Canaanites. Water had been transported hither in leathern bottles, and bread and fish in baskets. These baskets were like our beehives; they could be placed one above another, and in the several compartments various things could be put without danger of mixing.

As Jesus was going up through the crowd to the summit of the mountain, shouts greeted Him on every side: "Thou art the true Prophet! The Helper!" etc., and as He passed along, they bowed low before Him. It may have been nine o'clock when He reached the summit, for it was six to seven hours from Adama to this place.

Many possessed had been led up the mountain. They were raging and shouting. When Jesus saw them, He commanded them silence, and by His command and the glance of His eye, they became calm and were freed from the evil one.

When Jesus had reached the tribune and the crowd

had been brought to order and silence by the disciples, He first invoked His Heavenly Father, from
whom come all good gifts, the people likewise praying. Then He began His instruction. He made allusion to what had there occurred, spoke of the children
of Israel, of Joshua's once appearing in these parts
and freeing them from the Canaanites and from
paganism, and of the destruction of Azor. Of all these
events Jesus explained the spiritual meaning. Thus
came truth and light to them anew, with grace and
mildness to free them from the power of sin. He
exhorted them not to resist as did the Canaanites,
that God's punishment might not come upon them
as it had done upon Azor. He also related a parable
of which He again made use on a later occasion. It
is in the book of the Gospels, I think, something
about wheat and husbandry. He taught also of
penance and the coming of the Kingdom, speaking
significantly of Himself and the Heavenly Father as
He had done in the neighboring towns.

The sons of Johanna Chusa and Veronica came
here to Jesus. They had been sent by Lazarus, to
warn Him against the two spies whom the Pharisees
had despatched from Jerusalem to Adama. The disciples brought them to Jesus during a pause in the
instruction. He told them not to be at all disquieted
on His account, that He would fulfill His mission,
and He thanked them for their devotedness, etc. The
spies sent by the Pharisees were also on the mountain with the disaffected Jews from Adama. Jesus
did not address them, but He said aloud in the course
of His instruction that enemies would lie in wait for
Him and persecute Him, still they would not succeed in hindering Him from accomplishing what the
Father in Heaven had entrusted to Him. He would
soon appear among them again to announce the Kingdom of God and the truth.

Many mothers were present with their children,
demanding Jesus' blessing. But the disciples were

disquieted and thought, on account of the presence
of the spies, that He should not give it. Jesus, however, reproved them for their anxiety, saying that He
regarded the intention of the mothers as good, and
that the children would thereby derive benefit, and
so He went down through the rows that they formed
and gave them His benediction.

The instruction lasted from ten in the morning till
near evening, when the people were ranged in order
to take some food. On one side of the mountain there
were grated fires whereon the fish were roasted. The
order observed was beautiful. Not only the inhabitants of each separate city encamped together, but
even the residents of the same streets were divided
into families with their neighbors. To the guests of
each street, one man was appointed to bring and
divide the food. Each person or one person in each
group, had a leather cover which, being spread out,
served for plates. They had with them also such things
as are used at table: bone knives and spoons with
jointed handles. Some had brought gourds, others
cups of bark, in which they received water from the
leathern bottles, while others, there and then, quickly
formed for themselves such cups if they had not done
so on the way. The superintendents received the food
from the disciples, and divided each portion among
the four or five sitting together, laying the fish and
bread on the leathern cover before them. Jesus had
blessed the food before it was divided, and by virtue
of that blessing it was multiplied, otherwise it would
have been far from sufficient for the two thousand
for whom it was intended. Each group received a
small portion only, but all were satisfied after eating, and much remained over to be collected into baskets and carried off by the poor.

There were some Roman soldiers going around
among instructions from him, for he had soldiers
under his command. Perhaps they had been charged
to bring him information of Jesus, for they went to

the disciples and begged some of the blessed bread, to take with them to Lentulus. On receiving it, they stowed it away in the knapsacks that hung from their shoulders.

It was already dark and torches lighted when the meal was over, Jesus blessed the multitude and left the mountain with the disciples, from whom, however, He soon separated. They took a shorter route back to Bethsaida and Capharnaum, while He with Saturnin and that disciple, His relative, went southward to a city lying off from Berotha, called Zedad, and spent the night at an inn outside the city.

8. Jesus Passes Through Gathheper To Capharnaum

On the night between Monday and Tuesday, I saw Jesus in the mountains with Saturnin and that other disciple. As He walked alone in prayer and they questioned Him about it, He spoke to them of prayer in private, illustrating by the example of the serpent and scorpion: "Were a child to ask for a fish, the father would not give him a scorpion," etc. During these days, I saw Him again in various little places among the shepherds healing and exhorting, also in Gathheper, Jonas' birthplace, and where some of His own relatives lived. He wrought cures in this latter place also, and then toward evening went as far as Capharnaum.

How indefatigable was Jesus! With what ardor He inspired the disciples and Apostles! At first they were often overcome by fatigue; but now what a difference! The disciples while travelling along the highways went forward to meet some and to hunt up the others, to instruct them themselves or invite them to attend Jesus' instructions.

Lazarus, Obed, Joseph of Arimathea's nephews, the bridegroom of Cana, and some other disciples, had arrived at Mary's house near Capharnaum. There were present also about seven women, relatives and friends, awaiting the return of Jesus. They went in and out the house and gazed along the road, to catch the first sight of Him. And now came some of John's disciples with the news of their master's imprisonment, which filled the hearts of the little company with anxiety. The disciples then went on to meet Jesus with whom they came up not far from Capharnaum, and made known to Him their errand. He consoled them, and continued His way to His Mother's alone. He had sent His disciples on in advance. Lazarus came out to meet Him, and washed His feet in the vestibule.

When Jesus entered the apartment, the men bowed low before Him. He greeted them, and went up to His Mother, to whom He stretched out His hands. She, too, most lovingly and humbly inclined to Him. There was no rushing into each other's arms; their meeting was full of tender and ingenuous reserve, which touched all present and made upon them the holiest impression. Then Jesus turned toward the other women, who lowered their veils and sank on their knees before Him. He was accustomed to give His blessing at such meetings and leavetakings.

I saw now a repast made ready, and the men reclining around the table, the women at one end sitting cross-legged. They spoke indignantly of John's imprisonment, but Jesus rebuked them. He said that they should not be angry and pass sentence upon it, for that it had to be. Were John not removed from the scene, He Himself would not be able to begin His work and go to Bethania. Then He told them of the people among whom He had been. Of Jesus' coming, none knew excepting those present and the confidential disciples. Jesus slept with the other guests in a side building. He appointed the disciples to meet Him after the next Sabbath at a house, high and solitary, in the neighborhood of Bethoron.

I saw Him conversing with Mary alone. She was weeping at the thought of His exposing Himself to

danger by going to Jerusalem. He comforted her, telling
her that she must not be anxious, that He would
accomplish His mission, and that the sorrowful days
had not yet come. He encouraged her to persevere in
prayer, and exhorted the others to refrain from all
comments and judgments upon John's imprisonment
and the action of the Pharisees against Himself, for
such proceedings on their part would only increase
the danger, that the Pharisees' manner of acting was
permitted by Divine Providence, though thereby they
were working out their own destruction.

Some mention was made of Magdalen also. Jesus
again told them to pray for her and think of her
kindly, for she would soon be converted and become
so good as to be an example for many.

Early next morning, Jesus went to Bethania with
Lazarus and about five of the disciples belonging to
Jerusalem. It was the beginning of the Feast of the
New Moon, and I saw floating from the synagogues
of Capharnaum and other places, long streamers of
knotted drapery and festoons of fruit on the principal houses.

9. John the Baptist Arrested by Herod and Imprisoned at Machaerus

Herod had once before caused the Baptist to be
arrested at the place of baptism and brought to him
where he kept him in custody some weeks in the
hope of intimidating him and leading him to a change
of sentiment. But through fear of the immense crowds
that were hurrying to hear John, he had released
him. John then retired to the place where he had
formerly baptized near Ainon and opposite Salem. It
was one hour and a half east of the Jordan and about
two hours south of Socoth. The baptismal well was
in the region of a lake, about a quarter of an hour
long, from which two streams, after bathing the foot
of a hill, flowed into the Jordan. On this hill were

the remains of an old castle, whose towers were still
habitable, and scattered around were gardens and
walks and other dwellings. Between the lake and the
hill was John's baptismal well. In the center of the
spacious, caldron-shaped summit of the hill, John's
disciples had raised an awning over a terraced elevation formed of stone, and it was there that he
taught. This region was under Philip's jurisdiction.
But it ran like a point into Herod's country, who on
that account was somewhat reserved in executing
his designs against John.

An uncommonly great concourse of people had
assembled to hear John: whole caravans from Arabia on camels and asses, and hundreds of people
from Jerusalem and all Judea, both men and women.
The crowds came and went by turns, covered the
caldron-shaped plateau, encamped at the base of
the hill, and stood on the heights around. The most
beautiful order was established and maintained by
John's disciples. Those nearest the preacher reclined
on the ground, those behind them sat on their heels,
while the outer rows stood; in this way all could
see. The heathens were separated from the Jews,
and the men from the women, who always stood
back in the last row. On the slope of the hill were
other groups squatting, head and arms resting on
their knees, or again, clasping one knee and lying
or sitting on the other hip.

Since his return from Herod, John was as if penetrated by a new spirit. His voice sounded usually
sweet, and yet was so powerful and far-reaching that
every word was understood. He again wore his mantle of skins, and was more roughly clothed than at
On where he had sometimes appeared in a flowing
robe. His teaching was of Jesus and His persecution
in Jerusalem. Pointing toward Upper Galilee where
Jesus was at that instant going about working miraculous cures, John said: "But He will soon reappear
in those parts. His persecutors will gain nothing over

Him until His mission shall have been fulfilled."

Herod also and his wife came with a guard of soldiers to John's place of instruction. He had travelled from his castle of Livias twelve hours, passing near Dibon where he had to cross two branches of a little river. As far as Dibon the road was good, but after that it became very rough and difficult, properly speaking fit only for foot-passengers and beasts of burden. Herod rode upon a long, narrow chariot on which one could recline or sit sideways. There were several with him. The wheels proper were heavy, low, round disks without spokes, though there were other larger ones and rollers at the back. The road was so uneven that on one side the chariot rested on the high wheels, and on the other upon low ones. The journey was a painful one. Herod's wife, along with her ladies in waiting, rode upon a similar chariot. They were drawn by asses preceded and followed by soldiers and courtiers.

Herod had undertaken this journey because John was now preaching again, and that more boldly and zealously than before. He was anxious to hear him and learn whether he said anything personally against himself. His wife was only waiting for an opportunity to excite him to extreme measures against John; she hid her crafty designs, however, under a fair appearance. Herod had still another motive in making this journey. He knew that the Arabian king Aretas, father of his repudiated first wife, had come hither to John and, to escape observation, had mingled with the disciples. He wanted to see whether Aretas had any design to stir up the people against himself. His first wife, a good and very beautiful lady, had returned to her father who, having heard of John's teaching and of his opposition to Herod's unlawful desires, had come to satisfy himself of the truth of what had been told him. But anxious to attract no attention, he was dressed simply, like John's disciples with whom he identified himself.

Herod alighted at the old castle on the hill and sat during John's instruction upon the graded terrace in front. His wife, surrounded by her guards and attendants, sat on cushions under an awning. John was preaching in a loud voice and at that moment crying out to the people that they should not be scandalized at Herod's second union, that they should honor him without imitating him. These words pleased Herod at first, though on second thought they irritated him. The force with which John spoke was indescribable. His voice was like thunder, and yet sweet and intelligible. He seemed to be exerting himself for the last time. He had already warned his disciples that his days were drawing to a close, but that they should not abandon him, they should visit him when in prison. For three days he had neither eaten nor drunk. The whole time had been spent in teaching, proclaiming aloud his testimony to Jesus, and in rebuking Herod for his adultery. The disciples implored him to discontinue and take a little nourishment, but he listened not; he was wholly under the spirit of inspiration.

The view from the height upon which John taught was uncommonly beautiful. One could see off in the distance the Jordan, the cities lying around, fields, and orchards. There must have been here in days gone by a great building, for I could still see stone arches like those of bridges, overgrown with thick green moss. Two of the towers of the castle at which Herod stopped, had been lately restored and it was in them that he lodged. This region was rich in springs and the baths were kept in perfect order. The water that supplied them was brought through a skillfully constructed, vaulted canal from the hill upon whose summit John taught. The baptismal pool was oval in form and encircled by three beautiful green terraces through which five pathways were cut. This region was indeed much smaller, but richer in appearance than that of Bethsaida at Jerusalem, which is

here and there rendered unsightly and impure by
reeds and by the leaves that fall into it from the surrounding trees. The baptismal pool lay behind the
hill, and about one hundred and fifty feet beyond
was the great pond in which were numbers of fish.
They seemed to be crowding to the side at which
John was teaching, as if they wanted to hear. On the
pond were little skiffs, trunks of trees hollowed out,
large enough at most for two men only, with seats
in the middle for fishing. John ate only a little poor
honey. When he took food with his disciples, it was
always in very small quantities. He prayed alone,
and spent much of the night gazing up to Heaven.

John knew that the time of his arrest was near;
therefore had he spoken as if under inspiration and
as if taking leave of his auditors. He had announced
Jesus more clearly than ever. He was now coming,
he said; consequently he himself should retire and
they should go to Jesus. He, John, was soon to be
apprehended. They were, he continued addressing
his audience, a hard and indocile people. They should
recall how he had come at first and prepared the
ways for the Lord. He had built bridges, made foot
paths, cleared away stones, arranged baptismal pools,
and conducted thither the water. He had a difficult
task, struggling against stony earth, hard rocks, and
knotty wood. And these labors he had had to continue toward a people stubborn, obdurate, and unpolished. But they whom he had stirred up should now
go to the Lord, to the well-beloved Son of the Father.
They whom He received would be truly received; they
whom He rejected should indeed be rejected. He was
coming now to teach, to baptize, to perfect what he
himself had prepared. Then turning toward Herod,
John earnestly reproached him several times before
the people for his scandalous connection. Herod, who
both reverenced and feared him, was inwardly furious, though preserving a cool exterior.

The instruction was ended and the crowd began

to disperse on all sides, the people from Arabia and
Aretas, Herod's father-in-law going with them. Herod
had not caught sight of him. Herod's wife had already
gone, and now he himself departed, concealing his
rage and taking a friendly leave of John.

John sent several disciples to different quarters
with messages, dismissed the others, and retired to
his tent to give himself up to prayer. It was already
dark and the disciples had departed, when about
twenty soldiers, after placing guards on all sides,
surrounded the tent and one entered. John told him
that he would follow quietly, that he knew his time
had come and that he must make way for Jesus, they
needed not to fetter him, for he would willingly accompany them, and that, in order to avoid a tumult, they
should lead him away with as little noise as possible. And so the twenty men hurried him off at a
rapid pace. He had only his rough mantle of skins
thrown about him, and his staff in his hand. Some
of his disciples met him as he was being led away.
He took leave of them with a glance, and bade them
visit him in his imprisonment. But soon the disciples and people mobbed together and cried aloud:
"They have arrested John!" and then arose weeping
and lamentations. They wanted to follow, but they
knew not what direction to take, for the soldiers had
turned quickly out of the usual way and proceeded
southward by an unknown route. Intense excitement,
grief, and mourning prevailed. The disciples scattered and fled in all quarters just as they did later,
at the time of Jesus' arrest, and the news was soon
spread throughout the whole country.

After marching with the soldiers the whole night,
John was conducted first to a tower at Hesebon.
Toward morning some soldiers of the place came to
meet the prisoner, for it was already known there
that John had been arrested, and the people were
gathering together in groups. The soldiers who had
charge of John seemed to be a kind of bodyguard to

Herod. They wore helmets, their breasts and shoulders protected by armor formed of metal plates and rings, and they bore long lances in their hands.

The people of Hesebon gathered in crowds before John's prison, and the guards had enough to do to drive them off. The upper part of the tower had several exterior openings. John stood in his prison crying in a voice loud enough to be heard without. His words were to this effect, that he had prepared the ways, had broken rocks, had directed streams, had dug fountains, had built bridges; he had had to cope with obstacles the most adverse and contradictory, and it was owing to the obstinacy of those whom he now addressed that he had been arrested. But they should turn to Him whom he had announced, to Him who would soon come by the paths he himself had made straight. When the Master approached, then should they who had prepared His way withdraw, and all should turn to Jesus, the latchets of whose shoes he himself was not worthy to loose. "Jesus," he continued, "is the Light, the Truth, and the Son of the Father," etc. He called upon his disciples to visit him in his confinement, for no one would yet venture to lay hands upon him, his hour was not yet come. John uttered the above in a voice as loud and distinct as if he were addressing the multitude from an orator's stand. Again and again the guard dispersed the crowd, but the throng soon reassembled, and John's instructions recommenced.

He was afterward led by the soldiers from Hesebon to the prison of Machaerus, the access to which was up a high and steep mountain. He rode with several in a low, narrow, covered chariot like a box, drawn by asses. Arrived at Machaerus, the soldiers conducted him up the steep mountain path to the fortress. But they did not enter by the principal gate, but through a postern in the wall nearby, which overhanging moss almost concealed. Traversing a passage somewhat inclined, they reached a brazen door which opened into another that ran under the gateway of the fortress, and thence led into a large underground vault. It was lighted from above and was clean, though destitute of every species of comfort.

From the place of baptism, Herod went to his castle of Herodium, which had been built by Herod the Elder, and where once, for mere sport, he had caused some persons to be drowned in a pond. Here, filled with dejection, Herod hid himself away and would see nobody, although many had already presented themselves to express to him their disapproval of John's arrest. A prey to inquietude, he shut himself up in his own apartments.

After some time John's disciples, provided they came in small numbers, were allowed to approach the prison, converse with him, and pass things to him through the grating. But if many came together, they were turned away by guards. John ordered the disciples to go on baptizing at Ainon, until Jesus came to establish Himself there for the same purpose. The prison was large and well-lighted, but its only resting place was a stone bench. John was very serious. His countenance always wore an expression of thoughtfulness and sadness. He looked like one that loved and heralded the Lamb of God, but who knew the bitter death in store for Him.

10. Jesus in Bethania. Inns Established for the Accommodation of Jesus and the Disciples on Their Journeys. The Pearl Lost and Found

With Lazarus and the five disciples belonging to Jerusalem, Jesus traversed the road from Capharnaum to Bethania through the region of Bethulia. But to Bethulia itself, which lay high in the distance, they did not go. Their way ran around it toward Jezrael, outside of which Lazarus owned a kind of accommodation inn with a garden.

The disciples had gone on ahead and prepared a luncheon. One of the trusty servants of Lazarus had charge of the place. It was early in the morning when they washed their feet here, shook the dust from their clothes, ate something, and took a little rest. From Jezrael they went over a little river, leaving Scythopolis and afterward Salem to the left, crossed a mountain spur, and approached the Jordan. Continuing their course southward, they crossed the river below Samaria and, because it was already night, rested some hours on an eminence of the river's bank where some faithful shepherds dwelt. Before daybreak next morning they started again and directed their steps between Hai and Gilgal through the desert of Jericho. Jesus and Lazarus journeyed together, while the disciples went ahead by another route. Jesus and Lazarus walked the whole day by unfrequented paths without touching at any place, not even at the inn that Lazarus owned on this side of the desert. When within a few hours of Bethania, Lazarus went on ahead and Jesus continued His journey alone.

There were assembled at Bethania with Lazarus and the five disciples from Jerusalem, about fifteen disciples and followers of Jesus and seven women: Saturnin, Nicodemus, Joseph of Arimathea, his nephews, Simeon's sons, and those of Johanna Chusa, Veronica, and Obed respectively. Among the women were Veronica, Johanna Chusa, Susanna, Mary Marcus the widow of Obed, Martha, and the discreet old servant of the last named, who afterward joined the holy women who cared for the wants of the Lord and His disciples. All were gathered in a large, subterranean vault of Lazarus' castle, quietly and, it seemed, secretly awaiting the coming of Jesus.

Toward evening He arrived and entered the garden by a back gate. Lazarus went out to meet Him in a reception hall, where he washed His feet. There was here a deep basin connected with the house by pipes, through which Martha poured tepid water for the use of their Guest. Jesus, sitting on the rim of the basin, immersed His feet, which Lazarus washed and dried. After that he shook out Jesus' garments, put on His feet fresh sandals, and handed Him a little food and drink.

Then Jesus accompanied Lazarus through a long, shady walk up to the house and down into the vaulted chamber. The women drew their veils and bowed low on their knees before Him, while the men inclined profoundly. Jesus greeted all and blessed them, after which they took their place at table. The women sat on cushions at one side of the table, their feet crossed under them.

Nicodemus was remarkably impressed and very desirous of hearing every word of Jesus. The men spoke indignantly of John's imprisonment. But Jesus said that it had to be, it was the will of God, and that they should not speak of such things in order not to attract attention and thereby give rise to danger. If John had not been removed from the scene of action, He Himself would not yet have been able to labor here. The blossoms must fall, if the fruit is to appear.

Then they spoke angrily of the spying and persecution set on foot by the Pharisees, whereupon Jesus again commanded them to be at peace. He deplored the action of the Pharisees and related the parable of the unjust steward. The Pharisees, too, were unjust stewards, though not so prudent as the subject of the parable, therefore would they have no resource on the day of reckoning.

After the meal, they retired to another apartment where lamps were lighted. Jesus prayed aloud, and they began the exercises of the Sabbath. After that Jesus conversed awhile with the men, and all retired to rest.

When silence reigned in the house and the inmates were sunk in slumber, Jesus arose from His couch and went out unperceived to the cave on Mount Olivet in which, on the day before His bitter Passion, He would wrestle in prayer. He prayed several hours to His Heavenly Father for strength to accomplish His work, and before daybreak returned unnoticed to Bethania.

The sons of Obed, who were servers in the Temple, now returned with some others to Jerusalem, but the rest of the guests remained quietly in the house, and none but themselves knew of Jesus' presence.

During the meal today, Jesus told them of His stay among the people of Upper Galilee, at Amead, Adama, and Seleucia. And as the men in their zeal vehemently inveighed against the sects, He reproved them for their bitterness, and related to them a parable. He told them of a man who on the way to Jericho had fallen among robbers, and who had received more pity from a Samaritan than from a Levite. I have always heard this parable related in the same way, though with different applications. He spoke also of the calamities about to befall Jerusalem.

At night when all were asleep, Jesus went again to pray in the cave on the Mount of Olives. He shed many tears and endured intense fear and anguish. He was like a son going forth to great labors, and who first threw himself on the bosom of his father to receive strength and comfort. My guide told me that whenever Jesus was in Bethania and had an hour to spare, He used to go to that cave to pray. This was a preparation for His last agony on Mount Olivet. It was also shown to me that Jesus chiefly on Mount Olivet prayed and sorrowed, because Adam and Eve when driven from Paradise had here first trodden the inhospitable earth. I saw them in that cave sorrowing and praying, and it was on this mountain, which Cain was cultivating for the first time, that he became so enraged as to resolve to kill Abel. I thought of Judas, I saw Cain murdering his brother in the vicinity of Mount Calvary, and on Mount Olivet called by God to account for the same. Daybreak found Jesus back again in Bethania.

The Sabbath over, that took place on account of which principally Jesus had come to Bethania. The holy women had heard with sorrow what hardships Jesus and His followers had had to endure upon their journeys, and that Jesus especially, on His last hurried journey to Tyre, had suffered such want; they had heard of His having to soften the hard crusts, which Saturnin had begged on the way, in order to be able to eat them. They had therefore offered to establish inns and furnish them with all that was necessary. Jesus accepted their offer, and came hither to make with them the necessary arrangements. As He now declared that He would henceforth publicly teach everywhere, Lazarus and the women again offered to establish inns, especially since the Jews in the cities around Jerusalem, instigated by the Pharisees, would furnish nothing to Him and His disciples. They also begged the Lord to signify to them the principal stopping places on His journeys and the number of His disciples, that they might know how many inns would be needed and what quantity of provisions to supply.

Jesus replied by giving them the route of His future journeys, also the stopping places, and the probable number of disciples. It was decided that about fifteen inns should be made ready and entrusted to the care of confidential persons, some of them relatives either of Lazarus or of the Holy Family. They were scattered throughout the whole country, with the exception of the district of Cabul toward Tyre and Sidon.

The holy women then consulted together as to what district each should see to and what share each should take in the new establishments, to supply furniture, covers, clothes, sandals, etc., to provide for washing and repairing, and to attend to the furnishing of bread and other necessaries. All this took place before and during the meal. Martha was in her element.

After the meal Jesus, Lazarus, the other friends, and the holy women assembled secretly in another of the subterranean halls. Jesus sat on a raised seat at one side of the hall, the men standing and sitting around Him; the women were on the opposite side on steps covered with carpets and cushions. Jesus spoke of the mercy of God to His people. He had sent them Prophets one after another whom they had disowned and ill-treated; now they would reject the Supreme Grace, and He predicted what would betide them. After He had dwelt upon this at length, some of His hearers said to Him: "Lord, relate this to us in a beautiful parable," and Jesus told them the parable of a king who after all his servants had been killed by the unfaithful vinedressers, sent his son into the vineyard where he too was murdered.

Some of the men withdrew at the close of this instruction and Jesus went with others into the hall and walked up and down. Martha, who was passing to and fro, approached Him and had a long talk about her sister Magdalen. She related what she had heard of her from Veronica, and her own consequent anxiety.

While Jesus was walking up and down the hall with the men, the women sat playing a kind of lottery for the benefit of their new undertaking. On the elevated platform was a table on rollers around which they sat. The plane of the table, which projected into five angles like the rays of a star, covered a box about two inches in depth. From the five points to the center of this partitioned box, ran deep furrows on the surface, and between them were slits connecting the interior. Each of the women had some long strings of pearls and many other little precious stones. Each in turn placed some of them in one of the furrows on the table. Then resting a delicate little bow on the outer end of the furrow, she shot a tiny arrow at the nearest pearl or stone. The shock received by this one communicated itself to the rest, which rolled into the other furrows or dropped through the holes into the compartments in the interior of the box. When all the pearls and stones had been shot from the surface, the table, which was upon rollers, was agitated to and fro, by which movement the contents fell into other little compartments which could be drawn out at the edge. Each of these little drawers had previously been assigned to one of the players, so that when the holy women drew them out, they saw at once what they had won for their new undertaking or which jewel they had lost. Obed had died not long before and his widow was still mourning for him. Before the baptism, he had been at Lazarus' with Jesus.

During the game the holy women lost a very precious pearl that had fallen down among them. All moved back and looked for it most carefully. When at last they found it and were expressing their joy, Jesus came over to them and related the parable of the lost drachma and the joy of the owner upon finding it again. From their pearl, lost, carefully sought, and joyfully found, He drew a new similitude to Magdalen. He called her a pearl more precious than many others that, from the lottery table of holy love, had fallen and were going to destruction. "With what joy," He exclaimed, "will ye find again the precious pearl!" Then the women, deeply moved, asked: "Ah, Lord! Will that pearl be found again?" and Jesus answered: "Seek ye more earnestly than the woman in the parable sought the lost drachma, or the shepherd his stray sheep." Profoundly touched at this answer, all promised to seek after Magdalen more diligently than after their lost pearl, and assured Him that their joy upon finding her would far exceed what they now felt. Some of the women begged the Lord to receive among His disciples the young man of Samaria who, after the Pasch, had besought this favor of Him on the road to that city. They praised his great wisdom

and virtue. I think he was related to one of them.
But Jesus replied that He could not count upon him
as he was blinded by love of riches.

That evening several of the men and women began
their preparations to go to Bethoron, where Jesus
was to preach next day. That night Jesus again retired
secretly to the Mount of Olives and prayed with His
whole heart and soul, after which He went with
Lazarus and Saturnin to Bethoron, about six hours
off. It was then one hour past midnight. They cut
through the desert on their way. When about two
hours distant from Bethoron, they were met by the
disciples whom Jesus had appointed to join Him there,
and who had arrived at the inn near Bethoron the
day before. They were Peter, Andrew, and their half-
brother Jonathan, James the Greater, John, James
the Less, and Judas Thaddeus, who was with them
now for the first time, Philip, Nathanael Chased, also
the bridegroom of Cana, and one or two of the widow's
sons. Jesus rested with them under a tree in the
desert for a long time, and gave them an instruction. He spoke again on the parable of the lord of
the vineyard who had sent his son to the vinedressers.
At the conclusion of the discourse, they proceeded to
the inn and took something to eat. Saturnin had
received from the women a purse of money with which
to procure provisions for the little party.

11. Jesus in Bethoron. The Hardships and Privations of the Disciples

It was toward eight o'clock in the morning when
Jesus arrived in Bethoron. A couple of the disciples
went to the dwelling of the Elders and demanded
the keys of the synagogue, as their Master wanted
to deliver an instruction; others scattered through
the streets and summoned the people to the school,
while Jesus went with the rest to the synagogue,
which was soon filled with auditors. He taught again

in severe terms on the parable of the lord of the vineyard whose servants were murdered by the unfaithful vinedressers, whose son whom he had sent to them shared the same fate, and who at last gave the vineyard into the hands of others. He spoke likewise of the persecution of the Prophets and the imprisonment of John, saying that they would persecute Him also and lay hands upon Him, and He ended by predicting the judgment and woe that were to come upon Jerusalem. This discourse occasioned great excitement among the Jews. Some rejoiced, while others muttered angrily to one another: "Whence came this Man so unexpectedly here? No one knew of His arrival!" And some who had heard that there were women, followers of Jesus, at the inn in the valley, went out to question them on the designs of their Master.

Jesus cured several that were sick of a fever, and after some hours left the city.

Veronica, Johanna Chusa, and Obed's widow had arrived at the inn, and prepared a luncheon. Jesus and the disciples partook of it standing, after which they girded themselves and recommenced their journey. Jesus taught on this same day in Kibzaim on similar subjects as at Bethoron, also in some small shepherd settlements. All the disciples were not present in Kibzaim, but they met again at a large house belonging to a shepherd. It was surrounded by outbuildings and stood on the confines of Samaria. Mary and Joseph had been hospitably received there on their journey to Bethlehem, after having vainly sought admittance elsewhere. Here Jesus and the disciples, about fifteen in all, ate and slept. Lazarus and the women had returned to Bethania.

On the next day Jesus and the disciples sometimes together, sometimes in separate groups, passed rapidly through several large cities and small towns that lay in a district of some hours in extent. Gabaa and Najoth, about four hours from Kibzaim, were among them.

In none of these places did Jesus take time to go to
the synagogues to teach, but instructed the crowds
that gathered to hear Him on hills in the open air,
on the public places, and in the streets. Several of
the disciples remained with Jesus, while the others
scattered through the valleys and shepherd villages
to call the dwellers to the places which Jesus was to
pass. The whole day's work was performed with in-
credible hardship and fatigue, with constant going
from place to place. Jesus cured many sick, some of
whom were carried to Him, but others cried out themselves for His aid. There were some lunatics among
them. Many possessed ran clamoring after Him, but
He commanded them to be silent and to retire.

What made that day's work still more wearisome,
was the bad dispositions of the people and the insults
of the Pharisees. These places, being near Jerusalem,
were full of people who had taken part against Jesus.
It was then as it is now in little places, they talk of
everything without understanding anything. It was
to such people that Jesus suddenly appeared with
His band of disciples and His grave and denuncia-
tory preaching. He repeated the instructions delivered at Bethoron, spoke of the graces now offered
for the last time, after which would come the day of
Justice, and again alluded to the ill-usage of the
Prophets, the imprisonment of John, and the persecution directed against Himself. He brought forward
above all the parable of the Lord of the vineyard,
who had now sent His Son. He said that the Kingdom would soon come and the King's Son would enter
into possession of it. He often cried, "Woe!" to
Jerusalem and to them that would not receive His
Kingdom, would not do penance. These severe and
menacing discourses were interrupted by many acts
of charity and by the cure of the sick. In this way,
Jesus journeyed from place to place.

The disciples had much to endure, and it was often
very hard for them. On reaching a town or village

and announcing the coming of Jesus, they often heard the scornful words: "What! Is He coming again! What does He want? Whence comes He? Has He not been forbidden to preach?" And they laughed at them, derided and insulted them. There were, indeed, a few that rejoiced to hear of Jesus' coming, but they were very few. No one ventured to attack Jesus Himself, but wherever He taught, surrounded by His disciples, or proceeded along the street followed by them, the crowd shouted after them. They stopped the disciples and plied them with impertinent questions, pretending that they had misunderstood or only half comprehended His severe words, and demanding an explanation. Meanwhile other cries resounded, cries of joy at some cure just wrought by Jesus. This scandalized the crowd and they fell back and left Him. And so He continued till evening these rapid and fatiguing marches without rest or refreshment.

I noticed how weak and human the disciples still were in the beginning. If during Jesus' instructions, they were questioned as to His meaning, they shook their head as if they had not understood what He really meant. Nor were they satisfied with their condition. They thought to themselves: "Now we have left all things, and what have we for it but all this tumult and embarrassment? Of what kind of a kingdom is He always speaking? Will He really gain it?" These were their thoughts. They kept them concealed in their own breast, though often manifesting discouragement in their countenance. John alone acted with the simplicity of a child. He was perfectly obedient and free from constraint. And yet the disciples had seen and were still witnessing so many miracles!

It was indeed touching to think that Jesus knew all their thoughts, and yet acted as if wholly ignorant of them. He changed nothing in His manner, but calmly, sweetly, and earnestly went on with His work.

Jesus journeyed far into the night of that day. When on this side of a little river that forms the

boundary of Samaria, He and His disciples stopped
for the night among some shepherds from whom they
received little or nothing. The river water was not
fit for drinking. It was a narrow stream and here,
not far from its source at the foot of Garizim, made
a rapid turn toward the west.

12. Jesus at Jacob's Well Near Sichar. Dina, The Samaritan

On the following day Jesus crossed the little river
and, leaving Mount Garizim to the right, approached
Sichar. Andrew, James the Greater, and Saturnin
accompanied Him, the others having scattered in different directions. Jesus went to the Well of Jacob, on
a little hill in the inheritance of Joseph to the north
of Mount Garizim and south of Mount Ebal. Sichar
lay about a quarter of an hour to the west in a valley which ran along the west side of the city for
about an hour. About two good hours northward from
Sichar stood the city of Samaria upon a mountain.

Several deeply rutted roads ran from different
points around the little hill and up to the octangu-
lar buildings that enclosed Jacob's Well, which was
surrounded by trees and grassy seats. The springhouse was encircled by an open arched gallery under
which about twenty people could find standing room.
Directly opposite the road that led from Sichar and
under the arched roof was the door, usually kept
shut, that opened into the springhouse proper. There
was an aperture in the cover of the latter, which
could be closed at pleasure. The interior of the little springhouse was quite roomy. The well was deep
and surrounded by a stone rim high enough to afford
a seat. Between it and the walls, one could walk
around freely. The well had a wooden cover, which
when opened disclosed a large cylinder just opposite
the entrance and lying across the well. On it hung
the bucket which was unwound by means of a winch.

Opposite the door was a pump for raising the water
to the top of the wall of the springhouse, whence it
flowed out to the east, south, and west under the
surrounding arches into three little basins dug in
the earth. They were intended for travellers to perform their ablutions and wash their feet, also for
watering beasts of burden.

It was toward midday when Jesus and the three
disciples reached the hill. Jesus sent them on to Sichar
to procure food, for He was hungry, while He Himself ascended the hill alone to await them. The day
was hot, and Jesus was very tired and thirsty. He
sat down a short distance from the well on the side
of the path that led up from Sichar. Resting His head
upon His hand, He seemed to be patiently waiting
for someone to open the well and give Him to drink.
And now I saw a Samaritan woman of about thirty
years, a leathern bottle hanging on her arm, coming
up the hill from Sichar to draw water. She was beautiful, and I remarked how briskly and vigorously,
and with what long strides she mounted the hill.
Her costume appeared somewhat studied, and there
was an air of distinction about it. Her dress was
striped blue and red embroidered with large yellow
flowers; the sleeves above and below the elbow were
fastened by yellow bracelets, and were ruffled at the
wrist. She wore a white stomacher ornamented with
yellow cords. Her neck was entirely concealed by a
yellow woolen collar thickly covered with strings of
pearl and coral. Her veil, very fine and long, was
woven of some rich, woolen material. It hung down
her back, but by means of a string could be drawn
together and fastened around her waist. When thus
worn, it formed a point behind and on either side
folds in which the elbows could comfortably rest.
When both sides of the veil were fastened on the
breast, the whole of the upper part of her person
was enveloped as if in a mantle. Her head was bound
with fillets that entirely concealed the hair. From

her headdress there arose above the forehead something like a little tower or a crown. Tucked up behind it lay the forepart of the veil which, when let down over her face, reached to the breast.

She had her large, brownish goat or camel-hair apron with its open pockets, thrown up over her right arm, so that the leather bottle hanging on that arm was partly concealed. This apron was similar to those usually worn at such work as drawing water. It protected the dress from the bucket and water bottle.

The bottle was of leather, and like a seamless sack. It was convex on two sides, as if lined with a firm, arched, wooden surface; but the two others, when the bottle was empty, lay together in folds like those of a pocketbook. On the two firm sides were leather-covered handles through which ran a leather strap used for carrying it on the arm. The mouth of the bottle was narrow. It could be opened like a funnel for receiving the contents, and closed again like a work pouch. When empty, the bottle hung flat on the side, but when filled it bulged out, holding as much as an ordinary water bucket.

It was under this guise that I saw the woman briskly ascending the hill, to get water from Jacob's Well for herself and others. I took a fancy to her right away. She was so kind, so frank, so openhearted. She was called Dina,[1] was the child of a mixed marriage, and belonged to the sect of Samaritans. She lived in Sichar, but it was not her birthplace. Her peculiar circumstances were unknown to the inhabitants, among whom she went by the name of Salome. Both she and her husband were very much liked on account of their open, friendly, and obliging manners.

The windings of the path by which she mounted the hill prevented Dina's seeing the Lord until she actually stood before Him. There was something startling in the sight as He sat there exhausted and all

---

1. In the Roman Martyrology she is called Photina.

alone on the path leading to Jacob's Well. He wore
a long, white robe of fine wool like an alb, bound
with a broad girdle. It was a garment such as the
Prophets wore, and which the disciples usually carried for Him. He made use of it only on solemn occasions when He preached, or fulfilled some Prophecy.

Dina coming thus suddenly upon Jesus was star-
tled. She lowered her veil and hesitated to advance,
for the Lord was sitting full in her path. I saw passing through her mind the characteristic thoughts: "A
man! What is he doing here? Is it a temptation?" She
saw that Jesus was a Jew as, beaming with benevolence, He graciously drew His feet back, for the path
was narrow, with the words: "Pass on, and give Me
to drink!"

These words touched the woman, since the Jews
and the Samaritans were accustomed to exchange
only glances of mutual aversion, and so she still lingered, saying: "Why art Thou here all alone at this
hour? If anyone should happen to see me here with
Thee, he would be scandalized." To which Jesus
answered that His companions had gone on to the
city to purchase food. Dina said: "Indeed! The three
men whom I met? But they will find little at this
hour. What the Sichemites have prepared for today,
they need for themselves." She spoke as if it were
either a feast or a fast that day in Sichar, and named
another place to which they should have gone for
food.

But Jesus again said: "Pass on, and give Me to
drink!" Then Dina passed by Him. Jesus arose and
followed her to the well, which she unlocked. While
going thither, she said: "How canst Thou, being a
Jew, ask a drink from a Samaritan?" And Jesus
answered her: "If thou didst know the gift of God
and who He is that sayeth to thee: 'Give Me to drink,'
thou wouldst perhaps have asked of Him, and He
would have given thee living water."

Then Dina loosened the cover and the bucket, mean-

while saying to Jesus, who had seated Himself on
the rim of the well: "Sir, thou hast nothing wherein
to draw, and the well is deep. Whence then hast Thou
living water? Art thou greater than our father Jacob
who gave us this well, and drank thereof himself and
his children and his cattle?" As she uttered these
words, I had a vision of Jacob's digging the well and
the water's springing up. The woman understood
Jesus' words to refer to the water of this well and
so, as she was speaking, she put the bucket on the
cylinder, which turned heavily, lowered it and drew
it up again. She pushed up her sleeves with the
bracelets until they puffed out high above the elbow,
and in this way with bare arms she filled her leather
bottle out of the bucket. Then, taking a little vessel
made of bark and shaped like a horn, she filled it
with water and handed it to Jesus, who sitting on
the rim of the well drank it and said to her: "Whosoever drinketh of this water, shall thirst again, but
he that shall drink of the water that I shall give
him, shall not thirst forever. Yes, the water that I
will give him, shall become in him a fountain of water
springing into life everlasting."

Dina replied eagerly: "Sir, give me that living water,
that I may no more thirst nor have to come with so
much fatigue to draw." She was struck by His words
"living water" and had a presentiment, though without being fully conscious of it, that Jesus meant by
the "living water" the fulfillment of the Promise. And
so it was under prophetic inspiration that she uttered
her heartfelt prayer for that living water. I have
always felt and understood that those persons with
whom the Redeemer treated are not to be considered as mere individuals. They perfectly represented
a whole race of people, and they did so, because they
belonged to the plenitude of time. And so in Dina
the Samaritan, there stood before the Redeemer the
whole Samaritan sect, so long separated from the
true faith of Israel, from the fountain of living water.

Jesus at the Well of Jacob thirsted after the chosen souls of Samaria, in order to refresh them with the living waters from which they had cut themselves off. It was that portion of the rebellious sect still open to salvation that here thirsted after this living water and, in a certain way, reached out an open hand to receive it. Samaria spoke through Dina: "Give me, O Lord, the Blessing of the Promise! Help me to obtain the living water from which I may receive more consolation than from this temporal Well of Jacob, through which alone we still have communication with the Jews."

When Dina had thus spoken, Jesus said to her: "Go home, call thy husband, and come back hither!" and I heard Him give the command twice, because it was not to instruct her alone that He had come. In this command the Redeemer addressed the whole sect: "Samaria, call hither him to whom thou belongest, him who by a holy contract is lawfully bound to thee." Dina replied to the Lord: "I have no husband!"

Samaria confessed to the Bridegroom of souls that she had no contract, that she belonged to no one. Jesus replied: "Thou hast said well, for thou hast had five husbands, and he with whom thou now livest is not thy husband. Thou hast spoken truly." In these words the Messiah said to the sect: "Samaria, thou speakest the truth. Thou hast been espoused to the idols of five different nations, and thy present alliance with God is no marriage contract."[2] Here Dina, lowering her eyes and hanging her head, answered: "Sir, I see that Thou art a Prophet," and she drew down her veil. The Samaritan sect recognized the divine mission of the Lord, and confessed its own guilt.

As if Dina understood the prophetic meaning of Jesus' words: "and he with whom thou livest is not

---

2. These words of Jesus refer to the five different pagan colonies with their idolatry, placed by the King of the Assyrians in Samaria after the greater part of its inhabitants had been led into the Babylonian Captivity. What remained of the original people of God in Samaria, had become mixed up with the heathens and their idol-worship.

thy husband," that is, thy actual connection with the
true God is imperfect and illegal, the religion of the
Samaritans has by sin and self-will been separated
from God's covenant with Jacob; as if she felt the
deep significance of these words, she pointed toward
the south, to the temple not far off on Mount Garizim,
and said questioningly: "Our Fathers adored on that
mountain, and you say that Jerusalem is the place
where men must adore?" Jesus replied with the words:
"Woman! Believe Me, the hour cometh when neither
in Garizim nor in Jerusalem wilt thou adore the
Father." In this reply He meant to say: "Samaria, the
hour cometh when neither here nor in the sanctuary of the Temple will God be adored, because He
walks in the midst of you," and He continued: "You
adore that which you know not, but we adore that
which we know, for salvation is of the Jews." Here
He related to her a similitude of the wild, unfruitful suckers of trees, which shoot forth into wood and
foliage, but produce no fruit. It was as if He had said
to the sect: "Samaria, thou hast not security in thy
worship. Thou hast no union, no sacrament, no pledge
of alliance, no Ark of the Covenant, no fruit. The
Jews, from whom the Messiah will be born, have all
these things, the Promise, and its fulfillment."

And again Jesus said: "But the hour cometh and
now is when the true adorers will adore the Father
in spirit and in truth, for the Father wills such to
adore Him. God is a spirit, and they that adore Him
must adore Him in spirit, and in truth." By these
words the Redeemer meant: "Samaria, the hour
cometh, yea, it now is, when the Father by true adorers will be honored in the Holy Ghost and in the
Son, who is the Way and the Truth." Dina replied:
"I know that the Messiah cometh. When He is come,
He will tell us all things." In these words here at
the Well of Jacob, spoke that portion of the Samaritan sect, which might lay some legitimate claim to
the Promise: "I hope for, I believe in the coming of

the Messiah. He will help us." Jesus responded: "I am He, I who now speak to thee!"

By this He said to all Samaria that would be converted: "Samaria! I came to Jacob's Well athirst for thee, thou water of this well. And when thou didst give Me to drink, I promised thee living water that would never let thee thirst again. And thou didst, hoping and believing, make known to Me thy longing for this water. Behold, I reward thee, for thou hast allayed My thirst after thee by thy desire after Me! Samaria, I am the Fountain of living water. I who now speak to thee, am the Messiah."

As Jesus pronounced the words: "I am the Messiah," Dina, trembling with holy joy, gazed at Him in amazement. But suddenly recovering herself, she turned and, leaving her water bottle standing and the well open, she fled down the hill to Sichar, to tell her husband and all whom she met what had happened to her. It was strictly forbidden to leave the Well of Jacob open, but what cared Dina now for the Well of Jacob! What cared she for her bucket of earthly water! She had received the living water, and her loving, joyous heart was longing to pour its refreshing streams over all her neighbors. But as she was hurrying out of the springhouse, she ran past the three disciples who had come with the food and had already been standing for some time at a little distance from the door, wondering what their Master could have to say for so long with a Samaritan woman. But through reverence for Him, they forebore to question. Dina ran down to Sichar and with great eagerness said to her husband and others whom she met on the street: "Come up to Jacob's Well! There you will see a man that has told me all the secret actions of my life. Come, He is certainly the Christ!'

Meanwhile the three disciples approached Jesus, who was still by the well, and offered Him some rolls and honey out of their basket, saying: "Master, eat!"

Jesus arose and left the well with the words: "I have
meat to eat which you know not." The disciples said
to one another: "Hath any man brought Him to eat?"
and they thought to themselves: "Did that Samaritan woman give Him to eat?" Jesus would not stop
to eat, but began descending the hill to Sichar. The
disciples followed, eating. Jesus said to them as He
went on before: "My meat is to do the will of Him
that sent Me, that I may perfect His work." By that
He meant, to convert the people of Sichar, after whose
salvation His soul hungered. He spoke much more
to the same purport.

When near the city, Dina the Samaritan again appeared hurrying back to meet Jesus. She joined Him
respectfully, but full of joy and frankness, and Jesus
addressed many words to her, sometimes standing
still and sometimes moving slowly forward. He
unfolded to her all her past life with all the dispositions of her soul. She was deeply moved and
promised that both she and her husband would abandon all and follow Him. He pointed out to her many
ways by which she could do penance for her sins and
repair her scandals.

Dina was an intelligent woman of some standing
in the world, the offspring of a mixed marriage, a
Jewish mother and a pagan father, born upon a country seat near Damascus. She had lost her parents at
an early age, and had been cared for by a dissolute
nurse by whom her evil passions had been fostered.
She had had five husbands one after another. Some
had died of grief, others had been put out of the way
by her new lovers. She had three daughters and two
half-grown sons, all of whom had remained with the
relatives of their respective fathers when their mother
was obliged to leave Damascus.

Dina's sons at a later period joined the seventy-
two disciples. The man with whom she was now living was a relative of one of her former husbands. He
was a rich merchant. As Dina followed the Samari-

tan religion, she had induced the man to remove to Sichar, where she superintended his household and lived with him, though without being espoused to him. They were looked upon in Sichar as a married couple. The husband was a vigorous man of about thirty-six years with a ruddy face and a reddish beard. There we're many things in Dina's life similar to those of Magdalen's, but she had fallen more deeply than the latter. Still I once saw that in the beginning of Magdalen's evil career at Magdalum, one of her lovers lost his life at the hand of a rival. Dina was an uncommonly gifted, open-hearted, easily influenced, pleasing woman of great vivacity and impetuosity, but she was always disturbed in conscience. She was living now more respectably, that is with this her reputed husband, in a house that stood alone and surrounded by a moat, near the gate leading from Sichar to the spring house. Though not held in contempt by the inhabitants, still they did not have much communication with her. Her manners were different from theirs, her costume elaborate and studied, all which, however, they pardoned in her as she was a stranger.

While Jesus was speaking with Dina, the disciples followed at some distance, wondering what He could have to say to the woman. "We have brought Him food, and that with a good deal of difficulty. Why, now, does He not eat?"

When near Sichar, Dina left the Lord and hurried forward to meet her husband and many of the citizens, who came pouring out of their houses, all curiosity to see Jesus. Full of joy, they exulted and shouted salutations of welcome to Him. Jesus, standing still, motioned with His hand for silence, and addressed them kindly for some moments, telling them among other things to believe all that the woman had told them. Jesus was so remarkably gracious in His words, His glance was so bright and penetrating that all hearts beat more quickly, all were borne toward

Him, and they were instant in their solicitations for
Him to enter and teach in their city. He promised
that He would do so, but for the present passed on.
This scene took place somewhere between three and
four o'clock in the afternoon.

While Jesus was thus addressing the Samaritans
outside the gate, all the other disciples, among them
Peter, who in the morning had gone on commissions
in a different direction, returned to their Master.
They were surprised and not any too well pleased to
see Him talking so long with the Samaritans. They
felt somewhat embarrassed at it, for they had been
reared in the preconceived idea that they were to
have no communication with these people, consequently they had never before seen anything like
this. They felt tempted to take scandal at it. They
reflected upon the hardships of yesterday and the
day before, on all the scorn and insult, on the cruel
treatment that they had endured. They had expected
an easier time, since the women of Bethania had
advanced so much money for that end. Seeing now
this intercourse with the Samaritans, they thought
to themselves it was certainly no wonder when things
went on in this way that they were not better
received. Their heads were always full of extravagant, worldly fancies of the Kingdom that Jesus was
to establish, and they thought if all this should become
known in Galilee, they would indeed be derided.

Peter had in Samaria a long conversation with
that young man who wanted to join the disciples,
but who was still wavering. He afterward spoke with
Jesus on the subject.

Jesus went with them all about a half-hour around
the city to the north, and there rested under some
trees. On the way thither the Lord had been conversing with them about the harvest, a subject which
He now continued. He said, "There is a proverb often
on the lips, 'yet four months, and the harvest cometh.'
Sluggards are ever desirous of putting off their work,

but they should look around and see all the fields standing white for the harvest." Jesus meant the Samaritans and others who were ripe for conversion. "Ye, disciples, are called to the harvest, though ye have not sown. Others have sown, namely, the Prophets and John and I Myself. He that reapeth, receiveth wages and gathereth fruit for eternal life, that both He that soweth and he that reapeth may rejoice together. For in this is the saying true, that it is one man that soweth and it is another that reapeth. I have sent you to reap that in which you did not labor. Others have labored and you have entered into their labors." In this way Jesus spoke to the disciples in order to encourage them to the work. They rested only a short time and then separated, Andrew, Philip, Saturnin, and John remaining with Jesus, while the others went on to Galilee passing between Thebez and Samaria.

Jesus, leaving Sichar to the right, journeyed about an hour southward to a field around which were scattered twenty shepherd huts and tents. In one of the larger huts, the Blessed Virgin and Mary Cleophas, the wife of James the Greater, and two of the widows were awaiting Him. They had been there the whole day, having brought with them food and little flasks of balsam. They now prepared a meal. On meeting His Mother, Jesus extended both hands to her, while she inclined her head to Him. The women saluted Him by bowing their head and crossing their hands on their breast. There was a tree in front of the house, and under it they took the meal.

Among the shepherds dwelling around these parts were the parents of the youths whom Jesus, after the raising of Lazarus, took with Him on His journey to Arabia and Egypt. These people had come to Bethlehem in the suite of the three Holy Kings, had on account of the hasty departure of the latter remained behind in this country, and had married some of the shepherds' daughters in the valley near

Bethlehem. Shepherd settlements like that just mentioned were frequent in the winding valleys between
this place and Bethlehem. The people dwelling here
cultivated also the field of Joseph's inheritance which
they had rented from the Sichemites. There were
many of them gathered here, but no Samaritans.

The first noteworthy incident that took place here
was the Blessed Virgin's begging Jesus to cure a lame
boy whom some of the neighboring shepherds had
brought thither. They had before doing so implored
Mary's intercession. Such things happened very often,
and it was quite affecting to see her asking Jesus
for these favors. Jesus commanded that the boy should
be brought, and the parents bore him on a little litter to the door of the house in which Jesus was. The
child was about nine years old. Jesus addressed some
words of exhortation to the parents and, as they fell
back, somewhat timidly awaiting the result, the disciples gathered around Jesus. He spoke to the boy,
leaned a little over him, then took him by the hand
and raised him up. The boy jumped out of the litter,
took a few steps, and then ran into the arms of his
parents, who cast themselves with him at Jesus' feet.
The crowd uttered cries of joy, but Jesus reminded
them to thank the Heavenly Father. He then
addressed a short instruction to the assembled shepherds and took with the disciples a light repast, which
the women had prepared in an arbor under the great
tree in front of the house. Mary and the women sat
apart at the end of the table. I am under the impression that this house was taken for one of the private inns, and was prepared and served by the holy
women of Capharnaum.

There approached now, and that rather timidly,
several persons from Sichar, among them Dina, the
woman of the well. They did not venture to draw
near, because they were not accustomed to have intercourse with the Jewish shepherds. Dina, however,
made bold to advance first, and I saw her talking

with the women and the Blessed Virgin. After the repast, Jesus and the disciples took leave of the holy women, who immediately set about preparing for their return journey to Galilee whither Jesus Himself was to go the next day but one.

Jesus now returned with Dina and the other Samaritans to Sichar, a city not very large, but with broad streets and open squares. The Samaritan house of prayer was a finer looking building, more ornamented than the synagogues of small Jewish places. The women of Sichar were not so reserved as the Jewish women; they communicated more freely with the men. As soon as Jesus entered Sichar, He was surrounded by a crowd. He did not go into their synagogue, but taught walking around here and there on the streets, and in one of the squares where there was an orator's chair. Everywhere was the concourse of people very great, and they were full of joy at the Messiah's having come to them.

Dina, though very much moved and very recollected, was of all the women the one that approached nearest to Jesus. Her neighbors now looked upon her with special regard, as she had been the first to find Jesus. She sent the man with whom she was living to Jesus, who spoke to him a few words of exhortation. He stood before Jesus quite embarrassed, and ashamed of his sins. Jesus did not tarry long in Sichar, but went out by the opposite gate and taught here and there among the houses and gardens that extended for some distance along the valley. He put up at an inn distant from Sichar a good half-hour, promising, however, to return to the city on the following day and give them an instruction.

When Jesus went again to Sichar, He taught the whole day, dividing the time between the orator's chair in the city and the hills outside, and in the evening He taught again in the inn. From the whole country around came crowds to hear Him, and they followed Him from place to place. The cry was: "Now

He is teaching here! Now He is teaching there!" The
young man of Samaria also listened to the instructions, but he did not speak with Jesus.

Dina was everywhere foremost, everywhere made
her way through the crowd to Jesus. She was very
attentive, very earnest, and deeply impressed. She
had had another interview with Jesus and was now
about to separate from her reputed husband. They
had resolved for Jesus' sake to consecrate all their
riches to the poor and the good of the future Church,
Jesus told them how to proceed in the affair. Many
of the Samaritans were profoundly touched by what
they had seen and heard, and they said to Dina:
"Thou hast spoken truly. We have now heard Him
ourselves. He is the Messiah!" The good woman was
quite out of herself, and so in earnest, so joyous! I
have always loved her dearly.

Here as in former places, Jesus took for the subjects of His discourse: the imprisonment of John, the
persecution of the Prophets, the Precursor charged
to prepare the ways, and the son sent to the vineyard, but who was murdered by the wicked servants.
He declared plainly that the Father had sent Him.
He taught also upon all that He had said to the
woman at the well, namely, the living water, Mount
Garizim, salvation from the Jews, the nearness of
the Kingdom and the Judgment, and the punishment inflicted upon the wicked servants who had
put to death the son of the lord of the vineyard.
Many of His hearers questioned Him as to where
now they should be baptized and cleansed, since
John was imprisoned. Jesus answered that John's
disciples were again baptizing near Ennon across
the Jordan, and that, until He Himself should appear
there with His disciples to give Baptism, they should
go thither. On the following day, accordingly, crowds
flocked to Ennon.

Next day Jesus taught at the inn and on the surrounding hills. His audience consisted of laborers, of

all kinds of people, and those slaves whom, after His baptism, He had once consoled in the field of the shepherds near Bethabara. There were present also many spies sent by the Pharisees from the environs around. They listened to Him with anger in their hearts, stuck their heads together, and muttered jeeringly. But they did not attempt to accost Him, and He took no notice of them. Several Samaritan Doctors and others remained unmoved by His words, receiving them into a disaffected heart.

13. Jesus in Ginnaea and Ataroth.
He Confounds the Wickedness of the Pharisees

When Jesus with His five disciples left the inn near Sichar, He journeyed leaving Thebez to the right and Samaria to the left, six hours further on to the city of Ginnaea, or Ginnim, situated in a valley on the boundary of Samaria and Galilee. Late in the evening they entered Ginnaea, their garments still tucked up and, as the Sabbath had begun, they went straight to the synagogue. The disciples who had journeyed on before them were likewise present. On leaving the synagogue, they went all together to a country seat belonging to Lazarus and which lay up among the mountains. Nearby was Little Thirza, where Jesus had already put up, and where also Mary and Joseph on their journey to Bethlehem had received lodgings. The steward, a man whose manners breathed the simplicity of ancient times, had many children. Jesus and His disciples spent the night there. The country seat may have been about three-quarters of an hour distant from Ginnaea. The holy women, on their return journey from Sichar, had spent the night in Thebez. The day of Jesus' arrival here, the day before the Sabbath, was a fast in expiation of the murmuring of the Children of Israel. On the Sabbath Jesus taught in the synagogue. The

passages read from Holy Scripture referred to the
journey through the Wilderness, the parcelling out
of the Land of Canaan, and to something in Jeremias. Jesus interpreted all as bearing reference to
the nearness of the Kingdom of God. He spoke of the
murmuring of the Children of Israel in the desert,
saying that they would have taken a much shorter
way to the Promised Land, had they kept the Commandments that God gave them on Sinai, but on
account of their sins they were obliged to wander,
and they that murmured died in the desert. And so,
too, would they among His present hearers wander
in the desert and die therein, if they murmured
against the Kingdom that was now at hand and with
it the final mercy of God. Their life had been an
image of that wandering in the desert, but they should
now go by the shortest way to the promised Kingdom of God, which would be pointed out to them. He
referred also to the dissatisfaction of the Children
of Israel with the judgeship of Samuel, their clamoring after a king, and their receiving one in Saul.
Now, when the Prophecy was fulfilled, when on
account of their impiety the scepter had passed from
Juda, they were again sighing for a king and for the
reestablishment of the kingdom. God would send them
a King, their true King, just as the lord of the vineyard had sent his own son after his servants had
been murdered by the unfaithful vinedressers. But
in the same way would they, too, expel their King
and put Him to death. He also explained those verses
of the Psalms that speak of the cornerstone rejected
by the builders, applying them to the son of the lord
of the vineyard, and spoke of the punishment that
would fall upon Jerusalem. The Temple, He said,
would not exist much longer, and Jerusalem itself
would soon be unrecognizable. He referred likewise
to Elias and Eliseus.

There were twelve obstinate Pharisees at this
instruction, and when it was over they disputed

with Jesus. They pointed to a roll of parchment, and asked what was meant by Jonas' lying three days in the whale's belly. Jesus answered: "In like manner will your King, the Messiah, lie three days in the grave, descend into Abraham's bosom, and then rise again." They laughed at that. Then three of the Pharisees came forward and, full of hypocrisy, said: "Venerable Rabbi, you speak always of the *shortest way*. Tell us, which is that shortest way?" Jesus answered: "Know ye the Ten Commandments given on Sinai?" They answered: "Yes." He went on: "Observe the first of them, and love your neighbor as yourself. Lay not upon those under you heavy burdens that you do not impose upon yourselves. That is the way!" They replied: "We know all that!" Jesus rejoined: "That ye know all this and yet do nothing of it, constitutes your guilt, therefore will ye be chastised." And He reproached them for burdening the people with unnecessary prescriptions while they themselves did not observe the Law itself, for that was especially the case in this city. He alluded also to the priestly robes prescribed by God to Moses, and of their mysterious signification. He convicted them of their nonfulfillment of these matters, for which they substituted many perversions and external forms. The Pharisees were highly exasperated, but they could not get the better of Jesus. They repeated to one another: "He is the Prophet from Nazareth! The carpenter's Son, forsooth!" Most of them left the synagogue before Jesus had concluded His discourse. One only remained till the end and invited Jesus and His disciples to a repast. He was better than the rest, though still a lurker.

Some sick persons had been brought and placed outside the synagogue, and the Pharisees requested Jesus to cure them, that thereby they might see a sign. But Jesus refused to perform any cure, saying that they would not believe in Him, therefore

they should see no sign. Their real aim was to
tempt Him to heal on the Sabbath, that they might
have something for which to bring an action against
Him.

When the Sabbath was over, most of the disciples
from Galilee returned to their homes, but Jesus with
Saturnin and two other disciples went back to
Lazarus' country seat. How touching to see Him giving instructions to the children of the steward and
those of the neighbors, first to the boys and then to
the girls. He spoke of obedience to parents and of
reverence for old age. The Father in Heaven had
appointed for them their fathers; as much as they
honored them, so much also would they honor their
Heavenly Father. He spoke likewise of the children
of the sons of Jacob and of these of Israel, telling
how they had murmured and for that reason had not
been allowed to enter the Promised Land, a land that
was so beautiful. Then He pointed to the fine trees
and fruits in the garden, and told them of the heavenly Kingdom promised to them that keep the Commandments of God. It was far more glorious and
beautiful than the lovely garden in which they were;
that garden, compared with the heavenly one, was
nothing more than a desert. They must then be obedient and submit thankfully to the decrees of God
in their regard; they must never murmur, that thereby
they might not be excluded from the Kingdom of
Heaven; they must not doubt concerning the beauty
of that Kingdom, as the Israelites did in the desert;
they must believe it to be far above, yes, a thousand
times more magnificent than what they then saw
before them; and lastly, they should have it often in
their thoughts, in order to merit it by their daily toil
and labors. During these instructions Jesus had the
smaller ones right in front of Him. He lifted some
of them up to His breast, or encircled a couple of
them with His arms.

From Lazarus' country seat, Jesus went with the

three disciples again southward about four hours,
back toward Ataroth, one of the chief cities of the
Sadducees, lying among the mountains. The Sadducees of this place, like the Pharisees of Gennabris,
had in consequence of what had taken place at the
Pasch persecuted the disciples, imprisoned several
of them and tormented them with judicial interrogatories. Some of them also had lately been in Sichar
and had listened insidiously to Jesus' instructions in
which He had censured the harshness of the Pharisees and Sadducees toward the Samaritans. They
had then resolved upon a plan to ensnare Jesus, and
it was in pursuance of the same that they had engaged
Him to celebrate the Sabbath of Ataroth. But He
knew of their doings, and so went by a different route
to Ginnaea. They had, however, concerted with the
Pharisees of Ginnaea and, on the morning of the
Sabbath, they sent messengers to say to Jesus: "Thou
hast taught beautiful things concerning the love of
one's neighbor. Thou sayest that one should love his
neighbor as himself. Come, then, to Ataroth and heal
one of our sick. If Thou showest us this sign, we, as
well as the Pharisees of Ginnaea, will all believe in
Thee and we shall spread Thy doctrines throughout
the country."

Jesus knew their wickedness and the plot they
had laid to entrap Him. The man whom, as they
pretended, they wanted Him to cure, had already
for several days lain stiff and dead, but they declared
to all the people of the city that he was only in a
trance. His wife herself did not know that he was
dead. Had Jesus raised him up, they would have
said that he was not dead. They went to meet Jesus
and conducted Him to the house of the dead man,
who had been one of the leaders of the Pharisees
and had been most active in annoying the disciples.
They were carrying the corpse on a litter out into
the street as Jesus came up. There were about fifteen Sadducees and a crowd of people standing

around. The corpse presented quite a fine appearance, for they had opened and embalmed it, the better to deceive Jesus. But Jesus said: "This man is dead and dead he will remain." They replied that he was only in a trance, and if he was indeed dead, he had only just now died. Jesus responded: "He denied the resurrection of the dead, therefore he will not now arise! Ye have filled him with spices, but behold, with what spices! Uncover his breast!" Thereupon I saw one of them raise the skin like a lid from the dead man's breast, when there broke forth a swarm of worms, squirming and straining to get out. The Sadducees were furious, for Jesus rehearsed aloud and openly all the dead man's sins and delinquencies, saying that these were the worms of his bad conscience, which he had in life covered up, but which were now gnawing at his heart. He reproached them with their deceit and evil design, and spoke very severely of the Sadducees and of the judgment that would fall upon Jerusalem and upon all that would not accept salvation. They hurried the corpse back again into the house. The scene was one of frightful alarm and confusion. As Jesus with the disciples was going to the gate of the city, the excited rabble cast stones after them. They were incited thereto by the Sadducees whom the discovery of the worms and their own wickedness had infuriated.

Among the wicked mob, there were, however, some well-intentioned persons who shed tears. In a bystreet lived some infirm women sick with a bloody flux. They believed in Jesus, and from a distance implored His aid, for, as unclean, they dared not approach Him. Knowing their need, He compassionately went through their street. When He had passed, they followed in His footsteps kissing them. He looked around upon them, and they were healed.

Jesus went on for almost three hours to a hill in the neighborhood of Engannim, a place lying almost

in a line with Ginnaea, though in another valley
some hours to the south. It was on the direct route
to Nazareth through Endor and Naim, about seven
hours from the latter.

Jesus spent the night on this hill, in the shed of
a public inn where, too, He took some refreshment
brought from Galilee by the disciples who had come
thither to meet Him. They were Andrew, the bridegroom Nathanael, and two servants of the so-called
centurion of Capharnaum. They urged Jesus to hurry,
as the man's son was so ill. Jesus replied that He
would go at the right time.

This centurion was a retired officer who had once
been Governor of a part of Galilee under Herod
Antipas. He was a well-disposed man and, in the late
persecution, had protected the disciples against the
Pharisees; he had also provided them with money
and other necessaries. As yet, however, he was not
quite believing, although he put faith in the miracles. He was very desirous of one in behalf of his
son, both through natural affection and also to put
the Pharisees to shame. The disciples likewise were
eager for it, saying with him: "Then the Pharisees
will be furious! Then they will see who He is that
we follow!"

It was in this spirit that Andrew and Nathanael
had undertaken the commission to Jesus, who knew
well the bottom of the their heart. He gave another
instruction the next morning when the two servants
of the centurion were converted. They were pagan
slaves, and had brought food with them. They now
returned with Andrew and Nathanael to Capharnaum.

14. Jesus in Engannim and Naim

From the inn on the hill Jesus proceeded to Engannim, which was not far off. He was accompanied by
Saturnin, by the son of the bridegroom of Cana's
maternal aunt, and by the son of the widow of Obed
of Jerusalem, a youth of about sixteen years. Jesus
had some distant relatives in this place. They were
Essenians of Anne's family. They received Jesus very
respectfully and as an intimate friend. They dwelt
apart at one side of the city, and led a very pure life,
many of them being unmarried and living together
as in a cloister. They, however, no longer strictly
observed the ancient discipline of the Essenians; they
dressed like others and frequented the synagogue.
They supported in Engannim a kind of hospital that
was full of the sick and suffering of all sects, and
where the poor were fed at long tables. They received
all that presented themselves, supported them, and
cared for them. In the dormitories of the sick, they
always put the bed of a bad man between two good
ones that, by their exhortations, they might try to
make him better. Jesus visited this hospital, and
healed some of the sick.

Jesus taught the whole day in the synagogue of
Engannim. Crowds had come thither from the country around, and because the synagogue could not
accommodate them all, they remained in troops outside. When one crowd came out, another went in.
Jesus taught here as at other places on this journey,
only not so severely since these people were well-
disposed. It was then as now, the people of the different localities being well or ill-disposed according
to the good or bad dispositions of their priests.

Jesus told them that He would cure the sick after
the instructions. He taught of the nearness of the
Kingdom and of the coming of the Messiah, citing
passages from the Scriptures and the Prophets and
proving that the time had arrived. He mentioned

Elias, his words and his visions, giving the date of the latter, and telling His hearers that the Prophet had raised an altar in a grotto to the honor of the Mother of the future Messiah. He made a calculation of the time which could be no other than the present, warned them that the scepter had been taken from Juda, and recalled to them the journey of the Three Kings. Jesus referred to all these facts in a general way, as if speaking of a third person, making no mention at all of His Mother and Himself. He spoke also of compassion, recommending them to treat the Samaritans kindly, and explained the Parable of the Samaritan, though without mentioning Jericho. He told them of His own experience of the Samaritans, that they were more willing to assist the Jews than the Jews them. He related the circumstance of the Samaritan woman, of her giving Him to drink (a piece of courtesy that a Jew would not so easily have shown a Samaritan), and how well her people in general had received Him. He taught here also of the chastisement in store for Jerusalem and the Publicans, of whom some dwelt in the country around.

While Jesus was teaching in the synagogue, numbers of sick from the city and the whole surrounding district were brought thither. They were laid on litters and cushions under awnings all along the streets by which Jesus was to pass, their friends standing by them. It was the rule that all sick of the same disease should be placed together. It was like a great fair of suffering people.

Jesus came out from the instruction, passed along through the sick, who humbly implored His aid, and while instructing and admonishing cured about forty persons, lame, blind, dumb, gouty, dropsical, feverstricken, etc. I did not see any possessed here. As the multitude was so great, Jesus went upon a little hill that was in the city, and there taught; but the throng at last became such that the people pressed into houses, mounted to the roofs, and even broke down the walls.

Seeing this confusion, Jesus disappeared in the crowd, left the city, and took a steep byway into the mountains where there was a solitary place. His three disciples followed, but after long seeking found Him not till night. He was praying. They asked Him how they, too, should occupy themselves in prayer, and He gave them in few words some petitions of the "Our Father," for instance: "Hallowed be Thy Name! Forgive us our trespasses as we forgive those that trespass against us, and deliver us from evil!" He added: "Now say these words and put them in practice," and He gave them on this point some admirable instructions. They were very faithful in following His injunction whenever He did not converse with them or when He walked alone.

The disciples always carried with them now some food in pouches, and when other wayfarers passed, even off on the byways, they hurried after them in obedience to the words of Jesus, and shared with them, especially if they were poor, whatever they needed.

Engannim was a Levitical city. It was built on the declivity of a valley that extended toward Jezrael across the claw of a mountain range that ran in an easterly direction. A brook flowed northward through the valley. The inhabitants carried on spinning and the manufacture of cloth for priests' vestments. They made also tassels, silk fringes, and balls for trimming the borders of these robes, upon which the women sewed. The people here were very good.

Jesus passed Jezrael and Endor, and toward evening arrived at Naim. He went unnoticed to an inn outside the city.

The widow of Naim, the sister of the wife of James the Greater, had been informed by Andrew and Nathanael of Jesus' near approach, and she was awaiting His arrival. With another widow she now went

out to the inn to welcome Him. They cast themselves
veiled at His feet. The widow of Naim begged Jesus
to accept the offer of the other good widow, who wished
to put all she possessed into the treasury of the holy
women for the maintenance of the disciples and for
the poor, whom she herself also wanted to serve. Jesus
graciously accepted her offer, while He instructed and
consoled her and her friend. They had brought some
provisions for a repast, which along with a sum of
money they handed over to the disciples. The latter
was sent to the women at Capharnaum for the common treasury.

Jesus took some rest here with the disciples. He
had on the preceding day taught in Engannim with
indescribable effort and had cured the sick, after
which He had journeyed thence to Naim, a distance
of about seven hours. The widow, lately introduced
to Jesus, told Him of another woman named Mary
who likewise desired to give what she possessed for
the support of the disciples. But Jesus replied that
she should keep it till later when it would be more
needed. This woman was an adulteress, and had
been, on account of her infidelity, repudiated by her
husband, a rich Jew of Damascus. She had heard of
Jesus' mercy to sinners, was very much touched, and
had no other desire than to do penance and be
restored to grace. She had visited Martha, with whose
family she was distantly related, had confessed to
her her transgression, and begged her to intercede
for her with the Mother of Jesus. She gave over to
her also a part of her wealth. Martha, Johanna
Chusa, and Veronica, full of compassion for the sinner, interested themselves in her case, and took her
at once to Mary's dwelling at Capharnaum. Mary
looked at her gravely and allowed her to stand for
a long time at a distance. But the woman suppli-
cated with burning tears and vehement sorrow:
"O Mother of the Prophet! Intercede for me with
thy Son, that I may find favor with God!" She was

possessed by a dumb devil and had to be guarded, for in her paroxysms she could not cry for help and the devil drove her into fire or water. When she came again to herself, she would lie in a corner weeping piteously. Mary sent in behalf of the unhappy creature a messenger to Jesus, who replied that He would come in good time and heal her.

JESUS' TEACHING MISSION IN THE COUNTRY OF GENESARETH AND ON THE BANKS OF THE JORDAN

1. The Messengers of the Centurion of Capharnaum

From Naim Jesus, leaving Nazareth on the left, journeyed past Thabor to Cana, where He put up near the synagogue with a Doctor of the Law. The forecourt of the house was soon full of people who had anticipated His coming from Engannim, and were here awaiting Him. He had been teaching the whole morning, when a servant of the Centurion of Capharnaum with several companions mounted on mules arrived. He was in a great hurry and wore an air of anxiety and solicitude. He vainly sought on all sides to press his way through the throng of Jesus, but could not succeed. After several fruitless attempts, he began to cry out lustily: "Venerable Master, let Thy servant approach Thee! I come as the messenger of my lord of Capharnaum. In his name and as the father of his son, I implore Thee to come with me at once, for my son is very sick and nigh unto death." Jesus appeared not to hear him; but encouraged at seeing that some were directing Jesus' attention to him, the man again sought to press through the crowd. But not succeeding, he cried out anew: "Come with me at once, for my son is dying!" When he cried so impatiently, Jesus turned His head toward him and said loud enough for the people to hear: "If you see not signs and wonders, you do not believe. I know your case well. You want

to boast of a miracle and glory over the Pharisees,
though you have the same need of being humbled
as they. My mission is not to work miracles in order
to further your designs. I stand in no need of your
approbation. I shall reserve My miracles until it is
My Father's will that I should perform them, and I
shall perform them when My mission calls for it!"
And thus Jesus went on for a long time, humbling
the man before all the people. He said that that man
had been waiting long for Him to cure his son, that
he might boast of it before the Pharisees. But miracles, Jesus continued, should not be desired in order
to triumph over others, and He exhorted His hearers to believe and be converted.

The man listened to Jesus' reproaches without
being at all disturbed. Not at all diverted from his
design, he again tried to approach nearer, crying out:
"Of what use is all that, Master? My son is in the
agony of death! Come with me at once, he may perhaps be already dead!" Then Jesus said to him: "Go,
thy son liveth!" The man asked: "Is that really true?"
Jesus answered: "Believe Me, he has in this very
hour been cured." Thereupon the man believed and,
no longer importuning Jesus to accompany him,
mounted his mule and hastened back to Capharnaum. Jesus remarked that He had yielded this time;
at another time He would not be so condescending.

I saw this man not as invested with the royal commission, but as himself the father of the sick boy.
He was the chief officer of the Centurion of Capharnaum. The latter had no children, but had long desired
to have one. He had, consequently, adopted as his
own a son of this his confidential servant and his
wife. The boy was now fourteen years old. The man
came in quality of messenger, though he was himself the true father and almost indeed the master. I
saw the whole affair, all the circumstances were clear
to me. It was perhaps on account of them that Jesus
permitted the man to importune Him so long. The

details I have just given were not publicly known.

The boy had long sighed after Jesus. The sickness was at first slight and the desire for Jesus' presence arose from the feeling entertained against the Pharisees. But for the last fourteen days, the case becoming aggravated, the boy had constantly said to his physicians: "All these medicines do me no good. Jesus, the Prophet of Nazareth, alone can help me!" When the danger had become imminent, messages had been dispatched to Samaria by means of the holy women, while Andrew and Nathanael had been sent to Engannim; and at last the father and steward himself rode to Cana, where he found Jesus. Jesus had delayed to grant his prayer, in order to punish what was evil in his intentions.

It was a day's journey from Cana to Capharnaum, but the man rode with such speed that he reached home before night. A couple of hours from Capharnaum, some of his servants met him and told him that the boy was cured. They had come after him to tell him that if he had not found Jesus, he should give himself no further trouble, for the boy had been suddenly cured at the seventh hour. Then he repeated to them the words of Jesus. They were filled with astonishment, and hurried home with him. I saw the Centurion Zorobabel and the boy coming to the door to meet him. The boy embraced him. He repeated all that Jesus had said, the servants that accompanied him confirming his words. There was great joy, and I saw a feast made ready. The youth sat between his adopted father and his real father, the mother being nearby. He loved his real father as much as he did the supposed one, and the former exercised great authority in the house.

After Jesus had dismissed the man of Capharnaum, He cured several sick persons, who had been brought into a court of the house. There were some possessed among them, though not of the vicious kind. The possessed were often brought to Jesus' instructions. At first sight of Him, they fell into frightful raging and threw themselves on the ground, but as soon as He commanded them to be at peace, they became quiet. After some time, however, they seemed no longer able to restrain themselves, and began again to move convulsively. Jesus made them a sign with His hand, and they again recovered themselves. The instruction over, He commanded Satan to go out of them. They lay, as was usual on such occasions, for about two minutes as if unconscious, and then, coming to themselves, thanked Jesus joyfully, not exactly knowing what had happened to them. There are such good possessed, people of whom the demon has taken possession by no fault of their own. I cannot clearly explain it, but I saw on this occasion, as well as upon others, how it happens that a guilty person may, by the mercy and long-sufferance of God be spared, while Satan takes possession of one of his weak, innocent relatives. It is as if the innocent took upon himself a part of the other's punishment. I cannot make it clear, but it is certain that we are all members of one body. It is as if a healthy member, in consequence of a secret, intimate bond between them, suffers for another that is not sound. Such were the possessed of this place. The wicked are much more terrible and they cooperate with Satan, but the others merely suffer the possession and are meanwhile very pious.

Jesus afterward taught in the synagogue. There were present from Nazareth several Doctors of the Law, and they invited Him to return with them. They said that His native city was ringing with the great miracles He had wrought in Judea, Samaria, and Engannim; that He knew very well the opinion prevalent in Nazareth that whoever had not studied in the school of the Pharisees could not know much; therefore they desired Him to come and teach them better. They thought by these arguments to seduce Jesus. But He replied that He would not yet go to

Nazareth, and that when He did, they would not obtain what they were now demanding.

After the instruction in the synagogue, Jesus was present at a great feast in the house of the father of the bride of Cana. The bride and bridegroom with the widowed aunt of the latter were there. Nathanael the bridegroom had joined Jesus as a disciple on His coming to Cana, and had helped to keep order during the instruction and the curing of the sick. The bridegroom and bride dwelt alone. They carried on no housekeeping, for they received their meals from the parents of the latter. Her father limped a little. They were good people. Cana was a clean, beautiful city on a lofty plateau. Several highways ran through it, and one straight to Capharnaum, about seven hours distant. The road inclined a little before reaching Capharnaum.

After the feast, Jesus returned to His abode and again healed several sick persons who were patiently awaiting Him. He did not always cure in the same way. Sometimes it was by a word of command, sometimes He laid His hands upon the sick, again He bowed Himself over them, again He ordered them to bathe, and sometimes He mixed dust with His saliva and smeared their eyes with it. To some He gave admonitions, to others He declared their sins, and others again He sent away without being cured.

2. Jesus in Capharnaum

When Jesus, with the disciples who had accompanied Him to Cana, left for Capharnaum, He was followed by Nathanael, whose wife with her aunt and others had already gone on before. The road, about seven hours in length, was tolerably straight. It ran by a little lake like that of Ennon, around which lay country seats and gardens. The magnificently fruitful region of Genesareth began here, and in many places there were watchtowers.

When Jesus approached the environs of Capharnaum, several possessed began to rage outside the gate and to call into the city: "The Prophet is coming! What does He want here? What business has He with us?" But when He reached the city, they ran away. A tent had been erected outside. The Centurion and the father of the boy came out to meet Jesus, the child walking between them. They were followed by the entire family, all the relatives, servants, and slaves. These last were pagans who had been sent to Zorobabel by Herod. It was a real procession, and all cast themselves down before Jesus giving thanks. They washed His feet and offered Him a little luncheon, a mouthful to eat and a glass of wine. Jesus spoke some words of admonition to the boy, laying His hand on his head as he knelt before Him. He now received the name of Jesse, whereas he had before been called Joel. The Centurion's name was Zorobabel. He earnestly besought Jesus to stay with him while at Capharnaum and to accept a feast in His honor. But Jesus refused, still reproaching him with his desire to see a miracle in order to vex others. He said: "I should not have cured the boy, had not the faith of the messenger been so strong and urgent." And thereupon Jesus went on His way.

But Zorobabel had a great banquet prepared to which all the servants and laborers of his numerous gardens around the city were called. The miracle had been related to them, and all deeply moved believed in Jesus. During the entertainment the domestics and many of the poor, to whom presents had been made, entoned a song of praise and thanksgiving in the entrance porch.

The news of the miracle soon spread throughout Capharnaum. Zorobabel sent an account of it to the Mother of Jesus and the Apostles. I saw the latter again busy at their fisheries. I saw the news taken also to Peter's mother-in-law, who was then lying sick.

Jesus went around Capharnaum to His Mother's dwelling, where about five women together with Peter, Andrew, James, and John were assembled. They went out to meet Him, and there were great rejoicings at His coming and His miracles. He took a meal here, and then went straight back to Capharnaum for the Sabbath. The women remained at home.

A great concourse of people and many sick were gathered at Capharnaum. The possessed ran crying about the streets as Jesus approached. He commanded them to be silent, and passed along through them to the synagogue. After the prayer, a stiff-necked Pharisee by the name of Manasses was called upon, for it was his turn to read the Scriptures aloud. But Jesus told them to give Him the roll, that He would do the reading. They obeyed, and He read from the beginning of the First Book of Moses down to the account of the murmuring of the Children of Israel. He spoke of the ingratitude of their fathers, of the mercy of God toward them, and of the nearness of the Kingdom, warning them to beware of acting as their fathers had done. He explained all the errors and crooked ways of their fathers by a comparison with their own erroneous notions, drawing a parallel between the Promised Land of those far-off times and the Kingdom now so near. Then He read the first chapter of Isaias, which He interpreted as referring to the present. He spoke of crime and its punishment, of their long waiting for a Prophet, and of how they would treat Him now that they had Him. He cited the various animals, all of which knew their master, although they, His hearers, knew Him not. He spoke of the One that longed to help them, picturing to them the woeful appearance He would present in consequence of their outrages upon Him, also of the punishment in store for Jerusalem, and of the small number of the elect when all this would take place. The Lord would, nevertheless, multiply them while the wicked would be destroyed. He called upon them to be converted, saying that even were they all covered with blood, if they cried to God and turned from their evil ways, they would become clean. Again He referred to Manasses who had given so much scandal, who had committed so much iniquity before the Lord; therefore had God permitted him in punishment to be led away captive to Babylon, where he had been converted, had cried to God for pardon, and had received a share in the Promise. Jesus then opened the Scriptures as if by accident at Isaias[1], and read the passage: "Behold a virgin shall conceive," which He applied to Himself and the coming of the Messiah.

He had given the same explanation at Nazareth some time before His baptism, whereupon His hearers had mocked, saying: "We never saw Him eating much butter and honey when with His father, the poor carpenter."

The Pharisees and many others of Capharnaum were not well satisfied at Jesus' having spoken to them so severely about ingratitude; they had expected some pleasant, flattering words on the score of the good reception they had extended to Him. The instruction lasted tolerably long and, when Jesus was going out of the synagogue, I heard two of the Pharisees whispering to each other: "They have brought some sick. Let us see whether He will dare to heal them on the Sabbath." The streets had been lighted with torches, and many of the houses illuminated with lamps. Some, however, were dark; they were the homes of the evil-minded. Wherever Jesus passed, He found sick in front of the houses and lights by them; some had been carried to the door in the arms of their relatives, while near them stood others bearing torches. There was great bustling to and fro in the streets, and shouts of joy were heard on all sides. Many of the possessed cried after Jesus, and He delivered

---

1. "Behold a virgin shall conceive, and bear a son, and his name shall be called Emmanuel. He shall eat butter and honey." (*Is.* 7:14, 15).

them with a word of command. I saw one of them
with a fearful countenance and bristling hair springing toward Him in rage and fury, and crying out:
"Thou! What dost Thou want here? What business
halt Thou here?" Jesus repulsed him, saying: "Withdraw, Satan!" And I saw the man dashed to the ground
as if his neck and every bone in his body were broken. When he rose up, he was quite changed, quite
gentle, and he knelt at Jesus' feet weeping and thanking. Jesus commanded him to be converted. I saw
Him curing many as He thus passed along.

After that Jesus went with the disciples to His
Mother's. It was night. On the way Peter spoke of
his household affairs: He had neglected many things
connected with his fishery, from which he had been
so long absent; he must provide for his wife, his children, and his mother-in-law. John replied that he
and James had to take care of their parents, and
that was more important than the care of a mother-
in-law. And so they bandied words freely and jocosely.
Jesus observed that the time would soon come when
they would give up their present fishing, in order to
catch fish of another kind. John was much more childlike and familiar with Jesus than the others. He was
so affectionate, so submissive in all things, without
solicitude or contradiction. Jesus returned to His
Mother's; the others, to their homes.

Early next day Jesus left His Mother's, which was
about three-quarters of an hour from Capharnaum
in the direction of Bethsaida, and went to the first-
named city with His disciples. The road was at first
somewhat of an ascent, but near Capharnaum it
began to decline. Before reaching the gate of the city,
the traveller came to a house belonging to Peter, who
had allotted it to Jesus and the disciples and placed
in it a pious old man as steward. It was about an
hour and a half from the lake. All the disciples from
Bethsaida and the country around were gathered in
Capharnaum, whither also Mary and the holy women

had come. Numbers of sick were ranged along the streets by which Jesus was to pass. They had been brought the day before, but had not been cured. Jesus healed a great many on His way to the synagogue in which, during His instruction, He related a parable. When He left the synagogue, He still continued teaching, and several persons threw themselves at His feet begging pardon for their sins. Two of them were adulteresses who had been put away by their husbands, and there were four men, among them the seducers of those women. They burst into tears and wanted to confess their sins before the multitude. But Jesus replied that their sins were already known to Him, that a time would come when the open confession of them would be necessary, but at present it would only scandalize their neighbor and attract upon them persecution. He exhorted them to watch over themselves that they might not relapse into sin, but if they should be so unhappy as to do so, not to despair, but to turn to God and do penance. He forgave them their sins, and when the men asked to which baptism they should go, to that of John's disciples, or wait for His own, He told them to go to the former.

The Pharisees present wondered very much that Jesus should undertake to forgive sin, and called Him to account for it. But Jesus silenced them by His answer, that it was easier for Him to forgive sins than to heal, for to him that sincerely repents, sin is forgiven, and he will not lightly sin again; but the sick who are cured in body often remain sick in soul, and make use of their body to relapse into sin. Then they asked Him whether the husbands of those women whose sins had been forgiven should take back their once-repudiated wives. Jesus answered that time did not permit Him to discuss that point, but later on He would instruct them upon it. They questioned Him also upon His curing on the Sabbath. Jesus defended Himself with the query: "If one of you had an animal that should fall into a well on the Sabbath, would you not draw it out?"

In the afternoon Jesus retired with all His disciples to the house outside Capharnaum, where the holy women were already assembled. They partook of an entertainment, which the Centurion Zorobabel had provided. He and Salathiel, the father of the boy, reclined at table with Jesus and the disciples, while Jesse, the boy, served. The women sat at a separate table. Jesus taught. They brought the sick to Him, making their way into the house, yes, even crowding with cries for help into the dining hall. He cured many. The meal over, Jesus returned to the synagogue, and I heard Him discoursing, among other things, of Isaias and his Prophecy to King Achaz: "Behold, a virgin shall conceive and give birth to a son," etc. (*Is.* 7:14).

When He left the synagogue, He cured numbers on the streets, and that until night had closed. Among them were many women afflicted with a bloody flux. Sad and mournful, they stood at a distance enveloped in their veils, not daring to approach Jesus or the crowd around Him. Jesus knew their suffering, turned toward them, and healed them with a glance. He never touched such sufferers. There was some mystery in the prohibition to that effect which I cannot now express. A fast day began on that evening.

When Jesus returned with His disciples to His Mother's, the question arose as to whether they should go with Him next morning to the lake, and I heard Peter excusing himself on account of the bad state of his barque.

The people whose sins Jesus had forgiven were clothed in penitential garb and enveloped in large veils. From the last Sabbath but one, the Jews wore black and the whole time was a season of penance commemorative of the destruction of Jerusalem, hence the severity of Jesus' words when speaking of the chastisement awaiting that city. On leaving

Capharnaum, the road ran by a large building surrounded by water. Here the dangerous possessed were
shut up at night. As Jesus went by, they raged and
cried: "There He goes! What does He want? Is it that
He thinks to drive us out?" When Jesus responded:
"Be silent, and remain until I come again. Then it
will be your time to retire," they became quiet.

When Jesus left the city, the Pharisees and magistrates held a meeting at which the Centurion Zorobabel was present. They deliberated upon all they had
seen, upon what they should do, what line of conduct they should pursue with respect to Jesus. They
said: "What commotion, what agitation this Man cre-
ates! Peace is no longer found in the land! The people leave their daily avocations and follow His
menacing speeches. He is constantly talking of His
Father, but is He not from Nazareth? Is He not the
Son of a poor carpenter? Whence comes it that He
has so great assurance and audacity? Upon what
does He rest His titles? He heals on the Sabbath,
thus disturbing its peace! He forgives sins! Is His
power from On High? Has He some secret arts? How
has He become so familiar with the Scriptures, so
ready in explaining them? Was He not reared in the
school of Nazareth? Perhaps He is connected in some
way with foreigners, with a strange nation! He is
always speaking of the approaching establishment
of a kingdom, of the nearness of the Messiah, of the
destruction of Jerusalem. Joseph, His father, was of
illustrious birth; but perhaps He is not Joseph's Son,
or He may be the supposititious Child of some other,
of some powerful man who wants to get a foothold
in our country, and thus become master in Judea.
He must have some great protector, some secret
resources upon which to count, else He could never
be so bold, so audacious, He would never act with
such disregard of legitimate authority and established
customs, just as if He had a perfect right to do so.
He absents Himself for long periods at a time. Where

and among whom is He then? Whence has He His knowledge and His skill in working miracles? What must we do about Him?" And so they went on discharging their wrath and interchanging conjectures. The Centurion Zorobabel alone remained calm; he even had some influence in pacifying the rest. He urged them to patience. "Wait," said he. "If His power is from God, He will certainly triumph; but if not, He will come to naught. So long as He cures our sick and labors to make us better, we have reason to love Him and to thank Him who sent Him."

Early next day Jesus went with about twenty of His disciples toward the lake, not by the direct road, but off to the south around the height upon which Mary's house stood toward the west. That elevation, though separated from it by a valley, was only a projection from the foot of a mountain chain running northward. Jesus chose this route as being better suited to teaching. There were many beautiful brooks running down from the height into the lake, and the little river near Capharnaum flowed along in this direction. This part of the country was watered and fertilized by the numerous streams that flowed around Bethsaida. Jesus paused several times with His disciples to rest in those pleasant spots, and often stood still to teach of the tithes. The disciples complained of the great severity with which the tithes were levied at Jerusalem, and asked whether it would not be well to suppress them. Jesus answered that God had commanded the tenth part of all the fruits of the earth to be given to the Temple and its servers, in order to remind men that they had not the propriety, but only the usufruct of them; even of vegetables and green things, the tenth part ought to be given by abstaining from their use. Then the disciples spoke of Samaria, expressing their regret for having perhaps hurried His departure thence. They did not know, they said, that the people of Samaria were so anxious to receive His teaching, so disposed

to receive Him well; had it not been for their impor-
tunity, He might have remained longer among them.
To this Jesus replied that the two days He had spent
in Sichar were sufficient, that the Sichemites were
hot-blooded and quickly roused, but of all that had
been converted, it was likely that only about twenty
would remain steadfast. The coming great harvest
He would resign to them, the disciples.

Touched by Jesus' last instructions, the disciples
spoke compassionately of the Samaritans, recalling
to their praise the history of the man that had fallen
among robbers near Jericho. Priest and Levite had
passed by, the Samaritan alone had taken him up
and poured wine and oil into his wounds. This fact
was generally known. It had really happened in the
neighborhood of Jericho. From their compassion for
the wounded man and their rejoicing over the kind
dispositions of the Samaritans, Jesus took occasion
to relate to them another parable of the same kind.
He began with Adam and Eve, and recounted their
Fall in simple words, as given in the Bible. They had,
He said, been driven from Paradise, had sought refuge
with their children in a desert full of robbers and
murderers, and like the poor man of the parable, lay
there struck and wounded by sin. Then did the King
of Heaven and earth make use of all means in His
power to procure help for poor humanity. He had
given them His Law, had sent them chosen priests
and Prophets with all that was necessary to cure
their ills. But suffering humanity had been helped
by none of these aids, it had even at times rejected
them with contempt. At last the King sent His own
Son in the guise of a poor man, to help the fallen
race. And then Jesus described His own poverty, no
shoes, no covering for the head, no girdle, etc., and
yet He pours oil and wine into the poor traveller's
wounds in order to heal them. But they who with
full power had been sent to cure the wounds of the
sufferer, had not had pity on him; they had seized

the King's Son and put Him to death, killed Him
who had poured oil and wine into the sufferer's
wounds. Jesus related this parable to His disciples
that, reflecting upon it, they might express their
thoughts, and He might clear up any misconceptions
they might have concerning it. But they did not understand Him. Noticing that He had described the King's
Son under characteristics that belonged to Himself,
they began to entertain all kinds of thoughts and to
whisper among themselves: "Who can that Father of
His be of whom He is always speaking?" Then Jesus
touched upon the solicitude they had expressed on
the preceding day for the loss experienced by the
neglect of their fisheries, and compared it with the
disposition of the King's Son. He had abandoned all
things and, when others in their abundance had left
the wounded man to die, He had anointed him with
oil and wine. And He went on: "The Father will not
abandon the servants of His Son. They shall receive
all back with a rich reward when He gathers them
around Him in His Kingdom."

In the midst of these and similar instructions,
they reached the lake a little below Bethsaida, where
lay the barques of Peter and Zebedee. A part of the
shore was entirely fenced in, and up on the bank
were little mud cabins for the fishermen's use. Jesus
went down to it with His disciples. On the ships
were the heathen slaves, but no Jews were engaged
in fishing because of the fast day. Zebedee was in
one of the huts on the shore. Jesus told those in the
ships to discontinue their fishing and come to land.
He was at once obeyed, and then He gave them an
instruction.

Jesus afterward proceeded up the lake toward
Bethsaida, a half-hour distant. Peter's license to fish
embraced about an hour's distance along the shore.
Between the harbor and Bethsaida was a little bay
into which emptied several streams, branches of that
which flowed from Capharnaum through the valley,

and which received in its course other rivulets and
creeks. It formed a great pool outside Capharnaum.
Jesus did not go to Bethsaida. He went to the west
and then by the north side of the valley to Peter's
house, which stood on the eastern side of that
high ground upon whose opposite side was Mary's
dwelling.

Jesus entered with Peter. Mary and the other holy
women were already there. The other disciples did
not go in. They waited nearby in the garden, or went
on ahead to Mary's. As Peter entered the house with
Jesus, he said: "Master, we have had a fast day, but
Thou hast fed us." Peter's house was very neatly
built with forecourt and garden. It was very long,
and on the roof, one could promenade and enjoy a
beautiful view toward the lake. I saw neither Peter's
step-daughter nor his wife's sons. They may have
been at school. His wife was with the holy women.
Peter had no children by her. His mother-in-law was
a tall, thin woman, so weak and sickly that, in going
around the house, she had to lean against the walls
for support.

Jesus held a long conference with the women on
the subject of the house they had hired up on the
borders of the lake, where He intended often to be.
He warned them against extravagance and indiscre-
tion, though they were to guard likewise against anxiety and solicitude. As for Himself, He said, He needed
very little, it was chiefly for the disciples and for the
poor they should provide. Leaving Peter's, He crossed
with His disciples to His Mother's. There He conversed for some time and then went out alone to
pray.

The stream of Capharnaum flowed along by Peter's
house. He could in his little boat, in the middle of
which was a seat, sail down to the lake with his fishing tackle.

When the holy women heard from Jesus that He
was going to Nazareth for the coming Sabbath, a dis-

tance of nine or ten hours, they did not like the idea.
They begged Him to remain where He was, or at
least to come back soon. Jesus replied that He did
not think He would stay long at Nazareth, since the
inhabitants would not be very well pleased with Him
for not complying with their wishes. He mentioned
several points upon which they would reproach Him,
and drew His Mother's attention to them, adding
that He would let her know if things turned out as
He said.

3. Jesus in Bethsaida

From Mary's, Jesus went with the disciples along
the north side of the valley to the declivity of the
mountain which stretched on to Bethsaida, distant
not quite an hour. The holy woman also left Peter's
house and went to that of Andrew at the northern
extremity of Bethsaida. It was in good condition,
though not so large as Peter's.

Bethsaida was a little fishing place. Only the central part of the city extended some distance inland;
the two extremities stretched around the lake like
slender arms. From Peter's fishery, one could see it
lying off toward the north. The inhabitants were made
up for the most part of fishermen, blanket weavers,
and tentmakers. They were people, simple and untu-
tored, reminding me of our turfcutters. The blankets
were made of goats' and camels' hair. The long hairs
from the camel's neck and breast fell over the edges
and shone so beautifully that they looked like fringe
and lace.

The old Centurion Zorobabel had not come to Bethsaida. He was too infirm for so long a walk. He might
indeed have gone on horseback, but then he would
have missed Jesus' instructions on the way; besides,
he was not yet baptized. Bethsaida was full of people from the surrounding towns and villages, along
with strangers from the other side of the lake, from

the country of Corozain and Bethsaida-Julias.

Jesus taught in the synagogue, which was not a very large building, He spoke of the nearness of God's Kingdom, saying in very plain words that He Himself was the Monarch of that Kingdom, and arousing the usual amount of wonder in His disciples and hearers. As on the preceding days, He taught in general terms and cured many sick who had been brought and laid outside the synagogue. Several possessed cried after Him: "Jesus of Nazareth! Prophet, King of the Jews!" He commanded them silence, for the time had not yet come to make Him known.

When Jesus had finished teaching and healing, He went with His disciples to Andrew's to get something to eat. But He did not go in—He said that He had another kind of hunger. Taking with Him Saturnin and another of the disciples, they went up the shores of the lake about seven minutes' walk from Andrew's. There in a lonely hospital were some poor lepers, simpletons, and other miserable, forlorn creatures languishing, quite forgotten by the rest of the world; some of them were entirely nude. No one from Bethsaida had followed Jesus for fear of contracting impurity. The cells of these poor creatures were built around a court. They never left them, their food being given them through an aperture in the door. Jesus commanded the superintendent of the hospital to bring out the miserable patients. The disciples covered all in need with the clothing they had brought with them. Then Jesus instructed and consoled them, going from one to another around the circle, and healing many by the imposition of His sacred hands. He passed some in silence, others He commanded to bathe or fulfill different prescriptions. The cured sank on their knees before Him, giving thanks with abundant tears. It was truly touching. These people were utterly neglected. Jesus took the superintendent back to Andrew's to dine with Him. As they were leaving the hospital, the relatives of

some of the cured presented themselves from Bethsaida bringing them clothes. They took them joyfully first to their homes and next to the synagogue,
to give thanks to God.

There was a grand dinner prepared at Andrew's
consisting of fine, large fish. They ate in an open
hall, the women at a separate table. Andrew himself
served. His wife was very active and industrious,
rarely leaving the house. She carried on a kind of
trade in net weaving, employing a number of poor
girls for the work. The greatest system and order
reigned throughout her establishment. Among those
so employed were some poor, fallen women, once honorable wives, but afterward repudiated for miscon-
duct. They had no place of refuge, and so the good
mistress, pitying their distress, gave them work,
instructed them in their duty, and prevailed upon
them to implore the mercy of God.

That evening Jesus taught in the synagogue, and
then recommenced His journeying with the disciples.
He passed many sick, but without curing them, for,
as He said, their time had not yet come. After taking leave of His Mother, He returned with all His
disciples to the house near Capharnaum that Peter
had placed at His service. Jesus conversed there a
long time with His disciples, and then left them to
go spend the night in prayer on a hill, which tapered
to a point and was covered with cypresses.

Capharnaum lay in a half-circle up on a mountain.
It had numerous vineyards and terraced gardens. On
the top of the mountain grew wheat, thick and stout
as rushes. It was a large and pleasant place. It had
once been still more extensive, or another city had
stood in the vicinity, for not far off I saw all kinds of
ruins like tokens of a destructive war.

4. Jesus in and Around Lesser Sephoris. His Different Ways of Curing the Sick

Jesus went from Capharnaum to Nazareth, the Galilean disciples accompanying Him for about five hours. He instructed them on the way concerning their future vocation. He counseled Peter to leave the borders of the lake, take up his abode in his house near Capharnaum, and give up his business. They passed several cities, also the little lake with the country seats around it. In a shepherd field two possessed men came running to Jesus and implored to be cured. They were the owners of the herds browsing around, and were only now and then tormented by the devil. Just at that time they were free from his influence. Jesus would not cure them, but commanded them first to amend their ways. He made use of an example: If a man was sick from overloading his stomach, and wanted to get well in order to indulge in new excesses, what would they think of him? The men turned away quite ashamed. The disciples left Jesus a couple of hours from Sephoris and returned to Peter's, Saturnin among them. There were only two with Him now. They were from Jerusalem, and were on their way home. Jesus went to Lower Sephoris, or Lesser Sephoris, and put up with the relatives of St. Anne. It was not, however, at Anne's paternal home, for that was between this Sephoris and Upper Sephoris, the latter distant about an hour. There were many houses lying around in a circle of five hours, all belonging to the city of Sephoris. Jesus did not go at this time to Upper Sephoris, where were schools of the various sects and tribunals of justice.

There were not many rich people in Lower Sephoris. They manufactured cloth and the rich women made silk tassels and laces for the service of the Temple. The whole region was like an enchanting garden, consisting of many little hamlets with coun-

try seats, gardens, and walks scattered among them.
Greater Sephoris was a far more important place; it
was very large and possessed many castles. The country around was lovely and abounded in springs. The
cattle were of extraordinary size.

Jesus' relatives had three sons, one of whom, by
name Colaja, was His disciple. The mother wanted
Jesus to admit the others also into the number of
His disciples, and brought forward the sons of Mary
Cleophas as an argument in her own favor. Jesus
gave her room to hope. After the death of Christ,
these sons were ordained to the priesthood at
Eleutheropolis by Joses Barsabas, the Bishop of that
place.

Jesus taught in the synagogue before a great concourse assembled from the country around. He went
also with His cousins out of the city, and gave instructions here and there to little crowds of people that
followed Him or were waiting for Him. On His return
He cured many sick persons outside the synagogue,
then entering, He taught of marriage and divorce.
He reproached the Doctors with having made additions to the Law. He pointed to a certain place in a
roll of parchment, accused one of the oldest among
them of having inserted it, convicted him of fraud,
and commanded him to erase the passage. The old
man humbled himself before Jesus, even prostrating
at His feet in presence of all the others, acknowledged his fault, and thanked for the lesson just
received.

Jesus spent the night in prayer. From the house
of His relatives in Lesser Sephoris He went to that
which had in former times belonged to Anne's father.
It was situated between Lesser Sephoris and Greater
Sephoris. There was now only one disciple with Him.
The present occupants of the house were, in consequence of frequent marriages, no longer related to
Jesus. There was only one old woman who could still
claim relationship. She was dropsical and bedridden.

Her usual companion was a little blind boy, who sat
by her bedside. Jesus prayed with the old woman,
making her repeat after Him. He laid His hand for
an instant on her head, then on the region of the
stomach. She began to grow faint, remained unconscious for about a minute, and then found herself
quite relieved. Jesus ordered her to rise. The dropsy
had not entirely disappeared, but the woman could
walk, and soon after, without difficulty, through copi-
ous perspiration and the healthful action of nature,
she was entirely freed from her trouble. She interceded with Jesus for the blind boy. He was about
eight years old, and had never seen nor spoken,
although he could hear. The old woman praised his
piety and obedience. Jesus put His forefinger into the
child's mouth, then breathing upon His thumbs or
moistening them with saliva, He held them upon the
closed eyes of the boy while He prayed, His eyes
raised to Heaven. Suddenly the child opened his eyes,
and the first object he beheld was Jesus His Redeemer!
Out of himself with joy and amazement, he threw
himself into Jesus' arms, stammering his thanks, and
then fell weeping at His feet. Jesus admonished him
affectionately to be obedient and to love his parents.
He told him that if, when blind, he had exercised
those virtues, he should more faithfully practice them
now that he could see, and never use his eyes to sin.
Then in came the parents and the whole family, and
there were intense joy and thanksgiving.

Jesus did not always operate His cures in the
same manner, though performing them in much the
same way as the Apostles, the saints, and the priests
after them down to our own day. He laid hands upon
and prayed with the sick, but His action was quicker
than that of the Apostles. He performed His cures
and other miracles as models for His followers and
disciples. He always made the manner of their per-
formance conform to the evil and the special needs
of those that had recourse to Him. He touched the

lame, their muscles were loosened, and they stood upright. The broken parts of fractured members He placed together, and they united. He touched the leprous, and immediately at the touch of His divine hand, I saw the blisters drying and peeling off, leaving behind the red scars. These, little by little, though more quickly than was usual in ordinary cures, disappeared. The greater or less merit of the invalid often determined the rapidity of his cure. I never saw a humpback instantly become straight, nor a crooked bone suddenly become a perfectly formed one. Not that Jesus could not have produced such effects, but His miracles were not intended as spectacles for a gazing multitude. They were works of mercy, they were symbolical images of His mission, a releasing, a reconciliation, an instruction, a development, a redeeming. As He desired man's cooperation in the work of his own Redemption, so too did He demand from those that asked of Him a miraculous cure their own cooperation by faith, hope, love, contrition, and reformation of life. Every state had its own manner of treatment. As every malady of the body symbolized some malady of the spiritual order, some sin or the chastisement due to it, so did every cure symbolize some grace, some conversion, or the cure of some particular spiritual evil. It was only in presence of pagans that I saw Jesus sometimes operating more astonishing, more prodigious miracles. The miracles of the Apostles and of saints that came after them were far more striking than those of Our Lord and far more contrary to the usual course of nature, for the heathens needed to be strongly affected, while the Jews needed only to be freed from their bonds. Jesus often cured by prayer at a distance, and often by a glance, especially in the case of women afflicted by a bloody flux. They did not venture to approach Him, nor dared they do so according to the Jewish laws. Such laws as carried with them some mysterious signification He

followed, others He ignored. Jesus went afterward
to a school situated at an equal distance from
Nazareth and from Lesser Sephoris. Parmenas, the
disciple from Nazareth, went thither to meet Him.
He had been one of the companions of Jesus' boy-
hood, and he would have joined the disciples at once,
were it not for his aged parents at Nazareth. He
supported them by executing commissions.

There were many Doctors and Pharisees in the
school of Lesser Sephoris and Greater Sephoris, also
some people who had assembled to argue with Jesus
on that passage relating to divorce which He had
declared unlawful, and for the insertion of which
passage He had reprehended the Doctor in the synagogue. That reprehension of Jesus had been very
badly received in Greater Sephoris, for the addition
made to the Law on that point was in keeping with
the teaching of the Pharisees. In this city divorces
were obtained on most insignificant pretexts, and
there was even an asylum for the reception of repudiated wives. The Doctor who had been guilty of the
interpolation had transcribed a roll of the Law and
inserted little false interpretations here and there.
They disputed a long time with Jesus, affirming that
they could not understand how He could presume
to expunge that passage. He reduced them to silence,
though not to the acknowledgment of their error, as
He had done the first. He showed them the prohibition against any interpolation, and consequently
the obligation of expunging such a passage. He
demonstrated to them the falsity of their explanations, and sharply rebuked them for the facil-
ity with which the marriage bond was dissolved in
their city. He enumerated some cases in which it
would be quite unlawful for the the husband to put
away his wife, but said that if one party could not
live in peace with the other, they might with permission separate. The stronger party, however, ought
not without cause drive away the weaker one against

the will of the latter. But Jesus' words did not effect much among His opponents. They were vexed and proud, but they could not gainsay His arguments. The Doctor of the Law who had been reprimanded and converted by Jesus in Lower Sephoris separated entirely from the Pharisees and made known to the people that he would for the future teach the Law without addition. If they were unwilling to retain him on those conditions, he would withdraw. The interpolated passage in the Law of divorce ran as follows: "If before marriage one of the parties has had illicit communication with a third person, the marriage is invalid. The third person has the right to claim the one with whom he or she has sinned, even though the parties of the present marriage desire to remain united." Jesus inveighed against this, and declared the law of divorce to have been given to a barbarous people only. Two of the most distinguished Pharisees engaged in the dispute were precisely in that predicament. They were preparing to avail themselves of that interpolation with regard to divorce, and therefore had they been zealous in proclaiming that part of their so-called law. This fact was not publicly known, but Jesus knew it and therefore He said to them: "In defending this distortion of the Law, are you not perhaps defending your own case also?" at which words they fell into a fury.

5. Jesus in Nazareth.
The Pharisees Want to
Cast Him Down a Mountain

Jesus went from this place to Nazareth, the distance being about two hours. He taught outside the city in the dwelling belonging to the children of His deceased friend, Eliud the Essenian. They washed His feet, gave Him some refreshment, and remarked how rejoiced the Nazarenes would be at His coming.

Jesus replied that their joy would be of short dura-
tion, since they would not care to hear what He
must say to them, and then He went into the city.
Someone had been appointed to wait for Him at the
gate. Scarcely had He made His appearance when
several Pharisees and a crowd of people came forward to meet Him. They received Him very ceremoniously and wanted to conduct Him to a public inn
where they had prepared for Him a feast of welcome before the Sabbath. But Jesus refused to partake of it, saying that He had just now other work
on hand. He went immediately to the synagogue,
whither He was followed by the Pharisees and a
concourse of people. The hour of the Sabbath had
not yet sounded.

Jesus taught of the coming of the Kingdom and
the fulfillment of the Prophecies. Asking for the Book
of Isaias, He unrolled it and read as follows: "The
Spirit of the Lord is upon Me, because the Lord hath
anointed Me: He hath sent me to preach to the meek,
to heal the contrite of heart, and to preach a release
to the captives, and deliverance to them that are
shut up." (*1 Is.* 61:1). The manner in which Jesus
read this text gave His hearers to understand that
it was spoken of Himself, that the Spirit of God had
descended upon Himself, that He Himself had come
to announce salvation to poor, suffering humanity,
that all wrong should be made right, widows should
be consoled, the sick cured, sinners forgiven. His
words were so beautiful, so loving that, wondering
and full of joy, they said one to another: "He speaks
as if He Himself were the Messiah!" They were so
carried away with admiration for Him that they
became quite vain of the fact that He belonged to
their own city. Jesus went on teaching after the Sabbath began. He spoke of the voice of the Precursor
in the desert, and said that all things should be made
even, the crooked ways straight, etc.

The instructions over, Jesus accepted a meal that

had been prepared for Him. The people behaved toward Him in a very friendly manner, and told Him that they had many sick whom He must cure. Jesus excused Himself. But they thought that He meant: "Not today. Wait till tomorrow." After the meal, He returned to the Essenians outside the city. As they were congratulating Him upon the kind reception He had received, He told them to wait till the following day when they would have another story to tell.

When Jesus went next morning to the synagogue, a Jew whose turn it was to read was about to take the roll of Scriptures. But Jesus desired them to hand it to Him. He taught from Deuteronomy, chapter 4, of the obedience due to the Commandments, from which nothing must be taken and to which nothing must be added. He reminded them that, although Moses had zealously repeated to the Children of Israel all that God commanded, yet they had frequently violated His ordinances. The Ten Commandments presented themselves in the course of the reading, and Jesus explained the first, that on the love of God. He spoke very severely, reproaching them with the additions they made to the Law, laying burdens upon the poor people, and not fulfilling the Law itself. He assailed them so sharply on this point that they became angry, for they could not say that He was uttering falsehood. But they murmured and said one to another: "How does He dare all at once to speak so boldly! He has been away from His native city only a short time, and now He wants to pass Himself off for some extraordinary personage. He speaks as if He were the Messiah. But we know His father, the poor carpenter, well, and we know Him too. Where did He learn the Scriptures? How can He dare presume to interpret for us?" And so they went on, growing more and more excited against Him, for they were mortified to have been thus convicted before all the people.

But Jesus quietly continued His teaching, and went when it suited Him out to the Essenian family. Here He was visited by the sons of the rich man, the youths who some time previously had so earnestly asked to be received among the disciples, and whose parents were aiming only at worldly renown and science for them. They pressed Jesus to dine with them, but He declined. Then they renewed their entreaties to be received among His followers, saying that they had fulfilled all that He had on a former occasion commanded them. Jesus replied: "If ye have done that, there is no need of becoming My pupils. You are yourselves masters," and with these words He dismissed them.

Jesus ate and taught in the family circle of the Essenians, who told Him in how many ways they were annoyed by their neighbors. He counseled them to remove to Capharnaum, where He Himself would dwell in the future.

Meantime the Pharisees had consulted together, had incited one another against Jesus, and had come to the determination that, if He spoke so boldly again that evening, they would show Him that He had no right to do so in Nazareth, and would perpetrate upon Him what had so long been desired in Jerusalem. Still they were not without hope that He would yield to their wishes and, through respect for them, work some miracle in their presence. When He returned to the synagogue for the close of the Sabbath, He found lying in front of it some sick who had been brought there by order of the Pharisees. But He passed through them without curing any. He went on with His discourse in the synagogue, speaking of the plenitude of time, of His own mission, of the last chance of grace, of the depravity of the Pharisees and the punishment in store for them if they did not reform, and impressed upon them the fact of His own coming to help, to heal, and to teach. They became more and more displeased, especially when He said:

"But ye say to Me, 'Physician, cure Thyself! In Capharnaum and elsewhere, Thou hast wrought miracles. Do the same here in Thy native city!' But I say to you no prophet is accepted in his own country." Then comparing the present to a time of famine and the different cities to poor widows, He said: "There was great famine throughout the land in the time of Elias, and there were many widows in those days, but the Prophet was sent to none but the widow of Sarepta. And there were many lepers in the days of Eliseus, but he cleansed none but Naaman the Syrian," and so Jesus compared their city to a leper who was not healed. They became terribly furious at being likened unto lepers, and, rising up from their seats, they stormed against Him and made as if they would seize Him. But He said: "Observe your own laws and break not the Sabbath! When it is over do what you propose to do." They allowed Him to proceed with His discourse, though they kept up the murmuring among themselves and addressed scornful words to Him. Soon after they left their places and went down to the door.

Jesus, however, continued to teach and explain His last words, after which He, too, left the synagogue. Outside the door, He found Himself surrounded by about twenty angry Pharisees who laid hands on Him, saying: "Come on up with us to a height from which Thou canst advance some more of Thy doctrines! There we can answer Thee as Thy teaching ought to be answered." Jesus told them to take their hands off, that He would go with them. They surrounded Him like a guard, the crowd following. The moment the Sabbath ended, jeers and insults arose on all sides. They raged and hooted, each trying to outdo his neighbor in the number and quality of his scoffing attacks upon Jesus. "We will answer Thee!" they cried. "Thou shalt go to the widow of Sarepta! Thou shalt cleanse Naaman the Syrian! Art Thou Elias? And art Thou going to drive up to Heaven?

Well, we'll show Thee a good starting place! Who art
Thou? Why didst Thou not bring Thy followers with
Thee? Ah, Thou wast afraid. Was it not here that
Thou, like Thy poor parents, gained Thy daily bread?
And now that Thou hast whereon to live, wilt Thou
turn us to scorn! But we will listen to Thee! Thou
shalt speak in the open air before all the people, and
we will answer Thee!" and thus shouting and raging they led Jesus up the mountain. He, meanwhile,
quietly went on teaching as usual, answering their
vain talk with passages from Holy Scripture and significant words that sometimes put them to shame,
and at others threw them into greater rage.

The synagogue was in the western part of Nazareth.
It was already dark and two of the crowd bore torches.
They led Jesus around by the eastern side of the
synagogue, then turned into a broad street that ran
westward out of the city. Ascending the mountain,
they reached a lofty spur which on the northern side
overlooked a marshy pool, and on the south formed
a rocky projection over a steep precipice. It was from
this point they were in the habit of precipitating
malefactors. Here they intended once more to call
Jesus to account, and then to hurl Him down. The
abyss ended in a narrow ravine. They were not far
from the scene of action when Jesus, who had been
led as a prisoner among them, stood still, while they
continued their way mocking and jeering. At that
instant I saw two tall figures of light near Jesus,
who took a few steps back through the hotly pursuing crowd, reached the city wall on the mountain
ridge of Nazareth, and followed it till He came to
the gate by which He had entered the evening before.
He went straight to the house of the Essenian. The
good people had not been anxious about His safety.
They believed in Him and were expecting His return.
He spoke to them of the late occurrence, reminded
them that He had foretold it, again bade them go to
Capharnaum and, after about half an hour, left the

city in the direction of Capharnaum.

Nothing was more laughable than the perplexity, the alarm, the silly plight of the Pharisees when, all on a sudden, they found Jesus no more among them. The cry was raised: "Halt! Where is He? Halt!" The crowd came rushing on, the Pharisees pressed back upon them, the narrow path became a scene of confusion and uproar. They laid hold of one another, they squabbled and shouted, they ran to all the ravines, and poked their torches into the caves, thinking that He had hidden therein. They endangered neck and limb in their fruitless search, and one upbraided the other for having allowed Him to slip away. Quiet was not restored until long after Jesus had left the city, and then they set guards upon and around the whole mountain. Returning to the city, the Pharisees said: "Now we have seen what He is— a magician. The devil has helped Him. He will soon spring up again in some other place, and throw all around Him into confusion."

Jesus had ordered His disciples to leave Nazareth at the close of the exercises in the synagogue, and await Him at a certain place on the road to Tarichaea. Saturnin and other disciples from Capharnaum had received the same directions. All met Jesus at dawn and with Him took a little rest in a retired vale. Saturnin had brought some bread and honey. Jesus told them of what had taken place at Nazareth, and bade them be calm and obedient, in order not to interfere with His work by stirring up too great excitement among the populace of different cities. Then they took a retired route through the valleys and past cities toward the effluence of the Jordan from the Sea of Galilee. A large, fortified city lay at the southern extremity on a tongue of land not far from the outlet of the Jordan. A large bridge and a dam led to it. Between the city and the lake was a gently sloping plain covered with verdure. The city was called Tarichaea.

6. Cure of Lepers at Tarichaea. Jesus
Instructs His Disciples
In Similitudes

Jesus did not go into the city. Taking a bypath, He drew near the southern wall not far from the gate. On the exterior side of this wall was a row of huts built purposely for the leprous. As Jesus approached them, He said to the disciples: "Stand at some distance and call out the lepers. Tell them to follow Me, and I will cleanse them! When they come out, do ye stand at a distance that ye may not be alarmed nor contract stain. Moreover do not speak of what ye shall see, for ye remember the fury of the Nazarenes. Ye must not scandalize anyone." Then Jesus went on a little toward the Jordan while the disciples called to the sick: "Come out and follow the Prophet of Nazareth! He will help you!" When the disciples saw the poor sufferers coming out of their huts, they hurried away. Jesus, turning out of the road that led to the city, walked slowly toward the region of the Jordan. Five men of different ages answered the disciples' invitation and issued from the cells in the city wall. They were clothed in white garments long and wide, but wore no girdle. On their head was a cowl from which fell over the face a black flap with holes in it for the eyes. They followed Jesus in single file to a retired spot, where He paused. There the first threw himself at His feet and kissed the hem of His robe. Jesus turned, laid His hand upon the leper's head, prayed over him, blessed him, and bade him step aside. He did in like manner to the second, and so on even to the fifth and last. They now removed their masks, uncovered their hands, and the crust of the leprosy peeled entirely off. Jesus warned them against the sins by which they had brought upon themselves that sickness, told them how they should henceforth conduct themselves, and commanded them not to say anything about His having cured them. But they replied: "Lord, Thou didst come so suddenly to us! So long have we hoped for Thee, so long sighed for Thee, and we had no one to tell Thee of our misery, no one to bring Thee to us! Lord, Thou didst come to us so unexpectedly! How can we restrain our joy? How can we be silent about Thy miracle!" Jesus repeated that they must not speak of it until they had fulfilled the Law. They should show themselves to the priests that they might see they were clean, offer the prescribed sacrifices, and perform the prescribed purifications; then they might proclaim their cure. At these words the five men again fell on their knees giving thanks, and then went back to their cells. Jesus continued His way to the Jordan and there rejoined the disciples. These five lepers were not closely confined. There was a certain space marked out for them around which they could go. No one went near them, and it was only from a distance that anyone spoke to them. Their food was deposited in a certain place on platters, which were not used a second time. The lepers broke and buried them. A new dish of little value was given them with every fresh supply of food.

Jesus walked with the disciples some distance toward the Jordan through delightful groves and avenues, and in a retired spot rested and took some refreshment. After that they crossed the river in a little boat. Boats of this kind lay at intervals along the shore for the accommodation of travellers, who could by that means ferry themselves over. The workmen, living at different distances along the shore, saw that the boats were taken back to where they belonged. Jesus, with the four disciples, did not journey close to the lake, but up toward the east, to the city of Galaad. The four disciples with Him were Parmenas of Nazareth, Saturnin, and two brothers: one called Tharzissus, the other Aristobolus. Tharzissus afterward became the Bishop of Athens. Aristobolus

later on was associated to Barnabas. I heard that
with the word "brother"; but he was his spiritual
brother only. He was a great deal with Paul and
Barnabas, and I think he became a bishop of Bri-
tany.[1] Lazarus had brought the two brothers to Jesus.
They were foreigners, I think Greeks, whose father
had settled lately in Jerusalem. They were shipping
merchants. Some of their slaves, or servants, when
journeying with a caravan, had gone with their beasts
of burden to hear John's teaching and had been baptized by him. It was by means of these servants that
the young men's parents heard of John and Jesus.
Taking their sons, they went themselves to John, and
both father and sons were baptized and circumcised,
after which the whole family removed to Jerusalem.
They were not without means, but later on they relin-
quished all their wealth in favor of the rising community of Christians. Both the young men were tall,
dark-complexioned, and clever; both had received a
polite education. They were fine-looking young men,
active and skillful at arranging things and making
all comfortable on journeys.

A little river watered the country up which Jesus
was now journeying, and at a certain place He crossed
it. The Prophet Elias had once been in these parts.
Jesus recalled the fact and, during the whole journey, instructed the disciples in simple similitudes
borrowed from various conditions of life, from the
several professions, from the groves and stones and
plants and places that presented themselves on the
road. The disciples questioned Him upon all that had
happened to Him in Sephoris and Nazareth. He spoke
to them of marriage in connection with the dispute
He had had with the Pharisees, at Sephoris, upon
the question of divorce. The conjugal bond is indis-
soluble. Divorce was granted by Moses in favor of a
barbarous, sinful people only.

1. Dorotheus writes it "Bethania." (First Edition of *Das Leben Jesu*.)

The disciples questioned Jesus also upon the reproach made Him by the Nazarenes, that He had no love for His neighbor, and in His own city, which ought to be the nearest and dearest to Him, He would work no cures. They asked if one's fellow townsmen should not be looked upon as neighbors. Then Jesus gave them a long instruction upon the love of the neighbor, proposing to them all kinds of similitudes and questions, the former of which He drew from different states of life in the world. He dwelt long upon them and pointed out place after place that rose up in the distance, and said in which such or such an industry was especially pursued. He spoke, too, of those that were to follow Him. They were, He said, to leave father and mother, and yet obey the Fourth Commandment. They must treat their native city as He had done Nazareth, if so it deserved of them, and still exercise the love of the neighbor. God, their Heavenly Father, and He who had been sent by Him, had the first claim to their love. Then He spoke of the love of the neighbor such as the world understands it, and of the publicans of Galaad (which city they were then passing), who loved those most that paid them the highest tax. He pointed afterward to Dalmanutha, which lay to the left, and said: "Those tentmakers and carpet-weavers love as their neighbor those that buy many tents from them, but their own poor they leave without shelter."

He then borrowed a comparison from the sandalmakers, which had reference to the vain curiosity of the people of Nazareth. "I have no need," He said, "of their homage which they clothe in beautiful colors like the variegated sandals in the workshop of the sandalmaker, but which will afterward be trodden underfoot in the mud." And again, pointing to a certain city, He said: "They are like the sandalmaker of that city. They slight and disparage their own children, and so the latter are forced to go abroad. But when among strangers they have learned a new

style of making beautiful, green sandals, their fellow citizens recall them through desire to see their
work. They boast of the new-fashioned articles which,
like the glory attached to them, are soon to be trodden underfoot." Then Jesus put the question: "Sup-
pose a traveller tears one of his sandals and goes to
a sandalmaker's to buy one. Will the latter present
him with the other one, also?" In this way Jesus drew
comparisons from fishermen, architects, and other
avocations.

The disciples asked Him where He intended to fix
His abode, whether He would build a house in
Capharnaum. He answered that He would not build
upon sand, and He mentioned another city that He
had to found. I could not so well understand the conversation between Jesus and the disciples when they
were walking; when they were seated I could hear
better. I remember this much, however, that Jesus
expressed His desire for a little boat, that He might
go here and there upon the lake. He wanted to teach
on water as well as on land.

They now went into the country of Galaaditis. Abraham and Lot had sojourned here, and even at that
early period had divided the country between them.
Jesus referred to that circumstance. He told the disciples also that in order to avoid scandalizing anyone, they should not speak of the lepers who had
lately been cleansed. He warned them to be particularly circumspect now to cause no excitement, for
the Nazarenes would certainly stir up alarm and
hatred. He told them that on the Sabbath He would
again teach in Capharnaum. They should then have
a chance to see the love of the neighbor and the gratitude of men exemplified, for the welcome extended
to Him this time would be very different from that
received on the occasion of the cure of the Centurion's son.

They may have been journeying for some hours to
the northeast around a curve of the lake, when they

arrived near Galaad to the south of Gamala. As in most of the cities in this district, the population was made up of heathens and Jews. The disciples were disposed to enter the city. But Jesus told them that, if He went to the Jews of the place, they would neither welcome Him nor give Him anything; and if to the heathens, the Jews would be scandalized and would pursue Him with calumny. He predicted the entire destruction of the city, saying that iniquity abounded in it.

The disciples spoke of a certain Agabus, a prophet living at that time in Argob, a city of that region. For a long time, he had had numerous visions of Jesus and His doings, and had lately uttered some prophecies regarding Him. Later on Agabus joined the disciples. Jesus informed them that Agabus was the son of Herodian parents, who had reared him in the errors of their sect, but he had afterward rejected them. He called the sects beautifully covered sepulchers full of corruption.

The Herodians were numerous on the west side of the Jordan in Perea, Trachonitis, and especially in Ituraea. They lived very privately and had some kind of mysterious organization by which they secretly helped one another. Many poor people applied to them, and received immediate relief. These Herodians were outwardly great sticklers for the prescriptions of the Pharisees; in secret they aimed at freeing Judea from the Roman yoke, and consequently were closely attached to Herod. They were something like the modern freemasons. I understood from Jesus' words that they feigned to be very holy and magnanimous, but in reality they were hypocrites.

Jesus and the disciples remained at some distance from Galaad at an inn resorted to by publicans. Quite a number of them were gathered there at the time, to whom the heathens paid taxes on their imported goods. They did not appear to know Jesus, and He did not address them. He taught, however, of the

nearness of the Kingdom, and of the father who had
sent his son into the vineyard. He gave them very
clearly to understand that He Himself was the Son,
adding that all who do His will are children of the
Father. But these last words perplexed them. Jesus
exhorted them to Baptism. Many were converted,
and asked whether or not they should be baptized
by John's disciples. He answered that they should
wait patiently until His own disciples baptized in
those parts. The disciples also asked their Master
today whether His Baptism was different from that
of John, because they had received the latter. Jesus,
in His answer, made a distinction between the two,
calling John's a baptism of penance.

In Jesus' instruction to the publicans, something
entered relating to the Trinity, something about the
Father, the Son, and the Holy Ghost in their Unity,
though expressed in other terms. The disciples were
not at all reserved before the publicans of this place.

As Jesus when in Nazareth had stopped with the
Essenians, a circumstance that drew upon Him the
reproaches of the Pharisees, the disciples put questions to Him concerning that sect. I heard Jesus
answering in sentences expressive of praise, though
interrogative in form. Mentioning various ways by
which justice and fraternal love might be wounded,
He asked after each: "Do the Essenians do this? Do
the Essenians do that?" etc.

Near Galaad some possessed, who were running
around in a desolate region outside the city, began
to cry after Jesus. They were perfectly abandoned.
They robbed and killed anyone that ventured within
their reach, and committed diverse kinds of excesses.
Jesus looked back after them and gave them His
blessing. They instantly ceased to rave, were freed
from the evil spirit and, hurrying to Him, fell at His
feet. He exhorted them to penance and Baptism,
though bidding them wait for the latter until His disciples should go to Ennon to baptize. The country

about Galaad was rocky, of a white, brittle formation.

Jesus and the disciples went from here across the mountain, to the south of which lay Gamala, and took a northwesterly direction to the lake. He passed Gerasa which, at about one hour's distance, lay between two ridges of the mountain. Nearby was a kind of morass formed from a brook whose waters were dammed up, and whose only outlet into the lake was through a ravine. Jesus related to the disciples some incidents connected with this place: The people of Gerasa had once upon a time ridiculed a Prophet, on account of his misshapen form, whereupon he had said to them: "Listen, O ye that insult my misfortune! Your children shall remain obdurate when One greater than I shall teach and heal in this place. Troubled at the loss of their unclean herds, they will not rejoice at the salvation that is offered them." This was a prophecy regarding Jesus Christ and the driving of Satan into the swine.

Jesus told the disciples what awaited Him in Capharnaum: that the Pharisees of Sephoris, exasperated by His teaching upon divorce, had sent their emissaries to Jerusalem; that the Nazarenes had joined their complaints to theirs; and that a whole troop of Pharisees from Jerusalem, Nazareth, and Sephoris was now despatched to Capharnaum, to be on the watch for Him and to dispute against Him.

Just at this moment they encountered several immense caravans of heathens with mules and oxen. The latter had great, thick jaws, broad, heavy horns, and went along with lowered head. It was a trading caravan going from Syria into Egypt. They had come over into the country of Gerasa partly in ships, and partly over the bridge of the Jordan higher up. There were many among them who had joined the caravan for the purpose of hearing the Prophet. A company waited upon Jesus to know whether the Prophet would teach in Capharnaum. But He told them that they should not now go to Capharnaum, but encamp on the declivity of the mountain to the north of Gerasa, whither the Prophet would soon go. There was something in Jesus' tone and manner that made them respond: "Master, Thou too art a Prophet!" and His glance roused in them the doubt as to whether He might not Himself be the one for whom they were in search.

When Jesus entered the inn outside Gerasa with His disciples there to lodge, the crowd of heathens and travellers was so great that He left at once, but the disciples stayed with the heathens, talking to them of the Prophet and instructing them.

Gerasa lay on the declivity of a valley about an hour and a half from the lake. It was larger and cleaner than Capharnaum and, like almost all the cities of these parts, it had a mixed population of heathens and Jews. The former had their own temples. The latter formed the poor and oppressed portion of the inhabitants, although they had their synagogue and Rabbi. There was much business carried on and the trades were numerous, for the caravans from Syria and Asia passed through Gerasa going down into Egypt. I saw before the city gate a long building, seven and a half minutes in length, wherein were manufactured long iron bars and pipes. They forged the bars flat, and then soldered them together into a circular form. Leaden pipes also were made. The furnaces at which they worked were not fed with wood, but with some kind of a black mass dug out of the earth. The iron they used came from Argob.

The heathens of the caravan had encamped to the north of Gerasa and on the southern side of the rising mountain. To the same place some heathens belonging to the city had come, also some Jews; but these latter stood apart by themselves. The heathens were differently clad from the Jews, their tunics reaching only halfway down the lower limbs. Some of them must have been rich, for I saw women who had their hair so braided with pearls as to form a perfect cap. Some wore it on the top of the head above their veil, braided with pearls into a little basket.

Jesus ascended the mountainside, where walking about He taught the crowds. He went among them, here and there, and at times He stood still, keeping up a kind of conversation with the travellers. He addressed them questions, which He answered Himself in words full of instruction. He asked, for instance: "Whence are ye? What impelled you to take this journey? What do ye expect from the Prophet?" and then He taught them what they must become, in order to share in salvation. He said: "Blessed are they that have journeyed so long and so toilsome a way, to seek salvation! But woe to them among whom it arises and who will not receive it!" He explained the Prophecy of the Messiah and the call of the heathens, told of that of the Three Kings (of whom these people knew) and also of their expedition in obedience to it.

In the caravan were some people from that country and city where the envoy of Abgarus of Edessa had stayed overnight near the brick kilns, on his return journey with Jesus' picture and letter. Jesus did not cure any sick here. The strangers were for the most part well-disposed, but there were some among them who regretted having undertaken such a journey. They had expected to hear something very different from the Prophet's words, something more flattering to the senses.

After these instructions, into which Jesus introduced many similitudes, He went with His four disciples to dine with a Jewish Doctor of the Law, a Pharisee, who dwelt outside the city. He had invited Jesus to be his guest, though his pride prevented his appearing at the instruction given the heathens. There were present at table some other Pharisees from the city. They received Jesus in a friendly manner which, however, was only feigned, for they were hypocrites.

A circumstance occurred during the course of the meal that gave Jesus a suitable opportunity for telling them the truth. A heathen slave, or servant, laid upon the table a beautiful dish of many colors filled with confectionery, made of spices kneaded together in the shape of birds and flowers. One of the guests raised the alarm. There was, he said, something unclean on the dish, and he pushed the poor slave back, called him opprobrious names, and put him last among the other servants. Jesus interposed: "Not the dish, but what is in it is full of uncleanness." The master of the house replied: "Thou mistakest, those sweetmeats are perfectly clean and very costly." Jesus responded in words like these: "They are truly unclean! They are nothing else than sensual pleasures made of the sweat, the blood, the marrow, and the tears of widows, orphans, and the poor," and He read them a severe lesson upon their manner of acting, their prodigality, their covetousness, and their hypocrisy. They grew wrathy, but could make no reply. They quitted the house, leaving Jesus alone with the host. This latter was very smooth and affable toward Jesus, but it was all hypocrisy. He was hoping in this way to entrap Him and get something at last to report against Him to the committee at Capharnaum.

Toward evening Jesus again taught the heathens on the mountain. When they asked Him whether they should be baptized by John and expressed a wish to settle in Palestine, Jesus counseled them to put off their Baptism until better instructed. He told them, moreover, to go first of all across the Jordan to Upper Galilee and into the region of Adama, where they would find good people and heathens already instructed, and where He Himself would again teach. It was dark and Jesus taught by torchlight. The instruction over, He left His hearers, and went to the shore of the lake and down to the spot where Peter's men were waiting for Him with a boat. It was late. The three sailors made use of lights when they disembarked about half an hour below Bethsaida-Julias. Peter and Andrew, with the help of their servants, had built especially for His use the little boat in which Jesus had crossed. They were not only mariners and fishermen, but shipbuilders also.

Peter owned three vessels, one of them very large, as long as a house, Jesus' little boat held about ten men. It was oval in form, almost like an egg. In the forepart and stern were enclosed places for storing, and affording accommodations for washing the feet. In the center rose the mast with poles extended from it to the sides of the vessel for support; above and around these poles swung the sails. The seats were ranged around the mast. Jesus often taught from this little barque, which He used likewise to cross from point to point and to sail about among the other ships. The large vessels had around the lower part of the mast decks formed like terraces, or galleries, one above another. They were supported by posts placed at regular intervals, so that a view could be had through them from side to side. They were furnished with canvas curtains that could be drawn so as to form separate compartments like little cells. The poles supporting the mast had projecting rounds to facilitate climbing, and on either side of the vessel were floating chests, or barrels like wings or fins, to prevent its being overturned in a storm. They could be filled with water or emptied, according as it was necessary for the ship to ride more lightly or sink to a greater depth. The fish caught was sometimes preserved in them. At either end of the vessel were movable planks which, on being shoved out, facilitated access to the casks, to neighboring boats, or to the nets. When not in use for fishing purposes, the vessels were held in readiness to transport caravans and travellers across the lake. The sailors and servants of the fishermen were, for the most part, pagan slaves. Peter owned some.

7. Jesus in Peter's House.
Measures Taken by the
Pharisees. Cures

Jesus landed above Bethsaida not far from the house of the lepers where Peter, Andrew, John, James the Greater, James the Less, and Philip were awaiting His coming. He did not go with them through Bethsaida, but took the shorter route over the height to Peter's dwelling in the valley between that city and Capharnaum, where Mary and the other women were assembled. Peter's mother-in-law was in bed sick. Jesus went to see her, but did not cure her yet. They washed the Master's feet and then sat down to a meal, during which the conversation turned principally upon the fact that, from the several most famous schools in Judea and Jerusalem, fifteen Pharisees had been sent to Capharnaum to spy Jesus' actions. From the larger places, two had been sent; from Sephoris only one; and from Nazareth came that young man who had several times begged of Jesus to be admitted to His disciples, and whom Jesus had again rejected at His last visit to His native city. He had married lately, and was now appointed Scribe of the commission. Jesus said to the disciples: "Behold, for whom you interceded! He desired to become My disciple, and yet he is now come to lay snares for Me!" This young man wanted to join Jesus through a motive of vanity and, not being allowed to do so, he took part with Jesus' enemies. The Pharisees forming the commission were empowered to remain for some time in Capharnaum. Of those that came in pairs, one returned to report, the second remaining to spy Jesus' conduct and teaching. They had already held a meeting before which the Centurion Zorobabel, the son, and father had to appear and answer interrogatories respecting the boy's cure and Jesus' doctrine. They could neither deny the cure nor challenge the doctrine, nevertheless they could not reconcile themselves to what had happened. They were angry because Jesus had not studied under them; they found fault with His frequenting the company of common people, such as the Essenians, fishermen, publicans, and sinners; they were indignant at His presuming to teach without a mission from Jerusalem, from the Sanhedrin; they were offended at His not having recourse to themselves for counsel and instruction; and they could not endure that He was neither Pharisee nor Sadducee, that He taught among the Samaritans, and cured on the Sabbath day. They were in short furious at the thought that to render Him justice would be to denounce and condemn themselves. The young man from Nazareth was a violent enemy of the Samaritans, whom he persecuted in many ways.

Jesus' friends and relatives did not want Him to teach in Capharnaum on the Sabbath. Even His Mother was full of anxiety, and she expressed her opinion that it would be more advisable for Him to go to the other side of the lake. From such objections, Jesus turned aside with a few brief words and without explanations.

There were in Bethsaida and Capharnaum immense numbers of sick, of heathens, and Jews. Several troops of the travellers that Jesus had lately met on the other side of the lake were here awaiting Him. Near Bethsaida were large open inns covered with reeds, some for heathens, some for Jews. Above this place were the heathen baths; below were the Jewish.

Peter accommodated many of the Jewish sick in the precincts of his dwelling, and Jesus next morning healed a large number of them. Jesus had said to Peter the evening before that he should leave his fishery on the following day and help Him to fish after men; soon would He call upon him to quit it entirely. Peter obeyed, though not without some inward embarrassment. He was always of the opinion

that life with the Master was too high for him, he
could not understand it. He believed in Jesus, he
saw His miracles, he shared freely his substance
with the other disciples, he did willingly all that
was enjoined upon him, but yet he felt unfit for such
a vocation. He thought himself too simple, too unworthy, and to this was added a secret anxiety for the
welfare of his business. Sometimes also it was very
vexatious to him to find himself the object of such
railleries as, "He is only a poor fisherman, and yet
look at him going around with the Prophet! And his
house is a perfect rendezvous for fanatics and seditious persons. See how he neglects his business!" All
this made it a struggle for Peter since, though full
of faith and love, he was not at that time so enthusiastic, so zealous as Andrew and the other disciples. He was timid and humble, attached to his
ordinary occupations, and in his simplicity would
have preferred being left in the peaceful discharge
of them.

Jesus went from Peter's dwelling over the mountain ridge to the north side of Bethsaida. The whole
road was full of sick, pagans and Jews, separate however, the leprous far removed from all others. There
were blind, lame, dumb, deaf, paralytic, and an
exceedingly large number of dropsical Jews. The ceremony of curing was performed with the greatest
order and solemnity. The people had already been
two days here, and the disciples of the place, Andrew,
Peter, and the others whom Jesus had notified of His
coming, had arranged them comfortably in the nooks,
retired and shady, and the little gardens on the road.
Jesus instructed and admonished the sick, who were
carried or led and ranged around Him in groups.
Some desired to confess their sins to Him, and He
stepped with them to a more retired spot. They sank
on their knees before Him, confessing and weeping.
Among the heathens were some that had committed
murder and robbery on their journeys. Jesus passed

by some, leaving them lying unnoticed for a time
while He turned to others; but afterwards coming
back to them, He exclaimed: "Rise! Thy sins are forgiven thee!" Among the Jews were adulterers and
usurers. When Jesus saw in them proofs of repentance, He imposed on them a penance, repeated some
prayers with them, laid His hands upon them, and
cured them. He commanded many to purify themselves in a bath. Some of the heathens He ordered
to receive Baptism or to join their converted brethren
in Upper Galilee. Band after band passed before Him,
and the disciples preserved order.

Jesus went through Bethsaida also. It was crowded
with people, as if upon a great pilgrimage. He cured
here in the different inns and along the streets.
Refreshments had been prepared in Andrew's house.
I saw some children there: Peter's stepdaughter and
some other little girls of about ten years, two others
between eight and ten, and Andrew's little son who
wore a yellow tunic with a girdle. There were also
some females of advanced age. All were standing on
a kind of covered porch outside the house, speaking
of the Prophet, asking whether He would soon come,
and running from side to side to see whether He
were in sight. They had assembled here in order to
get a glimpse of Him, though ordinarily the children
were kept under greater restraint. At last Jesus
passed, turned His head toward them, and gave them
His blessing. I saw Him going again to Peter's and
curing many. He cured about one hundred on that
day, pardoned their sins, and pointed out to them
what they should do in the future.

I saw again that Jesus exercised many different
manners of curing, and that probably He did so in
order to instruct the disciples as to how they should
act, also the ministers of the Church till the end of
time. All the actions of Jesus, even His sufferings,
appeared to be of a purely human nature. There were
no sudden, no magical transformations in the cures

He wrought. I saw in them a certain transition from sickness to health analogous to the nature of the malady and the sins that had given rise to it. I saw stealing upon those over whom He prayed or upon whom He laid His hand a certain stillness and inward recollection, which lasted for some moments, when they rose up as if from a slight swoon, cured. The lame rose without effort and cast themselves cured at His feet, though their full strength and agility returned to some only after a few hours, to others not for days. I saw some sick of the dropsy who could totter toward Him without assistance, and others who had to be carried. He generally laid His hand on their head and stomach and pronounced some words, after which they at once arose and walked. They felt quite relieved, the water passing from them in perspiration. The leprous, on being cured, immediately lost the scales of their disease, though still retaining the red scars. They that recovered sight, speech, or hearing, had at first a feeling of strangeness in the use of those senses. I saw some swollen with gout cured. Their pains left them, and they could walk, but the swelling did not go down at once, though it disappeared very soon. Convulsions were cured immediately and fevers vanished at His word, though their victims did not instantly become strong and vigorous. They were like drooping plants regaining freshness in the rain. The possessed usually sank into a short swoon from which they recovered with a calm expression of countenance and quite worn-out, though freed from the evil one. All was conducted quietly and methodically. Only for unbelievers and the malevolent had the miracles of Jesus anything frightful in them.

The heathens present on this occasion had been influenced to come chiefly by people that had been to the baptism and teaching of John, and by other heathens from Upper Galilee where Jesus had formerly taught and cured. Some had already received

John's baptism, and some had not. Jesus did not order them to be circumcised. When questioned on this point, He instructed them upon the circumcision of the heart and the senses, and taught them how to mortify themselves. He spoke to them of charity, temperance, frugality, ordered them to keep the Ten Commandments, taught them some parts of a prayer like the petitions of the Lord's Prayer, and promised to send them His disciples.

8. Jesus Teaches and Cures In Capharnaum

On the preceding evening, flags with knots and strings of fruit were raised on the synagogues and public buildings of Bethsaida, to herald the last day of the month Ab. With the Sabbath, the first day of the month Elul began. Next morning after Jesus had healed many sick Jews in Bethsaida, He went with the disciples to Peter's, near Capharnaum. The women had preceded Him thither, and crowds of sick were again awaiting Him. There were two deaf men into whose ears Jesus put His finger. Two others were brought forward, who could scarcely walk, besides which their arms were perfectly stiff and their hands swollen. Jesus laid His hand on them and prayed; then grasping them by both hands, He swung their arms up and down, and they were cured. The swelling did not, however, disappear at once, but only after a couple of hours. He exhorted them for the future to use their hands for the glory of God, for it was sin that had reduced them to this state. He cured many others, and then went into the city for the Sabbath.

The concourse of people at Capharnaum was very great. The possessed had been released from their place of confinement and ran crying out along the streets to meet Jesus. He commanded them to be silent and delivered them; whereupon, to the aston-

ishment of the multitude, they followed Him quietly
to the synagogue and listened to His instruction.
The Pharisees, and among them those fifteen from
the other cities, sat around His chair, forced to treat
Him with respect and hypocritical reverence. They
gave Him the Scriptures, and He taught from *Isaias* 49, that God had not forgotten His people. He
read aloud: "If even a woman should forget her child,
yet would not God forget His people"; and then
explained from the following verses that the impiety of men could not restrain God, could not hinder
Him from realizing His thoughts of mercy. The time
of which the Prophet speaks, that the eyes of God
are always on the walls of Sion, had now come, now
should the destroyers flee and the builders com-
mence their labor. The Lord would gather together
nations to ornament His sanctuary. There will be so
many good and pious souls, so many benefactors and
leaders of the poor nations that the sterile synagogue will say: Who has begotten to me so many
children? The Gentiles shall be converted to the
Church, the kings of the earth shall serve her! The
God of Jacob shall snatch from the enemy, from the
perverted synagogue, her children; and they that
like murderers lay hands on the Saviour, shall rage
against one another, and choke one another. (*Isaias*
50:1 *et seq.*) Jesus explained this as referring to the
destruction of Jerusalem, since it would not receive
the Kingdom of grace. God demands whether He has
separated from the Synagogue, whether He has given
her a bill of divorce, whether He has sold His people. Yes, on account of their sins, have they been
sold! On account of her transgressions, has the Synagogue been abandoned! He has called, He has
warned, and no one has heeded. But He is the mighty
God, He can cause Heaven and earth to tremble,
Jesus applied all to His own time. He showed that
all had been led astray, those that had been for-
saken by the synagogue. And then, as if speaking

to Himself, He uttered the words of this passage of
Isaias: "The Lord hath given me a learned tongue,
that I should know how to uphold by word him that
is weary: He hath opened His ears to Him in the
morning to hear His commands, and He hath not
resisted." The Pharisees took these words as foolish
self-praise, though they were ravished by His preaching, and said to one another at the end of it: "Never
before has any Prophet so taught!" They whispered,
nevertheless, some malicious remarks into one
another's ears, Jesus went on with the explanation
of this passage: "I have given My body to the strik-
ers, and My cheeks to them that plucked them,"
applying it to the persecutions that He had already
endured and to what He had still to suffer. He spoke
of the ill-treatment He had received at Nazareth,
saying: "Let him who can condemn Me, come forward!" His enemies, He said, would grow old and
come to naught in their vain teachings, the Judge
would come upon them. The godly would hear His
voice, while the ignorant, the unenlightened should
call to God and hope in Him. The Day of Judgment
would come, and they that had kindled the fire would
go to ruin. (*Is.* 1:11). This passage, also, Jesus
explained of the destruction of the Jewish people
and Jerusalem.

The Pharisees had not a word to reply. They listened in silence, transported by His words, though
occasionally whispering a jeering remark into their
neighbor's ear. Jesus then explained something from
Moses as He always did at the termination of His
sermons, and added a parable, which He addressed
more particularly to the disciples and to the faith-
less young Scribe of Nazareth. The parable was that
of the talent put out at interest, for the young Scribe
was vain of his acquirements. He was humbled interiorly by it, but not improved. Jesus related the parable in terms similar to, though not quite the same
as those given in the Gospel.

In front of the synagogue, Jesus cured the sick on the streets, and then went with His disciples to Peter's outside the city gate. Nathaniel Chased and the bridegroom, also Thaddeus, had come hither from Cana for this Sabbath. Thaddeus was often in Capharnaum, for he travelled a great deal throughout the country, dealing in fishing nets, sailcloth, and tackling. That night the house was again full of sick persons, and separated from the rest were several women afflicted with a flow of blood. Some women, completely enveloped, were brought on portable beds by their friends. They were pale and emaciated, and had already sighed long after Jesus' help. This time I saw that He imposed hands on the sufferers, and blessed them. Then He commanded those on the beds to throw off their covers and arise. They obeyed, one helping the other. Jesus exhorted them and bade them adieu. During the night, He retired to pray.

The spying Pharisees had not spoken openly in Capharnaum of the object of their mission; even the Centurion Zorobabel had been questioned only secretly. They had sufficient pretexts to account for their presence: The Jews were in the habit of going from one place to another for the celebration of the Sabbath, especially if a distinguished Doctor was expected to preside; it was customary, besides, for crowds to retire into the country of Genesareth, to rest from business and enjoy the beauty and luxuriance that everywhere abounded.

On the following day Jesus went very early to Capharnaum. There was an innumerable concourse gathered before the synagogue, among them crowds of sick, of whom He healed many. When He entered the synagogue wherein the Pharisees were assembled, some possessed who were present began to cry out after Him. One in particular, more noisy than his fellows, went running toward Him crying: "What have we to do with Thee, Jesus of Nazareth? Thou hast come to destroy us! I know that Thou art the

Holy One of God!" Jesus commanded the demon to be silent and to go out of the man. The latter, tearing himself, ran back among his companions, but the devil, uttering great cries, went out of him. The man then became perfectly calm, and cast himself at Jesus' feet. Many of those present, and especially the disciples, said in the hearing of the Pharisees, who were scandalized at what they saw: "What kind of a new doctrine is this? Who can this Teacher be? He has power over the impure spirits!"

The crowd was so dense, there were so many sick in and around the synagogue, that Jesus had to take His stand on a spot to be seen and heard not only from within, but also from the court, which was crowded. The Pharisees stood around Him inside, while Jesus turned toward the court to address the people. Sometimes He turned toward the interior of the synagogue, and again toward those outside. The halls around the building were open for the accommodation of the immense throng of hearers, who filled not only the court, but mounted the steps leading to the flat roofs of the buildings that enclosed it. Below were the cells and oratories reserved for penitents and those that came to pray. There were some places specially reserved for the sick.

Jesus again clearly and energetically expounded Isaias, applying all to their own time and to Himself. The times, He said, were fulfilled and the Kingdom was near. They had always longed after the fulfillment of the Prophecies, they had sighed for the Prophet, the Messiah, who would relieve them of their burdens. But when He would come, they would not receive Him, because He would fail to realize their erroneous notions of Him. Then taking the signs of the coming of the Prophet for whose accomplishment they always sighed, those signs that were still read from the Scriptures in their synagogues and for which they prayed, He proved that they had all been fulfilled. He said: "The lame shall walk, the blind

see, the deaf hear. Is there not something of this
now? What mean these gatherings of the Gentiles to
hear instruction? What do the possessed cry out?
Why are the demons expelled? Why do the cured
praise God? Do not the wicked persecute Him? Do
not spies surround Him? But they will cast out and
kill the Son of the Lord of the vineyard, and how
shall it be with them? If ye will not receive salvation, yet shall it not be lost. Ye cannot prevent its
being given to the poor, the sick, to sinners and publicans, to the penitent, and even to the Gentiles in
whose favor it shall be taken from you." Such was
the substance of Jesus' discourse. He added: "That
John whom they have imprisoned ye acknowledge to
be a Prophet! Go to him in his prison and ask him
for whom did he prepare the ways and of whom did
he bear witness?" While Jesus spoke, the rage of the
Pharisees increased, and they whispered and muttered together.

During Jesus' discourse, four distinguished men of
Capharnaum, sick of an unclean malady, were carried by eight others less sick to the synagogue and
placed in such a position in the court that Jesus
could see them and they could hear His teaching.
On account of their sickness, they were allowed to
enter only by one particular gate, but that being just
at present obstructed by the crowd, the eight semi-
invalids had to lift them in their beds to a place over
a wall and force their own way through the crowd,
which at once retreated before the unclean sickness.
When the Pharisees saw the newcomers, they became
angry and began to snarl at them as public sinners
suffering from an unclean malady. They spoke aloud
against them, asking what kind of irregularity was
this, that such people should venture into their vicinity? When their remarks ran through the crowd and
reached the objects of them, the poor sick men
became sad and frightened lest Jesus, being informed
of their sins, should refuse to cure them. They were

full of contrition, and had long sighed for Jesus' assistance. But when Jesus heard the murmuring of the Pharisees, He turned on the instant to where the sick men were lying in fear and anxiety, addressed His discourse to the crowd in the court and, casting a look full of earnestness and love on the sufferers, cried out to them: "Your sins are forgiven you!" At this the poor men burst into tears, while the Pharisees, highly exasperated, growled out: "How does He dare say so? How can He forgive sins!" Jesus said: "Follow Me down there, and see what I am going to do! Why are ye offended at My doing the will of My Father? If ye do not want salvation yourselves, yet should you not grudge it to the repentant! Ye are angry that I cure on the Sabbath? Does the hand of the Almighty rest on the Sabbath day from doing good and punishing evil? Does He not feed the hungry, cure the sick, and shed around His blessings on the Sabbath? Can He not send sickness on the Sabbath? May He not let you die on the Sabbath? Be not vexed that the Son does the will and the works of His Father on the Sabbath!" When He reached the sick men, He ordered the Pharisees to stand in a row at some distance, saying: "Stay here, for to ye these men are unclean, though to Me not, since their sins have been forgiven them! And now, tell Me. Is it harder to say to a contrite sinner, 'Thy sins are forgiven thee,' than to say to a sick man, 'Arise, and carry thy bed hence?'" The Pharisees had not a word to answer. Then Jesus approached the sick men, laid His hands on them one after the other, uttered a few words of prayer over them, raised them up by the hand, and commanded them to render thanks to God, to sin no more, and to carry away their beds. All four arose. The eight who had carried them and who were themselves half-sick, had become quite vigorous, and they helped the others to throw off the covers in which they were wrapped. These latter appeared to be only a little fatigued and embarrassed. Putting

together the poles of their portable beds, they shoul-
dered them, and all twelve went off through the wondering and exulting crowd joyfully entoning the song
of thanksgiving: "Praised be the Lord God of Israel!
He has done great things to us. He has had mercy
on His people, and has cured us by His Prophet!"

But the Pharisees, full of wrath and deeply mortified, hurried away without taking leave of the Saviour. Everything about Jesus exasperated them: His
actions and His manner of performing them, that
He was not of the same opinion with them, that He
did not esteem them just, wise, and holy, that He
associated with people whom they despised. They
had a thousand objections to make to Him; namely,
that He did not keep the fasts strictly, He associated with sinners, pagans, Samaritans, and the rabble at large, that He was Himself of mean extraction,
that He gave too much liberty to His disciples and
did not keep them in proper respect—in a word,
everything in Him displeased them. Still they could
bring no special charge against Him. His wisdom
and His astonishing miracles they could not deny;
consequently, they took refuge in ever-increasing rage
and calumny. When one considers the life of Jesus
in detail, the priests and people of His time are
found to be pretty much the same as they are nowadays. If Jesus actually returned to earth, from many
Doctors of the Law, from many politicians, He would
have to endure still worse things.

The sickness of the lately cured consisted in a discharge of impure humors. They were, before their
cure, quite exhausted and motionless, as if they had
had an apoplectic stroke. The eight others were partially lame on one side. The beds consisted of two
poles with feet, a crosspiece in the middle, on which
a mat was stretched. They rolled the whole together,
and carried them on their shoulders like a couple of
poles. It was a touching sight—those men going
through the crowd singing!

9. Jesus Cures Peter's Mother-in-Law.
Peter's Great Humility

Jesus now went without delay with the disciples out of the city gate and along the mountain to Peter's in Bethsaida. They had urged Him to do so, for they thought that Peter's mother-in-law was dying. Her sickness had very much increased, and now she had a raging fever. Jesus went straight into her room. He was followed by some of the family; I think Peter's daughter was among them. He stepped to that side of the bed to which the sick woman's face was turned, and leaned against the bed, half-standing, half-sitting, so that His head approached hers. He spoke to her some words, and laid His hand upon her head and breast. She became perfectly still. Then standing before her, He took her hand and raised her into sitting posture, saying: "Give her something to drink!" Peter's daughter gave her a drink out of a vessel in the form of a little boat. Jesus blessed the drink and commanded the invalid to rise. She obeyed and arose from her low couch. Her limbs were bandaged, and she wore a wide nightdress. Disengaging herself from the bandages, she stepped to the floor and rendered thanks to the Lord, the entire household uniting with her.

At the meal that followed, she helped with the other women and, perfectly recovered, served at table. After that, Jesus, with Peter, Andrew, James, John, and several of the other disciples, went to Peter's fishery on the lake. In the instruction He gave them, He spoke principally of the fact that they would soon give up their present occupations and follow Him. Peter became quite timid and anxious. He fell on his knees before Jesus, begging Him to reflect upon his ignorance and weakness, and not to insist on his undertaking anything so important, that he was entirely unworthy, and quite unable to instruct others. Jesus replied that His disciples should have no

worldly solicitude, that He who gave health to the
sick would provide for their subsistence and furnish
them with ability for what they had to do. All were
perfectly satisfied, excepting Peter who, in his humility and simplicity, could not comprehend how he was
for the future to be, not a fisherman, but a teacher
of men. This, however, is not the call of the Apostles
related in the Gospel. That had not yet taken place.
Peter had nevertheless already given over a great
part of his business to Zebedee. After this walk by
the lake, Jesus again went to Capharnaum and found
an unusual number of sick around Peter's house outside the city. He cured many, and taught again in the
synagogue.

As the concourse of people continued to increase,
Jesus, without being noticed, disengaged Himself from
the crowd, and went alone to a wild but very pleasant ravine which extended to the south of Capharnaum, from Zorobabel's mansion to the dwellings of
his servants and workmen. In it were grottos, bushes,
and springs, numerous birds, and all kinds of tame,
rare animals. It was a skillfully cared-for solitude
belonging to Zorobabel, besides being a part of that
garden of pleasure, Genesareth, thrown open to the
public. Jesus spent the night alone and in prayer,
the disciples being ignorant of His whereabouts.

Early next morning, He left the wilderness, but
not to return to Capharnaum. He ordered Peter and
another of the disciples who had come to seek Him
to send Parmenas, Saturnin, Aristobolus, and Tharzissus to a certain place where He would meet them,
and thence go to the Baths of Bethulia. He went
around the height of the valley on which lay Magdalum, which He passed a couple of hours eastward
to the left. On the south side of this height was the
city of Jetebatha.

10. Jesus at the Baths of Bethulia
And in Jetebatha

At first I thought that Jesus was going to Gennabris, situated among the mountains, about three hours west of Tiberias. But He did not go there, but to the north side of the valley where was the fountain of Bethuel. A great many wealthy and distinguished people from Galilee and Judea owned villas and gardens here, which they occupied in the beautiful season of the year. On the south side of the lake, formed by the northern declivity of the heights of Bethuel, were rows of houses and warm baths, those toward the east being the warmer. The baths had one large reservoir in common, around which were private apartments formed by tents; in them were tubs sunk to a greater or lesser depth in the water, according to the convenience of the bathers. These private apartments communicated with the reservoir. There were many inns in the neighborhood of the baths. A private house and garden could also be hired for the season with everything else free. The revenues belonged to the city of Bethulia, and were used principally to keep up the baths. The waters of the lake were uncommonly pure, clear as a mirror to the very bottom, which was paved with beautiful, little white pebbles. It was fed by a stream from the east which flowed from the baths in the valley of Magdalum. The lake swarmed with little pleasure boats, which in the distance looked like ducks. On the north side of the lake, but facing south, were dwellings for the accommodation of female visitors at the baths. Their walks and pleasure grounds, however, were near the brook that flowed through those of the men. Both sides of the valley formed a gentle declivity toward the lake. From the dwellings and baths there ran around the lake, crossing and opening into one another, shady avenues, embowered walks with wide-stretching trees and luxuriant foliage, among which lay meadows of very high and beautiful grass, orchards, vegetable gardens, and grounds for riding and games. The view was enchantingly beautiful—hills and mountains, all teeming with the most exuberant fertility, rich especially in grapes and fruits. The second harvest of the year was now ripe.

Jesus remained on the side of the lake by which He had come, and put up at a traveller's inn. People soon gathered around Him, and He taught them with great sweetness outside the inn. Many women were among His hearers. Next morning I saw a number of little boats coming over from the south side of the lake where the bathers were. It was a deputation of the most distinguished men come to invite Jesus courteously to return with them and preach. Jesus ferried across with them and went to an inn where they presented Him with a little luncheon. He taught in the cool of the morning and evening under shady trees, on a hill not far from the inn. Most of His hearers stood around Him, the women on one side veiled. The order observed was truly pleasing. The people were, for the most part, well-bred and well-inclined, cheerful and good-humored. As there were no factions among them, one did not fear to give vent to his feelings before the others, consequently they were all most reverential and attentive to Jesus. They were perfectly carried away and rejoiced by His very first discourse. He taught of purification by water, of the union, equality, and the feeling of confidence that reigned among them, of the mystery of water, of the washing away of sin, of the bath of baptism as administered by John, of the charity and good understanding that ought to unite the baptized, the converted, etc. He borrowed, moreover, subject matter and graceful similitudes from the lovely season, from the country around, the mountains, trees, fruit, and herds, in short from everything they saw about them. I saw His audience around

Jesus in a circle, and at times exchanging places
with newcomers to whom He repeated the substance
of His last discourse.

I saw some gouty invalids moving slowly about.
They were mostly government officials and officers
who were enjoying a vacation. I recognized them by
the uniforms they wore when leaving for their different garrisons around the country. During their
stay at the baths, all were dressed alike with nothing to distinguish them from other people. The men
wore fine, yellow woolen stuff made into tunics of
four separate skirts, one above the other, the lower
one wrapped into a kind of trousers down to the
knees; some went barefoot, others wore sandals. The
upper part of the body was covered with a scapular
open at the sides and bound at the waist by a broad
girdle. The shoulders were covered with an armflap
that reached halfway to the elbow; the head was
uncovered. They played at games, fighting with little sticks and armed with shields made of leaves.
They attacked one another in rows and also singly,
aiming at pushing their opponents from their places.
They ran toward a goal for a wager, jumped over
ropes, sprang through hoops upon which all sorts of
glittering things were hanging. These they were not
to touch in passing through, otherwise they tinkled
and fell off. The contestant for the prize lost in pro-
portion to the number thus displaced. The prizes consisted of fruit which I saw lying ready for the winners.
I saw some playing on reed flutes; others had long,
thick reeds through which they gazed into the distance and into the lake. Sometimes they blew balls
or little arrows through them, as if they were shooting after fishes. I saw that these reeds were flexi-
ble; they could be bent to form a ring and then hung
on the arm. I saw them also sticking glass globes of
different colors on the ends of the reeds and waving
them to and fro, thus reflecting the light of the sun.
The whole landscape was mirrored in the globes, but

in an inverted position. When the globes were
revolved, the whole lake appeared to be passing over-
head. This greatly diverted the beholders.

The fruits, and especially the grapes, were truly
magnificent. I saw some persons very respectfully
and courteously bringing some of the finest to Jesus.

The dwellings of the women were on the opposite
side of the valley; but their baths were on this side,
more toward the east and out of sight of those of the
men. On the banks of the stream that flowed into
the lake, I saw little boys in short, white woolen
tunics with willow switches of various colors in their
hands, driving flocks of different kinds of aquatic
birds. The water from the stream and lake was conducted up to the inns on the height and also to the
baths. It was received in channels from which it was
raised to higher reservoirs, and from them to others, and so on. I saw the women also playing at different games on the green. They were very modestly
clothed in fine, white woolen wrappers that fell around
them in numerous folds and were girded twice, over
the breast and again at the waist. The wide sleeves
could be raised or lowered by means of buckles.
Around the wrists they had large, stiff frills with
many folds, like the tail of a peacock. Their headdress consisted of a cap of circular puffs graduated
lower and narrower, wound with silk or small feathers of natural whiteness. It looked like a snail's shell
made of feathers. It was tied behind and a long point
made of tassels hung down the back. They wore no
veil, but over the face were two sections of finely
plaited, white, transparent stuff like half fans, which
reached to below the nose, and had holes for the
eyes. They could lower them in part if they wished
to guard against the sun, or throw them entirely
back. Before men they were lowered.

I saw the women amusing themselves lustily at
the following game. Each had a girdle ending in a
ring, or a loop, around her waist. They formed a cir-

cle, each holding her neighbor fast by the loop with
one hand, the other being free. A trinket was concealed in the grass and they turned round here and
there in a circle until one of the players spied it.
When she stopped to pick it up, the others in the
circle gave a sudden jerk; those following likewise
stooped after the treasure, each one trying not to
fall. Sometimes they tumbled over one another amid
shouts of laughter.

Bethulia was situated on a plateau in a mountainous region, solitary and wild. It was an hour and a
half south of the lake. Above it was a great, rough-
looking tower and many ruined walls and towers.
Once upon a time, the city must have extended much
further and been very strongly fortified. Trees were
now growing on those walls, upon which vehicles
could be driven, and I saw the visitors at the baths
promenading on them. The city lay high up around
the mountain. Here it was that Judith became illustrious. The camp of Holofernes stretched from the
lake through the ravine of Jetebatha around to
Dothan, a couple of hours to the south of Bethulia.
From Jetebatha also there were visitors at the baths.
They did not wait to hear Jesus' instructions but,
returning to Jetebatha, spread the news of His presence in Bethulia. Jetebatha was situated about an
hour and a half to the southeast, built in the bosom
of the mountains as in an immense cave. Before it
rose a mountain from which the descent into the city
was over deep, wild ditches. It appeared to be built
in a deep quarry, the mountain hanging high over
it. To the north of this mountain, not quite two hours
distant, was Magdalum, on the edge of a deep dale,
with its surroundings of avenues, gardens, and towers of all kinds stretching off into the middle of it.
Between the mountain and Magdalum were still
standing the remains of the channel of an aqueduct
through whose arches one could look far off into the
country. The channel was now overgrown by vines

and foliage. Southward from Jetebatha rose another
wild mountain pierced right and left by broad ravines.
It was a region full of wonderful hiding places. There
were numerous Herodians in Jetebatha. In a wall of
the fortifications they had a secret meeting place.
The sect was composed of shrewd, intelligent people
ranged under a secret superior. They had signs
whereby they recognized one another, and the chiefs
could also tell (how, I do not now know) if a member had betrayed anything. Secret enemies of the
Romans, they were plotting a revolution in favor of
Herod. Although in reality followers of the Sadducees,
yet in the exterior they conformed to the Pharisees,
thinking in this way to draw over both parties to
their designs. They knew indeed that the time had
come for the appearance of the Messiah, the King of
the Jews, and they resolved to make use of the general belief for the furtherance of their ends. Exteriorly and through motives of cunning, they were very
bland and tolerant, though really treacherous sneaks.
They had, properly speaking, no religion at all; but
under the cloak of piety, they labored at the found-
ing of an independent kingdom of this world, and
Herod supported them in their intrigues.

When the synagogue of Jetebatha heard of Jesus'
presence in the neighborhood, they sent two Herodians to the baths of Bethulia, to find out what sort
of a person He was and to invite Him to Jetebatha.
Jesus, however, gave them no decided answer as to
whether He would go or not. About seven of the disciples that had journeyed with Him a couple of weeks
before met Him here again. Two of them were John's
disciples, some relatives of his who also were disciples, from the country of Hebron, and one was a
cousin from Lesser Sephoris. They had been seeking
Him in Galilee, and had now found Him, During
those days, I saw Jesus speaking confidentially with
several of the guests at the baths. There must have
been some of His own followers among them.

When the Herodians returned to Jetebatha, one of them set about preparing the people in case Jesus should come to their city. He told them that Jesus, the Prophet of Nazareth, who was now nearby at the Baths of Bethulia, would probably visit their city for the coming Sabbath. He was the one who had made a great uproar in Capharnaum on the preceding Sabbath and on the Sabbath before that in Nazareth. He warned them not to be seduced by Him, not to applaud Him, not even to let Him speak for any length of time, but to interrupt Him with murmurs and contradictions whenever He said anything singular or unintelligible; and so the people were prepared for Jesus' coming.

Jesus delivered at the Baths of Bethulia another discourse full of beauty and simplicity. Numbers of men formed around Him a circle in which He moved about among them. At a distance in the background, several men lame with the gout were timidly standing. They had come to make use of the baths, but had not yet ventured to approach Jesus. Jesus repeated what He had taught yesterday and the day before, exhorting His audience to purification from sin. All hearts were touched and turned to Him. Many exclaimed: "Lord, who could hear Thee and resist Thy words!" Jesus replied: "Ye have heard much about Me, and now ye listen to My words. Who do ye think I am?" Some said: "Lord, Thou art a Prophet!" Others answered: "Thou art more than a Prophet! No Prophet ever taught such things as Thou dost teach. None has ever done the things that Thou hast done!" But others, again, kept silence. Jesus, penetrating the thoughts of these last, pointing to them, said: "These men's thoughts are the right ones." Someone then said: "Lord, Thou canst do all things! Is it not so? They said that Thou hast even raised the dead, the daughter of Jairus. Is it so?" The speaker alluded to that Jairus who dwelt in a city not far from Gibea, where Jesus had at an

earlier period instructed the poor, depraved inhabitants. Jesus answered the question addressed to
Him by a simple "Yes!" and then His questioner
went on to inquire why Jairus still remained in so
disreputable a place. Thereupon Jesus began to speak
of fountains in the desert, applying the similitude
to the necessity of the weak for a powerful leader.
Jesus' hearers were full of confidence and they questioned Him with simplicity. Then He asked them:
"What do ye know of Me? What evil do men say of
Me?" Some answered: "They complain that Thou dost
not discontinue Thy works on the Sabbath day and
that Thou healest the sick on that day." Then Jesus,
pointing to a little neighboring field near a pond,
in which shepherd boys were guarding tender lambs
and other young cattle, said: "See those young shepherd boys and their tender lambs! If one of the little animals should fall into the pond on the Sabbath
and bleat for help, would not all the others stand
around the brink bleating piteously also? Now, the
poor little shepherds could not help the lamb out.
But supposing the son of the master of the flocks
were passing by—supposing he had been charged
to look after the lambs and see to their pasture—
would he not be touched with pity at the sound of
the poor little thing's bleating? Would he not hasten to draw it out of the mire?" Here all raised their
hands like children at catechism, and cried out: "Yes,
yes! He would!" Jesus went on: "And if it were not
a lamb, if it were the fallen children of the Heavenly Father, if it were your own brethren, yes, if it
were yourselves! Should not the Son of the Heavenly Father help you on the Sabbath?" All cried out
again: "Yes! Yes!" Then Jesus pointed to the men
sick of the gout standing afar off, and said: "Behold
your sick brethren! Shall I not help them if they
implore My assistance on the Sabbath day? Shall
they not receive pardon of their sins, if they bewail
them on the Sabbath day? If they confess them on

the Sabbath and cry to their Father in Heaven?"
With uplifted hands, they all cried out: "Yes, yes!"
Then Jesus motioned to the gouty patients, and
they moved slowly and heavily into the circle. He
spoke a few words to them on faith, prayed for awhile,
and said: "Stretch out your arms!" They stretched
out their afflicted arms toward Him. Jesus passed
His hand down them, breathed for an instant on
their hands, and they were cured, were able to use
their limbs. Jesus commanded them to bathe, and
warned them to abstain from certain drinks. They
cast themselves at His feet giving thanks, while the
whole assembly sang canticles of praise and glory.

Jesus wanted to depart, but they begged Him to
remain with them. They were full of love and good
intentions, they were very much impressed. He told
them that He had to proceed further and fulfill His
mission. They accompanied Him a part of the way
with the disciples. He dismissed them with His blessing, and went on to Jetebatha about an hour and a
half to the east.

It was afternoon when Jesus arrived at His des-
tination. He washed His feet and took a luncheon
at an inn outside the city. The disciples went before
Him into Jetebatha to the chief of the synagogue,
and requested the key for their Master, who wished
to teach. The people hurriedly gathered in crowds,
and the Doctors of the Law and the Herodians were
all expectancy to ensnare Him in His doctrine. When
He had taken His place in the synagogue, they put
to Him questions upon the approach of the Kingdom, the computation of time, the fulfilling of the
weeks of Daniel, and the coming of the Messiah.
Jesus answered in a long discourse, showing that
the Prophecies were now fulfilled. He spoke, too, of
John and his Prophecies, whereupon they took occasion to warn Him hypocritically to be careful as to
what He said in His instructions, not to set aside
the Jewish customs, and to take a lesson from John's

imprisonment! What He said of the fulfillment of
the weeks of Daniel, of the near coming of the Messiah, and of the King of the Jews, was excellent and
quite in accordance with their own ideas. But, as
He told them, *they* might seek where they would,
they would still nowhere find the Messiah. Jesus
had, though rather vaguely, applied the Prophecies
to Himself. They understood Him well enough, but
they pretended that such things could not happen
to anyone, and that they had failed to catch His
meaning. In reality they wanted to force Him to
speak out more clearly, so that they might get something of which to accuse Him. Jesus said to them:
"How ye play the hypocrite! What turns ye away
from Me? Why do ye despise Me? Ye lay snares for
Me, and ye seek to form new plots with the Sadducees, as ye did in Jerusalem at the Pasch! Why
do ye caution Me, citing John and Herod?" Then He
cast into their face Herod's shameful deeds, his mur-
ders, his dread of the newborn King of the Jews, his
cruel massacre of the Innocents, and his frightful
death, the crimes of his successors, the adultery of
Antipas, and the imprisonment of John. He spoke
of the hypocritical, secret sect of the Herodians who
were in league with the Sadducees, and showed them
what kind of a Messiah and what sort of a Kingdom of God they were awaiting. He pointed to different places in the distance, saying: "They will be
able to do nothing against Me until My mission is
fulfilled. I shall twice traverse Samaria, Judea, and
Galilee. Ye have witnessed great signs wrought by
Me, and seeing still greater, ye shall remain blind."
Then He spoke of judgment, of the death of the
Prophets, and of the chastisement that was to over-
take Jerusalem. The Herodians, that secret society,
seeing themselves discovered, blanched with rage
when Jesus referred to Herod's misdeeds and laid
open the secrets of the sect before the people. They
were silent and, one by one, left the synagogue, as

did also the Sadducees who here had charge of the
schools. There were no Pharisees in Jetebatha.

Jesus now found Himself alone with His seven disciples and the people. He continued to teach some
time longer, and many were very much impressed.
They declared that they had never listened to such
instructions, and that He taught better than their
own teachers. They reformed their lives, and followed
Him later. But a large part of the people, instigated
by the Sadducees and Herodians, murmured against
Him and raised a tumult. Jesus therefore left the
city with the disciples and went southward through
the valley, and then up for a couple of hours into a
harvest field between Bethulia and Gennabris. Here
He put up at a large farmhouse, whose occupants
were well known to Him. The holy women had often
stayed here overnight on their journeys to Bethania,
and the messengers between them and the Saviour
used to put up at the same place.

11. Jesus in the Harvest Field of Dothain and in Gennabris

Jesus in the harvest field of Dothain taught of
reaping, gleaning, and binding into sheaves. This was
the field in which later on He and the disciples
plucked the ears of wheat. He went around the field,
here and there, talking of seeds and stony soil, for
such was the character of this region. He said that
He was come to gather the good ears, and explained
the parable of rooting up the tares at the harvest.
He likened the harvest to the Kingdom of God. He
instructed at intervals during the work and while
going from one field to another.

The stalks remained standing high, the ears only
having been cut off and bound together in the form
of a cross.

In the evening after the harvest, Jesus from a hill-
top delivered a long discourse before the laborers.

Borrowing a similitude from a brook that flowed in their vicinity, He applied it to the life, gentle and beneficent, of some men; He spoke of the flowing waters of grace, and of the conducting of those waters to our own field, etc. He sent John's two disciples to Ennon with a commission to say to His own disciples there that they should go to Machaerus and calm the people, for He knew that an insurrection had broken out in that place. Aspirants to baptism had crowded to Ennon; immense caravans had arrived. But when they found out that the Prophet had been arrested, they proceeded to Machaerus, their numbers increasing on the way. They raged and shouted, crying for John to be released, that he might instruct and baptize them. They even threw stones at Herod's palace, all the approaches to which the guards hastily closed. Herod pretended that he was not at home.

That evening Jesus put up near Gennabris in another farmhouse, and taught again of the grain of mustard seed. The master of the house complained to Him of a neighbor who for a long time had encroached upon his field and in many ways infringed his rights. Jesus went to the field with the owner, that he might point out to Him the injury done. As the present state of affairs had lasted some time, the damage was considerable, and the owner complained that he could not do anything with the trespasser. Jesus asked whether he still had sufficient for the support of himself and his family. The man answered, yes, that he enjoyed competency. Upon hearing this, Jesus told him that he had lost nothing, since properly speaking nothing belongs to us, and so long as we have sufficient to support life, we have enough. The owner of the field should resign still more to his importunate neighbor, in order to satisfy the latter's greed after earthly goods. All that one cheerfully gives up here below for the sake of peace, will be restored to him in the Kingdom of his

Father. That hostile neighbor, viewed from his own standpoint, acted rightly, for his kingdom was of this world, and he sought to increase in earthly goods. But in Jesus' Kingdom, he should have nothing. The owner of the field should take a lesson from his neighbor in the art of enriching himself, and should strive to acquire possessions in the Kingdom of God. Jesus drew a similitude from a river which wore away the land on one side and deposited the debris on the other. The whole discourse was something like that upon the unjust steward, in which worldly artifice and earthly greed after enrichment should furnish an example for one's manner of acting in spiritual affairs. Earthly riches were contrasted with heavenly treasures. Some points of the instruction seemed a little obscure to me, though to the Jews, on account of their notions, their religion, and the standpoint from which they viewed things, all was quite plain and intelligible. To them all was symbolical.

The field in which lay Joseph's Well was in this neighborhood, and Jesus took occasion from the circumstance just related to refer to a somewhat similar struggle recorded in the Old Testament. Abraham had given far more land to Lot than the latter had demanded. After relating the fact, Jesus asked what had become of Lot's posterity, and whether Abraham had not recovered full propriety. Ought we not to imitate Abraham? Was not the kingdom promised to him, and did he not obtain it? This earthly kingdom, however, was merely a symbol of the Kingdom of God, and Lot's struggle against Abraham was typical of the struggle of man with man. But, like Abraham, man should aim at acquiring the Kingdom of God. Jesus quoted the text of Holy Scripture in which the strife alluded to is recorded, (*Gen.* 13:7 *et seg.*) and continued to talk of it and of the Kingdom before all the harvest laborers.

The unjust husbandman likewise was present with his followers. He listened in silence and at a distance. He had engaged his friends to interrupt Jesus from time to time with all kinds of captious questions. One of them asked Him what would be the end of His preaching, what would come of it all. Jesus answered so evasively that they could make nothing out of His words. They were, however, something to this effect: If His preaching seemed too long to some, to others it was short. He spoke in parables of the harvest, of sowing, of reaping, of separating the tares from the good grain, of the bread and nourishment of eternal life, etc. The good husbandman, the host of Jesus, listened to His teaching with a docile heart. He ceased to accuse his enemy, later on gave over all he possessed into the treasury of the rising Church, and his sons joined the disciples.

There was much talk here of the Herodians. The people complained of their spying into everything. They had recently accused and arrested here at Dothain and also in Capharnaum several adulterers, and taken them to Jerusalem where they were to be judged. The people of Dothain were well pleased that such persons should be removed from among them, but the feeling of being continually watched was very distasteful to them. Jesus spoke of the Herodians with perfect freedom. He told the people to beware of sin, also of hypocrisy and criticizing others. One should confess his own delinquencies before sitting in judgment upon his neighbor. Then Jesus painted the ordinary manner of acting among the Herodians, applying to them the passage from the Prophet Isaias read in the synagogue on the preceding Sabbath, which treats of dumb dogs that do not bark, that do not turn away from evil, and that tear men in secret. He reminded them that those adulterers were delivered over to justice while Herod, the patron of their accusers, lived in the open commission of the same crime, and He gave them signs by which they might recognize the Herodians.

There were in several of the huts nearby some men who had received injuries during their labor. Jesus visited them, cured the poor creatures, and told them to go to the instruction and resume their work. They did so, singing hymns of praise.

Jesus sent some shepherds from Dothain to Machaerus with directions to John's disciples to induce the people to disperse, for their rebellion, He said, might render John's imprisonment more rigorous, or even give occasion for his death.

Herod and his wife were in Machaerus. I saw that Herod caused the Baptist to be summoned to his presence in a grand hall near the prison. There he was seated surrounded by his guard, many officers, Doctors of the Law, and numerous Herodians and Sadducees. John was led through a passage into the hall and placed in the midst of guards before the large, open doors. I saw Herod's wife insolently and scornfully sweeping past John as she entered the hall and took an elevated seat. Her physiognomy was different from that of most Jewish women. Her whole face was sharp and angular, even her head was pointed, and her countenance was in constant motion. She had developed a very beautiful figure, and in her dress she was loud and extreme, also very tightly laced. To every chaste mind she must have been an object of scandal, as she did everything in her power to attract all eyes upon her.

Herod began to interrogate John, commanding him to tell him in plain terms what he thought of Jesus who was making such disturbance in Galilee. Who was He? Was He come to deprive him (Herod) of his authority? He (Herod) had heard indeed that he (John) had formerly announced Jesus, but he had paid little attention to the fact. Now, however, John should disclose to him his candid opinion on the subject, for that Man (Jesus) held wondrous language on the score of a Kingdom, and uttered parables in which He called Himself a King's Son, etc., although He was only the

son of a poor carpenter. Then I heard John in a loud
voice, and as if addressing the multitude, giving testimony to Jesus. He declared that he himself was
only to prepare His ways; that compared with Him,
he was nobody; that never had there been a man, not
even among the Prophets, like unto Jesus, and never
would there be one; that He was the Son of the Father;
that He was the Christ, the King of Kings, the Saviour, the Restorer of the Kingdom; that no power was
superior to His; that He was the Lamb of God who
was to bear the sins of the world, etc. So spoke John
of Jesus, crying in a loud voice, calling himself His
precursor, the preparer of His ways, His most insignificant servant. It was evident that his words were
inspired. His whole bearing was stamped with the
supernatural, so much so that Herod, becoming terrified, stopped his ears. At last he said to John: "Thou
knowest that I wish thee well. But thou dost excite
sedition against me amongst the people by refusing
to acknowledge my marriage. If thou wilt moderate
thy perverse zeal and recognize my union as lawful
before the people, I shall set thee free, and thou canst
go around teaching and baptizing." Thereupon John
again raised up his voice vehemently against Herod,
rebuking his conduct before all the assistants, and
saying to him: "I know thy mind! I know that thou
recognizest the right and tremblest before the judgment! But thou hast sunk thy soul in guilty pleasures, thou liest bound in the snares of debauchery!"
The rage of the wife at these words is simply indescribable, and Herod became so agitated that he
hastily ordered John to be led away. He gave directions for him to be placed in another cell which, having no communication outside, would prevent his being
heard by the people.

Herod was induced to hold that judicial examina-
tion because of his anxiety, excited by the tumult
raised by the aspirants to baptism and the news
brought him by the Herodians of the wonders wrought

by Jesus.

The whole country was discussing the execution in Jerusalem of certain adulterers from Galilee who had been denounced by the Herodians. They dwelt upon the fact that sinners in humble life were brought to justice while the great ones went free; and that the accusers themselves, the Herodians, were adherents of the adulterous Herod who had imprisoned John for reproaching him with his guilt. Herod became dispirited. I saw the execution of the adulterers mentioned above. Their crimes were read to them, and then they were thrust into a dungeon in which was a small pit. They were placed at its edge. They fell upon a knife which cut off their heads. In a vault below waited some jailers to drag away the lifeless trunks. It was some kind of a machine into which the condemned were precipitated. It was in this same place that James the Great was executed at a later period.

On the following day Jesus was again teaching among the harvesters when Andrew, James, and John arrived. Nathanael was at his house in the suburbs of Gennabris. Jesus informed His disciples that He would next go through Samaria to the place of baptism on the Jordan. The well of Dothain, at which Joseph was sold, was not far from the field in which Jesus was then teaching.

The people of the place asked whether or not they did rightly in supporting the poor, crippled laborers that could no longer work. Jesus answered that in acting thus they acquitted themselves of a duty, but they should not pride themselves upon it, otherwise they would lose their reward. Then He entered the huts of the sick, cured many of them, bade them attend the instruction and return to their work. They obeyed, praising God.

Jesus then went to the synagogue in Gennabris for the Sabbath. Gennabris was as large as Munster, and about one hour's distance from the mountain

upon whose heights lay the harvest field in which
Jesus had last taught. It was situated toward the
east on a slope covered with gardens, baths, and pleasure resorts. On the side by which Jesus arrived, it
was defended by deep ditches of standing water. After
half an hour Jesus and the disciples reached the
walls and tower gates of the city precincts, where
were gathered many disciples from the country
around. With about twelve of them, Jesus entered
the city, where numbers of Pharisees, Sadducees, and
especially Herodians had assembled for the Sabbath.
They had undertaken with crafty words to entrap
Jesus in His speech. They said among themselves
that such a project would be more difficult to carry
out in small places, since in such Jesus was more
daring, but among them the thing could be easily
managed. They congratulated themselves beforehand,
quite sure of the success of their plans. The crowd
present, having been intimidated by these enemies
of Jesus, held their peace and made no manifestation upon Jesus' arrival. He entered the city quietly,
and the disciples washed His feet outside the synagogue. The Doctors of the Law and the people were
already assembled inside. They received Him coolly,
though with some hypocritical demonstrations of
respect, and permitted Him to read aloud and interpret the Scriptures. He opened at *Isaias* 54, 55, 56,
from which He read and explained some sentences,
treating of God's establishing His Church, of what
it cost Him to build it, of the obligation of all to
drink of her waters and, though without money, to
go and eat of her bread. Men, said Jesus, sought
earnestly to satisfy their hunger in the synagogue,
but no bread was there to be found. The Word come
forth from the mouth of God—namely, the Messiah—
should accomplish His work. In the kingdom of God,
that is, in the Church, strangers and Gentiles should,
if they had faith, labor and bear fruit; Jesus called
the Gentiles eunuchs because, unlike the Patriarchs,

they had not concurred in the lineage of the Messiah. He applied numerous texts of the Prophet to His Kingdom, to the Church, and to Heaven. He compared the Jewish teachers of His own day to dumb dogs which, instead of keeping guard, think but of fattening themselves, of eating and drinking immoderately. By these words He meant the Herodians and Sadducees who, lurking in secret, attack people without barking, yes, even assault the pastors of the flock. Jesus' words were very sharp and incisive.

Toward the close of His discourse, He read from *Deuteronomy* 11:29, of the blessing upon Garizim and the curse upon Hebal, and of many other things connected with the Commandments and the Promised Land. These different passages Jesus applied to the Kingdom of God.

One of the Herodians stepped up to Him and very respectfully begged Him to say a word upon the number of those that would enter His Kingdom. They thought to entrap Him by this question, because on the one side, all by circumcision had a share in the Kingdom; and on the other, while rejecting many of the Jews, He had spoken even of Gentiles and eunuchs as having a part in it. Jesus did not give them a direct answer. He beat around and at last struck upon a point that made them forget their former question. To another question put to Him, His answer consisted of a series of interrogations: How many of those that had wandered in the desert entered the land of Canaan? Nevertheless, had not all gone through the Jordan? How many really entered into possession of the land? Had they conquered it entirely, or were they not obliged to share it with the Gentiles? Would they not one day be chased out of it? Jesus added, moreover, that no one should enter into His Kingdom excepting by the narrow way and the gate of the Spouse. I understood that by this were signified Mary and the Church. In the Church we are regenerated by Baptism; from

Mary was the Bridegroom born, in order that through
her He might lead us into the Church, and through
the Church to God. He contrasted entrance by the
gate of the Spouse with entrance through a side door.
It was a similitude like unto that of the Good Shepherd and the hireling *(John* 10:1 *et seq.).* He added
that entrance is permitted only by the door. The words
of Jesus on the Cross before He died, when He called
Mary the Mother of John and John the son of Mary,
have a mysterious connection with this regeneration
of man through His death.

Not having succeeded that evening in ensnaring
Jesus, His enemies resolved to postpone further
attempts until the close of the Sabbath. It is indeed
wonderful! When Jesus' enemies were concocting their
schemes, they could boast of how they would catch
Him and pin Him down in His doctrine; but as soon
as He presented Himself before them, they could
bring nothing against Him; they were amazed and
almost persuaded of the truth of His words, though
at the same time full of rage.

Jesus quietly left the synagogue. They conducted
Him to a repast with one of the Pharisees, where,
too, they could neither attack nor surprise Him. He
spoke here a parable of a feast to which the master
of the house had invited the guests at a certain hour,
after which the doors were closed and tardy corners
were not admitted.

The repast over, Jesus went with the disciples to
sleep at the house of another Pharisee, an upright
man and an acquaintance of Andrew. He had honestly defended those disciples, among them Andrew,
who, in consequence of what had happened at the
Pasch, had been brought before the court of justice.
He had lately become a widower. He was still young,
and soon after he joined the disciples. His name was
Dinocus, or Dinotus. His son, twelve-years-old, was
called Josaphat. His house was to the west and outside the city. Jesus had come to Gennabris from the

south. He had descended the cultivated neighboring heights of Dothain, which lay more to the south than Gennabris, and then secretly turned back to the latter city. The Pharisee's house was on the west side, as I have said, while Nathanael's was on the north toward Galilee.

I saw today that Herod, after John's judicial hearing, sent officers to the tumultuous people. They were commissioned to deal very gently with them, to tell them not to be disquieted on John's account, but peaceably to return to their homes. The officers assured them that John was very well and kindly treated. They said, moreover, that Herod had indeed changed his prisoner's cell, but it was only that he might have him nearer to himself. In disobeying the orders given them to disperse quietly, they might cast suspicion upon their master and render his imprisonment more painful. They should therefore go home at once, for he would soon resume his work of baptizing. The messengers from Jesus and John arrived just as Herod's officers were haranguing the crowd, and they too having delivered similar messages, the people scattered by degrees. But Herod was a prey to the greatest anxiety. The execution of the adulterers in Jerusalem had reminded the public of his own adulterous marriage. They murmured loudly over John's imprisonment for having spoken the truth and maintained the Law, according to which those poor criminals had been put to death in Jerusalem. Herod had moreover heard of Jesus' miracles and discourses in Galilee, and it had also reached his ears that He was now coming down to the Jordan to teach. He was in great dread lest the excited populace might thereby be still more stirred up. Under the influence of these feelings, I saw him calling a meeting of the Pharisees and Herodians, to deliberate upon some means of restraining Jesus. The result of the conference was that he sent eight of the members to give Jesus to understand in the most deli-

cate manner possible that He should confine Himself, His miracles, and His teaching to Upper Galilee
and the far side of the lake; that He should not enter
Herod's dominions in Galilee, and still less that part
of the country around the Jordan under his jurisdiction. They were to intimidate Him with the example of John, since Herod might easily feel himself
constrained to make Him share John's captivity. This
commission started for Galilee that same day.

Next morning Jesus again taught in the synagogue
and without much contradiction, for His enemies had
resolved to wait for the afternoon instruction when
they might attack Him all together. He again chose
His texts alternately from *Isaias* and *Deuteronomy*.
Occasion offered to speak of the worthy celebration
of the Sabbath, and He dwelt upon it at length. The
sick of Gennabris had been so intimidated by the
threats of the Herodians that they did not dare to
implore Jesus to help them.

Jesus spoke also in the synagogue of the embassy
sent by Herod to lie in wait to catch Him in His
speech. "When they come," said He, "ye may tell the
foxes to take word back to that other fox not to trouble himself about Me. He may continue his wicked
course and fulfill his designs in John's regard. For
the rest, I shall not be restrained by him. I shall
continue to teach wherever I am sent in every region,
and even in Jerusalem itself when the time comes.
I shall fulfill My mission and account for it to My
Father in Heaven." His enemies were very much
incensed at His words.

In the afternoon Jesus and the disciples left the
house of Dinotus the Pharisee, to take a walk. When
they reached the gate near which was Nathanael's
house, Andrew went in and called him out. He came
and presented to Jesus his cousin, a very young man
to whom he intended to resign his business, in order
to follow Jesus uninterruptedly. I think he attached
himself to Jesus irrevocably at that time.

After their walk, they entered the city at the side upon which the synagogue was situated. About twelve poor day laborers, sick from hard work and privation, having heard of the cure of cases like their own effected by Jesus in the harvest field, had dragged themselves from the country to the city in the hope of receiving a similar favor. They had stationed themselves in a row outside the synagogue, ready to cry to Jesus for help as He passed. Jesus approached, and said to them in passing some words of comfort. To their entreaties to help them, He bade them have patience. Close behind Him followed the Doctors of the Law, who were enraged that these strangers had dared petition Jesus for a cure since up to this time they had succeeded in restraining the sick of the city from a similar proceeding. They roughly repulsed the poor, miserable creatures, telling them under cloak of a good intention that they must not excite trouble and disturbance in the city; that they must take themselves off right away, for Jesus had important questions to treat with themselves; there was now no time for Him to busy Himself with them. And as the poor men could not retire quickly enough to suit their wishes, they had them removed by force.

In the synagogue Jesus taught chiefly of the Sabbath and its sanctification. The Commandment to that effect was contained in the passage from Isaias read on that day. After teaching some time, He pointed to the deep moats around the city near which their asses were grazing, and asked: "If one of those asses should fall into a moat on the Sabbath day, would ye venture to draw it out on the Sabbath day in order to save its life?" They were silent. "Supposing it was a human being that fell in, would ye venture to help him out?" Still they were silent, "Would ye allow salvation of body and soul to be meted out to yourselves on the Sabbath day? Would ye permit a work of mercy to be performed on the Sabbath day?" Again they were silent. Then said Jesus: "Since ye

are silent, I must take it for granted that ye have
nothing to oppose to My doctrine. Where are those
poor men who implored My help outside the synagogue? Bring them hither!" As they whom He
addressed showed no inclination to obey, Jesus said:
"Since ye will not execute My orders, I shall have
recourse to My disciples." At these words, His enemies changed their minds, and sent messengers to
seek for the sick men. Soon the poor creatures made
their appearance, dragging in slowly. It was a piti-
ful sight. There were about twelve of them, some
lame, and some so frightfully swollen with dropsy
that even their puffed-up fingers stood wide apart
from one another. They entered rejoicing and full of
hope, although they had shortly before departed very
sad, on account of the rebuff received from the Doctors of the Law.

Jesus commanded them to stand in a line, and it
was touching to see the less afflicted placing those
worse than themselves in front, that Jesus might
cure them first. Jesus descended a couple of steps
and called the first up to Him. Most of them were
paralyzed in the arms. Jesus silently prayed over
them, His eyes raised to Heaven, and touched their
arms, gently stroking them downward. Then He
moved their hands up and down, and ordered them
to step back and give thanks to God. They were cured.
The dropsical could scarcely walk. Jesus laid His
hand on their head and breast. Their strength
instantly returned, they were able to retire briskly,
and in a few days the water had entirely disappeared.

During this miraculous healing the people began
to press forward in crowds, among them many other
poor, sick creatures who, uniting their voices with
those of the cured, proclaimed aloud the praises of
God. The concourse was so great that the Doctors of
the Law, filled with shame and rage, had to give
place to the people, and some of them even left the
synagogue. Jesus went on instructing the multitude

until the close of the Sabbath. He spoke to them of the nearness of the Kingdom, of penance and conversion. The Scribes with all their opposition and cunning had not another word to say. It was extremely ridiculous to see those men, who had so loudly boasted to one another, not once daring to open their mouths. They could not in even the least thing carry their point against Jesus, they could not answer even His simplest question.

After the Sabbath, a great banquet was spread in one of the public pleasure resorts of the city. It was intended to celebrate the close of the harvest, and Jesus with His disciples was invited. The guests were made up of the most distinguished citizens of the place, also many visitors to the city, and even some rich peasants. At several tables, laden with the products of the harvest, all kinds of fruit and grain and even poultry were eaten. Whatever had yielded an abundant crop was here represented with profusion. The flocks also yielded their share to the entertainment. Some of the animals were roasted ready to be eaten, while others were slaughtered and ready for cooking, as symbols of abundance.

The first places had been assigned to Jesus and His disciples, notwithstanding which, a haughty Pharisee had put himself foremost. When Jesus went to the table, He asked him in a low voice how he had come by the place that he occupied. The Pharisee replied: "I am here because it is the praiseworthy custom of this city for the learned and distinguished to sit first." Jesus responded: "They that strive after the first places upon earth, shall have no place in the Kingdom of My Father." The Pharisee, quite ashamed, resigned the seat for a lower one, though at the same time he tried to make it appear that he did so on an inspiration of his own. During the repast Jesus spoke of some things regarding the Sabbath, especially of that passage of *Isaias* 58:7: "Deal thy bread to the hungry, and bring the needy and the

harborless into thy house," and asked whether it was
not customary at such feasts, feasts of thanksgiving
for a plentiful harvest, to invite the poor as guests
and let them take part. He expressed His surprise
at their having omitted that custom. "Where," He
asked, "are the poor?" "Since," He continued, "ye have
invited Me, have given Me the first place, have made
Me the Master of your feast, it behooves Me to see
about the guests that have a right to be present. Go,
call in those people that I cured, and bring all the
rest of the poor!" But as they were in no hurry to
fulfill Jesus' commands, His disciples hastened out
and collected the poor in all the streets. They soon
came trooping in, and Jesus and the disciples gave
up their seats to them, while the Scribes, one by one,
slipped out of the hall. Jesus, the disciples, and some
right-minded people among the guests served the
poor at table. When their meal was over, they divided
among them all that was left, to the great joy of the
recipients. Then Jesus and His followers returned to
the house of Dinotus the Pharisee on the west side
of the city, and there rested.

The next day crowds of sick from Gennabris itself
and from the country around came to the house at
which Jesus was staying, and He devoted the whole
morning to their cure. They were mostly paralyzed
in their hands and dropsical. The son of the Pharisee Dinotus, at whose house Jesus was stopping,
was about twelve years old, and was named Josaphat. When his father gave up all to follow Jesus,
he accompanied him. The Jewish boys wore a long
tunic gored on both sides, buttoned in front and laced
down to the feet. When more grown, they exchanged
the long tunic for a shorter one like those of their
elders, and bound their limbs in something like pan-
taloons. When the boys' tunic was girded at the waist,
it hung in gathers; but it was usually worn flowing
like a loose shirt, though often it was tucked up a
little. When Jesus took leave of Dinotus, He pressed

him to His Heart, and the man shed many tears.

Jesus with Nathanael, Andrew, James, Saturnin, Aristobulus, Tharzissus, Parmenas, and about four other disciples, went between two to three hours southward through the valleys. They spent the night under an empty shed belonging to the harvesters, on a declivity between two cities. The one on the left was called Ulama; that to the right was, I think, named Japhia. The distance between Ulama and Tarichaea was about the same as between Gennabris and Tiberias. The city to the right was less elevated than Bethulia, and was at a good distance from it, but to one far away, the mountain between them not being visible, Bethulia appeared to rise above and directly behind Japhia. The locality seemed to lie quite near to Jesus' route as He journeyed along, but the road soon made a bend that hid it from sight.

That field in which Jesus instructed the harvesters was the very same in which Joseph met his brethren with their herds, and the long four-cornered well the same into which he was let down.

12. Jesus in Abelmahula

Next morning Jesus left the shed under which He had passed the night, and journeyed with His disciples about five hours to the south. It was almost two o'clock when they reached the little city Abelmahula, where the Prophet Eliseus was born. It lay on one of the heights of Mount Hermon, its towers rising to the summit of the mountain ridge. It was only a couple of hours from Scythopolis, and to the west ran the valley of Jezrael. With the city of Jezrael itself, Abelmahula lay in a straight line. Not far from Abelmahula, and nearer the Jordan, was the town of Bezech. Samaria was several hours to the southwest. Abelmahula was in or upon the confines of Samaria, but inhabited by Jews.

Jesus and His disciples sat down on the resting

place outside the city, as travellers in Palestine were
accustomed to do. Hospitable people from the city
used then to take them to their houses for entertainment. And thus it happened now. Some people
going by recognized Jesus. They had seen Him once
before when He was journeying through these parts
at the feast of Tabernacles. They hurried into the
city and spread the news. Soon out came a well-to-
do peasant with his servants, bringing to Jesus and
the disciples bread and honey and something to drink.
He invited them into his house, and they followed
him. They having arrived there, he washed their feet
and provided them with fresh garments while their
own were being shaken and brushed. Then he ordered a repast straightaway to be prepared, and to
it he invited several Pharisees with whom he was
on good terms. They soon made their appearance.
The host showed himself hospitable and friendly to
a degree, though he was a rascal in disguise. He
wanted to be able to boast before the people of the
city that he had entertained the Prophet in his house,
and to offer to the Pharisees an opportunity to sound
Jesus. They thought they could do that better when
alone with Him at table than in the synagogue before
the people.

But hardly was the table set when all the sick of
the place, all that were able to be moved, appeared
before the house and gathered together in the courtyard—to the great displeasure of the owner, as well
as of the Pharisees. The former hurried out to drive
them away, but Jesus, turning from the table with
the words: "I have other food after which My soul
hungers," followed, His disciples after Him, and began
curing the sick. There were among them several possessed who set up a shout after Jesus. He cured them
with a glance and a word of command. Many others
were lame in one or both hands. Jesus passed His
hand down their arms and raised them up and down.
On the head and breast of the dropsical He laid His

hand. Others were consumptive, others were covered
with small, though not infectious sores. Some He
ordered to bathe. To others He commanded certain
works, and told them that they would be perfectly
well in a few days. Far in the background, and leaning against the wall for support, stood several women
afflicted with an issue of blood. They were veiled
and, in their shame, ventured only now and then to
cast a sidelong glance toward Jesus. When they raised
a fold of their veil for this purpose, the countenance
disclosed bore signs of suffering. At last Jesus
approached them, touched and cured them, and they
cast themselves at His feet.

The whole crowd set up shouts of joy and intoned
hymns of thanksgiving. The Pharisees inside had
closed all the doors and windows of the house. They
sat down to table vexed and disappointed, but jumped
up from time to time to peep through the lattice.
The work of healing went on for so long that, when
they wanted to go home, they were forced to pass
through the courtyard filled with the sick, the cured,
and the exulting crowd. The sight stabbed them to
the very heart. The crowd became at last so great
that Jesus had to take refuge in the house until
they had dispersed.

It was already dusk when five Levites presented
themselves to invite Jesus and the disciples to pass
the night in the schoolhouse over which they presided.
The guests of the pharisaical peasant took leave of
him with thanks for his hospitality. Jesus gave him
a short exhortation before leaving, and made use of
an expression similar to those He had used among
the Herodians, something about foxes. But the man
preserved his friendly exterior. Jesus and the disciples partook of a little luncheon in the schoolhouse.
They slept in a long corridor on which carpets had
been spread, their couches separated from one
another by movable screens. There was a boys' school
in one part of the building, and in another, young

pagan girls desirous of embracing Judaism received thorough instruction. This school was in existence even in Jacob's time. When Jacob was persecuted in diverse ways by Esau, Rebecca sent him secretly to Abelmahula where he owned herds and servant, and dwelt in tents. Rebecca established there a school for the young Canaanite girls and other Gentile maidens. Like Esau, his children, his servants, and others of Isaac's family intermarried with these Gentiles. Rebecca, who held such alliances in abhorrence, had the young girls that desired it instructed in this school in the customs and religion of Abraham. The ground on which the school was built belonged to her.

Jacob long remained hidden at Abelmahula. When Rebecca was questioned as to his whereabouts, she used to answer that he was far away herding flocks for strangers. At times he returned secretly to see her, but on Esau's account she had to keep him hidden. Jacob dug a well near Abelmahula, the same by which Jesus had been seated before entering the city. The people held it in great reverence and always kept it covered. He had also made a cistern in the neighborhood. It was long, four-cornered, and had a flight of steps leading down into it. Later on, Jacob's abode became known. Rebecca noticed that, like Esau, her younger son was likely to espouse a Canaanite wife, so she and Isaac sent him to her native place to his Uncle Laban, where he served for Rachel and Lia.

Rebecca had established the school so far from her own home in the land of Heth because Isaac had so many quarrels with the Philistines, who did all in their power to ruin him. She had confided the direction of the school to a man from her own country, Mesopotamia, and to her nurse who, I think, was his wife. The young girls dwelt in tents and were instructed in all that a wife in a migratory household of the pastoral times ought to know. They

learned the religion of Abraham and the special
duties of wives of his race. They had gardens in
which they planted all kinds of running vines, such
as gourds, melons, cucumbers, and a kind of grain.
They had very large sheep whose milk was used for
food. They were taught also to read, but this as well
as writing came very hard to them. The writing of
those days was done in a very strange way on thick
brown tablets, not on rolls of skin as in later times,
but upon the bark of trees. I saw them peeling it
off, and burning the letters into it. They had a little box full of zigzag compartments, which I saw
shining on the surface, and filled with all kinds of
metal signs. These the writer heated in a flame and
burnt one after another into the bark tablet. I saw
the fire in which they heated the metal. It was the
same as that used for boiling, roasting, and baking,
also for giving light. Upon seeing it used in this last
way, I thought: "They do indeed place their light
here under a bushel." In a vessel, whose form
reminded me of the headdress that many of the
pagan idols wore, there burned a black mass. A hole
was bored in the middle of it, for the passage of air,
perhaps. The little round towers encircling the vessel were hollow, and into them some part of the cooking could be placed. Over the pan of coals, something
like a cover was turned upside down. It was tapering toward the top and pierced by a number of holes.
On this, too, was a circle of little towers in which
things could be warmed. All around this bushel-like
cover were openings with sliding screens. When they
wanted light, all they had to do was to open one of
these little windows and the glare from the flame
shone forth. They always opened them toward the
quarter from which no draught came, a precaution
very necessary in tents. Below the coal pan, was a
little place for ashes in which they could bake flat
cakes, and on top of the whole arrangement water
could be boiled in shallow vessels. This they drew

off for bathing, washing, and cooking. They could also broil and roast on these stoves. They were thin and light, could be carried on journeys, and easily moved from place to place. It was over such stoves that the metal letters were heated before being burnt into the tablets of bark.

The people of Canaan had black hair and were darker than Abraham and his countrymen, who were of a ruddy, olive complexion. The costume of the Canaanite women was different from that of the daughters of Israel. They wore a wide tunic of yellow wool down to the knee. It consisted of four pieces which could be drawn together by a running string below the knee, thus forming a kind of wide pantalet. It was not bound around the upper part of the limbs like that of the Jewish women, but its wide folds fell front and back from the waist to the knee. The upper part of the body was covered with a similarly doubled lappet that fell over the breast and back. The pieces were bound together on the shoulders, forming a sort of wide scapular, likewise open on both sides and fastened around the waist with a belt, above which it hung loose like a sack. The whole costume from shoulder to knee looked like a wide sack bound at the waist and ending abruptly below the latter. The feet were sandaled and the lower limbs wound crosswise with straps, through the openings of which the skin could be seen. The arms were covered with pieces of fine, transparent stuff which, by several shining metal rings, were formed into a sleeve. They wore on the head a pointed cap of little feathers, from the top of which hung something like the crest of a helmet ending in a large tuft. These people were beautiful and well-made, but much more ignorant than the Children of Israel. Some of them had long mantles also, narrow above and wide below. The women of Israel wore over a kind of bandage wrapped around the body a long tunic, and lastly a long gown fastened in front with buttons.

They wound their heads in a veil or with several rows of ruffs, such as are worn nowadays around the neck.

I saw that they studied in Rebecca's time the religion of Abraham: the creation of the world, about Adam and Eve and their entrance into Paradise, Eve's seduction by Satan, and the Fall of the first man and woman by their violation of the abstinence commanded them by God. By the eating of the forbidden fruit arose sinful appetites in man. The young girls were taught also that Satan had promised our first parents a divine illumination and knowledge, but that after sin they were blinded. A film was drawn over their eyes; they lost the gift of vision they had possessed. Now they had to labor in the sweat of their brow, bring forth children in pain, and with difficulty acquire the knowledge of which they had need. They learned, too, that to the woman a son was promised who should crush the serpent's head. They were taught about Abel and Cain and the latter's descendants, who became degenerate and wicked. The sons of God, seduced by the beauty of the daughters of men, formed unions with them from which sprang a mighty, godless race of giants, powerful in enchantment and the art of magic, a race that discovered and taught to others all kinds of pleasure and false wisdom, all that buried the soul in sin and tore it away from God, a race that had so seduced and corrupted men that God resolved to destroy them all with the exception of Noe and his family. This people had fixed their principal abode on a high mountain range up which they ever pressed higher and higher. But in the Deluge that mountain was submerged, and a sea now covers its site. They (the scholars of Rebecca's school) learned also all about the Deluge, about Noe's escape in the ark, about Sem, Cham, and Japhet, about Cham's sin, and the reiterated wickedness of men at the Tower of Babel. They were told of the building of that Tower, of its destruction, of the confusion of tongues, and of the dispersion of men now become enemies to one another. All this recalled to the youthful minds of the scholars the impiety of the giants on that high mountain, those wicked, powerful men, those dealers in witchcraft, and they saw the fatal consequences of unions forbidden by the Law of God. Necromancy and idolatry were practiced likewise at the Tower of Babel.

By such teachings were the converted Gentile maidens warned against alliances with idolaters, idle efforts after necromancy and the hidden arts, against the seductions of the world, sensual delights, vain adornments—in a word, against all that did not lead to God. They were taught to look upon such things as tending to those sins on whose account God had once destroyed mankind. They were, on the other hand, instructed in the fear of God, obedience, subjection, and in the faithful, simple exercise of all duties devolving upon the pastoral life. They were also taught the Commandments that God gave to Noe, for instance, abstinence from uncooked meat. They learned of God's having made choice of the race of Abraham, to make of his descendants His chosen people from whom the Redeemer was to be born. For this purpose He had called Abraham from the land of Ur, and had set him apart from the infidel races. They were told of God's sending *white men* to Abraham, that is, men who appeared white and luminous. These men had confided to Abraham the Mystery of God's Blessing, owing to which his posterity was to be great above all the nations of the earth. The transmitting of that Mystery they referred to only in general terms, as of a Blessing from which Redemption should spring. They were told also about Melchisedech's being a *white man* like those sent to Abraham, of his sacrifice of bread and wine, and of his blessing Abraham. The chastisement inflicted by God upon Sodom and Gomorrha formed a part of the instruction given.

When Jesus visited the school, the young girls were computing a chronological table upon the coming of the Messiah. All agreed in their reckoning, which brought the result down to their own time. Just at that moment, in stepped Jesus and His disciples, a circumstance that produced a very powerful impression upon the scholars. Jesus took up the subject then engrossing their attention, and explained to them with the utmost clearness that the Messiah was already come, though not yet recognized. He spoke of the unknown Messiah, and of the signs that were to herald His coming, and that had already been fulfilled. Of the words: "A virgin shall bring forth a son," Jesus spoke only in veiled terms, since those children were too young to comprehend them. He exhorted them to rejoice that they lived in a time after which the Patriarchs and Prophets had so long sighed. He dwelt upon the persecutions and sufferings the Messiah was to endure, and explained some texts of Prophecy to that effect. He told them to be on the watch for what would take place in Jericho at the approaching feast of Tabernacles. He spoke of miracles, and particularly of the curing of the blind. He made for them also a chronology of the Messiah, spoke of John and of the baptism, asked whether they too wanted to be baptized, and, lastly, related to them the parable of the lost drachma.

The girls sat in school cross-legged, sometimes with one knee raised. Each was provided with a kind of table and bench combined. She leaned sideways against the one, and when writing, supported her roll on the other. They often stood while listening to the instruction given them.

In the house at which Jesus put up there was also a boys' school. It was a kind of orphanage, an institution for the education of children abandoned by their parents. There were some of Jewish parentage who had been rescued from slavery, in which they had grown up without instruction in the religion of their forefathers. Both Pharisees and Sadducees taught in the school. Little girls also were received, the youngest of whom received instruction from the larger ones.

At the moment of Jesus' entrance into this school, the boys were making some calculation connected with Job. As they could not readily do it, Jesus explained it and wrote it down for them in letters. He also explained to them something relating to measure, two hours of distance or time, I do not now know which. He explained much of the Book of Job. Some of the rabbis at this period attacked the truth of the history therein contained, since the Edomites, to which race Herod belonged, bantered and ridiculed the Jews for accepting as true the history of a man of the land of Edom, although in that land no such man was ever known to exist. They looked upon the whole story as a mere fable, gotten up to encourage the Israelites under their afflictions in the desert. Jesus related Job's history to the boys as if it had really happened. He did so in the manner of a Prophet and Catechist, as if He saw all passing before Him, as if it were His own history, as if He heard and saw everything connected with it, or as if Job himself had told it to Him. His hearers knew not what to think. Who was this Man that now addressed them? Was He one of Job's contemporaries? Or was He an angel of God? Or was He God Himself? But the boys did not wonder long about it, for they soon felt that Jesus was a Prophet, and they associated Him with Melchisedech, of whom they had heard and of whose origin man knows not. Jesus spoke likewise of the signification of salt. He made it clear by a parable, and related that of the Prodigal Son. The Pharisees arrived during Jesus' instructions, and were highly displeased to find Him applying to Himself all the signs and Prophecies quoted by Him in reference to the Messiah.

That evening Jesus went with the Levites and the children to take a walk outside the city. The little girls followed last, in the charge of the larger ones. Jesus, letting the boys go on ahead, stood still from time to time until these little ones came up, and then instructed them in examples drawn from nature, from all the objects around them, the trees, fruits, flowers, bees, birds, sun, earth, water, flocks, and field labors. In indescribably beautiful words, He next taught the boys about Jacob and the well that he had dug in that locality. He told them that now the living water was about to be poured upon them, and how perfidious a thing it was to fill up, choke up the well, as the enemies of Abraham and Jacob had done. He applied it to those that wanted to suppress the doctrine and miracles of the Prophets, namely, the Pharisees.

When on the following morning Jesus went to the synagogue, He found there all the Pharisees and Sadducees of the place, as also a great concourse of people. He opened the Scriptures and expounded the Prophets. Some of the Pharisees and Sadducees obstinately disputed with Him, but He put them all to shame. A man whose arms and hands were paralyzed had meantime been slowly making his way to the door of the synagogue. He had been so long trying, and had at last succeeded in getting a position by which Jesus must pass on going out. One of the Pharisees eyed the poor creature with displeasure, and ordered him away. As he refused to obey, they tried to push him out. But he supported himself as well as he could against the door and looked piteously at Jesus, who was on a high seat at a considerable distance from the entrance and separated from him by an immense crowd. Jesus turned toward him and said: "What do you desire of Me?" The man answered: "Master, I implore Thee to cure me. Thou canst do it, if Thou wilt!" Jesus replied: "Thy faith hath saved thee. Stretch forth thy hands above the people," and

in that moment the man was healed at a distance.
He raised up his hands praising God. Then Jesus
said: "Go home, and raise no excitement!" But the
man replied: "Master, how can I be silent on so great
a benefit?" and he went out and told it to all that
he met. And now crowds of sick gathered before the
synagogue, and Jesus cured them as He passed out.
After that He dined with the Pharisees who, in spite
of their inward displeasure, always treated Him courteously. This was part of their policy, that they might
the more easily entrap Him. He performed more cures
that evening.

13. Jesus Goes From Abelmahula To Bezech

Next morning found Jesus still at the school of
Abelmahula. He was quite surrounded by the little
girls who crowded close upon Him, holding on to His
garments and clasping His hand. He was unspeak-
ably kind to them, and exhorted them to obedience
and the fear of God. The larger ones stood back. The
disciples present were somewhat annoyed and uneasy.
They were anxious for their Master to take His departure. According to their Jewish notions, such familiarity with children was not becoming in a Prophet,
and they feared it would injure His reputation.

Jesus did not trouble Himself about their thoughts.
After He had instructed all the children, addressed
some exhortations to the larger ones, and encouraged their teachers in their good resolutions, He
directed one of the disciples to give the little girls a
present, and each in effect received two small coins
fastened together. I think they were two drachmas.
Then Jesus blessed them all in general and left the
place with the disciples, starting eastward toward
the Jordan.

During the journey Jesus taught in a field before
some huts where a crowd of laborers and shepherds

had gathered. About four o'clock that afternoon, they reached the neighborhood of Bezech about two hours east of Abelmahula and near the Jordan. It was like two distinct cities, lying as it did on both sides of a stream that flowed into the Jordan. The country around was hilly and rugged, the houses stood somewhat scattered. Bezech was less a city than two united villages. The inhabitants lived to themselves with very little intercourse with strangers. They were chiefly engaged in husbandry, and they leveled their rugged and hilly farmlands with great labor. They also manufactured agricultural implements for sale, and wove coarse carpets and canvas for tents.

About an hour and a half from this place, the Jordan made a bend toward the west, as if about to flow straight to Mount Olivet. It turned back, however, thus forming a kind of peninsula on its eastern bank, upon which stood a row of houses. In coming from Galilee to Abelmahula, Jesus had to cross a little river. Ennon was on the opposite side of the Jordan, about four hours, perhaps, from Bezech.

Jesus taught in an inn outside the city, the first of those erected for His and the disciples' accommodation that He had met on this journey since leaving Bethania. It was in the charge of a pious, upright man, who went out to meet the travellers, washed their feet and gave them refreshments, after which Jesus entered the city. The superintendents of the school came out into the street to receive Him, and He visited several houses and cured the sick.

There were now thirty disciples with Jesus. Those from Jerusalem and its environs had arrived with Lazarus, and several of John's disciples had come. Some of the latter were just from Machaerus with a message to Jesus from their master, a pressing request to reveal Himself more clearly and to say only that He was the Messiah. Among these messengers of John was the son of the widower Cleophas. I think he was Cleophas of Emmaus, a relative of

Cleophas, the husband of Mary's eldest sister. Another
of these disciples was Judas Barsabas, related to
Zachary of Hebron. His parents, though living now in
Cana, had once dwelt in Nazareth. Among these disciples of John, I still recall others. The sons of Mary
Heli, the eldest sister of the Blessed Virgin, were
John's disciples. They were born so long after their
sister Mary Cleophas that they were scarcely older
than her sons. They clung to the Baptist until he
was beheaded, and then joined the disciples of Jesus.

The married couple who directed the inn at Bezech
were good, devout people. They observed continence
by virtue of a vow, although they were not Essenians. They were distant relatives of the Holy Family.
During His stay here, Jesus had several private interviews with these good people.

All the friends and disciples ate and slept with
Jesus in the newly erected inn. They found ready for
them, thanks to the forethought of Lazarus and the
holy women, table furniture, covers, carpets, beds,
screens, and even sandals and other articles of clothing. Martha had near the desert of Jericho a house
full of women whom she kept busy preparing all
these things. She had gathered together many poor
widows and penniless girls, who were striving to lead
a good life. There they lived and worked together.
All was carried on quietly and unknown to the public. It was no little thing to provide for so many inns
and so many people and to superintend them constantly—above all, to send messengers around to
them, or give them personal attention.

Next morning Jesus delivered a long and magnificent discourse on a hill in the middle of the city,
where the inhabitants had erected for Him a teacher's
chair. The crowd was great, and among them were
about ten Pharisees, who had come from the places
around with the intention of catching Jesus in His
words. His teaching here was mild and full of love,
for the people, who were well disposed, had profited

by John's visit and instructions, and especially by
the baptism which many of them had received. Jesus
exhorted them to remain contented with their humble condition, to be industrious, and to show mercy
to their neighbor. He spoke of the reign of grace, of
the Kingdom, of the Messiah, and more significantly
than ever of Himself. He alluded to John and his
testimony, to his imprisonment and the persecution
directed against him. He spoke likewise of the royal
adulterer for the denunciation of whom John had
been cast into prison, though in Jerusalem certain
men guilty of the same crime, but who had carried
on their evil doings less openly than Herod, had been
condemned and executed. Jesus spoke significantly
and to the point. He gave particular admonitions
to each condition, age, and sex. A Pharisee having
asked whether He was going to take John's place, or
whether He was the one of whom John had spoken,
Jesus answered indirectly and reproached the questioner with his evil intention to entrap Him.

After that Jesus gave a very touching instruction
to the boys and girls. He counseled the boys to bear
with one another. If one should strike a companion
or throw him down, the ill-treated party should bear
it patiently and think not of retaliating. He should
turn away in silence, forgiving his enemy, and his
love should become twice as great as it was before,
yes, for they should show affection even to enemies.
They should not covet the goods of others. If a boy
wanted the pen, the writing materials, the plaything,
the fruit belonging to his neighbor, the latter should
relinquish not only the object coveted, but give him
still more if allowed to do so. They should fully satisfy their neighbor's cupidity if permitted to give the
things away, for only the patient, the loving, and the
generous should have a seat in His Kingdom. This
seat Jesus described to them in childlike terms as a
beautiful throne.

He spoke of earthly goods which a man must give

up in order to attain those of Heaven. Among other admonitions to the girls, He warned them not to seek to excel others, not to envy others for their fine clothes, but to be gentle and obedient, to love their parents and fear God.

At the close of the public instruction, Jesus turned to His disciples, consoled them with more than ordinary tenderness, and exhorted them to bear all things with Him and not to be preoccupied with the cares of this world. He promised that they should be richly rewarded by their Father in Heaven and, with Himself, should possess the Kingdom. He spoke to them of the persecutions that He and they would have to suffer, and said plainly: "If the Pharisees, the Sadducees, or the Herodians should love or praise ye, it would be a sign that ye had wandered from My teachings and were no longer My disciples." He mentioned those sects with significant nicknames. Then He praised the people of the place, particularly for their charitable compassion, for they often took poor orphans from the school at Abelmahula into their service. He congratulated them on the new synagogue they had built by contribution, in which some of the devout souls of Capharnaum also had joined. Then He cured many of their sick, took a repast with all the disciples at the inn, and in the evening when the Sabbath began, went to the synagogue.

Jesus taught in the synagogue from *Isaias* 51:12, "I, I myself will comfort you." He spoke against human respect, telling them that they should not fear the Pharisees and other oppressors, but remember that God had created them and preserved them till the present. He explained the words: "I have put My words in thy mouth," to mean that God had sent the Messiah, that this Messiah was God's Word in the mouth of His people, that this Messiah gave utterance to God's Word, and that they themselves were God's people. Jesus applied all this so clearly to Himself that the Pharisees whispered among themselves that He was palming Himself off for the Messiah. Then He said that Jerusalem should awaken from her intoxication, for the hour of wrath had passed and that of grace had dawned. The unfruitful synagogue had given birth to not one that could lead and raise up the poor people, but now should sinners, hypocrites, and oppressors be chastised and oppressed in their turn. Jerusalem should arise, Sion should awaken! Jesus applied all in a spiritual sense to the pious and holy, to the penitent, to those that through the Jordan—that is, through Baptism—should go into the Promised Land of Canaan, into the Kingdom of His Father. The uncircumcised, the impure, the licentious, the sinful should no longer corrupt the people. He taught of Redemption and of the Name of God, which should now be announced among them. Then from *Deuteronomy* 16, 17, and 18, He spoke of judges and public officers, of prevarication and bribery, and inveighed vehemently against the Pharisees. After that He cured many sick outside the synagogue.

The next day Jesus again taught in the synagogue, taking His texts from *Isaias* 51 and 52, and from *Deuteronomy* 16-21. He spoke of John and the Messiah. He gave signs by which the latter might be recognized, and they were different from those by which He usually designated Him. He said plainly that He Himself was the Messiah, for many of His hearers were already, through the teaching of John, well prepared for the announcement. Jesus based this part of His discourse upon *Isaias* 52:13-15. He said: "The Messiah will gather ye together. He will be full of wisdom, He will be exalted and glorified. Many of ye have shuddered at the thought of Jerusalem's being laid waste and desolate under the rule of the Gentiles, and in like manner will your Redeemer be persecuted and despised by men. He will be a man without repute among other men. And yet He will baptize, will purify the Gentiles. He will

teach kings, who will be silent before Him, and they
to whom He has not been announced will both hear
of Him and see Him." Then Jesus recounted all that
He had done, all the miracles He had wrought since
His baptism, the persecution He had undergone at
Jerusalem and Nazareth, the contempt He had
endured, the spying and scornful laughter of the
Pharisees. He alluded to the miracle at Cana, to the
healing of the blind, the dumb, the deaf, the lame,
and to the raising from the dead of the daughter of
Jairus of Phasael. Pointing in the direction of
Phasael, He said: "It is not very far from here. Go
and ask whether I say the truth!" Then He continued: "Ye have seen and known John. He proclaimed
himself the precursor of the Messiah, the preparer
of His ways! Was John an effeminate man, one given
to the softness and delicacy of high life? Was he not
rather reared in the wilderness? Did he dwell in
palaces? Did he eat of costly dishes? Did he wear
fine clothing? Did he make use of flattering words?
But he called himself the precursor—then did not
the servant wear the livery of his Lord? Would a
king, a rich, a glorious, a powerful king such as ye
expect your Messiah to be, have such a precursor?
And yet ye have the Redeemer in your midst, and
ye will not recognize Him. He is not such as your
pride would have Him, He is not such as ye are
yourselves, therefore ye will not acknowledge Him!"

Jesus then turned to *Deuteronomy* 18:18-19: "I will
raise them up a prophet out of the midst of their
brethren . . ." "And he that will not hear his words,
which he shall speak in my name, I will be the
revenger," and He delivered a powerful discourse upon
these texts. No one dared oppose a word to His teaching. He said: "John lived solitary in the desert. He
mingled not with men, and ye blamed the life he led.
I go from place to place, I teach, I heal, and that too
ye blame! What kind of a Messiah do ye want? Each
one would like to have a Messiah according to his

own ideas! Ye resemble children running in the streets. Each makes for himself the instrument he likes best. One brings forth low, bass notes from the horn he has twisted out of bark, and another screeches high on his flute of reeds." Then Jesus named all kinds of playthings used by children, saying that His hearers were like the owners of those toys. Each wanted to sing upon his own note, each was pleased with his own toy alone.

Toward evening, when Jesus left the synagogue, He found a great crowd of sick waiting for Him outside. Some were lying on litters over which awnings had been stretched. Jesus, followed by His disciples, went from one to the other, curing them. Here and there appeared some poor possessed, raging and crying after Him. He delivered them as He passed, and commanded them to be silent. There were paralytics, consumptives, the deaf, the dumb, and the dropsical with tumors or scrofulous swellings on their neck. Jesus healed all, one after the other, by the imposition of hands, though His manner and touch were different in different cases. Some were entirely cured at once, a little weakness alone remaining; others were greatly relieved, the perfect cure following quickly according to the nature of the malady and the dispositions of the invalid. The cured moved away chanting a Psalm of David. But there were so many sick that Jesus could not go around among them all. The disciples lent their aid in raising, supporting, and disembarrassing them of their wrappings and covers. At last Jesus laid His hands on the head of Andrew, of John, and of Judas Barsabas, took their hands into His own, and commanded them to go and, in His name, do to some of the sick as He had done. They instantly obeyed and cured many.

After that, Jesus and the disciples returned to the inn, where they took a repast at which no stranger was present. Jesus blessed the food. A great part of it was left, and this He sent to the poor heathens encamped outside Bezech and to the other poor. The disciples had instructed the pagans belonging to the caravans.

Immense multitudes had assembled in Bezech from both shores of the Jordan. All that had heard John were now eager to hear Jesus. The heathen caravans, though on their way to Ennon, had come hither to hear Him. Bezech was about three-quarters of an hour from the Jordan, on a swiftly flowing stream which divided the city into two parts.

14. Jesus Leaves Bezech and Goes to Ennon. Mary of Suphan

Jesus still taught and cured in the country around the inn. The neophytes, the pagan caravan, and many others took their way to the Jordan with the intention of crossing. The ferry was an hour and a half to the south of Bezech, below a city called Zarthan, which was one hour's distance from the first named, and lower down on the Jordan. On the opposite side of the river, between Bezech and Zarthan, was a place called Adam. It was near that city of Zarthan that the Jordan had ceased to flow while the children of Israel were crossing. Solomon once had some vases cast here. That industry was still carried on. West of the bend that the Jordan makes in this neighborhood was a mountain extending off to Samaria, and in it was a mine from which was obtained a metal something like that which we call brass. Jesus taught all along the route. When questioned as to whether He intended to teach in Zarthan, He answered: "There are other localities that need it more. John was often there, so ye may ask the people whether he feasted and lived on dainty fare." The Jordan was here crossed by a great ferry, just below which began the detour of the river toward the west. After crossing, Jesus and His followers went on for about two

hours eastward and along the northern bank of a
little stream that flowed into the Jordan somewhere
below the ferry. Then they crossed another stream
near which lay Socoth to their left, looking as if they
had just stepped over it. They rested under tents
between Socoth and Ennon, which places may have
been about four hours apart. If they had again crossed
the river and gone up a little distance, they could
have seen Salem, which was hidden from them by
the hilly bank. It was opposite Ennon, and somewhat below the middle of another bend of the Jordan westward.

Crowds innumerable were collected at Ennon. The
pagans were encamped between the hill upon which
it was built, and the Jordan. There were ten Pharisees present, some from Ennon, some from other
places, among them the son of Simeon of Bethania.
Some of them were reasonable enough and animated
by upright intentions.

The little city of Ennon lay on the north side of
the hill, as if built up entirely of beautiful villas. On
this side and beyond the city was the source of the
basin destined for Baptism, which was on the east
side of the hill. The stream was conducted through
the hill in metal pipes, which could be closed and
opened when needed. There was a springhouse over
the source.

The Pharisees, among them the son of Simon the
Leper, came out to this place to meet Jesus and the
disciples. They welcomed them cordially and politely,
led them into a tent, washed their feet, brushed their
garments, and presented them refreshments of honey,
bread, and wine. Jesus congratulated them on the
good dispositions of many among them though, as
He said, it grieved Him that they belonged to that
sect. He accompanied them to the city where He soon
came to a court in which a crowd of sick of all kinds,
some natives of the city, some strangers, were awaiting His arrival. Some were lying under tents, others

were in the halls that opened into the court. Many
could walk, and Jesus helped them one after another
with imposition of hands and words of admonition.
The disciples assisted in bringing the sick forward,
in raising them and freeing them from their covers,
etc. The Pharisees and many others were present.
Several women stood at a distance, pale and enveloped
in their mantles. They were afflicted with an issue
of blood. When Jesus had finished with the rest, He
approached them, laid His hands upon them, and
cured them. Among the sick were paralytics and dropsical; consumptives, some with abscesses on their
necks and other parts of the body (though not such
as to render them unclean); the deaf and the dumb;
in a word, sufferers of all kinds.

At the extremity of this court was a large portico
opening into the city. I saw in it many spectators,
Pharisees and women. To the Pharisees of Ennon,
since there were upright souls among them and also
because they had received Him frankly and respectfully, Jesus showed a certain indulgence that He had
not exhibited in other places. He wished thereby to
make void the reproach that He associated only with
publicans, sinners, and vagrants. He wanted to show
them that He would pay them due honor if they
demeaned themselves properly and with upright
intentions. They showed great activity in preserving
order among the people on this occasion, and Jesus
allowed them to do it.

While Jesus was busy curing the sick, a beautiful
woman of middle age and in the garb of a stranger
entered the large portico by the gate leading from
the city. Her head and hair were wound in a thin
veil woven with pearls. She wore a bodice in shape
somewhat like a heart, and open at the sides, something like a scapular thrown over the head and fastened together around the body by straps reaching
from the back. Around the neck and breast it was
ornamented with cords and pearls. From it fell, in

folds to the ankle, two deep skirts, one shorter than the other. Both were of fine white wool embroidered with large, colored flowers. The sleeves were wide and fastened with armlets. To the shoulder straps that connected the front and back of the bodice was attached the upper part of a short mantle that fell over the arms. Over this flowed a long veil, of the whiteness of wool.

The woman, ashamed and anxious, entered slowly and timidly, her pale countenance bespeaking confusion and her eyes red from weeping. She wanted to approach Jesus, but the crowd was so great that she could not get near Him. The Pharisees keeping order went to her, and she at once addressed them: "Lead me to the Prophet, that He may forgive my sins and cure me!" The Pharisees stopped her with the words: "Woman, go home! What do you want here? The Prophet will not speak to you. How can He forgive you your sins? He will not busy Himself with you, for you are an adulteress." When the woman heard these words, she grew pale, her countenance assumed a frightful expression, she threw herself on the ground, rent her mantle from top to bottom, snatched her veil from her head and cried: "Ah, then I am lost! Now they lay hold of me! They are tearing me to pieces! See, there they are!" and she named five devils who were raging against her, one of her husband, the other four of her paramours. It was a fearful spectacle. Some of the women standing around raised her from the ground, and bore her wailing to her home. Jesus knew well what was going on, but He would not put the Pharisees of this place to shame. He did not interfere, but quietly continued His work of healing, for her hour had not yet come.

Soon after, accompanied by the disciples and Pharisees, and followed by the people, Jesus went through the city to the hill upon which John had formerly taught. It was in the center of moss-covered ram-

parts and there were some buildings around. On the
side by which they approached was a half-ruined
castle, in one of whose towers Herod took up his
abode during John's teaching. The whole hill was
already covered with the expectant crowd. Jesus
mounted to the place where John had taught. It was
covered with a large awning open on all sides. Here
He delivered a long discourse in which He spoke of
the mercy of God to men, particularly to His own
people. He ran through the entire Scriptures, showed
God's guidance of His chosen nation, His promises
to them, and proved that they were all being realized in the present. Jesus did not, however, say so
openly at Ennon as He had done at Bezech that He
was Himself the Messiah. He spoke also of John,
his imprisonment and his mission. One crowd of listeners was at intervals supplanted by another, that
all might hear His words. Jesus questioned some of
them as to why they wanted to receive Baptism,
why they had put it off till the present, and what
they thought the ceremony to be. He divided them
into classes, some of which were to be baptized at
once, and others only after further instruction. I
remember the answer of one group of neophytes to
the question why they had delayed till now. One of
the number said: "Because John constantly taught
that a Man was to come who would be greater than
himself. We waited consequently in order to receive
still greater grace." At these words, all that approved
the response raised their hands. They formed a special class to receive more particular instructions as
preparation for Baptism.

The discourse ended at about three o'clock in the
afternoon. Then Jesus and the disciples went with
the Pharisees down the hill and into the city, where
a great entertainment had been prepared for Him
in one of the public halls. But when He drew near
the hall, He stopped short, saying: "I have another
kind of hunger," and He asked (though He already

knew) where that woman lived whom they had sent
away from Him in the morning. They pointed out the
house. It was near the hall of entertainment. Jesus
left His companions standing where they were, while
He went forward and entered the house through the
courtyard.

As Jesus approached, I saw the fearful torture and
affliction of the woman inside. The devil, who had
possession of her, drove her from one corner to
another. She was like a timorous animal that would
hide itself. As Jesus was traversing the court and
drawing near to where she was, she fled through a
corridor and into a cellar in the side of the hill upon
which her house was built. In it was a vessel like a
great cask, narrow above and wide below. She wanted
to hide herself in it, but when she tried to do so, it
burst with a loud crash. It was an immense earthen
vessel. Jesus meantime halted and cried: "Mary of
Suphan, wife of . . ." (here He pronounced her husband's name, which I have forgotten) "I command
thee in the Name of God to come to Me!" Then the
woman, enveloped from head to foot, as if the demon
forced her still to hide in her mantle, came creeping
to Jesus' feet on all fours, like a dog awaiting the
whip. But Jesus said to her: "Stand up!" She obeyed,
but drew her veil tightly over her face and around
her neck as if she wanted to strangle herself. Then
said the Lord to her: "Uncover thy face!" and she
unwound her veil, but lowering her eyes and avert-
ing them from Jesus as if forced to do so by an interior power. Jesus, approaching His head to hers, said:
"Look at Me!" and she obeyed. He breathed upon
her, a black vapor went out of her on all sides, and
she fell unconscious before Him. Her servant maids,
alarmed by the loud bursting of the cask, had hurried thither and were standing nearby. Jesus directed
them to take their mistress upstairs and lay her on
a bed. He soon followed with two of the disciples
that had accompanied Him, and found her weeping

bitter tears. He went to her, laid His hand on her head, and said: "Thy sins are forgiven thee!" She wept vehemently and sat up. And now her three children entered the room, a boy about twelve years old, and two little girls of about nine and seven. The girls wore little short-sleeved tunics embroidered in yellow. Jesus stepped forward to meet the children, spoke to them kindly, asked them some questions, and gave them some instruction. Their mother said: "Thank the Prophet! He has cured me!" whereupon the little ones fell on the ground at Jesus' feet. He blessed them, led them one by one to their mother, in order of age, and put their little hands into hers. It seemed to me that, by this action, Jesus removed from the children the disgrace, and thus legitimatized them, for they were the fruits of adulterous unions. Jesus still consoled the woman, telling her that she would be reconciled with her husband, and counseling her thenceforth to live righteously in contrition and penance. After that He went with the disciples to the entertainment of the Pharisees.

This woman was from Suphan in the land of Moab. She was a descendant of Orpha, the widow of Chelion, and daughter-in-law of Noemi, who upon the latter's advice did not go with her to Bethlehem, though Ruth, the widow of Orpha's other son Mahalon, accompanied Noemi thither. Orpha, the widow of Chelion, who was the son of Elimelech of Bethlehem, married again in Moab, and from that union sprang the family of Mary the Suphanite. She was a Jewess and rich, but an adulteress. The three children that she had with her at the time of her conversion were illegitimate. Her legitimate children had been retained by their father when he repudiated his unfaithful wife, their mother. She was living at this time in a house of her own at Ennon. For a long time she had conceived sentiments of sorrow for her disorders and had done penance, her conduct being so reserved and proper that she had

won the esteem of even the most respectable women
of Ennon. The Baptist's preaching against Herod's
unlawful connection had strongly affected her. She
was often possessed by five devils. They had again
seized upon her when, as a last resource, she had
gone to the court where Jesus was curing the sick.
The rebuff of the Pharisees and their words, which
in her deep dejection she had taken as true, had
driven her to the brink of despair. Through her
descent from Orpha, Ruth's sister-in-law, she was
connected with the House of David, the ancestral
line of Jesus. It was shown me how this stream,
deviating in her from its course and troubled by her
abominable sins, was purified anew in her by the
grace of Jesus and flowed once more in its direct
course toward the Church.

Jesus went into the entertainment hall in which
were the Pharisees and the rest of the disciples, and
took His place with them at table. The Pharisees
were somewhat displeased that Jesus had left them
and gone to seek the woman whom they had so
harshly repulsed that morning before so many people. But they said nothing, fearing to receive a reproof
themselves. Jesus treated them with much consideration during the meal, and taught in numerous
similitudes and parables. Toward the middle of the
entertainment, the three children of the Suphanite
entered in their holiday dresses. One of the little
girls bore an urn full of odoriferous water, the other
had a similar one of nard, and the boy carried a
vessel. They entered the hall by the door opposite
the unoccupied side of the table, cast themselves
down before Jesus, and set their presents on the
table in front of Him. Mary herself followed with
her maids, but she dared not approach. She was
veiled, and carried a shining crystal vase with colored veins like marble in which, surrounded by
upright sprays of delicate green foliage, were various kinds of costly aromatics. Her children had

offered similar vases, but smaller. The Pharisees cast
forbidding glances upon the mother and children.
But Jesus said: "Draw near, Mary!" and she stepped
humbly behind Him, while her children, to whom
she had handed it, deposited her offering beside the
others on the table. Jesus thanked her. The Pharisees murmured as later on they did at Magdalen's
present to Jesus. They thought it a great waste,
quite opposed to economy and compassion for the
needy; however, they only wanted something to bring
against the poor woman. Jesus spoke to her very
kindly, as also to the children, to whom He presented
some fruit which they took away with them. The
Suphanite remained veiled and standing humbly
behind Jesus. He said to the Pharisees: "All gifts
come from God. For precious gifts, gratitude gives
in return what it has the most precious, and that
is no waste. The people that gather and prepare
these spices must live." Then He directed one of the
disciples to give the value of them to the poor, spoke
some words upon the woman's conversion and repentance, restored her to the good opinion of all, and
called upon the inhabitants of the city to treat her
affectionately. Mary spoke not a word, but wept quietly under her veil the whole time. At last she cast
herself in silence at Jesus' feet, rose, and left the
dining hall.

Jesus took this occasion to give some instruction
against adultery. Which among them, He asked, felt
himself free from spiritual adultery. He remarked
that John had not been able to convert Herod, but
that this poor woman had of her own accord turned
away from her evil life, and then He related the parable of the sheep lost and found. He had already consoled the woman in her own house, assuring her that
her children would turn out well, and holding out to
her the hope that she should one day join the women
under Martha's supervision and work for the benefit of the inns. I saw the disciples after the entertain-

ment giving abundantly of what was left to the poor. Jesus then went down to the west side of the hill of Ennon where the camp of the heathens lay at some distance. There was also, I think, a tent inn on this side. There Jesus instructed the heathens. Ennon was in the dominion of Herod, but it belonged, like a property across the boundary, to the Tetrarch Philip. Many soldiers of Herod were again there trying to find out news for their master.

15. Jesus in Ramoth-Galaad

From Ennon Jesus went with twelve disciples to the Jabok and the neighboring places. Andrew, James, John, and some other disciples remained at Ennon, in order to baptize at the pool of Baptism east of the hill. The water ran from the hill into the baptismal basin, formed a little lake behind it, watered some meadows as a little brook, and then fell into a reservoir on the north of Ennon from which it could be turned at pleasure into the Jordan.

I saw Jesus with the disciples teaching in a city about one hour east of Socoth and on the south side of the Jabok. Among the numerous sick that He healed was a man who since his birth had one eye closed, Jesus moistened it with His saliva. The eye opened, and the man enjoyed perfect sight.

Jesus crossed the Jabok, which flows through a valley, and turned to the east until He came into the vicinity of Mahanaim, a nice, clean city in two sections. He sat down by the well outside, and soon out came the Elders of the synagogues and the chief men of the city with goblets, food, and drink. They bade Jesus welcome, washed His and the disciples' feet, poured ointment on Jesus' head, gave Him and the disciples a little luncheon, and conducted Him with great love and simplicity into the city. Jesus delivered a short discourse upon the Patriarch Jacob and of all that had happened to him in those parts.

Most of these people had been baptized by John. A patriarchal simplicity reigned in all the cities around this region, and many of the ancient customs were still observed. Jesus did not tarry long here, only time enough to receive the honors paid Him on His route.

From Mahanaim He went along the northern bank of the Jabok for about an hour eastward to the place where Jacob and Esau met. The valley here sinks deep. During the whole way Jesus taught His disciples. After some time they recrossed to the southern bank not far from where two little streams united to form the Jabok. Then they continued their journey for about a mile to the east with the desert of Ephraim on their right.

After traversing the valley they found, upon a mountainridge to the east of the forest of Ephraim, Ramoth-Galaad, a beautiful city, clean and regularly built. In it the heathens had their own quarter and temple. The sacred services were celebrated by Levites. One of the disciples went on ahead to announce Jesus' approach. The Levites and others of distinction were already awaiting Him in a tent near the well outside the city. They washed the newcomers' feet, gave them the usual refreshments as a pledge of hospitality, and conducted them into the city. There they found a crowd of poor sick gathered on an open square to implore Jesus' help. He cured many of them. That evening He taught in the synagogue, for it was the beginning of the Sabbath that commemorated the sacrifice of Jephte's daughter, which in this city was celebrated as a mourning and national festival. There were crowds of young maidens and other people from the country around.

Jesus and the disciples took a repast with the Levites and stayed overnight in a house near the synagogue. There were in these parts no special inns prepared for Jesus. In Ennon, Kamon, and Mahanaim they were hired in advance, and the number of guests limited. Ramoth was built in terraces on a hill behind which, in a little vale flanked by a steep, rocky wall, was the quarter of the city inhabited by the pagans. They had a temple. One could always recognize their abodes by the figures erected on the roofs. On the roof of this temple was a whole group. The central figure wore a crown and stood in a reservoir or fountain, holding a basin in its hand. Around it were several figures of children dipping up the water and pouring it from one to another until at last it fell into the basin held by the middle finger.

The cities in this region were more beautiful, more neatly built than the old Jewish ones. The streets were laid off in the form of a star, all verging to a central point, and the extremities were rounded, thus making the circumference assume something of a zigzag form, as did also the city walls. Ramoth-Galaad was formerly a city of refuge for criminals. (*Deut.* 4:43, *Jos.* 20:8). There was a large solitary building in which they were lodged, but at the time of Jesus' visit it had fallen to ruin and appeared to be no longer used. They made tapestry here, embroidered with figures of all kinds of animals and flowers, partly for trade, and partly for the use of the temple. I saw numbers of women and young maidens working at it in long tents. The costume of the people resembled more the patriarchal style, and they were very clean. Their clothing was of fine wool.

Jesus assisted at a solemn memorial feast of the sacrifice of Jephte's daughter. He went with His disciples and the Levites to a beautiful open square outside the city to the east where preparations for the festival had been made. The inhabitants of Ramoth-Galaad were already assembled and ranged in large circles. Here were still the hill and the altar upon which Jephte's daughter was immolated. In front of it was a semicircle of grassy seats for the maidens, and nearby were seats for the Levites and magistrates of the city. All went in a long and orderly procession to their places. The young girls of Ramoth and many from the neighboring cities assisted at the feast in robes of mourning. One young girl, clothed in white and veiled, personated Jephte's daughter herself. A troop of others clad in somber robes, their faces veiled to the chin and wearing black, fringed sashes on the forearm, represented her lamenting companions. Tiny girls scattering flowers and playing on little flutes mournfully headed the procession in which three lambs were led. The ceremonies were long and of the most touching nature. They comprehended different parts, chanting, religious instructions, and representations of the sad drama, while Psalms and songs commemorative of it were sung. The maiden that personated Jephte's daughter was comforted and lamented in chorus by her companions, though she herself was sighing only after death. Among the Levites also in some of the choirs of singers, there seemed to be held a conference upon the heroine's fate; but she presented herself before them and in earnest words begged to be allowed to accomplish the vow. They made use of different rolls of writing in the different scenes, some parts being recited from memory, others read from the rolls.

Jesus took an active part in the celebration. He personated the supreme Judge, or High Priest, and besides the speeches assigned His role, He delivered instructions before and during the ceremonies. Three lambs were sacrificed in memory of Jephte's daughter, their blood sprinkled around the altar, and the roasted flesh given to the poor. Jesus gave the young maidens some words of instruction on the danger of yielding to vanity. I understood from it that Jephtias would have been liberated had she not been so vain.

The feast lasted until afternoon. During the whole celebration, the maidens successively replaced one another in personating Jephtias. As soon as one fin-

ished her part, the next in order rose from the stone
seat upon which she had been sitting in the midst
of the circle, retired with her into a tent nearby, and
assumed the costume of the victim, that worn by her
at the moment of immolation.

The tomb of the young heroine was on a neighboring hill, and on it the lambs were sacrificed. It
was a four-cornered sarcophagus opening on top.
When the fat of the lambs and the other portions to
be sacrificed were almost consumed, what was left
of the victims was introduced slantingly into the opening, that with the ashes it might fall into the tomb.
When the lambs were slaughtered, I saw the blood
sprinkled around the altar, and the maidens putting,
with a little rod, a drop of it on the end of the long,
narrow veil hanging over their shoulder. Jesus said:
"Jephtias! Thou shouldst have thanked God in the
retirement of thine own home for the victory He had
granted thy people. But becoming vain and seeking
praise as a hero's daughter, thou didst with frivo-
lous ornaments and festive sounds go forth boasting
before the other daughters of the land."

When the festive ceremonies were ended, all retired
to a pleasure garden nearby where arbors and tents
had been erected and an entertainment prepared.
Jesus took part in it. He placed Himself at the table
at which the poor were fed, and related a parable.
The maidens ate in the same tent, but separated
from the others by a screen about three feet high.
Lying at table, one could not see over it, though to
one standing, it did not obstruct the view. After the
meal Jesus with the Levites, the disciples, and many
others returned to the city, where numbers of sick
were patiently awaiting His coming. He cured them,
as well as some lunatics and others afflicted with
melancholy. He taught in the synagogue, taking for
His subject Jacob and Joseph and the selling of the
latter to the Egyptians. He said: "One day another
also shall be sold by one of His brethren. But He

will pardon His penitent brethren and in the time
of famine feed them with the Bread of Eternal Life."
On that same evening, some of the pagans outside
the city accosted the disciples very humbly, asking
them whether they too might hope to share in the
great Prophet's teachings. The disciples informed
Jesus of their desire, and He promised to go to them
in the morning.

Jephte was the natural son of an idolatrous mother.
Driven by his father's legitimate children from
Ramoth, called also Maspha, he lived in the neighboring land of Tob. He joined some military adven-
turers and led a life of brigandage. His pagan wife
died young, leaving him an only daughter, who was
beautiful and extraordinarily talented, but rather
given to vanity. Jephte was an exceedingly rash,
absolute, and determined man, eager for victory, and
strongly wedded to his own word. He was more like
a pagan hero than a Jew. He was an instrument in
the hand of God. Fired with desire to conquer and
rule the land from which he had been expelled, he
made that solemn vow to offer to the Lord as a holocaust the first one that should come out of his own
house on his victorious return. He dreamed not that
it would be his only daughter; as for the rest of his
family, he had no love for them.

Jephte's vow was not pleasing to God; nevertheless He permitted it, decreeing that its fulfillment
should be a chastisement upon both father and
daughter and cut off the posterity of the former from
Israel. His daughter would perhaps have been perverted by the success and elevation of her father;
but as it was, she did penance during two months
and died for God. It is probable that she also influenced her father to a better way of thinking and
made him more faithful to God. The daughter went
out followed by a long train of maidens with songs
and flutes and timbals to meet her father. It was at
a whole hour's distance from the city that she met

him, still she was the first whom he saw belonging
to his own family. When she discovered her misfortune, she entered into herself and asked for a reprieve
of two months, that she might retire into solitude to
prepare by penance for her sacrifice, and to mourn
with her companions over her virginal death, which
would deprive her father of posterity in Israel. With
several of her young companions she went into the
mountains opposite the valley of Ramoth, where for
two months she dwelt under a tent in prayer, fasting, and sackcloth. The maidens of Ramoth took turns
in staying with her. She mourned especially her vanity and thirst for glory. The rulers held council as to
whether she could be freed from death, but it was
not possible since her father had sworn a solemn
oath. It was consequently a vow that could in nowise
be commuted. I saw too that the daughter herself
desired its fulfillment, and petitioned for it in words
both wise and touching.

Her sacrifice was accompanied by every mark of
grief, her companions chanting songs of mourning
around her. She was seated on the same spot upon
which the memorial feast was celebrated. Here again
a council was held for the purpose of delivering her
from death, but stepping forward, she expressed her
wish to die, just as I had seen at the feast. She was
clothed in a long, white garment that closely
enveloped her from the breast to the feet; but from
her head to her breast she wore a transparent, white
veil through which could be seen her face, neck, and
shoulders. She walked courageously to the altar. Her
father hurried from the scene without bidding her
adieu. Then she drank something red from a vessel
presented her. I think it was something to render
her unconscious. One of Jephte's warriors was deputed
to give the deathblow. His eyes were bandaged as a
sign that he did not incur the guilt of murder, since
he would not see the blow that was to kill the victim. She was then laid on his left arm, and he pierced

her throat with a short, sharp weapon. She had no
sooner drunk the red liquid than it produced its effect,
for she was perfectly unconscious when laid on the
warrior's arm. Two of her young companions, who
also were in white and appeared to act as bridemaids, caught the blood in a dish and poured it on
the altar. She was afterward enveloped by her companions in a winding sheet and laid at full length
on the altar, the upper surface of which was grated.
A fire was kindled below and, when her garments
were burned and the whole looked like a blackened
mass, some men raised the grate with the corpse
upon it. They rested the grate upon the edge of an
open tomb nearby, and then gently raising the grate,
let the body slide down into it. The tomb was then
closed. It was still to be seen even in Jesus' time.

The companions of Jephtias and many of the assistants steeped their veils and handkerchiefs in her
blood, while others gathered up the ashes of the holocaust. Before Jephtias made her appearance in her
sacrificial habiliments, her young companions had
retired with her into a tent where she bathed and
was prepared for the ceremony.

It was to the north of Ramoth, over two hours' distance in the mountains that Jephtias and her companions met her father. They were mounted upon
little asses adorned with ribands and hung with tinkling bells. One rode in front of Jephtias, one on
either side, and the rest followed with songs and
music. They sang the canticle of Moses upon the
defeat of the Egyptians. As soon as Jephte descried
his daughter, he rent his garments and became in-
consolable. Jephtias herself did not give way to grief,
but learned with calmness the fate that awaited her.

When she and her companions left her father's
house for the wilderness, taking with them such food
only as was allowed for a fast, Jephte spoke to his
daughter for the last time. This was in a certain
manner the beginning of the sacrifice. At the moment

of parting, he laid his hand, as was customary in offering sacrifice, upon his daughter's head with the simple words: "Go forth! Thou wilt never have a spouse!"—to which she responded: "No, I shall never have a spouse!"—and he never again spoke to her. After his daughter's death, Jephte had a beautiful monument erected in Ramoth and a little temple built over it. He ordered a memorial festival to be annually celebrated on the anniversary of his daughter's immolation as a remembrance of his sad vow and a warning to others against such rashness. (*Judges* 11:39-40).

Jephte's mother was a pagan who had been converted to Judaism. His wife was the daughter of a man born from the illicit union of a Jew with an idolatress. On his expulsion from his native place, his daughter did not accompany him. She remained in Ramoth where, meanwhile, her mother died. When, in time of danger, Jephte was recalled to Tob by his compatriots, he did not return into the city of his birth. He assembled the people and concerted measures with them in the camp outside of Maspha. His own home and his only daughter he did not see. When he made that vow, he never thought of her, but of his other relatives who had repudiated him, and therefore God punished him.

The feast lasted four days. Jesus with His disciples visited also the pagan quarters in Ramoth. The people met Him with marks of reverence at the head of their street. Not far from their temple was an open-air space used for public discourses. Several of the sick and aged had been brought thither, the former of whom Jesus healed. They that had solicited a visit from Him appeared to be learned men, priests, and philosophers. They knew about the journey of the Three Kings, and of their having seen the birth of the King of the Jews in the stars, for they, too, had a similar expectation and were likewise engaged in the observation of the stars. Not far from here was a kind of observatory similar to that in the land of the holy Three Kings, and from it they gazed at the stars. They had long sighed for instruction, and now they received it from Jesus Himself. He spoke to them of very profound mysteries, even of the Most Holy Trinity. I heard these words that especially astonished me: *"There are three that give testimony: the water, the spirit, and the blood, and these three are one."* He spoke of the Fall of man, of the promised Redeemer, of the guidance of mankind, of the Deluge, of the passage through the Red Sea and the Jordan, and of Baptism. He told them that the Jews had not obtained entire possession of the Promised Land, that many heathens still dwelt therein, but that He was now come to take possession of all that remained and unite it to His Kingdom—not, however, by the sword, but by charity and grace. His words made so deep an impression upon many of His hearers that He sent them to Ennon to be baptized. Seven aged men that could no longer travel, Jesus allowed to be baptized at once by two of the disciples. A basin was brought and placed before them while they stood up to the knees in the water in a bathing cistern near at hand. Above the basin was placed a railing upon which they could lean. Two of the disciples laid their hands on the neophyte's shoulders while Mathias, a disciple of John, poured on their heads, one after another, water from a shell at the end of which was a handle. Jesus dictated to the disciples the form of words they should use. The old men were clothed in beautiful white garments, all very neat and clean.

Then Jesus gave an instruction to the people in general, taking for His subject chastity and marriage. To the women He spoke especially of obedience, of humility, and the education of their children. These people were well-disposed. They conducted Jesus most affectionately back to the Jewish quarter, where He went to the synagogue and healed the

sick that He found before it. The Levites were not
well pleased at Jesus' having visited the heathens.
In the synagogue, where Jephte's festival was still
being celebrated, Jesus taught of the call of the Gentiles. He said that many of them would rank higher
in His Kingdom than the children of Israel, and that
He was come to unite with the rightful possessors
of the Promised Land, by grace, instruction, and Baptism, the idolaters whom the Israelites had not
expelled. He spoke also of Jephte's victory and vow.

While Jesus was preaching in the synagogue, the
maidens were celebrating their feast at the monument that Jephte had erected to his daughter. It had
been rebuilt, and every year at the recurrence of the
festival was beautified by the contributions of the
young girls. It stood in a round temple with an opening in the roof. In the center of this temple was a
smaller one of the same form. It consisted of a kind
of cupola supported by columns, in one of which was
concealed a staircase leading up to it. Around the
cupola wound a spiral walk upon which was a rep-
resentation of the triumphal procession of Jephtias,
the figures being the height of a child. This piece of
workmanship was of light material, but shining like
polished metal. The base supporting it was of open
work, through which the figures appeared to be gazing down into the little temple. The top of the cupola
was crowned by a circular, metal platform from which
a kind of ladder, consisting of a pole with projecting
rods on either side, led up to the roof of the exterior
temple. From this roof the view over the city and
surrounding country was very extended. The platform at the top of the ladder was wide enough to
allow two girls holding on to the pole to make a turn
around it hand in hand. A pedestal in the center of
the smaller temple supported a white marble figure
of Jephte's daughter seated on a chair of the same
material, just as she appeared before her immolation. Her head reached to the first coil of the spiral-

shaped cupola. Around the base of the statue, there
was space enough for three men to walk abreast.

The columns surrounding the little temple were
connected together by beautiful grates. The exterior
was of stone veined in different colors. The coils of
the cupola varied in degrees of whiteness from bottom to top, the upper ones of the purest white.

In the temple around this monument, the young
girls now celebrated Jephtias' feast. The maiden's
statue held a handkerchief to the eyes with one
hand as if shedding tears, while the other hanging
listlessly at her side held a flower or broken branch.
The young girls' celebration was conducted with
order. Sometimes they stretched curtains from the
outer circle of the temple to the interior of the monument and took their places in little groups apart
to pray and sigh and mourn in silence, their eyes
fixed on the statue. Sometimes they sang together
in chorus, sometimes in alternate choirs. Again, they
passed two by two before the statue, strewing flowers, adorning it with wreaths and, as if to console
Jephtias, chanting hymns on the shortness of life.
I remember the expressions: "Today for me! Tomorrow for thee!" Then they sang the praises of Jephtias' fortitude and resignation, lauding her highly
as the price of their victory. Then they mounted in
groups by the serpentine walk up to the top of the
cupola where they sang triumphal songs. Some went
up to the roof of the exterior temple, looked out over
the country as if to catch a glimpse of the conquer-
ing hero, and pronounced the fearful vow. The procession then returned lamenting to the monument,
mourned over the young virgin, and consoled her on
the privation of the privileges of maternity. The exercises were interspersed with canticles of thanksgiving to God and reflections upon His justice, the
various scenes being accompanied by very touching
pantomimes, expressive by turns of joy, grief, and
devotion. A grand entertainment was prepared for

the young girls in the temple. I saw them not reclining at one table, but sitting in tiers of three, one above another, all around the temple, with little round tables at their side. They sat cross-legged. They had all kinds of wonderful dishes and viands made up into figures—for instance, that of a lamb lying on its back and filled with fruit and other eatables.

16. Jesus Leaves Ramoth and Goes to Arga, Azo, and Ephron

After assisting at an entertainment given Him by the Levites, Jesus with seven disciples and some people belonging to Ramoth went northward and crossed the Jabok. After climbing the mountains westward for about three hours, they arrived at the ancient kingdom of Basan and reached a city with two very steep mountains on one side and a long one on the other. It was called Arga and belonged to the district Argob, in the half-tribe Manasses. An hour and a half or two hours eastward from Arga, near the source of the brook Og, was situated a great city named Gerasa. To the southeast of this and on an elevated site one could see Jabesch-Galaad. The country around was stony. At a distance one might think there were no trees in these parts, but many sections were covered with low, green bushes. The kingdom of Basan commenced here, and Arga was its first city. The family of the half-tribe of Manasses extended a little farther to the south. About an hour northward of the Jabok, I saw a boundary marked off by stakes.

Jesus stayed overnight with His companions about half an hour from the city in a public inn situated on a grand highway that ran from the east toward Arga. The disciples had food with them. In the night when all were asleep, Jesus arose and went alone into the open air to pray. Arga was a large, popu-

lous, and extraordinarily clean city. Like most of the
cities in these parts where pagans form a portion
of the population, it was built in the form of a star,
the streets wide and straight. The mode of life was
quite different from that observed in Judea and
Galilee, the customs being much better. Levites were
sent hither from Jerusalem and other localities to
teach in the synagogue. They were changed from
time to time, for if those sent did not give satisfaction, the people had the right to complain, and thus
get others. People of bad conduct were not allowed
to go at large. They were sent to a place of punishment and there detained. The inhabitants did not
carry on private housekeeping, that is, they did not
prepare their food in their own houses. They had
large public kitchens where all was cooked and
whither they went either to get their food and carry
it to their homes, or to partake of it in halls adjoining. They slept on the roofs of their houses under
tents. There were large dyeing establishments in this
city, for they were skillful in the art of coloring, producing especially beautiful violets. The manufacture
and embroidery of large carpets were also carried on
here with more skill and to a greater extent than in
Ramoth. Between the city and the wall ran tent after
tent where women sat and worked at long strips of
stuff stretched before them. On account of the delicate nature of their employments, the people of Arga
were famed of old for their exceedingly great cleanliness. Quantities of oil of superior quality were produced around Arga. The olive trees grew in long rows
neatly tied to trellises. Down in the valleys toward
the Jordan, the people had numbers of camels and
excellent pasture grounds. There grew also in this
region a precious wood, which was used in the building of the Ark of the Covenant and the table of showbread. The bark of the tree that produced it was
smooth and beautiful, the branches hung like those
of the willow, the leaves were like pear leaves, though

very much larger, green on one side and on the other covered with some gray-colored stuff. It bore berries like the fruit of the dogrose, though larger. The wood was exceedingly hard and tough, and could be split into very fine strips like bark. When dry and bleached, it became firm and beautiful and almost indestructible. The tree contained a very fine pith, which was extracted by incisions so as to leave in the center of the inmost plank only a delicate, reddish vein. The wood was made into little tables, and used for all kinds of inlaid work. They dealt also in myrrh and other spices, although these did not grow there. They obtained them from the caravans that often unloaded their camels and rested here for weeks at a time. They pressed the spices into balls and prepared them to be used by the Jews in embalming the dead. The cows and sheep of Arga were very large.

When on the following morning Jesus and His disciples went toward Arga, the Levites and chief men of the city met Him with every mark of respect, conducted Him to a tent, washed His feet, and presented Him refreshments. Some of the disciples had gone on before Jesus to apprise the townspeople of His coming. He taught in the synagogue, after which He cured a great many sick, among them numbers of consumptives. He went likewise to many of the sick in their homes. Toward three o'clock a dinner was spread. Jesus dined with the Levites in a public hall, the dishes having been brought thither from the eating house. In the evening, He taught again in the synagogue, for it was the commencement of the Sabbath. Next morning He gave another discourse, speaking at length of Moses in the wilderness on Mounts Sinai and Horeb, of the construction of the Ark of the Covenant, of the table of showbread, etc. As the ancestors of His hearers had sent offerings for the same, Jesus alluded to them as symbolical. He exhorted them now, in the time of their fulfillment, to bring heart and soul as an offering by penance and conversion, and He showed them the connection between that offering of their forefathers and their own present condition. But I do not remember it. The substance of this discourse was as follows:

While Jesus was speaking, I had an extended and circumstantial vision of the departure of the Israelites from Egypt. I saw that Jethro, the father-in-law, and Sephora, the wife of Moses, dwelt in Arga with the two sons and a daughter of the latter. I saw Jethro with the wife and children of Moses journeying to join him on Mount Horeb. Moses received them most joyfully, and related all the miracles wrought by God for the deliverance of His people from Egypt, whereupon Jethro offered sacrifice. I saw too that Moses at this time settled the disputes of all the Israelites himself, but Jethro counseled him to nominate subordinate judges. He then returned home, leaving Sephora and her sons with Moses. I saw Jethro recounting in Arga all the wonders he had seen, and many were thereby roused to great reverence for the God of the Israelites. Then Jethro sent Moses presents and offerings on camels, to which the Argites had contributed. The presents consisted of fine oil, which was afterward burned before the tabernacle; very fine, long strands of camel's hair for spinning and weaving into covers and curtains; and most beautiful setim wood, which was afterward made into the poles of the Ark of the Covenant and the table for the showbread, I think, too, they sent a species of grain out of which the showbread was made. It was made from the pith of a reedlike plant, from which long before I saw Mary making pap.

On the Sabbath Jesus taught in the synagogue from *Isaias* and from *Deuteronomy* 21:26. He spoke also of Balac and the Prophet Balaam. I saw many things connected with both, but I cannot now recall them. That evening in the Sabbath instructions, He related from the Law of Moses, which had previously been read, the history of Zambri and the Madianite stabbed by Phineas, (*Num.* 25:7.)

(Here Anne Catherine repeated in an admirable manner, although she had never heard nor read them, a number of the Laws of Moses as set forth in *Deuteronomy* 21:26. They were those that especially corresponded to her own position in childhood and the ideas peculiar to the occupations connected with it; for instance, the law forbidding one that has found a bird's nest to take the parent birds as well as the young; that which commands the gleanings of the harvest to be left for the poor; that which prohibits pledges to be taken from the poor, or borrowing from them, etc. Jesus touched upon all these points, dwelling at length upon the law that forbids defrauding laborers of their wages, because the people of Arga lived by labor, Sister Emmerich was rejoiced when told that all those laws could be found in the Bible, and she wondered at having heard them so correctly.)

The Sabbath over, Jesus went to an inn belonging to the pagans who had sent Him, by the disciples, a most pressing invitation to that effect. He was received with great humility and affection. He instructed them upon the call of the heathens, telling them that He was now come to gain over those that had not been conquered by the Israelites. They questioned Him upon the fulfillment of the prophecy that the scepter should be taken away from Juda at the time of the Messiah, and He gave them an answer full of instruction. They knew the story of the Three Kings, and begged for Baptism. Jesus explained what the ceremony meant, that it was to be for them a preparation for their sharing in the Kingdom of the Messiah. These good pagans were travellers, and had been a couple of weeks at Arga, awaiting the arrival of a caravan. They numbered five families, about

thirty-seven souls in all. They could not go to the
Baptism at Ennon, for fear of missing the caravan.
They asked Jesus where they should take up their
future residence, and He indicated to them the place.
I never heard Him speaking to the heathens of circumcision, but He always insisted on continence and
the obligation of having but one wife.

These heathens were at once baptized by Saturnin
and Judas Barsabas. They stepped into a bathing
cistern, and bowed over a large basin in front of it
which Jesus had blessed. The water was thrice poured
over their head.

All were clothed in white. After the ceremony they
presented to Jesus golden bracelets and earrings for
the money box of the disciples. Those articles formed
the principal part of their commerce. They were
changed into money, which by Jesus' orders was distributed to the poor. Jesus taught again in the synagogue, cured the sick, and dined with the Levites.

After the meal, accompanied by several people,
Jesus went a couple of hours farther on to the north
to a little place named Azo, where were many people gathered for the celebration of a feast commemorative of Gideon's victory begun that evening. Jesus
was received outside the city by the Levites. They
washed His feet and offered Him to eat, after which
He went into the synagogue and taught.

In Jephte's time, Azo was a fortified city, but was
destroyed during the war that called him from the
land of Tob. It was in Jesus' time a very clean little
place, the houses in one long row. There were no heathens in it, and the inhabitants were singularly good,
industrious, and well-behaved. They had many olive
trees skillfully planted on terraces outside the city,
and which they carefully tended. Stuffs were also
fabricated and embroidered here. The manner of living was the same as at Arga. The people of Azo looked
upon themselves as Jews of exceptional purity, since
they lived entirely apart from the pagans. Every-

thing was very clean in Azo. The road led down through a gently sloping valley, in which lay the city flanked on the west by a mountain.

When Deborah ruled in Israel and Sisara was slain by Jahel, there lived for a long time at Maspha a woman disguised as a man. She was descended from a woman who had survived the destruction of the tribe of Benjamin to which she belonged. This descendant assumed male attire and knew so well how to conceal her sex as to arouse the suspicion of no one. She had visions, she prophesied, and often served the Israelites in quality of spy. But whenever they employed her in that way, they met with defeat. The Madianites were encamped at that time near Azo, and that woman went out to them in the dress of a distinguished military officer. She called herself Abinoem after one of the heroes present at the defeat of Sisara. She passed unperceived through several quarters of the camp, spying as she went. At last she entered the general's tent and expressed her readiness to deliver all Israel into his hands. She had been accustomed to abstain from wine and to conduct herself with great reserve and circumspection. But upon this occasion she became intoxicated, and her sex was discovered. They nailed her hand and foot to a plank, and cast her into a pit with the words: "May even her name be here buried with her!"

It was from Azo that Gedeon went out against the camp of the Madianites. Gedeon was a very handsome, powerful man of the tribe of Manasses. He dwelt with his father near Silo. Israel was in a critical condition at that time. The Madianites and other idolatrous tribes overran the country, laid waste the fields, and carried off the harvest. Gedeon, a son of Joas the Ezrite, dwelling in Ephra, was very brave and liberal. He often threshed his wheat before his neighbors and generously divided it among the needy. I saw him going out at early morn before daybreak,

while the dew still lay on the ground, to a very large
tree with spreading branches under which his threshing floor lay concealed. The oak covered with its
broad branches the wide rocky basin in which it
stood. This basin was surrounded by a mound-like
wall that reached to the branches of the tree, so that
a person standing at the foot of the oak was as if
in a large vaulted cave and could not be seen from
without. The trunk was, as it were, formed of many
single branches wound together. The soil was firm
and rocky. Around in the walls were large cavities
in which the grain was stored in casks of bark. The
threshing was done with a cylinder that revolved
on wheels around the tree, and on it were wooden
hammers that fell upon the grain. High up in the
tree was a seat from which one could see around.
The Madianites pitched their tents from Basan down
across the Jordan, and even to the very field of
Esdrelon. The valley of the Jordan swarmed with
grazing camels, which circumstance greatly served
Gedeon's purpose. He reconnoitered for several
weeks, and with his three hundred men, moved slowly
toward Azo. I saw him slipping unperceived into the
camp of the Madianites, and listening to what was
said in one of the tents. Just at that moment, a soldier exclaimed to one of his companions: "I have
been dreaming that a loaf of bread fell down the
mountain and crushed our tent." The other answered:
"That is a bad omen! Gedeon will certainly fall upon
us with his Israelites." On the following night,
Gedeon and his handful of warriors, with lighted
torches in one hand and the trumpets upon which
they were blowing in the other, pressed into the
camp. Other bands did the same from opposite sides.
The enemy became panic-stricken. They turned their
swords against one another, while being slain and
routed on all sides by the Children of Israel. The
mountain from which the bread rolled down, as seen
in the soldier's dream, was directly back of Azo and

it was from there that Gedeon made his attack in person.

The annual commemoration of Gedeon's victory was now being celebrated in Azo. Outside the city was a large oak on a hill and at its foot an altar of stone. Between this tree and the mountain from which the soldier had seen the bread rolling down, the disguised prophetess lay buried. This tree was different from our oaks. It bore a large fruit with a green husk, under which was an exceedingly hard kernel in a little cup like our acorns. The Jews of Azo used these kernels for the tops of their walking sticks. For the accommodation of the large concourse of people, there was from that tree down to the city a whole row of tabernacles made of foliage and adorned with all kinds of fruit.

Jesus and the disciples went with the Levites in procession to the Ark. Five little he-goats, their necks adorned with red wreaths, were led in advance of the cortege. When they reached the oak, they were shut up in little grated caverns cut out of the side of the hill around the tree. Little cakes were also carried thither for sacrifice, and trumpets were blown. Different passages of Gedeon's life were read from rolls, and canticles of victory sung. Then the goats were slaughtered and cut up, several pieces along with some of the cakes being laid upon the altar around which the blood was sprinkled. A Levite blew fire from a tube into the wood lying under the grating of the altar, in memory of the angel's having enkindled Gedeon's sacrifice with a rod. (*Jgs.* 6:21).

Jesus delivered a discourse to the assembled crowd, and thus the morning passed. In the afternoon He went with the Levites and the principal citizens to a valley south of the city where, around a little fountain, were a public bathing place and pleasure garden. In a garden apart were the women and maidens playing at games and enjoying themselves. An entertainment had been prepared here and, according to

an ancient custom, the upper tables were assigned
to the poor. Jesus took His place at one of them. He
related the parable of the Prodigal Son and told of
the calf that his father commanded to be slaughtered for him. He passed the night under a tent on
the roof of the synagogue, for the people of this place
were accustomed to sleep on the roofs.

The feast was continued during the next day. The
tabernacles of foliage were intended for the Feast of
Tabernacles also, which was to begin in about fourteen days. Next morning Jesus delivered an instruction in the synagogue, and outside the school cured
many blind, many consumptives, and several harmless possessed. After that He partook of a dinner and
then left the city, accompanied by the Levites and
others, about thirty in all.

The road led first over that mountain from which
the soldier had seen the barley loaf rolling down into
the camp of the Madianites. (*Jgs.* 7:13). Then the
travellers climbed by a defile over another mountain
narrow, long, and high, on the opposite side of which
they journeyed northward through the valley for about
an hour. They reached at last a pleasant little lake
near which rose some buildings belonging to the
Levites of Azo. A brook flowed through it and down
through the valley into the Jordan. About six hours
northeastwardly from this point was Betharamphtha-Julias built around a mountain.

Jesus partook of a luncheon by the lake. It consisted of roasted fish, honey, bread, and a beverage
of balm from a little jug, all of which the party had
with them. The lake was about three hours' distance
from Azo. All along the route, Jesus had related parables of the sower and the stony soil, for it was over
such they were then journeying. He also related
another of fishes and how to catch them. There were
some little boats on the lake fishing with drawnets,
the capture being intended for the poor.

An hour and a half distant was Ephron. It could

not be seen from here, though the high mountains
in its vicinity were distinctly visible. Jesus now took
leave of those that had accompanied Him from Azo,
and proceeded to Ephron. Azo was the best place He
had met on His way in these parts. Jesus was as
usual received outside of Ephron by the Levites of
the place, and here too were found already waiting
for Him a crowd of sick. They lay in wooden chests
to which handles were attached for convenience in
carrying. Jesus cured them all. Ephron lay on the
southern height of a narrow pass through which
flowed a stream down into the Jordan. The latter
could be seen far away through the defile. The stream
of which I speak was often dried up. Opposite Ephron
rose a narrow but lofty mountain. It was upon it that
Jephte's daughter with her maids awaited the sig-
nal of her father's victory, namely, the rising of a column of smoke. The moment she descried it, she
hurried back to Ramoth whence with great pomp she
set out to meet her father. Jesus instructed and cured
many here.

The Levites of this place belonged to an ancient
sect called Rechabites. Jesus reproached them for
the hardness and severity of their opinions, and
advised the people not to observe many of their prescriptions. In His instruction He alluded to the punishment of those Levites of Bethsames that had
irreverently (too curiously) gazed upon the Ark of
the Covenant which had been brought back by the
Philistines. (*3 Kgs.* 6:15 *et seq.*). The Rechabites were
descended from Jethro, the father-in-law of Moses.
In early times they lived under tents, carried on no
husbandry, and abstained from the use of wine. They
exercised the office of chanters and gatekeepers in
the Temple. Those men that near Bethsames had,
contrary to orders, gazed upon the returning Ark
and had for so doing been punished with death, were
Rechabites who there dwelt under tents. Jeremias
tried once, but in vain, to make them drink wine in

the Temple. He afterward held up to Israel as an example the obedience of these men to their laws. In Jesus' time they no longer dwelt under tents, though they still preserved many of their peculiar customs. They wore a hairy ephod (a scapular) as a cilicium [hair shirt] next their skin, and over that a garment made from the skins of beasts. Their outer robe was white, beautiful and clean, and was confined by a broad girdle. One of the points in which they differed from the Essenians was in their better mode of dressing. Their rules relating to purity were excessively strict, and they had very singular customs with regard to marriage. They passed judgment after examining blood drawn from the candidate for marriage. According to this test they decided whether he should marry or not, enjoining it upon some of their sect and forbidding it to others. In early times they were to be found in Argob, Jabesch, and in Judea. They offered no opposition to the words of Jesus, but took His instructions and His reproaches alike humbly and in good part. He reprehended them most of all for their unmerciful severity to adulterers and murderers to whom they granted no quarter. There were on this mountain many foundries and forges. They made pots and gutters, also water pipes. These last were formed of two pieces soldered together.

17. Jesus in Betharamphtha-Julias. Abigail, the Repudiated Wife of Philip the Tetrarch

From Ephron, Jesus went with His disciples and several of the Rechabites about five hours to the north to Betharamphtha-Julias, a beautiful city situated on a height. On the way He gave an instruction near a mine from which was obtained the copper that was wrought in Ephron. There were some Rechabites in

Betharamphtha, and among them priests. Those of Ephron appeared to me to be under their jurisdiction.

The city was large and extended far around a mountain. The western part was inhabited by Jews, the eastern and a portion of the heights by idolaters. The two quarters were separated by a walled-in road and a pleasure garden full of shady walks. High on the mountain arose a beautiful castle with its towers, its gardens, and trees. It was occupied by a divorced wife of the Tetrarch Philip, who had settled upon her all the revenues of this part of his territory. She was descended from the kings of Gessur, and had with her five daughters already well grown. She was named Abigail and, although tolerably advanced in years, was still active and beautiful. Her disposition was full of goodness and benevolence.

Philip was older than Herod of Pera and Galilee. He was a pagan of peaceable inclinations, but a lover of pleasure. He was half-brother of the other Herod, born of a different mother, and had first married a widow with one daughter. When Abigail's husband was dispatched by Philip to a war or to Rome, I know not which, he left his wife behind. She meanwhile was seduced by Philip, who married her, whereupon her husband died of grief. When after some years Philip's first wife, whom he had repudiated for the sake of Abigail, was about to die, she begged him on her deathbed to have pity at least on her daughter. Philip, who had by this time grown tired of Abigail, married his step-daughter, and banished Abigail and her five daughters to Betharamphtha, called also Julias in honor of a Roman empress. Here she occupied herself in doing good. She was favorably disposed toward the Jews, and cherished a great desire after truth and salvation. She was, however, under the watchful guardianship of some of Philip's officers, who had to render an account of her. Philip had one son, and his present wife was much younger than himself.

Jesus was received cordially and hospitably in Betharam. The morning after His arrival He cured many sick Jews, and taught that evening in the synagogue, as also on the next morning, His instructions turning upon the tithes and the offering of the firstborn, and the sixtieth of Isaias. (*Deut.* 26-30, *Is.* 60).

Abigail was held in esteem by the inhabitants of Betharamphtha. She sent gifts down from her castle to the Jews for the more honorable entertainment of Jesus and His disciples. On the first of the month of Tisri the new year was celebrated, which fact was announced from the roof of the synagogue by all kinds of musical instruments, among them harps and a number of large trumpets with several mouthpieces. I saw again one of those wonderful instruments I had formerly seen on the synagogue of Capharnaum. It was filled with wind by means of a bellows. All the houses and public buildings were adorned on this feast day with flowers and fruit. The different classes of people had different customs. During the night many persons, most of them women clothed in long garments and holding lighted lanterns, prayed upon the tombs. I saw too that all the inhabitants bathed, the women in their houses and the men at the public baths. The married men bathed separate from the youths, as also the elder women from the maidens. As bathing was very frequent among the Jews and water not abundant, they made use of it sparingly. They lay on their back in tubs and, scooping up the water in a shell, poured it over themselves; it was often more like a washing than a bath. They performed their ablutions today at the baths outside the city, in water perfectly cold. Mutual gifts were interchanged, the poor being largely remembered. They commenced by giving them a good entertainment, and on a long rampart were deposited numerous gifts for them, consisting of food, raiment, and covers. Everyone that received presents from his friends bestowed a part of them upon the poor. The Rechabites present superintended and directed all things. They saw what each one gave to the poor and how it was distributed. They kept three lists, in which they secretly recorded the generosity of the donors. One of these lists was called the Book of Life; another, the Middle Way; and the third, the Book of Death. It was customary for the Rechabites to exercise all such offices, while in the Temple they were gatekeepers, treasurers, and above all, chanters. This last office they fulfilled on today's feast. Jesus also received presents in Betharamphtha of clothing, covers, and money, all of which He caused to be distributed among the poor.

During the feast Jesus went to visit the pagans. Abigail had pressed Him earnestly to come to see her, and the Jews themselves, upon whom she bestowed many benefits, had begged Him to have an interview with her. I saw Jesus with some of His disciples crossing the Jewish quarter of the city to that of the pagans. He reached the public pleasure grounds, pleasant and shady, that lay between the two quarters, and where the Jews and pagans usually met when necessary. Abigail was already there with her suite, her five grown daughters, many other heathen maidens, and some pagan followers. Abigail was a tall, vigorous woman of about fifty years, almost the same age as Philip. She wore an expression of sadness and anxious yearning. She sighed after instruction and conversion to a better life, but she knew not how to set about its attainment, for she was not allowed to act freely and was jealously watched by her wardens. She cast herself at Jesus' feet. He raised her up and, walking up and down, instructed her and her companions. He spoke of the fulfillment of the Prophecies, of the vocation of the Gentiles, and of Baptism. From all the places at which Jesus had

been since He left Ennon proceeded caravans of Jews
and Gentiles thither in uninterrupted succession, to
receive Baptism from the disciples left there for that
purpose. Andrew, James the Less, John, and the disciples of John the Baptist were all busy administering Baptism. Messengers were constantly going and
coming between them and the imprisoned Baptist.

Jesus received from Abigail the customary marks
of honor. She had appointed Jewish servants to wash
His feet and to offer Him the refreshments usually
extended to strangers as tokens of welcome. She very
humbly begged His pardon for desiring an interview
with Him, but, as she said, she had so long sighed
after His instructions. She begged Him to take part
in an entertainment she had prepared in His honor.
Jesus was very condescending toward all, but especially toward Abigail herself. His every word and
glance made a strong impression on her soul. She
was full of anxiety, and was not without some glimmering of the truth. This instruction to the pagans
lasted till nearly afternoon. Then at Abigail's invitation Jesus passed to the east side of the city not
far from the pagan temple. There were many baths
in the vicinity and a kind of public feast going on,
for the heathens also celebrated the new moon today
with special magnificence. In coming hither Jesus
took the road that separated the two quarters of the
city, the Jewish from the heathen. In the abodes
formed in the walls were many poor, sick pagans
lying in chests full of straw and chaff. The destitute
among the heathens were numerous. As yet Jesus
cured none of their sick.

On the pleasure grounds of the heathens, where
the entertainment was prepared, Jesus taught for a
long time, sometimes walking around, and again during the meal. He made use of all kinds of parables
relating to animals, in order to illustrate to them
their own vain and fruitless lives. He spoke of the
unwearied and often useless labor of the spider, of

the active industry of the ant and wasp, and placed before them as a contrast the beautifully ordered work of the bee. The viands of the entertainment, at which Abigail assisted in person, reclining at the table, were for the most part distributed at Jesus' request to the poor. There were also on this day great solemnities in the pagan temple, a very magnificent building with large open porticos on five sides through which was afforded a view into the interior. It was capped by a high cupola. There were many idols in the different halls of the temple, the principal one being named Dagon. The upper part of its body was like a human being, the lower part like a fish. There were others in the form of animals, but none so beautiful as the idols of the Greeks and Romans. I saw young maidens hanging wreaths on and around the idols, then singing and dancing before them, while the pagan priests burnt incense on a little three-legged table. On the cupola was a very wonderful and ingenious piece of mechanism which revolved the whole night. It was a brilliant globe covered with stars. As it slowly revolved, it could be seen from the interior of the temple as well as from without. It represented something connected with the course of the stars and the new moon, or the new year. The globe revolved slowly. When it had reached one of the extreme points in its orbit, the songs and rejoicings in the temple ceased on the opposite side, to be taken up on that to which the globe had turned.

Not far from the festive scene where Jesus had been entertained was a large pleasure garden, and in it were the young girls amusing themselves at various games. Their robes were slightly raised and their lower limbs strapped with bands. They were armed with bows, arrows, and little spears wreathed with flowers. A kind of race course had been ingeniously formed of branches, flowers, and decorations of all kinds, along which the girls ran, shooting their arrows

at the same time after the birds that were fastened
here and there for that purpose, and darting their
spears at the different animals, the kids and little
asses, that were fenced in around the course. On
this festal race course was a horrible idol with broad,
open jaws like a beast, and hands hanging before it
like a human being. It was hollow, and under it
blazed a fire. The animals killed by the girls were
placed in its jaws, where they were consumed, their
ashes falling into the fire below. Those that had
escaped the darts of the young huntresses were set
aside and regarded as sacred. The priests laid upon
them the sins of the people and set them free. It
was something like the Jewish scapegoat. Were it
not for the torture of the animals, so painful to
behold, and the horrible idol, the fleetness and skill
of the young girls would have been a very pleasing
sight. The feast lasted till evening and, when the
moon rose, animals were offered in sacrifice. When
night closed, the whole temple and Abigail's castle
were ablaze with torches.

Jesus taught again after the repast. Many of the
heathens were converted and went to Ennon for Baptism. That evening Jesus went up the mountain by
torchlight and had an interview with Abigail in the
portico of her castle. Near her were some of Philip's
officers, who watched her constantly. Her every action
was on that account one of constraint, and she gave
the Lord to understand her embarrassing position
by the look she cast upon those men. Jesus, however,
knew her whole interior and the bonds that held her
captive. He had compassion upon her. She asked
whether she might hope for pardon from God. One
thing in particular constantly harassed her, namely,
her infidelity to her lawful husband and his death.
Jesus comforted her, saying that her sins would be
forgiven her, she should continue her good works,
persevere and pray. She was of the race of Jebusites.
These heathens were accustomed to allow their

deformed children to perish, and were very super-
stitious about the signs that accompanied their birth.

In all the places through which Jesus had passed
lately, preparations were busily going forward for the
Feast of Tabernacles. They were transporting lath-
work from place to place and putting up light tents
and huts made of foliage here and there on the roofs
of Betharamphtha. The maidens were busied with
plants and flowers which they put into water and
set in the cellars to keep fresh. There were so many
fast days before the feast, and so much was needed
on account of the entertainments given upon it, that
everything had to be prepared some time before. Such
cares were entrusted to many of the poor, who
received food and money in return for their services.
When all was over they were entertained at a grand
feast and again recompensed. In all these places no
open shops were to be seen. Outside the Temple in
Jerusalem, there were some places around upon which
stood shops; in other cities, here and there, but chiefly
at the gate, was a tent in which covers were sold.
One never saw in Palestine people sitting together
in the public houses. Here and there in the corner
of a wall might be seen a man standing with a leathern bottle or pitcher. The traveller in passing got his
little jug replenished, but rarely did he sit down to
drink. A drunkard was never seen on the streets.
The water vendors carried a pole across the shoulder on which were hung two leathern bottles, one in
front, the other behind. As for dishes and vessels of
iron, to procure them a man had to mount his ass
and go to where they were fabricated.

On the following day Jesus cured, on the walled-
in road between the Jewish and the heathen quarters, all the poor, sick pagans who were lying so
miserably in the cavities of the wall, and the disciples distributed alms among them. After that until
the time of His departure, Jesus taught in the synagogue. As the feast then celebrated was likewise

commemorative of the sacrifice of Isaac, Jesus spoke of the true Isaac, but His hearers did not understand Him. In all these places, He alluded very significantly to the Messiah, though without saying in express terms that it was Himself.

18. Jesus in Abila and Gadara

Jesus with the disciples and accompanied by the Levites went three hours to the northwest toward a deep dale through which the brook Karith flowed to the Hieromax. In this dale lay the beautiful city of Abila built around the source of the brook Karith. The Levites accompanied Him to a mountain that stood halfway on the road, and then went back to Betharam. It was three o'clock in the afternoon when the Levites of Abila, among whom were several Rechabites, received Jesus outside the city. Three of the disciples from Galilee were with the Levites awaiting His arrival. They conducted Him at once into the city and to a very lovely fountain, the source of the brook Karith. The beautiful little edifice, supported by columns that had been built over the source, formed the central point, to which ran colonnades connecting it with the synagogue and other public buildings. The city was built on both sides of the gently rising height. The streets ran from these central buildings in the form of a star so that from every one of them the fountain could be seen. It was at this fountain that the Levites washed the feet of Jesus and the disciples, and offered them the customary refreshments. In the neighboring gardens and on the buildings around were men and maidens busily preparing for the Feast of Tabernacles.

From here Jesus accompanied the Levites northward about half an hour outside the city into the valley to where a broad, stone bridge was built over the stream. On it, in memory of Elias, was a low pedestal, or column, surmounted by a cupola resting

on eight pillars. The pedestal supported a pulpit to
which the teacher mounted by steps. Both banks of
the narrow stream were cut in tiers to afford seats
for the audience, and both were now crowded with
people. In addressing them Jesus turned from side
to side that all might hear.

Today was a feast in this city commemorative of
Elias, of something that had happened to him here
by the stream. The instruction was followed by a
banquet at the baths and pleasure garden outside
the city. The festival ended with the Sabbath, because
on the following day a fast was kept in remembrance
of the murder of Godolias. (*4 Kgs.* 25:22-25). The
sound of trumpets was still heard during the day.

On the declivity of the mountain west of the city
of Abila I saw a very beautiful sepulcher in front of
which was a little garden. In the latter were assembled the women belonging to three families of Abila.
They were celebrating a solemnity in honor of the
dead. They sat on the ground closely veiled, wept,
uttered lamentations, and frequently prostrated with
the face to the earth. They killed several birds of
very beautiful plumage, plucked them, and burned
the lovely, shining feathers on the tomb. The flesh
was afterward given to the poor. The tomb was that
of an Egyptian woman from whom the mourners had
descended. Before the departure of the Children of
Israel, there lived in Egypt an illegitimate relative
of the Pharaoh then reigning. She was very favorably disposed toward Moses, and rendered great services to the Israelites. She was a prophetess, and
she it was that had discovered Joseph's mummy to
Moses on the last night of his stay in Egypt. Her
name was Segola, and she was the mother of Aaron's
wife, from whom, however, he separated and married Elizabeth, the daughter of Aminadab of the tribe
of Juda. The repudiated wife also was connected in
some way with Aminadab, but how I do not now
know. She had by her mother Segola, as well as by

Aaron himself, been richly dowered. Taking with her
large treasure, she accompanied the Israelites on
their departure and married a second time during
their stay in the desert. She afterward attached herself to the Madianites, especially to the family of
Jethro. Her descendants settled near Abila where
they dwelt under tents, and it was here that she
was buried. After the time of the Prophet Elias, Abila
was built, and it was then that those descendants
settled there. I did not see the city in Elias' time;
it may have been destroyed before him. There were
still three families of those descendants in Abila,
and they were celebrating today the anniversary of
the death of their ancestress, Segola's daughter,
whose mummy had been transported hither from
the desert and entombed. The women made an offering of their earrings and other trinkets to the Levites
in memory of their deceased relative, Jesus praised
her from the pulpit of Elias and spoke of the goodness of Segola, her mother. The women listened attentively from where they stood behind the men.
There were numbers of poor at the banquet in the
bathing garden, and every guest was obliged before
partaking of the viands to give something from his
own plate to his poor neighbor.

I saw the Levites conducting Jesus next day into
a great court all around which were cells. Here were
found about twenty patients, some of them deaf and
dumb, others blind from their birth, who were cared
for by attendants and two physicians. It was a kind
of hospital. The deaf and dumb were exactly like children. Each had a little garden in which he amused
himself and raised flowers. Soon all gathered around
Jesus, laughing and pointing with their finger to
their mouth. Jesus stooped and wrote all kinds of
signs in the sand with His finger. They watched Him
attentively and, at every mark He made, pointed
around them to this or that object. It was in this
way that He made them understand something about

God. I know not whether He formed letters or figures, or whether the mutes had ever before been instructed in that way. After that Jesus put His finger
into their ears and touched them under the tongue
with His thumb and forefinger. They shuddered as
if a shock thrilled through their whole being, they
gazed around, they heard, they wept, they stammered,
they talked, they cast themselves down at Jesus' feet,
and broke forth into a most touching, monotonous
chant of a few words, It sounded almost like that
sweet singing I heard in the caravan of the holy
Three Kings.

Then Jesus turned to the blind men who were
standing still in a row. He prayed and laid His two
thumbs on their eyes. They opened their eyes, fixed
them upon their Saviour and Redeemer, and mingled their songs of praise with those of the once deaf
and dumb, but who could now extol His goodness
and listen to His words. Oh, what a charming, what
a joyous scene! No words can describe it! The whole
city crowded in joy and jubilation to hail Jesus as
He came forth from the court surrounded by the
miraculously cured, whom He had ordered to bathe.

After that, Jesus, with the disciples and Levites,
traversed the city to the pulpit of Elias. The excitement throughout the city was great. At the news of
the miracles just wrought, several possessed had been
set at large. On a corner of one of the streets some
women, poor simpletons, ran after Jesus, chattering
and repeating the words: "Jesus of Nazareth! Prophet!
Thou art a Prophet! Thou art Jesus! Thou art the
Christ! The Prophet!" They were harmless fools. Jesus
commanded them to be silent, and they became quiet.
He laid His hand on their heads, and they fell on
their knees in tears. Silent and confused, they allowed
themselves to be quietly led away by their friends.
Then several possessed pressed raging through the
crowd as if to tear Jesus to pieces. He cast upon them
a single glance, and they fell like whining dogs at

His feet. With a word of command, He drove the devil
forth. They sank down unconscious, a dark vapor
escaped from them, and then they arose weeping and
thanking and were led to their homes by their friends.
Jesus generally ordered such persons to perform certain purifications. He again taught from the pulpit
on the brook, alluding in the course of His instruction to Elias, to Moses, and to the departure of the
Israelites from Egypt. He spoke of the cures that had
just been effected in their midst, and of the Prophecies which declared that in the Messiah's time the
dumb would speak and the blind see. He also made
allusion to those that saw these signs and yet would
not acknowledge them.

I saw on that occasion many things connected with
Elias. He was a tall, spare man with hollow, reddish
cheeks, a bright, piercing glance, a long, thin beard,
and a bald head with only a circle of hair around
the back. On the top of his head were three large
protuberances almost of the form of bulbs, one in the
middle, two somewhat toward the forehead. He wore
a garment made of two skins fastened together on
the shoulder, open at the sides, and bound around
the waist with a cord. Over his shoulders and around
his knees hung the hair of the beast's skin. He carried a staff in his hand. His shins were far darker
than his face. He was nine months in Abila, and two
years and three months in Sarepta with the widow.
While at Abila, he dwelt in a cave on the eastern
slope of the valley not far from the brook. I saw how
the bird brought him food. At first there arose a little dark figure like a shadow out of the earth, holding in its hand a thin cake. It was neither man nor
beast, it was the evil one come to tempt the Prophet.
Elias would not touch the bread, but bade the tempter
begone. Then I saw a bird coming to the vicinity of
his cave with bread and other food, which it hid
under the leaves, as if for itself. It must have been
a waterfowl, for it was web-footed. Its head was some-

what broad, and by the side of the beak hung bags
something like pockets, and under the beak hung a
craw. It made a cracking noise with its bill, like a
stork. I saw that this bird was quite at home with
Elias, so much so that on a sign from the Prophet
it came and went. I saw him pointing to it right and
left. I have often seen the same kind of bird with
the hermits, also with Zozimus and Mary of Egypt.[2]
When Elias was with the widow of Sarepta, besides
the oil and meal that never decreased, other food
was sometimes brought him by ravens.

Jesus went with the Levites to the cave of Elias.
On the eastern declivity of the valley under a broad,
overhanging cliff was a narrow rocky bank upon which
Elias, under shelter of the upper rock, used to sleep
on a couch overgrown with moss. When the Sabbath,
on the fourth of the month Tisri, began, and the fast
was over, there was an entertainment in the bathing
gardens, at which again the poor were fed.

Next morning, after Jesus had again taught and
cured the sick in the synagogue, He went with the
disciples, the Levites, the Rechabites, and some of
the citizens to the western heights of the mountain.
There making a circuit of about an hour, He went
through the vineyards giving instructions. On this
mountain range, as far as Gadara, were numerous
rocky projections like mounds. Some had been raised
by nature, others formed by the hand of man, and
around them vines were planted, the vinestocks as
thick as one's arm. They were planted far apart and
threw out their branches to a great distance. The
bunches of fruit were often as long as one's arm,
while the single grapes were large as plums. The
leaves were larger than those of our vines, though
small when compared with the fruit. The Levites

---

2. The Hebrew word which is translated as "raven" ("corous," *3 Kings* 17)
   signifies, according to the interpreters of Holy Scripture, various kinds
   of birds, among them a *corvus aquaticus* with colored feathers and a
   long beak. See Calmet, *Diction. S. Script.* S. V. *corvus.*

put many questions to Jesus upon different portions of the Psalms that treated of the Messiah. They said: "Thou art certainly the greatest Prophet after the Messiah! Thou canst explain these points to us." Among other things there was question of the words: *"Dixit Dominus Domino meo,"* and of him that with blood-besprinkled garments trod the wine press alone. (*Is.* 63:3). Jesus explained all to them with its profound signification and applied it to Himself. During this little instruction they sat around one of the vinehills eating grapes. The Rechabites, however, would not touch the fruit, because they were forbidden to drink wine. But Jesus challenged them upon their abstinence and commanded them to eat, saying that if they sinned by so doing, He would take the guilt upon Himself. When they brought forward their Law as an excuse for not complying, I heard them saying that Jeremias, on the command of God, had once forbidden it and they had obeyed. But now that Jesus ordered otherwise, they hearkened to His word. Toward evening they returned to the city, and assisted at another entertainment to which the poor were admitted. Then Jesus taught in the synagogue and afterward went to the house of the Levites, where He passed the night on the roof under a tent.

Attended by the Levites, Jesus went from Abila to Gadara and reached the small Jewish quarter of the city in the evening. It was separate from the larger pagan quarter which had as many as four idolatrous temples. I knew at once that Gadara was a heathen city from seeing the idol of Baal standing under a large tree. Jesus was well received here. There were Pharisees and Sadducees among the inhabitants, also a Sanhedrim for the country around, although the male Jews of the place numbered from three to four hundred only. Jesus found some Galilean disciples awaiting Him in Gadara. They were Nathanael (Chased), Jonathan, Peter's half-brother, and I think

Philip. Jesus put up at the inn outside the Jewish quarter, where already a great number of arbors had been erected for the Feast of Tabernacles.

Next morning when Jesus went to the synagogue to preach He was met by a great crowd of sick, who had assembled outside to wait for Him, and also by several raging possessed. The Pharisees and Sadducees, though apparently well-disposed, wanted to drive these people away. They should not be so importunate, they said, it was not the time for that. But Jesus very graciously interposed, "Let them remain," He said, "for it was for them that I came," and He cured many of them.

The Jewish Sanhedrim of Gadara were meantime deliberating whether or not they should allow Jesus to teach, since so much was said against Him. They unanimously resolved to permit Him to do so, for they had heard Him very well spoken of, especially after the cure of the son of the Centurion of Capharnaum.

The disciples lately arrived spoke to Jesus of another person at Capharnaum who greatly needed His assistance.

In the synagogue Jesus taught of Elias, of Achab and Jezabel, and of the idol of Baal erected in Samaria. In speaking of Elias, Jesus said that he had not received bread from ravens, because he had been disobedient. There was also some allusion made to King Balthasar of Babylon, who had desecrated the sacred vessels and had seen the writing on the wall. Jesus taught long and earnestly from Isaias, most strikingly applying the Prophet's words to Himself and uttering profound thoughts upon His own approaching Passion and victory. He spoke of the wine press, of the red, bloody garments, of the lonely worker, of the nations trodden down in wrath. He had previously spoken of the rebuilding of Sion, of the watchmen upon the walls of the Holy City, and I felt that He was alluding to the Church. To me His teaching, though so profound and earnest, was so

clear, and yet the Jewish Doctors, though surprised
and deeply affected, failed to understand Him. That
night they met together, consulted the Scriptures,
weighed and compared various passages. They
thought that He must surely be allied to some neighboring nation, and that He would soon return with
a powerful army and conquer Judea.

The idol Baal, under a wide-spreading tree outside the entrance of the pagan quarter, was of metal.
It had a broad head and an immense mouth. The
head went up in a point like a sugarloaf, and around
it was a wreath of leaves like a crown. The idol,
short, broad, and chunky, looked like an ox sitting
upright. In one hand it held a bunch of corn, and in
the other some kind of plant, perhaps grapes, or
something similar. There were seven openings in its
body, and it sat in a kind of cauldron in which a fire
could be lighted under it. On its feasts, the idol was
clothed.

Gadara was a stronghold. The pagan quarter was
tolerably large and somewhat sheltered by the highest peak of the mountain, at whose northern base
were warm baths and beautiful buildings.

On the following morning as Jesus was curing
numbers of sick outside the city, the priests
approached to salute Him. "Why," said He addressing them, "Why were ye so disturbed last night over
My teaching of yesterday? Why should ye tremble
before an army, since God protects the just? Fulfill
the Law and the Prophets! Why then should ye fear?"
Jesus again taught in the synagogue as on the preceding day.

Toward noon a pagan woman timidly approached
the disciples and implored them to bring Jesus to
her house that He might cure her child. Jesus went
with several of His disciples into the pagan quarter.
The woman's husband met Him at the gate and led
Him into the house. The wife cast herself at Jesus'
feet, saying: "Master, I have heard of Thy wonders

and that Thou canst perform greater prodigies than
Elias. Behold, my only boy is dying, and our Wise
Lady cannot help him. Do Thou have pity on us!"
The boy, about three years old, lay in a little crib in
the corner. The evening before, the father had taken
the child into the vineyard and he had eaten a few
grapes. Soon after, the boy became sick, and the father
had to take him back home whimpering loudly. The
mother had held him all night in her arms, vainly
trying to relieve him. He already wore the appearance of death, indeed he looked as if he might really
be dead. At this point the mother had hastened to
the Jewish quarter to implore Jesus' aid, for the heathens had heard of the cures wrought by Him on the
day before. Jesus said to her: "Leave Me alone with
the child, and send to Me two of My disciples!" Then
came Judas Barsabas and Nathanael the bridegroom.
Jesus took the boy from his crib into His arms, laid
him on His breast, breast to breast, pressed him to
Himself, bowed His face upon the face of the child,
and breathed upon him. The child opened his eyes
and rose up. Then Jesus held him out in His arms
and commanded the two disciples to lay their hands
upon the child's head and to bless him. They obeyed,
and the child was cured. Jesus then took him to the
anxiously waiting parents who, embracing the child,
cast themselves down at Jesus' feet. The mother cried
out: "Great is the God of Israel! He is far above all
the gods! My husband has already told me that, and
henceforth I will serve no other god!" A crowd soon
gathered and several other children were brought to
the Lord. He cured one little boy of a year old by
the imposition of hands. Another of seven years was
a simpleton and subject to convulsions arising from
possession by the evil one. The child did not endure
any violent assaults, but he was often paralyzed and
speechless. Jesus blessed him and ordered him a bath
of three different waters: some from the warm spring
of Amathus north of the base of the mountain of

Gadara, some from the brook Karith near Abila, and lastly some from the river Jordan. The Jews of these parts kept on hand some of the water of the Jordan taken from the point over which Elias had crossed. They preserved it in leathern bottles, and used it in cases of leprosy.

The pagan mothers complained of the frequent illness of their children and of the little assistance they derived from their priestess in such trials. Jesus commanded the priestess to be summoned before Him. She obeyed reluctantly, for she did not want to enter Jesus' presence. She was closely enveloped in veils. Jesus ordered her to draw near. But she would not look at Him, she turned her face away and behaved exactly like the possessed. She was irresistibly forced to turn away from the glance of Jesus, though at His command she approached. Jesus, addressing the pagan men and women before Him, said: "I will show you now what wisdom you reverence in this woman and what is her skill," and He commanded the spirits to leave her. Thereupon a black vapor issued from her and all kinds of figures: noxious insects, snakes, toads, rats, dragons withdrew from her like shadows. It was a horrible sight, Jesus exclaimed: "Behold what doctrine ye follow!" The woman fell upon her knees weeping and sobbing. She was now quite changed, quite tractable, and Jesus ordered her to disclose by what means she had tried to cure the children. With many tears and half reluctantly she obeyed. She told that she had been taught to make the children sick by charms and witchcraft, that she might afterward cure them for the honor of the gods. Jesus then commanded her to accompany Him and the disciples to where the god Moloch was kept, and He directed several of the pagan priests to be called. A crowd had gathered, for the news of the child's cure was soon spread. The place to which Jesus now went was not a temple, but a hill surrounded by tombs. The god was in a subterranean vault in the midst of them. The vault was closed on top by a cover. Jesus told the pagan priests to call forth their god. When by means of machinery, they had caused the idol to rise into sight, Jesus expressed to them His regret that they had a god that was unable to help himself.

Then turning to the priestess, He commanded her to rehearse the praises of her god, tell how she served him, and what reward he gave her. Like Balaam the Prophet, the woman began to repeat aloud before all the people the horrors of Moloch's worship and the wonders of the God of Israel. Jesus then directed the disciples to upset the idol and to shake it violently. They did as commanded. Jesus said to the pagans: "Behold the god that ye serve! Behold the spirits that ye adore!" and in the sight of all present, there appeared all kinds of diabolical figures issuing from the idol. They trembled convulsively, crept around for awhile, and vanished into the earth among the tombs. The idolaters gazed at the scene in affright and confusion. Jesus said: "If we cast your god down again into his den, he will surely go to pieces." The priests implored Jesus not to destroy their idol, whereupon He allowed them to raise it as before and lower it into its place. Most of the idolaters were deeply touched and ashamed, especially the priests, although some were very indignant. The people were, however, on Jesus' side. He gave them a beautiful instruction and many were converted. Moloch was seated like an ox on his hind legs, his forepaws stretched out like the arms of one who is going to receive something upon them, but by means of machinery he could be made to draw them in. His gaping mouth disclosed an enormous throat, and on his forehead was one crooked horn. He was seated in a large basin. Around the body were several projections like outside pockets. On festival days long straps were hung around his neck. In the basin under him fire was made when sacrifices were to be offered. Around the rim of the basin numbers of lamps were kept constantly burning before the god. Once upon a time it was customary to sacrifice children to him, but now they dared no longer do so, and animals of all kinds were offered in their stead. They were consumed in the openings of his body or cast into his yawning jaws. The sacrifice most agreeable to him was an Angora goat. There was also a machine by which the priests and others could descend to the idol in the subterranean vault among the tombs. The worship of Moloch was, however, no longer in great repute. He was invoked chiefly for purposes of sorcery and especially by the mothers of sick children. Each pocket around his person was consecrated to special sacrifices. Children used to be laid on his arms and consumed by the fire under him and in him, for he was hollow. He drew his arms in when the victim was deposited upon them, and pressed it tightly that its screams might not be heard. There was machinery in the hind legs by which he could be made to rise. He was surrounded with rays.

19. Jesus in Dion and Jogbeha

The heathens whose children Jesus had cured asked Him whither they should remove, for they were determined to renounce idolatry. Jesus spoke to them of Baptism, exhorting them in the meantime to remain tranquil and persevere in their good resolutions. He spoke to them of God as of a father to whom we must sacrifice our evil inclinations, and who asks no other offering from us than that of our own heart. When addressing the pagans, Jesus always said to them more plainly than He did to the Jews, that God has no need of our offerings. He exhorted them to contrition and penance, to thanksgiving for benefits received, and to compassion toward the suffering. Returned to the Jewish quarter, He terminated the exercises of the Sabbath and took a repast, after which began a fast in atonement for the adoration of the golden calf. It was celebrated on the 8th of Tisri because the 7th, the fast day proper, fell this year on the Sabbath.

Jesus left the city the next afternoon. The pagans whose children He had cured thanked Him again outside their own quarter. He blessed them, and with twelve disciples went down through the valley to the south of Gadara. He crossed a mountain and reached a little stream flowing from the range below Betharamphtha-Julias where the mines were. It was three hours from Gadara to the inn near the stream at which Jesus and the disciples put up. The Jews dwelling around that part of the country were engaged in gathering in the fruits. Jesus instructed them. There was also a band of pagans near the stream busy gathering white flowers from a blooming hedge, but it was not the flowers alone that they gathered, but also great, ugly beetles and other insects. When Jesus approached them, they drew back as if in fear. It was shown me that these insects were intended for the idol Beelzebub at Dion. I saw the idol outside the gate of the city, sitting under a large willow. It had a figure something like a monkey with short arms and slender legs, and it was seated like a human being. Its head was pointed and furnished with two little horns bent like a crescent, and the face with its extremely long nose was horrible. The chin was short but projecting, the mouth large and like that of a beast, the body lank, the legs long and thin with clawed toes. It wore an apron. In one hand it grasped a vessel by the stem, and in the other held a butterfly just escaping the larva. The butterfly, which was something like a bird and something like a disgusting insect, shone with variegated colors. Around the head of the idol and just above the forehead was a wreath of loathsome beetles and flying vermin, forming as it were a compact mass, one appearing to hold the other fast. Above the forehead and in the center of the pointed head between the horns sat one of those disgusting things larger and more hideous than the others. They were glittering, and they radiated all the colors, but they were horrible, venomous things with long bodies, horns, feelers, and stings. When Jesus drew near to the pagans that were seeking these insects for the idol, the whole crown flew asunder like a dark swarm and hid in the holes and corners around the country, while all kinds of frightful black spirits crept with them, frightened, into the holes. They were the wicked spirits that were honored in Beelzebub with those beetles.

On the following forenoon, Jesus reached Dion, that is the Jewish quarter, which was much smaller than that of the pagans. The latter was beautifully situated on the declivity of a mountain and had several temples. The Jewish quarter was entirely distinct from it. Where Jesus arrived outside the city the arbors were, for the most part, finished. Under one of them He was ceremoniously received by the priests and magistrates of the place, His feet washed, and the customary refreshments offered. Immediately after, He went out among the sick, numbers of whom were lying and standing under the arbors that had been erected from this spot to the city. The disciples assisted and kept order. There were sick of all kinds: lame, dumb, blind, dropsical, and paralyzed. Jesus cured and exhorted many. There were some that stood upright on three-legged crutches, and there were other crutches upon which the invalid could rest without using the feet. These latter were almost like go-carts. At last Jesus came to the sick women. They were lying, leaning, and sitting nearer the city under a long arbor that had been erected over a terraced bank. This bank was covered with beautiful, fine grass that hung like soft, silky hair, and over it was spread a carpet. There were several

women afflicted by an issue of blood. They were
closely veiled and remained at a distance. Others
were hypochondriacal, their faces wan and sallow,
their countenance sad and gloomy. Jesus addressed
them graciously and cured them one after another.
He gave each at the same time hints and admonitions suited to her case for correcting her several
imperfections, for avoiding such and such sins, and
He instructed all as to what penances to perform.
He also blessed and cured several children presented
to Him by their mothers. This work lasted until the
afternoon and ended amid general rejoicings. The
cured went away singing canticles of thanksgiving,
joyously and merrily carrying their beds and
crutches. They returned to the city processionally in
beautiful order as they had been cured, accompanied by their rejoicing relatives, friends, and attendants. Jesus with the disciples and Levites walked
in their midst. The humility and gravity of Jesus on
such occasions are inexpressible. The women and
children led the procession chanting the fortieth
Psalm of David: *"Blessed is He that understandeth
concerning the needy and the poor."* They went to
the synagogue and thanked God, after which they
took a meal under an arbor. It consisted of fruit,
birds, honeycomb, and toasted bread. When the Sabbath began, all went in mourning garments to the
synagogue, for the great Feast of Atonement then
commenced for the Jews.

Jesus delivered in the synagogue a discourse on
penance. He spoke against those that limit themselves to corporal purification without restraining
the evil desires of the soul. Some of the Jews disci-
plined themselves under their wide mantles around
the thighs and legs. The pagans of Dion also celebrated a feast with an enormous quantity of incense.
The very seats upon which they sat were placed over
burning perfumes.

I saw, too, the celebration of the Feast of Atone-

ment in Jerusalem, the numerous purifications of
the High Priest, his arduous preparations and mortification, the sacrifices, the sprinkling of blood, the
burning of incense, also the scapegoat, and the casting of lots for the two goats. One was for sacrifice,
the other was chased away into the desert with something containing fire tied to its tail. It ran wildly
through the wilderness, and at last plunged down a
precipice. This desert, which was once traversed by
David, commenced above the Mount of Olives. The
High Priest was today violently agitated and troubled; he would have been glad if another could have
performed the duties of his office instead of himself.
He was full of dread at the moment of entering the
Holy of Holies, and he earnestly begged the people
to pray for him. The people thought he must have
committed some sin, and felt very anxious lest some
calamity might befall him in the Holy of Holies. The
truth was, his conscience smote him for the share
he had had in the murder of Zachary, the father of
John. This sin was chastised with interest in the person of his son-in-law, who passed sentence of death
on Jesus. I do not think this High Priest was Caiaphas,
but his father-in-law.

The Holy Mystery was no longer in the Ark of the
Covenant. There were in it only some little linen
napkins and the various compartments. This Ark of
the Covenant was new and quite different in form
from the first. The angels were different. They were
seated and surrounded by a triple scarf; one foot was
raised, the other hung at the side of the Ark, and
the crown was still between them. There were all
kinds of sacred things in the Ark, such as oil and
incense. I remember that the High Priest burned
incense and sprinkled blood, that he took one of the
little linen cloths from the Ark, that he mixed some
blood (which he either drew from his finger or had
on his finger) with water, and then presented it to
a row of priests to drink. It was a kind of figure of

Holy Communion. I saw also that the High Priest, chastised by God, was become very miserable and was struck with leprosy. There was great consternation in the Temple. I heard a most impressive lesson read in the Temple from Jeremias and at the same time I saw many scenes in the life of the Prophet and much of the horrors of idolatry in Israel.

I saw also during another reading in the Temple that Elias, after his death, wrote a letter to King Joram. The Jews would not believe it. They explained it in this way: They said that Eliseus, who brought the letter to Joram, had given it to him as a prophetical letter bequeathed to himself by Elias. I began myself to think it very strange, when suddenly I was transported to the East and, in my journey, passed the Mountain of the Prophets, which I saw covered with ice and snow. It was crowned with towers, presenting perhaps the appearance it wore in the time of Joram. I went on then eastwardly to Paradise, and saw therein the beautiful, wonderful animals walking and gamboling around. There, too, were the glistening walls and, lying asleep on either side of the gate, Henoch and Elias. Elias was in spirit gazing upon all that was then going on in Palestine. An angel laid before him a roll of fine, white parchment and a reed pen. Elias sat up and wrote, resting the parchment on his knees. I saw a little chariot something like a chair, or throne, coming over an eminence, or around by some steps from the inside of the garden. It was drawn by three marvelously beautiful white animals. I saw Elias mount it and, as if on a rainbow, journey quickly to Palestine. The chariot stood still over a house of Samaria. I saw Eliseus inside praying, his eyes raised to Heaven. I saw Elias letting the letter fall before him, and Eliseus bearing the same to King Joram. The animals were harnessed to Elias' chariot, one in front and two behind. They were indescribably lovely, delicately formed animals of the size perhaps of a large roe, snow-white,

with long, white, silken hair. Their limbs were very
slender, their head always in motion, and on their
forehead was an elegant horn bent somewhat toward
the front. On the day that Elias was taken up to
Heaven, I saw his chariot drawn by the same kind
of animals.

I saw also the history of Eliseus and the Suna-
mitess. Eliseus performed prodigies even more wonderful than those of Elias, and in his dress and
manners there was something more elegant and
refined. Elias was wholly a man of God with nothing in his manners modeled after other men. He was
something like John the Baptist; they were men of
the same stamp. I saw also how Giezi, the servant
of Eliseus, ran after the man whom his master had
cured of leprosy (Naaman). It was night and Eliseus
was asleep. Giezi overtook Naaman at the Jordan
and demanded presents from him in the name of his
master.

On the next day Giezi was pursuing his work as
if nothing had happened (he was making light wooden
screens to be used as partitions between sleeping
apartments) when Eliseus asked him: "Where hast
thou been?" and exposed to him all that had taken
place the previous night. The servant was punished
with leprosy, which he transmitted to his posterity.

As the idolatry practiced by the human race, the
adoration of animals and idols in the early times,
the repeated lapsing of the Israelites into the same,
and the great mercy of God in sending them the
Prophets were shown me, and I was wondering how
men could adore such abomination, I had a vision
in which I saw that the same abomination still exists
on the earth, though in a formless material, more
spiritual. I saw innumerable visions throughout the
whole world of idolatry infecting even Christianity,
and I saw it indeed in almost all the forms in which
it was formerly practiced. I saw priests adoring serpents in presence of the Most Blessed Sacrament,

their different passions assuming the various forms
of those serpents. I saw all kinds of similar animals
by the side of learned and distinguished men. They
adored them while at the same time they *thought
themselves above all religion!* I saw toads and all
kinds of hateful creatures near poor, low, depraved
people. I saw also entire churches in the practice of
idolatry, namely, a dark, reformed church in the North
with empty, horrible altars upon which stood ravens
receiving the adoration of the congregation. The
people saw not indeed such animals, but they were
adoring them in their own conceits and haughty self-
sufficiency. I saw ecclesiastics for whom little dis-
torted figures, little pugs, etc., were turning the leaves
of their breviary while they recited the Holy Office.
Yes, I saw with some even the idols of ancient times,
such as Moloch and Baal. They were placed on the
table among their books, and held sway over them.
I have seen them even presenting morsels of food
to those men who despised the holy simplicity of the
children of God, and made a mockery of it.

I saw that such horrors are as rife in our own day
as in the past, and that the visions of idolatry vouchsafed me were not accidental. If the ungodliness and
idolatry of men of our own day could assume a cor-
poreal form, if their thoughts and sentiments could
be reduced to exterior acts, we should find the same
idols existing now as in days gone by.

When Jesus again left Dion, several heathens from
the pagan quarter approached Him very timidly. They
had heard of the wonderful cures He had effected in
Gadara, and they now brought their children to Him.
Jesus cured them and induced the parents to determine to receive Baptism. After that He went with
twelve disciples five hours to the south and over the
brook that flowed down from the vale of Ephron. One
half-hour to the south of this brook lay Jogbeha, a
little, unknown place, quite hidden away in a hollow
behind a forest. It was founded by a Prophet, a spy

of Moses and Jethro, whose name sounds like
Malachai. He is not, however, one and the same with
the last Prophet, Malachias. Jethro, the father-in-law
of Moses, employed him as a servant. He was exceedingly faithful and prudent, on which account
Moses sent him to explore this country. He had come
two years before Moses arrived himself, had explored
the country for miles around even as far as the borders of the lake, and had given an account of all that
he saw. Jethro at that time dwelt near the Red Sea,
but upon Malachai's report, he went with the wife
and sons of Moses to Arga. Malachai was at last pursued as a spy. They hunted him to kill him. There
was no city here in those times, only a few people
living in tents. Malachai took refuge in a morass, or
cistern, and an angel appeared and helped him. He
brought him upon a long strip of parchment the command to continue three years longer reconnoitering
the country. The inhabitants, that is those who lived
in the tents, provided him with clothes such as they
themselves wore, long, red tunics and jackets of the
same color. Malachai also explored the country around
Betharamphtha. He lived for some time among the
tent-dwellers of Jogbeha, and by his superior intel-
ligence rendered them great assistance.

In the hollow in which Jogbeha was hidden was
a ditch filled with water and quite covered with
reeds, and on the spot in which Malachai lay concealed was a well that had been filled up. It began
later on to bubble and cast out quantities of sand
with occasional columns of vapor and sometimes pebbles. By degrees was formed around the well a hill,
which was soon clothed with verdure. The morass
was filled up by earth brought from a neighboring
mountain, and buildings were erected upon it. Thus
arose around the well, which was covered by a beautiful spring house, the city of Jogbeha, which name
signifies: "It will be elevated." The marshy cistern
must have been built around in far earlier times,

for lying near were the moss-covered ruins of walls in which were still discernible the holes destined probably for fish. There were other ruins in this locality like the foundation of an ancient tent castle. Malachias taught the inhabitants to use black mineral pitch in building.

Jesus was very graciously received in the isolated city of Jogbeha. Living apart from the other inhabitants was a sect called Karaites. They wore long, yellow scapulars, white garments, and aprons of rough skin. The youths wore shorter clothes and had their limbs wound with strips of stuff. There were about four hundred of these men. Once upon a time they were of far more importance, but suffered much from the oppression of enemies. They were of the race of Esra and a descendant of Jethro. One of their teachers had a great dispute once with a distinguished pharisaical Doctor. They clung strictly to the letter of the Law and rejected oral additions, led a life very simple and plain, and had all their goods in common. If a member withdrew from the community, he had to abandon whatever goods or property he had brought to it. There were no poor among them, for they mutually assisted one another; even strangers were supported by them. They reverenced old age, and among them were many aged persons, whom the young treated with the greatest deference. They called those holding a distinguished position "ancients." The Karaites were sworn enemies of the Pharisees, who added all sorts of oral traditions to the Law, though in some points they were somewhat similar to the Sadducees. In their manners and customs, however, they were different, being far stricter. One of them belonging to this place had married a woman of the tribe of Benjamin and on that account had been driven from the community. It was at the time of the great strife with that tribe. They suffered nothing in the least resembling an image, and they believed that the souls of the deceased passed into other bodies, even into those of the lower animals. They delighted in the thought of the beautiful animals in Paradise. They were in expectation of the Messiah, after whom they earnestly prayed, but they looked for Him to come as a worldly monarch, They regarded Jesus as a Prophet. They observed great cleanliness, but did not adhere to the numerous purifications, the throwing away of dishes, and similar annoying observances not in the Law. They followed the Law religiously, though interpreting it much more freely than did the Pharisees.

They lived here quietly, having little communication with other people, permitting neither luxury nor vanity, and supporting themselves by their modest labor. A great many willow trees grew in these parts, from which they wove baskets and beehives, for there were many bees around here. They also made coarse covers, and light wooden vessels, all working together under long tents. Their arbors for the Feast of Tabernacles now at hand stood already prepared outside the city. They entertained Jesus with honey and bread baked in the ashes. Jesus taught here. He instructed them in all things, and they listened to Him very reverently. He expressed to them the wish that they should live in Judea, and praised the reverence of their children toward their parents, of the scholars for their teachers, and the regard they entertained for age. He also commended their attention to the poor and the sick, for whom they provided in well-arranged hospitals.

FROM THE SECOND FEAST
OF TABERNACLES TO
THE FIRST CONVERSION
OF MAGDALEN

1. Jesus in Ennon and Socoth.
Mary of Suphan.
Conversion of an Adulteress

Arom Jogbeha, Jesus went through Socoth to
Ennon, a distance of about an hour along a pleasant road, enlivened by the camps of the caravans
and the pilgrims going to Baptism. It was already
lined with long rows of tents covered with foliage,
and the people were still busied with preparations,
because with the close of the coming Sabbath, the
Feast of Tabernacles began. Jesus taught at intervals on the way. Just outside Ennon they had erected
a beautiful tent, and a solemn reception was prepared for Jesus by Mary the Suphanite. The most
distinguished personages of the city were present,
also the priests, and Mary with her children. The
men washed the feet of Jesus and His disciples, and
costly refreshments were offered them, according to
custom. Mary's children and others of their age presented the viands. The women, closely veiled, prostrated before Jesus, their faces on the ground. He
saluted and blessed them graciously. Mary, with tears
of joy and gratitude, invited Jesus to repair to her
house. When He entered the city, Mary's children,
two girls and a boy, and others of their age with long
garlands of flowers and scarfs of woolen stuff walked
before Him and at His side.

Jesus, accompanied by His disciples, entered the

courtyard of Mary's house, passing under a flowery arch erected for the occasion. Mary again cast herself at His feet, weeping and thanking, her children following her example. Jesus caressed the little ones. Mary told Him that Dina the Samaritan had been there, and that the man with whom she had been living up to that time had received Baptism. Mary knew Dina, since her own husband and three legitimate children lived in Damascus. She and the Samaritan had together sounded Jesus' praises. She was radiant with joy, and showed Jesus many costly robes for the use of the priests, and a high miter which she herself had made for the Temple, for she was incredibly skillful at such work, and rich in money and property. Jesus was very gracious toward her. He spoke to her of her husband, advising her to go back to him, to be reconciled with him, for her presence near him would prove of use, and her illegitimate children could be provided for elsewhere. He directed her also to send a messenger to her husband to request him to come to her. On leaving her house Jesus went to the place of Baptism, where He mounted the pulpit and taught the people.

Lazarus, Joseph of Arimathea, Veronica, Simeon's sons, and some disciples from Jerusalem had come hither for the Sabbath. Andrew, John, and some of the Baptist's disciples were still here, but James the Less had gone back. The Baptist had again sent messengers to Jesus urging Him to go to Jerusalem and to say openly before the whole world who He was. John was now so impatient, so anxious, because though so powerfully impelled to announce Jesus, he was unable to do so.

When the Sabbath began, Jesus taught in the synagogue, taking for His subjects the creation of the world, the waters, and the Fall of man. He alluded very significantly to the Messiah, commenting in the most striking manner upon *Isaias* 42:5-43, and applying the same to Himself and the Jewish people. After the Sabbath, there was an entertainment given to Jesus at the public banqueting hall. It had been prepared by Mary of Suphan. The tables, as well as the hall, were beautifully decorated with foliage and flowers and lamps. The guests were numerous and among them were many whom Jesus had cured. The women sat on one side behind a screen. During the meal Mary went forward with her children and placed costly perfumes on the table. She then poured a flask of odoriferous balm over Jesus' head, and cast herself down before Him. Jesus received these attentions graciously, and related parables. No one found fault with Mary, for all loved her on account of her munificence.

Next morning Jesus cured several sick persons, and taught in the synagogue. He also taught in a place to which those pagans that had received Baptism and those still in expectation of the same were admitted. In His latter instruction He spoke so feelingly, so naturally, of the lost son, that one would have thought Him the father who had found his son. He stretched out His arms, exclaiming: "See! See! He returns! Let us make ready a feast for him!" It was so natural that the people looked around, as if all that Jesus was saying were a reality. When He mentioned the calf that the father had slaughtered for the newly found son, His words were full of mysterious significance. It was as if He said: "But what would not be that love which would lead the Heavenly Father to give His own Son as a sacrifice, to save His lost children." The instruction was addressed principally to penitents, to the baptized, and to the pagans present, who were depicted as the lost son returning to his home. All were excited to joy and mutual charity. The fruit of Jesus' teaching was soon apparent at the celebration of the Feast of Tabernacles, in the good will and hospitality shown by the Jews to their pagan brethren. In the afternoon Jesus with His disciples and a crowd of the inhabitants took a walk outside the city and along by the Jordan, through the beautiful meadows and flowery fields in which the tents of the heathens stood. The parable they had just heard, that of the Prodigal Son, formed the subject of conversation, and all were cheerful and happy, full of love toward one another.

The exercises of the Sabbath were today brought to a close at an earlier hour than usual. Jesus again taught and cured some sick before its close. Then all went out of the city, or rather to a quarter somewhat remote, for it was built very irregularly, the streets broken up by open squares and gardens. And now was celebrated a great feast. The tabernacles were arranged in three rows and adorned with flowers, green branches, all kinds of devices formed of fruit, streamers, and innumerable lamps. The middle row was occupied by Jesus, the disciples, the priests, and the chief men of the city disposed in numerous groups. In one of the side rows were the women, and in the other the school children, the youths, and the maidens forming three distinct bands. The teachers sat with their pupils, and every class had its own chanters. Soon the children, crowned with flowers, surrounded the tables with flutes and chimes and harps, playing and singing. I saw also that the men held in one hand palm branches on which were little tinkling balls, and branches of willow with fine, narrow leaves, also the branches of a kind of bush such as we cultivate in pots. It was myrtle. In the other they held the beautiful yellow Esrog apple. They waved their branches as they sang. This was done three times: at the commencement, in the middle, and at the end of the feast. That kind of apple is not indigenous to Palestine; it comes from a warmer clime. It may indeed be found here and there in the sunny regions, but it is not so vigorous nor does it ripen to maturity. It was transported hither by caravans from warm countries. The fruit is yellow and like a small melon; it has a little crown on top, is ribbed and somewhat flat. The pulp in the center of the fruit is streaked with red, and in it closely packed together are five little kernels, but no seed vessel. The stalk is rather curved, and the blossoms form a large, white cluster like our elderberry. The branches below the large leaves strike root again in the earth, whence new ones spring up and thus an arbor is formed. The fruit rises from the axil of the leaves.

The pagans also took part in this feast. They, too, had their tabernacles of green branches, and those that had received Baptism took their places next to the Jews, by whom they were cordially and hospitably entertained. All were still influenced by the impressions received at the instruction upon the Prodigal Son. The meal lasted until late into the night. Jesus went up and down along the tables instructing the guests, and wherever anything was needed supplying the want through one of the disciples. Joyous sounds of conversation and merriment arose from all sides, occasionally interrupted by prayer and canticles. The whole place was ablaze with lights. The roofs of Ennon were covered with tents and tabernacles, and there the occupants of the houses slept at night. In the tabernacles outside the city many poor people and servants, after the feast was over and all had gone to rest, passed the night as guards.

Jesus, accompanied by the disciples and many others, returned from Ennon to Socoth, which was at no great distance. The greater part of the way was covered with tabernacles and tents, for many from the surrounding districts celebrated the feast here, and the caravans, which were constantly coming and going, were now resting for the feast. The whole length of the road was like one triumphal march. Behind the tabernacles were stands covered with awnings at which provisions could be purchased. It took Jesus several hours to traverse this road, for He was everywhere saluted and from time to time He stood still

to instruct. He did not reach the synagogue of Socoth
till toward evening. Socoth on the north bank of the
Jabok was a beautiful city, and had a very magnificent synagogue. Besides the Feast of Tabernacles,
there was another celebrated today in Socoth, that
of the reconciliation of Jacob and Esau. The whole
day was devoted to it, and there were visitors from
all the country around. Among the school children
at Ennon were some of the orphans from the school
of Abelmahula, who were now in Socoth, having come
for the feast of today. It was the real anniversary of
Jacob and Esau's reconciliation, which, according to
the Jewish tradition, had taken place on this day.

The synagogue, one of the most beautiful that I
have ever seen, was rendered still more gorgeous
today by its festal decorations of countless crowns,
flowery garlands, and lovely, sparkling lamps. It was
lofty and supported by eight columns. On both sides
of the edifice ran corridors communicating with the
buildings that comprised the dwellings of the Levites
and the schools. One end of the synagogue was more
elevated than the rest, and here toward the center
rose an ornamented pillar with little cases and projections running up around it, in which were kept
the rolls of the Law. Behind the pillar was a table,
and near it a curtain that could be drawn to cut off
the neighboring space from the rest of the synagogue.
A couple of steps farther back was a row of seats for
the priests, with one more elevated in the middle for
the preacher. Back of these seats stood an altar of
incense above which, in the roof of the synagogue,
was an opening; and behind this altar, at the far end
of the edifice, were tables upon which the offerings
were deposited. The men, ranged according to their
classes, stood in the center of the synagogue. To the
left, on a slight elevation and separated by a grating, was the place for the women; and on the right
was that of the school children grouped in classes,
the boys and girls separate.

The feast of today celebrated the reconciliation between God and man. There was a general confession of sin made either in public or private, according to individual desire. All gathered round the altar of incense, offered gifts of expiation, received a penance from the priests, and made voluntary vows. This ceremony bore a striking resemblance to our Sacrament of Penance. The priest from the teacher's chair spoke of Jacob and Esau, who had today been reconciled with God and each other, also of Laban and Jacob who had again become friends and offered a sacrifice to the Lord, and he earnestly exhorted his hearers to penance. Many of those present had by John's teaching and that of Jesus during the past days been very much touched, and were waiting only for this great festival to do penance. Some men, whose consciences reproached them with grave faults, went through the door in the grating near the teacher's chair around behind the altar, and laid on the tables their offerings, which a priest received. Then, returning to the priests in front of the pillar containing the Law, they confessed their sins either publicly to the assembled priests, or privately to one of their own choice. In the latter case, both priest and penitent retired behind the curtain, the confession was made in a low voice, a penance imposed, and at the same time incense was cast upon the altar. If the smoke arose in a certain way, the people took it as a sign of the genuineness of the penitent's contrition and of the pardon accorded his sins. The rest of the Jews chanted and prayed during the confessions. The penitents made a kind of profession of faith, promising fidelity to the Law, to Israel, and to the Holy of Holies. Then they prostrated and confessed their sins, often with abundant tears. The female penitents followed after the men, and their offerings were received by the priests. Then retiring behind a grating, they called for a priest and confessed.

The Jews accused themselves of sins against the

Ten Commandments and of all violations of established usages. There was something singular in their
confession, which I hardly know how to repeat. They
bemoaned the sins of their forefathers. They spoke
of a soul prone to sin received from their progenitors, and of another, a holy one, received from God.
They appeared indeed to speak of two distinct souls.
The priests in their exhortation likewise said something to the same effect, namely, "May their" (the
ancestors') "sinful soul remain not in us, but may
our holy soul remain in us!" I cannot now recall what
was said of the influence mutually exerted by these
two souls upon, and by, and in, each other. Jesus
next spoke. He touched upon this same point, but
treated it differently from the Doctors. He said that
it should indeed be so no longer. The sinful soul
received from their forefathers should not remain in
them. It was a touching instruction, clearly signify-
ing that Jesus Himself was about to make satisfaction for all souls. They also lamented the sins of their
parents, as if knowing that all kinds of evils had
descended to them through their progenitors, as if
through them they were still in possession of the sad
heritage of sin.

The penitential exercises had already begun when
Jesus arrived. He was received at the entrance of
the synagogue, and for awhile He remained standing at one side on the platform among the Doctors,
one of whom was preaching. It was about five o'clock
when He arrived. The offerings of the penitents consisted of all sorts of fruits, money, articles of clothing for the priests, pieces of stuff, silken tassels and
knots, girdles, etc., and principally of frankincense,
some of which was burned at once.

And now I witnessed a touching spectacle. While
the confessions were going on and the offerings were
being made by the penitents, I noticed a distin-
guished-looking lady in a private seat near the
secluded place of penance. Her seat was cut off from

the rest by a grating. I noticed her troubled and agitated appearance. Her maidservant was nearby, having just deposited on a stool at her mistress' side a basket containing the gifts intended for the offering. The lady was impatient for her turn to come, and when at last she could no longer restrain her agitation and desire for reconciliation, she arose, drew her veil and, preceded by her maid with the offerings, passed through the grating and straight to the priests, into a place to which entrance was forbidden to women. The wardens tried to prevent her, but the maid would not be stopped. She forced her way in, exclaiming: "Make way! Make way for my mistress! She wants to make her offering, she wants to do penance! Make way for her! She wants to purify her soul!" The lady, agitated and bowed down by sorrow, advanced toward the priests, threw herself on her knees, and begged to be reconciled. But they told her to withdraw, they could not hear her there. One of them however, younger than his brethren, took her by the hand, saying: "I will reconcile thee! If thy corporal presence belongs not here, not so thy soul, since thou art penitent!" Then turning with her toward Jesus, he said: "Rabbi, what sayest Thou?" The lady fell on her face before Jesus, and He answered: "Yes, her soul has a right to be here! Permit this daughter of Adam to do penance!" and the priest retired with her into the curtained enclosure. When she reappeared, she prostrated in tears upon the ground, exclaiming: "Wipe your feet on me, for I am an adulteress!" and the priests touched her lightly with the foot. Her husband, who knew nothing of what was transpiring, was sent for. At his entrance, Jesus occupied the teacher's chair, and His words sank deep into the man's heart. He wept, and his wife, veiled and prostrate on the ground before him, confessed her guilt. Her tears flowed abundantly, and she appeared to be more dead than alive. Jesus addressed her: "Thy sins are forgiven thee! Arise, child of God!"

and the husband, deeply moved, reached out his hand
to his penitent wife. Their hands were then bound
together with the wife's veil and the long, narrow
scarf of the husband, and loosened again after they
had received a benediction. It was like a second nuptial ceremony. The lady was now, after her reconciliation, quite inebriated with joy. At the moment her
offerings were presented, she had cried out: "Pray!
Pray! Burn incense, offer sacrifices, that my sins may
be forgiven!" and she falteringly repeated various
passages from the Psalms, while being conducted to
her place by the priests.

Her offering consisted of many costly fruits such
as they were accustomed to use at the Feast of Tabernacles. They had been carefully arranged in the basket, so that they would not injure one another by
pressure. There were also borders, silk tassels, and
fringes for priestly vestments. She at the same time
committed to the flames several magnificent silk
robes in which her vanity had arrayed itself for the
gaze of her paramour. She was a tall, robust, beautifully formed woman of an ardent and vivacious
temperament. Her deep contrition and voluntary
avowal of guilt had won for her forgiveness, and her
husband was heartily reconciled with her. She had
had no children by her illicit connection, had been
the first to dissolve her sinful bonds, and had won
over her paramour to penance. She did not, however, make him known either to the priests or to
her husband. It was forbidden to the latter to make
inquiries, and to her to name the guilty one. The
husband was a pious man; he forgave and forgot
with all his heart. The multitude present did not
indeed catch the details of the scene. Still they saw
the interruption, they saw that something extraordinary was transpiring, and they heard the lady's
cry for prayer and sacrifice. All prayed earnestly for
her, and rejoiced over a soul doing penance. The people of this place were very good, as they generally

were on the east side of the Jordan, for they had retained more of the manners and customs of the ancient patriarchs.

Jesus continued teaching in beautiful and touching language. I recall distinctly His allusion to the sins of our forefathers and our own share in the same, and He rectified the ideas of some of His auditors on that subject. Once He used the expression: "Your fathers have eaten grapes, and your teeth have been set on edge."

The schoolteachers were then questioned upon the faults of their pupils, while the latter were reminded that if they accused themselves and were sorry, they would be forgiven,

There were many sick outside the synagogue and, although it was not customary for them to enter on the Feast of Tabernacles, yet Jesus directed the disciples to bring them into the corridor between the sacred building and the dwellings of the Doctors. At the close of the feast, the whole synagogue having long before been lighted up with lamps, He went out into the corridor and cured many of them. At the moment Jesus entered the corridor, a messenger appeared from the lately reconciled lady, begging Jesus to grant her a few words. Jesus went to her and retired apart with her a few instants. She threw herself at His feet and exclaimed: "Master, he with whom I sinned, implores Thee to reconcile him to God!" and Jesus promised to see him there in that same place after the repast.

The curing of the sick was followed by an entertainment in honor of the feast, and given on one of the open squares of the city. Jesus, the disciples, the Levites, and the most distinguished personages of the city took their places under a large and beautiful bower that formed the center of many others, the men and women separate. The poor were not forgotten. Everyone sent the best from his own table to them. Jesus went around from table to table, not

excepting that of the women. The reconciled sinner
was full of joy, as were also her female friends. They
gathered around her, heartily wishing her every happiness. As Jesus was making the rounds of the tables,
she seemed to be very uneasy about something, and
frequently cast anxious glances toward Him, hoping
that He would not forget His promise to reconcile
the partner of her guilt, for she knew that he was
already waiting at the place designated. When Jesus
drew near to where she sat, He quieted her anxiety,
telling her that He knew what was troubling her and
bidding her rest assured that all would be well in
its own good time. When the guests separated for
their homes, Jesus started for His lodgings near the
synagogue. He was met by the man who had been
waiting in the corridor for Him, and who now threw
himself at His feet and confessed his sin. Jesus
exhorted him to sin no more and imposed on him as
penance to give the priests every week for a certain
time something for a charitable purpose. He was not
obliged to make public offerings, but to mourn his
sin in private.

When Jesus returned from Socoth to Ennon, He
gave instructions at the place of Baptism, cured the
sick, and visited the Gentiles. Several little parties
of neophytes were baptized. There were still standing here some of the arrangements John had made
when baptizing for the first time at the Jordan near
On, a tent and the baptismal stone. The neophytes
leaned over a railing, their heads over the baptismal
pool. Jesus received the confessions of many and
granted them absolution from their sins, a power which
He had imparted to some of the older disciples—for
instance, to Andrew. John the Evangelist did not yet
baptize. He acted as witness and sponsor.

Before Jesus again left Ennon with His disciples,
He had an interview with Mary the Suphanite in
her own house. He gave her salutary advice. Mary
was entirely changed. She was full of love, zeal, humil-

ity, and gratitude; she busied herself with the poor
and the sick. When journeying after her cure through
Ramoth and Basan, Jesus had sent a disciple to Bethania to inform the holy women of it and of her reconciliation, in consequence of which announcement
Veronica, Johanna Chusa, and Martha had been to
visit her.

On His departure from Ennon, Jesus received rich
presents from Mary and many other people, all of
which were at once distributed to the poor. The gateway by which He left the city was decorated with an
arch of flowers and garlands. The assembled crowd
saluted Him with songs of praise, and He was met
outside the city by women and children who presented Him with wreaths. This was one of the customs at the Feast of Tabernacles. Many of the citizens
accompanied Him beyond the city limits. For two
hours His road ran to the south, through the valley
of the Jordan, and on this side of the river. Then it
wound for about half an hour to the west, then turned
again to the south and led to the city of Akrabis,
which was situated upon a ridge of the mountain.

2. Jesus in Akrabis, Silo, and Korea

Jesus was received in ceremony outside of Akrabis, for the inhabitants were expecting His coming.
The tabernacles of green branches were ranged for
some distance beyond the city, and into one of the
largest and most beautiful they conducted Jesus for
the customary washing of feet and offering of refreshments. Akrabis was rather a large place, about two
hours from the Jordan. It had five gates, and was
traversed by the highway between Samaria and Jericho. Travellers in this direction had to pass through
Akrabis, consequently it was well supplied with provisions and other necessaries. Outside the gate at
which Jesus arrived were inns for the accommodation of caravans. Tabernacles were erected before each

of the five gates, for each quarter of the city had its
own gate.

Next day Jesus made the rounds of the city, visited all the tabernacles, and gave instructions here
and there. The people observed many customs peculiar to this festival; for instance, they took only a
mouthful in the morning, the rest of the repast being
reserved for the poor. Their employment during the
day was interrupted by canticles and prayers, and
instructions were given by the Elders. These instructions were now delivered by Jesus. On His coming
and going, He was received and escorted by little
boys and girls carrying around Him garlands of flowers. This, too, was one of their customs. The residents of the different quarters sometimes went from
their own tabernacles to those of their neighbors,
either to listen to the instructions or to assist at an
entertainment. On such occasions they went processionally, carrying garlands such as were borne by
Jesus' escort.

The women were busied with all sorts of occupations in the tabernacles. Some were sitting embroi-
dering flowers on long strips of stuff, others were
making sandals out of the coarse, brown hair of goats
and camels. They attached their work to their girdle as we do our knitting. The soles were furnished
with a support like a heel both before and behind,
also with sharp points, in order to aid in climbing
the mountains. The people gave Jesus a very cordial
reception, but the Doctors of the Law were not so
simple-hearted as their confreres at Ennon and
Socoth. They were indeed courteous in their manner,
but somewhat reserved.

From Akrabis Jesus went to Silo, distant only one
hour in a direct line toward the southwest; but as
the road winds first down into the valley and then
over the mountain, it makes the distance a good two
hours. The inhabitants of Silo, like those of Akrabis, were assembled in the tabernacles outside the

gates of the city. They, too, knew of Jesus' coming
and were waiting for Him. They saw Him and His
companions from afar, climbing up the winding road
that led to their city. When they perceived that He
was not directing His steps to the gate nearest to
Akrabis, but was going around the city more to the
northwest, to that which led from Samaria, they
sent messengers to announce the fact to the people
of that quarter. These latter received Him into their
tabernacles, washed His feet, and presented the customary refreshments, He went immediately to the
central height of the city, where once the Ark of the
Covenant had rested, and taught in the open air
from a teacher's chair very beautifully wrought in
stone. Here, too, were tabernacles and houses of
entertainment, in which latter everything needed in
the former was cooked in common. Men were performing this duty, but they appeared to me to be
slaves and not real Jews.

The day following was one of the most solemn of
the feast, though I do not know whether what I saw
here was a purely local custom or one practiced generally. One of the Doctors of the Law annually on
this day delivered from the teacher's chair a casti-
gatory sermon, to which not one of his hearers dared
offer the least contradiction. It was principally for
the purpose of delivering this sermon that Jesus had
come here today. All the Jews, men, women, youths,
maidens, and children had assembled to hear Him.
They had come processionally from their different
tabernacles, carrying festoons and garlands of leaves
between the various divisions and classes. The
teacher's chair, under an awning decorated with
foliage, crowned a terraced eminence. Jesus taught
until midday. He spoke of the mercy of God toward
His people, of Israel's revolts and turpitude, of the
chastisements awaiting Jerusalem, of the destruction of the Temple, of the present time of grace, the
last that would be offered them. He said that if the

Jews rejected this last grace, never to the end of time
should they as a nation receive another, and that a
much more frightful chastisement should fall upon
Jerusalem than it had ever yet experienced. The whole
discourse was calculated to inspire fear. All listened
silent and terrified, for Jesus very clearly signified,
as He explained the Prophecies, that He Himself was
the One who was to bring salvation. The Pharisees
of the place, who were not of much account and who,
like those of Akrabis, had received Jesus with a show
of hypocritical reverence, kept silence, though filled
with wonder and irritation. The people, however, ap-
plauded Jesus and sang His praises. Jesus spoke
likewise of the Scribes, their misrepresentations of
the Holy Scriptures, their false interpretations and
additions.

That evening a public entertainment was given in
the tabernacles on the eminence. But Jesus was not
present at it. He went down to the tabernacles of
the poor, where He consoled and instructed. Wherever there were no Pharisees to spy their actions,
the people pressed around Jesus, cast themselves at
His feet, paid Him homage, confessed their sins, and
made known their needs. He consoled them and gave
them advice. It was a touching sight to see all this
going on in the darkness of night among the tabernacles, from which shone forth a faint and trembling
glimmer. No lights were to be seen for, on account
of the draught, the lamps had been covered with
screens, and the yellow glare they cast lit up the
green foliage, the fruits, and the people in a manner quite strange to behold. From the height of Silo,
many places around could be distinctly seen, and
everywhere shone the glimmering light of the taber-
nacle-feast, while the sound of singing came from
far and near. Jesus did not perform any cures here.
The Pharisees kept the sick back, and the people
appeared to be afraid. Here as in Akrabis, the song
of the Pharisees, when they heard of Jesus' coming,

was: "What new doctrine is He now going to bring us? What design has He in coming here?"

From Silo Jesus took a southwestwardly direction and went down for one and a half hours to Korea, a place that could be seen from the height of the former city. It had neither walls nor ramparts. The Pharisees of Korea went out some distance beyond the city to meet Jesus, taking with them one of their fellow citizens who had been blind from his birth. They thought to tempt Jesus. The blind man had over his garments, around his shoulder, and over his head a wide scarf like a linen cloth. He was a tall, handsome man. As Jesus drew near, to the astonishment of the bystanders, the blind man turned toward Him and cast himself at His feet. Jesus raised him and questioned him on his religion, the Ten Commandments, the Law, and the Prophecies. The blind man answered more intelligently than any had dared to hope—yes, he even seemed to utter prophecies. He spoke of the persecution awaiting Jesus, saying that He must not yet go to Jerusalem, because there His enemies would put Him to death. All present were struck with fear. The crowd gathered around was great. Jesus asked him whether he desired to see the tabernacles of Israel, the mountains and the Jordan, his own parents and friends, the Temple, the Holy City, and lastly Himself, Jesus, who was then standing before him. The blind man answered that he already saw Him, that he had seen Him as soon as He drew near, and he described His appearance and dress. "But," he continued, "I do desire to see all other things, and I know that, if Thou wilt, Thou canst give me sight." Then Jesus laid His hand on the man's forehead, prayed, and with His thumb made the Sign of the Cross on his closed eyelids, raising them at the same time. Thereupon the man cast off the scarf from his head and shoulders, looked gladly and wonderingly around, and exclaimed: "Great are the works of the Almighty!"

He fell at Jesus' feet, who blessed him. The Pharisees looked on in silence, the relatives of the blind man gathered around him, the crowd intoned Psalms, while the blind man himself in a prophetic strain spoke and chanted alternately of Jesus and the fulfillment of the Promise. Jesus went on into the city, where He healed many sick and restored sight to others that were blind, whom He found in the space between the houses and the earthen mounds. The usual courtesies of washing the feet and offering refreshments had already been tendered to Him in one of the tabernacles outside the city. The blind man, who accompanied Jesus the whole way, continued to speak under prophetic inspiration of the Jordan, of the Holy Spirit who had descended upon Him, and of the voice from Heaven.

That evening Jesus preached in the synagogue for the Sabbath. He spoke of the family of Noe, of the building of the ark, of the vocation of Abraham, and expounded the passages of Isaias in which mention is made of God's covenant with Noe, and of the rainbow as a sign in the heavens. (*Is.* 54-55). As He spoke I saw all very distinctly: the whole life and all the generations of the Patriarchs, the branches that separated from the parent stock, and the idolatry that arose from them. When I am actually gazing upon such things, all seems clear and natural, but when out of vision, when returned to the routine of daily life, I am saddened by its weary interruptions and can no longer comprehend what I have seen with the eye of the spirit. Jesus spoke likewise of the erroneous interpretation of the Scripture and of false computation of time. He proved by His own reckoning, which was quite simple and clear, that all things in the Scriptures could be made accurately to accord. I cannot understand how such things could have been thrown into confusion, while others had been totally forgotten.

One section of Korea lay upon a terraced mountain; the other, connected with the first by a row of small houses, extended eastward into a deep mountain dale. Some Pharisees and many sick from Silo were here awaiting Jesus. Although Korea lay a little more to the west than Akrabis, yet it was still nearer to the Jordan as the river made a bend in this locality. It was not a large place and the people were not rich. They did cheap basketwork, made beehives and long strips of straw matting, some coarse, some fine. The straw or reeds were bleached and of the best. They made also whole screens like entire walls of this matting for separating sleeping chambers one from another. There were in the neighborhood many other little places. The mountains of this region are steep and rugged. Across the Jordan from Akrabis was the region traversed by Jesus the preceding year at the Feast of Tabernacles when He went through the valley to Dibon.

Next morning Jesus preached in the synagogue and, while the Jews took their Sabbath promenade, cured many sick who had been brought to a large hall nearby. At the close of the Sabbath, while assisting at the entertainment given in the tabernacles, Jesus had a dispute with the Pharisees. The subject under discussion was the prophecies uttered lately by the man born blind and to whom Jesus had given sight. The Pharisees maintained that the same man had already predicted many things that had never come to pass, to which Jesus replied that the Spirit of God had not then descended upon him. During the conversation, mention was made of Ezechiel as if his early Prophecies relating to Jerusalem had not been fulfilled, to which Jesus responded that the Spirit of God had not come upon him until he was in Babylon near the river Chobar, when something was given him to swallow. Jesus' response reduced the Pharisees to silence.

The man restored to sight went around the city, praising God, singing Psalms, and prophesying. The

day before he had been to the synagogue, where he
was invested with a broad girdle and was admitted
by vow among the Nazarites. A priest performed over
him the ceremony of consecration. I think he afterward joined the disciples.

Jesus visited the parents of the man restored to
sight, he himself having prayed Him to do so. He
conducted Him to their home, which was in a retired
part of the city. They were Essenians, of the grade
that lived in marriage, distant relatives of Zachary,
and connected in some way with the Essenian community of Maspha. They had several sons and daughters, the one restored to sight being the youngest
child. There were several other Essenian families,
all related to them, living in their neighborhood. They
owned beautiful fields on a declivity just outside their
quarter of the city, and cultivated wheat and barley.
They retained for their own use only a third part of
the produce, one being given to the poor, the other
to the community at Maspha. These Essenians came
out hospitably to meet Jesus and welcome Him in
front of their dwellings. The father of the blind man
restored to sight presented him to Jesus with the
request that He would receive him as the least of
the servants and messengers of His disciples, the
one to go before Him and prepare the inns for His
reception. Jesus accepted him and sent him at once
to Bethania with Silas and one of the disciples from
Hebron. I think He intended to give Lazarus a joy-
ful surprise by means of the man restored to sight,
for he had known the latter as one born blind. The
young man's father was named Cyrus, Sirius, or Syrus,
the name of a king who reigned during the Jewish
Captivity. The son's name was Manahem. He had
always worn a girdle under his garments, but after
his cure he put it outside and made a formal vow
for a time. He possessed the gift of prophecy. Even
when blind he had always been present at John's
preaching, and had received baptism. He often gath-

ered many of the youths of Korea around him,
instructed them and, inspired by the Spirit, prophesied to them of Jesus. His parents loved him on
account of his piety and zeal, and provided him with
clothing of the best. When Jesus gave him sight, He
said: "I give thee a double gift, sight of soul and of
body." The Pharisees of Korea treated Manahem with
contempt on account of his prophecies. They called
them troubled fancies, foolish reveries, and said that
he was vain of his fine clothes. They had brought
him out themselves to meet Jesus, being firmly convinced that He could not cure him since no one had
ever seen any pupil in his eyes. And now that he
was restored to sight, the most wicked among them
dared to affirm that he had never been blind, that
being an Essenian, he had very likely made a vow
to feign blindness.

The Pharisees who spoke with Jesus of Ezechiel
had expressed their contempt for the Prophet. He
was, they said, only a servant of Jeremias and he
had, in the school of the Prophet, very preposterous,
very gloomy reveries. Things had fallen out quite differently from his predictions. Manahem also had
uttered very profound prophecies of Melchisedech,
Malachias, and Jesus.

3. Jesus in Ophra, Salem, and Aruma

One hour to the southwest of Korea was the city
of Ophra, hidden among the mountains. Starting
from Korea the traveller had first to ascend and
then to descend the mountain road. An hour and a
half at most westward from it, and on the north side
of the desert to Bethoron toward the west, stood the
mountain fortress of Alexandrium. Mount Garizim
lay on the northwest, to the south and west the
plain just mentioned and the mountains of the tribe
of Benjamin. Mary often traversed this plain. Many
lonely shepherd huts were scattered over it, and the

city of Bethel was built on its confines.

Three highroads ran through Ophra. Caravans from Hebron were constantly passing this way, consequently the whole place was made up of public inns and mercantile houses. The people were somewhat rude and greedy for gain. Once during the preceding year they had received a visit from some of Jesus' disciples, and since that they had improved a little. At the moment of Jesus' arrival, the men of the place were busy gathering grapes in the vineyards that lined the road on either side, for a solemn festival was to begin that evening. The tabernacles were deserted excepting by the children, the youths, and the maidens, who with banners were going through them processionally. The priests also were engaged removing the prayer rolls and other holy things from the tabernacles to the synagogue, where they laid a prayer roll on every seat. I saw the women in their homes. They were dressed in their holiday robes, and were praying from rolls of parchment.

Jesus was espied by some men outside the gate. They went to Him and conducted Him into the city. They washed His feet and He took a little luncheon at an inn near the synagogue. After that He visited several houses, healing the sick and giving instruction. That evening the roll of the Law was carried around in the school, and everyone read a little out of it. This ceremony was followed by a grand entertainment given in the public festive hall. I saw lambs on the table, and the Esrog apples also that had been procured for the Feast of Tabernacles were eaten. These apples were prepared with some ingredients. Each was cut into five parts, and these were again tied into one by a red thread. Five persons ate of one apple. The viands had all been prepared by Sabbath servants, that is, by pagans who appeared to be in a kind of slavery.

Next morning Jesus went from house to house, exhorting the people to turn away from their avarice and love of gain, and engaging them to attend the instruction to be given in the synagogue. He saluted all with a congratulatory word on the close of the feast. The people of Ophra were so usurious and unpolished that they were held in the same low esteem as the publicans. But they had now improved a little. That afternoon the branches of which the tabernacles had been formed were brought processionally by the boys to the square in front of the synagogue, there piled in a heap, and burned. The Jews watched with interest the rising of the flames, presaging from their various movements good or bad fortune. Jesus preached afterward in the synagogue, taking for His subjects the happiness of Adam, his Fall, the Promise, and some passages from Josue. He spoke also of too great solicitude for the things of life, of the lilies that do not spin, of the ravens that do not sow, etc., and brought forward examples in the person of Daniel and Job. They, He said, were men of piety, engrossed in occupations, but still without worldly solicitude.

Jesus was not entertained gratis in Ophra. The disciples had to pay all expenses at the inn. While He and they were still there a man from Cyprus came to see Him. He had been to see John at Machaerus, ten hours from Ophra, and had been conducted hither by a servant of Zorobabel, the Centurion of Capharnaum. He had been commissioned by an illustrious man of Cyprus to bring him some reliable news of Jesus, also of John, of whom he had heard so much.

The messenger did not tarry long at Ophra. He left as soon as he had executed his commission, for a ship was in waiting to carry him home. He was a pagan, but of a most amiable and humble disposition. The Centurion's servant had, at his request, conducted him from Capharnaum to John, at Machaerus, and from the latter to Jesus, at Ophra. Jesus conversed with him a long time, and the disciples put in writing before his departure all that he desired to know. One of the ancestors of his master had been King of Cyprus. He had received many Jews fleeing from persecution and had even entertained them at his own table. This work of mercy bore its fruit in one of his descendants, obtaining for him the grace to believe in Jesus Christ. In this vision I had a glimpse of Jesus retiring after the coming Pasch to Tyre and Sidon, and thence sailing over to the island of Cyprus to announce His doctrine.

From Ophra Jesus journeyed through the valley between Alexandrium and Lebona to Salem. He descended through the forest of Hareth into the plain of Salem. Gardens and beautiful walks lay around the outskirts of the city, which was most delightfully situated. It was not very large, but cleaner and more regular than many others in this region, laid out in the form of a star, the points radiating from a fountain in the center. All the streets ran toward the fountain, and were broken up by beautiful walks. The city at this period, however, had something in its appearance that bespoke decline. The fountain was regarded as sacred. It was once tainted like that near Jericho, but Eliseus had, like the one alluded to, purified it by casting into it salt and water in which the Holy Mystery had been immersed. The little edifice erected over it was very beautiful. In the center of the city and not far from the fountain arose a lofty castle, then in ruins, the large window casements destitute of windows. Nearby stood a high, round tower. On its flat top, which was surrounded by a gallery, a flag was waving. At about two-thirds of the height of the tower projected four beams toward the four quarters of the world, upon which hung large polished globes that glittered in the sun. They faced four different cities, and were a sort of memorial of David's time. He had once sojourned here with Michol and, when obliged to flee into the land of Galaad, he had by means of these globes received information from Jonathan concerning Saul and his movements against himself. The globes, by previous agreement, were hung sometimes this way, sometimes that, thus indicating by signs what was transpiring in those parts.

Jesus was very well received. People whom He met near the harvest ricks accompanied Him to the city, from which others were coming to meet Him. They conducted Him and the disciples to a house, in which they washed their feet and provided them with sandals and garments until their own were dusted and cleaned. Travellers were often presented with the dress thus provided, but Jesus never accepted it as a gift. He generally had a change with Him, of which one of the disciples took charge. The Salemites then took Jesus to their beautiful fountain and tendered to Him the customary refreshments. There were gathered around the fountain numbers of sick of all kinds, so numerous that even the streets were lined with them. Jesus at once began to cure, passing quietly from one to another until nearly four o'clock, when He assisted at a dinner given at an inn, and thence proceeded to the synagogue to preach. During the discourse He spoke of Melchisedech, also of Malachias who had once sojourned here and who had prophesied the Sacrifice according to the order of Melchisedech. Jesus told them that the time for that Sacrifice was drawing near, and that those ancient Prophets would have been happy to have seen and heard what they now saw and heard.

The people of Salem were of the middle class, neither poor nor rich, but well inclined and charitable toward one another. The Doctors of the synagogue likewise were well-intentioned, but they were often visited by Pharisees from the neighborhood—to their own great annoyance and that of the citizens. Salem enjoyed certain privileges. It had under its jurisdiction the district in its immediate vicinity and other neighboring places. Jesus was especially kind to these people and confirmed them in their good sentiments.

On the morning of the next day Jesus went about an hour southeast of Salem to a nook between the Jordan and the little river that flows into it from Akrabis. There was a pleasure garden in this hilly region, also three fish ponds, one above another, each fed by the waters of the little river. There were also baths that could be warmed. Jesus was followed thither by many from the city. From this garden Ennon could be distinctly seen across the Jordan, whose opposite bank was full of promenaders. Toward noon all returned to the city and found assembled some of the Pharisees from Aruma. This city was situated on a mountain two hours west of Salem and about one hour northwest of the newly built city of Phasael, which lay almost hidden in a corner of the mountains. It was there the devout Jairus dwelt, whose daughter Jesus had not long ago raised to life. Among those Pharisees was a brother of Simon the Leper, of Bethania. He was one of the most distinguished Pharisees of Aruma. There were also some Sadducees present. They had all come as guests, for it was customary for the Doctors of the Law to visit one another during the days immediately following the Feast of Tabernacles. Some from other places besides Aruma were present also. A banquet was given in one of the public houses of Salem, at which Jesus and all the Doctors assisted. The latter feared that Jesus was going to preach in Salem on the coming Sabbath. They did not relish the idea, since the inhabitants were already unfavorably disposed toward themselves; therefore Simon's brother invited Jesus to go to Aruma for the Sabbath, and Jesus accepted the invitation.

Phasael was a new place at which Herod stopped when in that part of the country. The city was surrounded by palm trees, and a little stream took its rise in the neighborhood, thence flowing into the Jordan almost opposite Socoth. The inhabitants appeared to be colonists. The city was built by Herod.

On Jesus' arrival at Aruma, He was not received by the Pharisees outside the city gate. Consequently, with His seven disciples, all like Himself with girded garments, He passed through into the city. There He was received according to the custom of the place by some of the well-disposed citizens, and as was always done to travellers that entered the gate with their garments girded. The fact of their entering in that style indicated that they had not yet received hospitality. Jesus and the disciples were taken to a house where their feet were washed, their clothes dusted, and refreshments offered them. After that Jesus went to the priests' house near the synagogue, where was Simon's brother together with several other Pharisees and Sadducees who had come hither from Thebez and other places. Providing themselves with rolls of the Scriptures, they went with Jesus to the public baths outside the city. There they deliberated upon the passages of Holy Writ that occurred in the lesson of the present Sabbath. It was like a preparation for a sermon. They were very courteous, very polished in their manner toward Jesus, whom they pressed to preach that evening, begging Him at the same time not to say anything that could make the people mutinous. They did not say this in plain terms, but they made themselves understood thus. Jesus replied sternly and unhesitatingly that He would teach what was in the Scripture, namely, the truth, and He went on to speak of wolves in sheep's clothing.

In the synagogue Jesus taught of Abraham's vocation and his journey to Egypt, of the Hebrew tongue, of Noe, Heber, Phaleg, and Job. The lessons were from *Genesis* 12 and *Isaias*. Jesus said that already in Heber's time God had separated the Israelites from the rest of mankind, for He had given Heber a new language, the Hebrew, which had nothing in common with other tongues then existing. This was done in order the more effectually to separate his race from all others. Before that, Heber, like Adam, Seth and Noe, had spoken that first mother tongue. But at the building of the Tower of Babel this had been confused and broken up into numerous dialects. In order to separate Heber entirely from the rest of men, God had given him a language of his own, the holy, ancient Hebrew, without which he and his descendants would never have been able to keep themselves pure and a distinct race.

While at Aruma, Jesus received hospitality at the house of Simon the Leper's brother. Simon himself, though now living in Bethania, was originally from Aruma. He was a person of little importance, though with aspirations to the contrary, but his brother of Aruma was well versed in the lore of the day. All things were perfectly regulated in this Pharisee's house. If Jesus was not received with the reverence that faith inspires, still He was treated conformably to the best laws of hospitality. He was given a separate oratory, the toilet linen and vessels were beautiful, and the master of the house himself paid the customary honors to his guest. The wife and children did not make their appearance.

Jairus of Phasael, whose daughter Jesus had raised from the dead, was also here for the Sabbath and had an interview with Jesus. He then went to see the disciples and took them around through the city. His daughter was not in Phasael, but at the girls' school up at Abelmahula. On this day many young girls came here in a body, as I had previously seen the men visiting different places in parties. Abelmahula may have been something over six hours from Phasael.

Outside of Aruma and to the east stood an immense old building occupied by aged men and widows. They were not Essenians, though they were habited in long, white robes and lived according to a certain rule. Jesus taught among them. When invited to a dinner or an entertainment, Jesus usually went from table to table and gave instructions.

The Feast of the Dedication of Solomon's Temple was being celebrated in Aruma. The synagogue was brilliantly illuminated. In the middle of it stood a pyramid of lights. The feast proper was already past. I think it was immediately after the Feast of Tabernacles. The present nocturnal celebration was a continuation of it. Jesus preached on the Dedication. He told of God's appearing to Solomon and saying to him that He would preserve the Israelites and the Temple as long as they remained faithful to Him, and that He would even dwell among them in the sacred edifice; but that He would destroy it if they fell away from Him. Jesus used severe language when alluding to this. He applied it to the present, to His own day, in which evil had reached its height. If, He said, they were not converted, the Temple would be destroyed. Then the Pharisees began to dispute with Him. They declared that God had not made use of such threats, that it was all a fable, an imagination of Solomon. The discussion became very lively, and I saw Jesus speaking with great animation. There was something in His appearance that affected them strongly and they could scarcely rest their eyes upon Him. He spoke to them upon the passages met today in the Sabbath lessons, of distorting and corrupting the eternal truths, of the history and chronology of ancient heathen nations, the Egyptians, for instance. He demanded of the Pharisees how they could venture to reproach these pagans, they themselves being even then in so miserable a condition, since what had been handed over to them as something so peculiarly theirs, something so sacred, the Word of the Almighty upon which His covenant with their holy Temple was founded, they could whimsically and capriciously reject as imaginations and fables. He affirmed and repeated God's promises to Solomon, and told them that in consequence of their false

interpretations and sinful explanations, Jehovah's
menaces were about to be fulfilled, for when faith
in His most holy promises was wavering, the foundation of His Temple also began to totter. He said:
"Yes, the Temple will be overturned and destroyed,
because ye do not believe in the promises, because
ye do not know that which is holy, because ye treat
it as a thing profane! You yourselves are laboring
at its downfall. No part of it shall escape destruction. It will go to pieces on account of your
sins!" In this wise spoke Jesus, and with such significance that He appeared to allude to Himself under
the name of the Temple, as before His Passion He
said still more plainly: "I will build it up again in
three days." His words on this occasion were not so
significant, though sufficiently so to fill His hearers
with fury not unmixed with dread, and make them
feel that there was something extraordinary and
mysterious in His speech. They expressed their indignation in loud mutterings. Jesus paid no attention to them. He coolly continued His discourse in
language they could not gainsay, for though against
their will, they were interiorly convinced of the truth
of His words. As He left the synagogue, the Pharisees offered Him their hand, as if desirous of apol-
ogizing for their violence. They wished to maintain
an appearance of friendliness. Jesus gently addressed
to them some earnest words, and left the synagogue,
which was then closed.

I had a vision of Solomon. He was standing upon
a column in the court of the Temple and near the
altar of incense, addressing the people and praying
aloud to God. The column was high enough for him
to be distinctly seen. There was an interior ascent to
the top upon which was a broad platform with a chair.
It was movable and could be transported from place
to place. I afterward saw Solomon in the fortress of
Sion, for he did not yet occupy his new palace. It was
there also that at an earlier period I saw God com-

municating with David, especially at the time of Nathan's embassy. There was also a terrace sheltered by a tent, upon which David slept. I saw Solomon praying on that terrace. A supernatural light of intense brilliancy shone around him, and from the light a voice proceeded.

Solomon was a handsome man. He was tall and his limbs were rounded, not spare and angular like those of most people of that place. His hair was brown and straight, his beard short and well trimmed, his brown eyes full of penetration, his face round and full with rather prominent cheekbones. He had not at that time devoted himself to his seraglio of pagan women.

To avoid scandalizing His enemies, Jesus did not publicly cure in Aruma. The people were besides intimidated by the Pharisees, and dared not make their appearance by day. It was an exceedingly touching sight to see Jesus, as I did, going on two successive nights through the moonlit streets and seeking admittance at some of the poorest gates where people were humbly awaiting Him. With the two disciples that accompanied Him, He entered the courtyards and cured many sick. They were pious souls who believed in Him and had implored His help through the intervention of the disciples. All this could be easily done without observation, since the streets in that quarter were very quiet. They were lined by the walls of the forecourt in which were little entrance gates; the windows of the houses were in the back, opening into the courtyards and little gardens. The people were patiently waiting for Jesus. I remember seeing a woman afflicted with an issue of blood. She was closely enveloped in a long veil, and was led by two young girls into the court. Jesus did not remain long by the sick when He cured at night. To arouse their faith, He usually put to them the question: "Dost thou believe that God can cure thee, and that He has given that power to One on earth?" These

were the words, or something to the same effect, for
I cannot clearly recall them. Then He presented His
girdle to the sick woman to kiss and spoke some
words that sounded like the following: "I heal thee
through the Mystery" (or it may have been: I heal
thee in the intention) "in which this girdle had been
worn from the beginning and will be worn till the
end." In curing others Jesus laid the ends of the girdle on their heads. It was a long, wide strip like a
towel. It was worn sometimes unfolded, sometimes
folded into a narrow band, and again with long, hanging ends ornamented with fringe.

The valley to the east of Aruma, which extended
from east to west in the direction of Sichar and northward to the mountain northeast of Sichem, was woody.
To the east of this mountain, which rose in the midst
of the plain of Sichar, was the little wood known as
the Grove of Mambre. It was there that Abraham
had first pitched his tent, there also that God
appeared to him and made to him the promise of a
numerous posterity. A large tree stood nearby. Its
bark was not so rough as that of the oak and it bore
flowers and fruit at the same time. The latter were
used for the knobs of pilgrim staffs. It was near this
tree that the Lord appeared.

The highroad ran from Sichar to the left of the
wood and around Mount Garizim. In the plain to the
north of the forest was a city that recalled Abraham's sojourn in those parts. Some vestiges of it must
still exist. It was three hours north of Aruma and
two northwest of Phasael. It was called Thanath-
Silo.

4. Jesus Leaves Aruma and Goes to Thanath-Silo and Aser-Machmethat

After Jesus had once more earnestly addressed the Pharisees, telling them that they had lost the spirit of their religion, that they now held only to empty forms and customs which, however, the devil had managed to fill with himself, as they might see if they looked around on the pagans, He left Aruma and went to the city Thanath-Silo, outside of which stood one of the inns established by Lazarus. He instructed the men and women whom He found at work on the immense corn ricks in the field. He introduced into His discourse parables relating to agriculture and the various kinds of land. These people were slaves and followers of the Samaritan creed. That evening Jesus taught in the synagogue. It was the feast of the new moon, consequently the synagogue and other public buildings were hung with wreaths of fruit.

A great many sick had assembled in front of the synagogue. They were mostly afflicted with paralysis, gout, or issue of blood, and some were possessed. Jesus blessed numbers of children, both sick and well. Many of those that were paralyzed in their hands and on one side owed their sickness in most cases to their labors in the field and to lying on the damp earth at night or in the daytime when in a profuse perspiration. I saw such cases in the fields outside of Gennabris, in Galilee.

Jesus went next day into the harvest field and cured many whom He found there. Some people brought out from the city baskets of provisions, and a great entertainment was spread in one of the tabernacles that still remained standing. Jesus afterward delivered a long discourse, in which He spoke against unnecessary and extravagant care for the preservation of life. He brought forward the example of the lilies. They do not spin, and yet they are clothed

more beautifully than Solomon in all his glory. Jesus
said many beautiful things to the same effect of the
different animals and objects around. He also taught
that they should not profane the Sabbath and feasts
by working for gain. Works of mercy, such as delivering a man or a beast from danger, were allowable;
but as for the harvest, they should commit the care
of its fruits to God's providence and not on account
of threatening weather gather them in on the Sabbath. Jesus' words on this subject were very beautiful and detailed. It was almost the same kind of a
sermon as that on the Mount, for He often repeated
the words: "Blessed are these! Blessed are those!"

Such instructions were much needed by the people of this place, for they were extraordinarily covetous and greedy for gain in trade and agriculture.
They were wholly engrossed in their calling, and
their servants were overburdened. They were charged
with the collection of the tithes from the surrounding country. The sums thus coming into their possession they used to hold back for a considerable
time, in order to put them out at usury. The products of their fields they sold. The old people worked
in wood, for which they often betook themselves to
the neighboring forest. I saw them cutting in large
numbers the wooden heels worn under the sandals.
There were many fig orchards around the city. There
were no Pharisees here. The people were rather
coarse, but very proud of their descent from Abraham. The sons of Abraham, however, whom the Patriarch had settled here, had soon degenerated. They
intermarried with the Sichemites, and when Jacob
returned to that region the law of circumcision was
already forgotten. Jacob had intended to fix his residence there, but was deterred from doing so by Dina's
seduction. He knew the children of Abraham who
dwelt in those parts, and sent them presents. Dina
had gone to take a walk by the well of Salem. Some
of the people in the fields, those to whom her father

had sent presents, invited her to visit them. She was accompanied by her maids, but leaving them, she ventured alone into the fields, desirous of gratifying her curiosity. It was then that the Sichemite saw and ensnared her.

Wherever Jesus went, the sick were collected in crowds. We shall not be surprised at this when we remember that, as soon as His presence became known in any place, they were hurried thither from the huts and villages around the whole country.

Here in Thanath the Jews and Samaritans lived separate, the former being the more numerous. Jesus preached to the Samaritans also, though remaining the while on Jewish territory. His hearers were gathered on the boundary of their own quarter at the head of one of the streets. He also cured their sick. The Jews of Thanath were not so hostile toward them as were those of other places, since here they held not so rigorously to the Law, and especially to the observance of the Sabbath.

Jesus cured here in diverse ways. Some cures were effected at a distance by a glance and a word, some by a mere touch, some by imposition of hands; over some of the sick He breathed, others He blessed, and the eyes of some He moistened with saliva. Many of the sick happening to touch Him were cured, and others at a distance were cured without His even turning to them. Toward the close of His career, He seemed to be more rapid in His movements than in the beginning. I thought that He made use of these different forms of healing to show that He was bound to no single one, but could produce a similar effect by the use of varied means. But He once said Himself in the Gospel that one kind of devil was to be expelled in one way, another in a different way. He cured each in a manner analogous to his malady, his faith, and his natural temperament, as in our own time we behold Him chastising some sinners and converting others. He did not interrupt the order of

nature, He merely loosened the bonds that bound
the sufferer. He cut no knots, He untied them, and
He did everything so easily for He possessed the key
to all. Inasmuch as He had become the God-Man, He
treated those that He cured in a human manner. I
had already been told that Jesus had healed in these
different forms in order to instruct the disciples how
to act in similar cases. The various forms of blessings, consecrations, and Sacraments made use of by
the Church, find their models in those then observed
by Jesus.

Toward noon Jesus left the city accompanied by
several persons. He proceeded along a tolerably broad
highway toward the northeast. It led to Scythopolis
with Doch upon the right and Thebez on the left at
the eastern extremity of the mountain upon which
Samaria was built. He descended toward the Jordan
and into a valley through which a stream flowed to
the river. Here He encountered a crowd of people,
most of them Samaritan laborers who, eager to
receive instruction, had hurried thither in advance
of Him. He found them waiting for Him, and He
stopped to address them. To the left of the valley
and upon a height stood a little place consisting of
one long row of houses. It was called Aser-
Machmethat, and into it Jesus entered toward
evening. Abelmahula may have been seven hours distant. Mary and the holy women passed by Aser on
their journeys to Judea when they did not take the
mountainous road past Samaria. The Blessed Virgin
and Joseph took this route on their flight into Egypt.
That same evening Jesus went to the well of Abraham and to the pleasure gardens outside of Aser-
Machmethat, and there cured many sick. Among them
were two Samaritans who had been brought thither.
Jesus was very affectionately received by the people
of this place. They were very good and each one coveted the honor of showing Him hospitality. But He
put up outside the place with a family whose mode

of life was patriarchal in its simplicity. The father was named Obed. Jesus and all the disciples were very lovingly entertained by him. The road through the country from Thanath-Silo to this place was far wider and better than that through Akrabis to Jericho. The latter was so very narrow, so uneven and rocky that beasts of burden could with difficulty traverse it with their loads of merchandise.

It was under the tree near Abraham's Well that, in the time of the Judges, the false prophetess carried on her sorcery and gave advice that always turned out disastrously. She used to perform all kinds of ceremonies there at night by the light of torches, calling up by her incantations singular figures of animals, etc. She was nailed to a board by the Madianites at Azo. This took place under the same tree beneath which Jacob buried the idols plundered from the Sichemites.

Joseph with the Blessed Virgin and Jesus had lain concealed a day and a night near that tree on their flight into Egypt, for Herod's persecution had been proclaimed and it was very unsafe to travel in these parts. I think too that, on the journey to Bethlehem when Mary was so chilled by the cold, it was near this tree she suddenly became warm.

Aser-Machmethat lay across a mountain ridge that descends toward the valley of the Jordan. The southern side of the mountain belonged to Ephraim; the northern, to Manasses. On the former stood Machmethat, on the latter Aser, the two forming but one city called Aser-Machmethat. The boundary ran between them. The synagogue was in Aser. The inhabitants of the two quarters were dissimilar in their customs, and had little communication. Machmethat, the quarter belonging to the tribe of Ephraim, extended up the mountain in one long line of houses; below in the valley was the little stream by which Jesus had instructed the Samaritans who had preceded Him thither. A little beyond this point and

nearer to the entrance of the city was the beautiful
well surrounded by baths and pleasure gardens. The
well, access to which was by a flight of steps, consisted of a solid basin in whose terraced center rose
the tree to which I have more than once alluded.
From this reservoir the surrounding bathing cisterns
were fed. It was here that Jesus cured the two Samaritan women.

Obed's house was on his large estate outside of
Machmethat. He was a kind of chief, or head magistrate of the place. The inhabitants of this quarter
were for the most part related to one another, and
several of the families were either those of Obed's
own children or those of his other relatives. In his
character of eldest and chief, Obed managed their
business, directed their agricultural and pastoral
affairs. His wife, with her housekeeping and the
female portion of the family, occupied a separate part
of the house. She was still quite a vigorous old Jewess. She had a kind of school, and taught the young
girls of the other families all sorts of handiwork,
Charity, wise counsels, and industry reigned throughout the whole house. Obed had eighteen children,
some of whom were still unmarried. Two of his daughters had wedded husbands from Aser, the quarter
belonging to Manasses. This was a cause of regret
to Obed, as I learned from his conversation with
Jesus, for the people of Aser were not the best in the
world and their customs were very different from
those of their sister city.

Next morning Jesus preached near the well to an
audience of about four hundred people, all ranged
around on the grass of the terraced declivity. He
spoke in significant terms of the approach of the
Kingdom, of His own mission, of penance, and of Baptism. He also prepared some for the last-named ceremony, among whom were Obed's children. After that,
accompanied by Obed, He went to some dwellings in
the fields where He consoled and instructed the ser-

vants and aged persons who had had to remain at home while the others repaired to His sermon. Obed conversed long with Jesus of Abraham and Jacob, who had once sojourned in this region, and of Dina's misfortune. The inhabitants of Machmethat looked upon themselves as descendants from Judah. Holofernes, the Median adventurer, had at his invasion quite ruined this place, and after that the ancestors of these people settled here with the firm determination to live together according to their ancient, pious customs. This they had done down to the present. Obed followed the ancient usages of the pious Hebrews, and reverenced Job in an especial manner. He amply provided for his sons and daughters on their settlement in life, and at every marriage in his family he gave large offerings to the poor and to the Temple.

Jesus blessed numbers of children everywhere presented to Him by their mothers.

That afternoon there was a grand entertainment given in the open space around Obed's house and in the courtyard under the tabernacles which were still standing everywhere. Almost all the inhabitants of Machmethat took part in it, especially the poor of the whole region. Jesus went around to all the tables, blessing and teaching and lovingly helping to the various dishes. He related many parables. The women were seated in a separate tabernacle. Afterward Jesus visited and cured some sick in their homes, and again blessed many little ones presented to Him by their mothers, who stood ranged in a row. There were a great many children present, especially around Obed's wife, for she had many pupils. Obed had a little son of about seven years, and with him Jesus exchanged many words. The boy lived in the field at the house of one of his elder brothers. He was an exceedingly pious child, and often knelt out in the field at night to pray. This did not please the elder brother, and Obed himself felt a little anxiety about the boy. But

Jesus' words restored peace to their anxious hearts. After His death, the boy joined the disciples.

In the war of the Maccabees, Machmethat remained true and rendered much help to the Jews. Judas Maccabeus himself sojourned here at different times. Obed took Job for his model in all things, and led in the bosom of his large family a life altogether patriarchal.

When Jesus went into the other part of the city, the quarter belonging to the tribe of Manasses, He found near the synagogue some Pharisees (not the best disposed toward Himself) and many arrogant citizens. They were friends and supporters of those that collected the taxes and imposts for the Romans, which they afterward put out at usury. Jesus taught, and then cured the sick. The Pharisees and proud citizens treated Jesus with coldness and indifference. They were displeased at His having visited the simple, rustic people of Machmethat before honoring their own city with His presence. They had no love for Him. And yet, they were ambitious for His first visit as a learned Doctor to be to themselves, rather than to their unsophisticated neighbors, upon whom they looked down.

Jesus, accompanied by a crowd of people, went back to the well outside Machmethat and began preparations for the ceremony of Baptism. Many confessed their sins in general terms, while many others, going in private to Jesus, made them known in detail, and asked for penance and pardon. Saturnin and Judas Barsabas performed the ceremony of Baptism, the other disciples acting as sponsors. It took place in an immense bathing cistern. After the Baptism, Jesus returned to Aser for the Sabbath. He preached from *Genesis* 18:23, *et seq.,* of the destruction of Sodom and Gomorrha, and then taking up the miracles recorded of Eliseus, He spoke in strong language on the necessity of penance. His words were not pleasing to the Pharisees, for He reproached them with their contempt for the publicans while they themselves were secretly practicing usury, though hiding the fact under their sanctimonious exterior.

After He had again taught in the synagogue at Aser, His subjects being Abraham and Eliseus, He cured many sick, some of them demoniacs and others possessed by the spirit of melancholy. That afternoon a dinner was given in the public house. The Pharisees had issued invitations; but ignoring that fact, Jesus invited many poor people, as also the inhabitants of Machmethat, and ordered the disciples to defray all expenses. While at table He had a warm discussion with the Pharisees, whereupon He related the parable of the unjust debtor who desired the remission of his own debts, though oppressing others on account of theirs. Jesus applied the parable to themselves. They extorted taxes from the poor and at the same time deceived the Romans by pocketing the proceeds and declaring the people unable to pay; or again, by levying high taxes, only a third part of which was delivered over to the Romans. The Pharisees tried to justify themselves, but Jesus silenced them with the words: "Render unto Caesar that which is Caesar's, and to God that which is God's." In their fury they exclaimed: "What's that to Him?"

A fast day commemorative of the putting out of Sedecias' eyes by Nabuchodonosor having begun, Jesus preached in the fields among the shepherds, also at Abraham's Well. He spoke of the Kingdom of God, declaring that it would pass from the Jews to the Gentiles, the latter of whom would even attain preeminence over the former. Obed afterward remarked to Jesus that if He preached to the Gentiles in that strain, they might possibly become proud. Jesus replied very graciously, and explained that it was just on account of their humility that they should reach the first place. He warned Obed and his people against the feeling of conscious rectitude and self-complacency to which they were predisposed. They in a measure distinguished themselves from their neighbors, and on account of their well-regulated life, their temperance, and the fruits of salvation amassed thereby, they esteemed themselves good and pleasing in the sight of God. Such sentiments might very easily end in pride. To guard against such a consequence, Jesus related the parable of the day laborers. He instructed the women also in their own separate pleasure garden, in which was a beautiful bower. To them He related the parable of the wise and the foolish virgins. While so engaged, Jesus stood, and they sat around Him in a terraced circle, one above another. They sat on the ground with one knee slightly raised, and on it resting their hands. All the women on such occasions wore long mantles or veils that covered them completely; the rich had fine, transparent ones, while those of the poor were of coarse, thick stuff. At first these veils were worn closed, but during the sermon they were opened for the sake of comfort.

About thirty men were here baptized. Most of them were servants and people from a distance who had come hither after John's imprisonment.

Jesus took a walk with the people through the vineyards, the fruits of which were ripening for the second time that year.

Jesus left Machmethat with five disciples (the two disciples of John had gone back to Machaerus) and descended the road by which He had come. The little stream in the valley to the south of Aser-Machmethat had its source in the fountain at which Jesus had given Baptism by means of the disciples. He proceeded about three hours westward along the valley at the southern foot of the mountain upon which Thebez and Samaria lay. He gave instructions to the shepherds whom He met along the way, and toward noon reached the field that Jacob had destined for the special inheritance of Joseph. (*Gen.* 48:22). It lay

in a valley to the south of Samaria and extended
from east to west, one hour long and a half broad.
A brook flowed westward through that valley. From
the vineyards on the heights around could be seen
Sichem a couple of hours to the south. It had everything to make it desirable: vineyards, pasture lands,
grain, orchards and water, besides the necessary buildings, all in good order. The landlord of this property
was leaseholder, for it now belonged to Herod. It was
the house at which the Blessed Virgin and the holy
women awaited the coming of Jesus from Sichem,
and in which He cured the boy. The people here were
very good. They assembled in crowds to hear Jesus'
instructions, after which they tendered to Him a dinner in the open air which He graciously accepted.
This special patrimony of Joseph was not the field
near Sichem which Jacob had purchased from Hemor.
It was another property upon which the Amorrhites
had a footing along with the rightful occupants. They
were dwelling on it at the time of purchase, and Jacob
was obliged to drive them off. He did not relish their
proximity, fearing lest his own people would inter-
marry among them. A kind of single combat or ami-
cable contention took place between the two parties.
It had been agreed upon that the one who broke his
opponent's sword, or shield, or struck it out of his
hand, should take possession of the land, the other
having to retire. They decided the question in another
way also, namely, by shooting at a certain boundary
with the bow and arrow. Jacob and the Amorrhite
leader took their places opposite each other, each attended by a certain number of his own followers standing in the rear. The struggle began. Jacob conquered
his adversary, and the latter had to remove. After
the contest they made a treaty. All this took place
soon after the purchase of the field. Jacob dwelt eleven
years near Sichem.

From this place Jesus again ascended the mountain
northwestwardly to Meroz, a city on the southern side

of a mountain on whose northern side stood Ataroth.
Meroz was built on a higher elevation than Samaria,
as well as Thebez off to the north and Aser-Machmethat to the east.

5. Jesus Teaches in Meroz and Receives Judas Iscariot to the Number of His Disciples. Ancestry and Character of Judas Iscariot

Jesus had never before been in Meroz. It was surrounded by a dry moat, which at times received some
water from the mountain streams. The place had a
bad name in Israel on account of the perfidy of its
inhabitants. It had been peopled by the descendants
of Aser and Gad, sons of Jacob and the handmaiden
Zelpha, some of whom had intermarried with the
Gentiles of Sichem. The other tribes refused to
acknowledge the offspring of these mixed marriages,
and they were despised likewise on account of their
faithlessness and perfidy. Meroz, in consequence,
became an isolated place, and its inhabitants, being
thus cut off from much good, were likewise shielded
from much evil. They had fallen into oblivion, per-
ished, as it were, from among men. Their chief occupations consisted in dressing skins, making leather,
preparing furs and garments of the same, and man-
ufacturing leather sandals, straps, girdles, shields,
and military jerkins. They brought the skins from
afar on asses and dressed them partly near Meroz,
using for that purpose a cistern supplied with water
from their fountain in the city. But because this
itself was fed from an aqueduct and had not always
a full supply, they tanned the skins near Iscariot, a
marshy region, a couple of hours to the west of Meroz
and northward from Aser-Machmethat. It was a desolate little place of only a few dwellings. Nearby was
a ravine through which a little stream flowed to the
valley of the Jordan. It was on its banks that the

people of Meroz prepared their skins. Judas and his parents had for some time dwelt in this locality, hence the surname borne by the former.

Jesus was very joyfully received at some distance from their city by the poor citizens of Meroz. They knew of His approach and went out to meet Him, carrying sandals and garments for His use while they cleaned and brushed His own. Jesus thanked them and went with the disciples into the city, where they washed His feet and offered the customary refreshments. The Pharisees came to salute Him. Toward evening He taught in the synagogue before a large audience, taking for His subject the slothful servant and the buried talent. By this parable Jesus designated the inhabitants themselves. Born of the maid servant, they had received one talent only which they should have put out at interest; but instead of that they had buried it. The Master was coming and they should hasten to gain something. Jesus rebuked them also for their little love for their neighbor and their hatred of the Samaritans.

The Pharisees were not well pleased with Jesus, but the people so much the more, as they were very greatly oppressed by them. They rejoiced likewise at Jesus' visit because their whole region seemed to lie forgotten by all the world, and no one ever came to help or instruct them in any way.

After the sermon, Jesus went with His disciples to an inn that stood outside the western gate of the city. Lazarus had erected it for their use on some ground that he owned in these parts. Bartholomew, Simon Zelotes, Jude Thaddeus, and Philip came here to see Jesus, by whom they were cordially received. They had already spoken with the disciples. They dined with Jesus and remained overnight. Jesus had often before seen Bartholomew, had given him an interior call to His service and had even spoken of him to the disciples, Simon and Thaddeus were his cousins. Philip also was related to him and, like

Thaddeus, was already among the disciples. Jesus had called all these to follow Him when, upon His last visit to Capharnaum at Peter's fishery on the lake, He had spoken of their soon being summoned to do so. It was then that Peter had expressed himself so desirous of being allowed to remain at home as unfit for such a calling. Then it was that Peter uttered the words that later on were recorded in the Gospel.

Judas Iscariot likewise had come with the above named disciples to Meroz. He did not, however, spend the evening with Jesus, but at a house in the city where he had often before stayed. Bartholomew and Simon spoke with Jesus of Judas. They said that they knew him to be an active, well-informed man, very willing to be of service, and very desirous of a place among the disciples. Jesus sighed as they spoke and appeared troubled. When they asked Him the cause of His sadness, He answered: "It is not yet time to speak, but only to think of it." He taught during the whole meal, and all slept at the inn.

The newly arrived disciples had come from Capharnaum where they had met Peter and Andrew. They had messages from there and had also brought Jesus some money for the expenses of the journey, the charitable gift of the women. Judas, having met them at Naim, accompanied them to Meroz. Even at this early period, he was already known to all the disciples, and he had recently been in Cyprus. His manifold accounts of Jesus, of His miracles, of the various opinions formed of Him, namely, that some looked upon Him as the Son of David, others called Him the Christ, and the majority esteemed Him the greatest of the Prophets, had made the Jews and pagans of the island very inquisitive with regard to Him. They had heard, too, many wonderful things of His visit to Tyre and Sidon. The Cyprian pagan, the officer who visited Jesus in Ophra, had in consequence of all these marvelous accounts been sent thither by his master, who was very much impressed by them.

Judas had accompanied the officer back to Cyprus. On his return journey he stopped at Ornithopolis where the parents of Saturnin, originally from Greece, then dwelt.

When Judas learned on the way that Jesus was going into the region of Meroz, where he himself was well-known, he went to seek Bartholomew in Debbaseth. He was already acquainted with him and he invited him to go with him to Meroz and present him to Jesus. Bartholomew expressed his willingness to do so. But he went first to Capharnaum with Jude Thaddeus to see the disciples there, thence with Thaddeus and Philip to Tiberias, where Simon Zelotes joined them, and then stopped at Naim for Judas who had journeyed thither to meet them. He begged them again to present him to Jesus as one desirous of becoming a disciple. They were well pleased to do so, for they took delight in his cleverness, his readiness to render service, and his courteous manner.

Judas Iscariot may have been at that time twenty-five years old. He was of middle height and by no means ugly. His hair was of a deep black, his beard somewhat reddish. In his attire he was perfectly neat and more elegant than the majority of Jews. He was affable in address, obliging, and fond of making himself important. He talked with an air of confidence of the great or of persons renowned for holiness, affecting familiarity with such when he found himself among those that did not know him. But if anyone who knew better convicted him of untruth, he retired confused. He was avaricious of honors, distinctions, and money. He was always in pursuit of good luck, always longing for fame, rank, a high position, wealth, though not seeing clearly how all this was to come to him. The appearance of Jesus in public greatly encouraged him to hope for a realization of his dreams. The disciples were provided for; the wealthy Lazarus took part with Jesus, of whom everyone thought that He was about to establish a kingdom;

He was spoken of on all sides as a King, as the Messiah, as the Prophet of Nazareth. His miracles and wisdom were on every tongue. Judas consequently conceived a great desire to be numbered as His disciple and to share His greatness which, he thought, was to be that of this world. For a long time previously he had picked up, wherever he could, information of Jesus and had in turn carried around tidings of Him. He had sought the acquaintance of several of the disciples, and was now nearing the object of his desires. The chief motive that influenced him to follow Jesus was the fact that he had no settled occupation and only a half-education. He had embarked in trade and commerce, but without success, and had squandered the fortune left him by his natural father. Lately he had been executing all kinds of commissions, carrying on all kinds of business and brokerage for other people. In the discharge of such affairs, he showed himself both zealous and intelligent. A brother of his deceased father, named Simeon, was engaged in agriculture in Iscariot, the little place of about twenty houses that belonged to Meroz and from which it lay only a short distance toward the east. His parents had lived there a long time, and even after their death he had generally made it his home, hence his appellation of Iscariot. His parents at one time led a wandering life, for his mother was a public dancer and singer. She was of the race of Jephte, or rather that of his wife, and from the land of Tob. She was a poetess. She composed songs and anthems, which she sang with harp accompaniment. She taught young girls to dance, and carried with her from place to place all sorts of feminine finery and new fashions. Her husband, a Jew, was not with her; he lived at Pella. Judas was an illegitimate child whose father was an officer in the army near Damascus. He was born at Ascalon on one of his mother's professional journeys, but she soon freed herself from the encumbrance by exposing the child. Shortly after his birth, he was abandoned on the water's edge. But being found by some rich people with no children of their own, they cared for the child and bestowed upon him a liberal education. Later on, however, he turned out to be a bad boy and, through some kind of knavery, fell again to the care of his mother, who assumed the charge for pay. It is in my mind that the husband of his mother, becoming acquainted with the boy's origin, had cursed him. Judas received some wealth from his illegitimate father. He was possessed of much wit. After the death of his parents, he lived mostly in Iscariot with his Uncle Simeon, the tanner, and helped him in his business. He was not as yet a villain, but loquacious, greedy for wealth and honor, and without stability. He was neither a profligate nor a man without religion, for he adhered strictly to all the prescriptions of the Jewish Law. He comes before me as a man that could be influenced as easily to the best things as to the worst. With all his cleverness, courteousness, and obligingness, there was a shade of darkness, of sadness, in the expression of his countenance, proceeding from his avarice, his ambition, his secret envy of even the virtues of others.

He was not, however, exactly ugly. There was something bland and affable in his countenance, though at the same time, something abject and repulsive. His father had something good in him, and thence came that possessed by Judas. When as a boy he was returned to his mother, and she on his account was embroiled in a quarrel with her husband, she cursed him. Both she and her husband were jugglers. They practiced all kinds of tricks; they were sometimes in plenty and as often in want.

The disciples in the beginning were favorably inclined toward Judas on account of his obliging ways, for he was ready even to clean their shoes. As he was an excellent walker, he made at first long journeys in the service of the little Community. I never saw

him work a miracle. He was always full of envy and
jealousy and, toward the close of Jesus' career, he had
become weary of obedience, of the wandering life of
the disciples, and of the—to him—inexplicable mystery that surrounded the Divine Master.

In the center of Meroz was a beautifully constructed
fountain, the water of which was conducted through
pipes from the neighboring mountain, at a little distance to the north of the city. There were five galleries around the well, each of which contained a
reservoir. Into these reservoirs the water of the well
could be pumped. In the outer gallery of all were little bathing houses, and the whole place could be
closed. Here to these galleries around the well had
numbers of very sick persons belonging to the city,
some of them considered incurable, been brought on
beds. The worst were placed in the little bathing
houses in the outside circle. Meroz, abandoned, despised, and helpless, possessed an astonishing number of sick, dropsical old people, paralytics, and
sufferers of all kinds. Jesus, accompanied by the disciples, Judas excepted (he had not yet been presented
to Jesus), went into the city. The Pharisees of the
place and some strangers who had come from a distance were present. They took their stand at the center of the fountain where they could see all that went
on. They appeared astonished and even somewhat
scandalized at the miracles of Jesus. They were old
people grounded in their own opinion, who had listened to previous accounts of such wonders with wise
shakes of the head, smiles, and shrugs, giving cre-
dence to none of it. But now they beheld with surprise and vexation those seriously affected, those
incurables of their own city, by whose deep-seated
maladies they hoped to see Jesus' healing power set
at naught, taking up their beds and going off to their
homes with songs of praise for their perfect cure.
Jesus preached, instructed and consoled the sick, and
gave Himself no trouble about the Pharisees. The

whole city resounded with joy and thanksgiving. This lasted from early morn till nearly noon.

Jesus and the disciples now returned to their inn by the western gate of the city. On their way through the streets, some furious possessed, that had been allowed to leave their place of confinement, cried after Jesus. He commanded them to be silent. They instantly ceased their cries and threw themselves humbly at His feet. Jesus cured them and admonished them to purify themselves. From the inn He went to the hospital of the lepers a short distance from the city, entered, called the lepers before Him, touched them, healed them, and commanded them to present themselves before the priests for the customary purifications. Jesus did not allow the disciples to follow Him into the leprous hospital. He sent them up to the mountain where, after healing the lepers, He was to deliver an instruction.

On the way the disciples were met by Judas Iscariot, and when Jesus again joined them, Bartholomew and Simon Zelotes presented him to Jesus with the words: "Master, here is Judas of whom we have spoken to Thee." Jesus looked at him graciously, but with indescribable sorrow. Judas, bowing, said: "Master, I pray Thee allow me to share Thy instructions." Jesus replied sweetly and in words full of prophetic meaning: "Thou mayst have a place among My disciples, unless thou dost prefer to leave it to another." These were His words or at least their purport. I felt that Jesus was prophesying of Matthias, who was to fill Judas' place among The Twelve, and alluding also to His own betrayal. The expression was more comprehensive, but I felt that such was the allusion.

They now continued the ascent of the mountain, Jesus teaching all the while. On the summit was gathered a great crowd from Meroz, from Ataroth off to the north, and from the whole region around. There were also many Pharisees from these places, Jesus had some days previously announced the sermon by

means of the disciples. He preached in vigorous terms
of the Kingdom, of penance, of the abandonment in
which the people of Meroz lived, and He earnestly
exhorted them to arise from their sluggishness. There
was no teacher's chair up here. The preacher took
his stand on an eminence, surrounded by a trench
and a low wall, upon which the listeners leaned or
stood.

The view from this point was very beautiful and
extended. One could see over Samaria, Meroz, Thebez, Machmethat, and away over the whole country
around. Mount Garizim, however, was not in view,
though the towers of its ancient temple were visible. Toward the southeast, the horizon stretched off
to the Dead Sea and eastward over the Jordan to
Gilead. To the north in an oblique direction rose the
heights of Thabor, the view further extending in the
direction of Capharnaum.

When evening closed, Jesus informed His hearers
that He would teach there again in the morning. A
great many of the people slept on the mountain under
tents as they were at so great a distance from home.
Jesus and the disciples went back to the inn near
Meroz. All along the way Jesus taught of the good
employment of time, of salvation so long looked for
and now so near, of abandoning their relatives in
order to follow Him, and of helping the needy. Arrived
at the inn, He dined with the disciples. While on the
mountain, He had caused to be distributed to the
poor the money that the disciples had brought with
them from Capharnaum. Judas regarded that distri-
bution with a covetous eye. During the meal at the
inn, Jesus continued His instructions, and indeed
after it far into the night. Today, for the first time,
Judas sat at table with the Saviour and spent the
night under the same roof with Him.

6. Sermon on the Mountain Near Meroz. The Daughters of Lais

Next morning Jesus went again to the mountain and there during the whole forenoon delivered a grand discourse similar to that known as the Sermon on the Mount. The multitude present was great, and food was distributed: bread and honey, along with fish taken from the ponds fed by the little brooks that watered the region. Jesus had by means of the disciples procured provisions for the poor. Toward the end of the discourse, He alluded again to the one talent that, as children of the handmaid, they had received and buried, and He inveighed severely against the Pharisees for their hatred toward them, asking why they had not long ago led these people back to the truth. His words vexed the Pharisees, and they began to retort. They reproached Jesus for allowing His disciples so much liberty, especially on the score of fasting, washing, purifications, the Sabbath, the shunning of publicans and the different sects. It was not in this way, they said, the children of the Prophets and the Scribes used to live.

Jesus replied in the words of the Commandment of fraternal love: "Love God above all things and thy neighbor as thyself. That is the first Commandment!" and He told the disciples that they should learn to practice it, instead of covering up its abuse by means of exterior practices. Jesus spoke somewhat figuratively; consequently, Philip and Thaddeus said to Him: "Master, they have not understood Thee." Then Jesus explained Himself quite significantly. He commiserated the poor, ignorant, sinful people whom they, the Pharisees, with all their outward observance of the Law, had allowed to go to destruction, and He ended by boldly declaring that they who acted so should have no part in His Kingdom. He then went down the mountain to His inn, which was one-half hour from the scene of the sermon and another from the city. He met all along the way, on litters under tents, a great number of sick of all kinds patiently awaiting His coming. Many of them had come too late for the first cures. They belonged to the country far around. Jesus cured them, addressing to them at the same time words of consolation and exhortation to a change of life.

A pagan widow of Naim, called Lais, was also here waiting for Jesus. She had come to implore His aid in behalf of her two daughters, Sabia and Athalia. They were in a fearful manner possessed by the devil, and were at home in Naim confined to their respective apartments. They were perfectly furious. They dashed themselves here and there, they bit their own flesh, and struck wildly around them; no one ventured to approach them. At other times their members were contracted by cramps, and they fell to the ground pale and unconscious. Their mother, accompanied by handmaids and menservants, had come to Jesus for help. She was waiting at a distance eagerly desirous of His approach, but to her disappointment, she saw Him always turning to others. The poor mother could not restrain her eagerness, but cried out from time to time as He drew near: "Ah, Lord, have mercy on me!" but Jesus appeared not to hear her. The women near her suggested that she should say: "Have mercy on my daughters!" since she herself was not a sufferer. She replied: "They are my own flesh. In having mercy on me, He will have mercy on them also!" and again she uttered the same cry. At last Jesus turned and addressed her: "It is proper that I should break bread to the children of My own household before attending to strangers." The mother replied: "Lord, Thou art right. I will wait or even come again, if Thou canst not help me today, for I am not worthy of Thy assistance!" Jesus had, however, finished His work of healing, and the cured, singing canticles of praise, were going off with their beds. Jesus had turned away from the disconsolate mother and appeared about to retire. Seeing this, the poor woman grew desperate. "Ah!" she thought, "He is not going to help me!" But as the words flashed through her mind, Jesus turned toward her and said: "Woman, what askest thou of Me?" She cast herself veiled at His feet and answered: "Lord, help me! My two daughters at Naim are tormented by the devil. I know that Thou canst help them if Thou wilt, for all things are possible to Thee." Jesus responded: "Return to thy home! Thy daughters are coming to meet thee. But purify thyself! The sins of the parents are upon these children." These last words Jesus spoke to her privately. She replied: "Lord, I have already long wept my sin. What shall I do?" Then Jesus told her that she should get rid of her unjustly acquired goods, mortify her body, pray, fast, give alms, and comfort the sick. She promised with many tears to do all that He suggested, and then went away full of joy. Her two daughters were the fruit of an illicit connection. She had three sons born in lawful wedlock, but they lived apart from their mother, who still retained property belonging to them. She was very rich and, notwithstanding her repentance, lived, like most people of her class, a life of luxury. The daughters were confined in separate chambers. While Jesus was speaking with their mother, they fell unconscious, and Satan went out of them in the form of a black vapor. Weeping vehemently and quite changed, they called their female attendants, and informed them that they were cured. When they learned that their mother had gone to the Prophet of Nazareth, they set out to meet her, accompanied by many of their acquaintances. They met her at about an hour's distance from Naim and related all that had happened to them. The mother then went on to the city, but the daughters with their maids and servants proceeded straight forward to Meroz. They wished to present themselves to Jesus who, they had heard, was going to teach there again the next morning. During the healing of the sick, Manahem, the blind disciple of Korea, who had been restored to sight and whom Jesus had sent on a message to Lazarus, returned from Bethania with the two nephews of Joseph of Arimathea. Jesus gave them an interview. The holy women had sent by them money and gifts of various kinds to Jesus. Dina the Samaritan had visited the holy women at Capharnaum, bringing with her a rich contribution. Veronica and Johanna Chusa had also visited Mary. On their return journey they called to see Magdalen, whom they found very much changed. She was depressed in spirits, her folly apparently undergoing a struggle with her good inclinations. The holy women took Dina with them to Bethania. There was at this epoch a rich, aged widow who joined Martha's little band and gave all she possessed for the benefit of the young community.

When the Pharisees invited Jesus to a dinner, they asked Him whether His disciples, young, inexperienced men, some of them quite rustic and unaccustomed to the society of the learned, should also be invited. Jesus answered: "Yes! For whoever invites Me, invites the members of My household also; and he that rejects them likewise rejects Me." At these words, they bade Him bring the disciples with Him. All repaired to the public house in the city, where Jesus still taught and explained parables.

The property upon which Lazarus had established the inn near Meroz, consisted of a beautiful field and numerous orchards interspersed with charming groves. Some of his servants lived there to attend to the fruit and provide for its sale. At this time they had charge also of the inn. At the last meeting of Jesus with Lazarus at Ennon, it had been agreed that Jesus should tarry for some time in these parts. The holy women had, in consequence, come thither to get the inn in order, and the people around the country had been notified to expect Jesus.

On the following morning, before going again to the mountain, Jesus taught at the fountain in Meroz,

and again reproached the Pharisees for the little care
they took of the people. After that He ascended the
mountain and delivered an instruction similar to that
known as the Sermon on the Mount. Before taking
leave of the people, He once more gave an explanation of the buried talent. Some of His hearers had
already been three days encamped on the mountain.
Those in need had been placed apart from the rest
and were provided with food and other necessaries
by the disciples. Judas' uncle, Simeon of Iscariot, a
devout, old man, dark complexioned and vigorous,
entreated Jesus to go to Iscariot, and Jesus promised
to do so. When He went down the mountain, He found
some sick awaiting Him. They were still able to walk.
Jesus cured them. This took place on the road between the inn and Lazarus' property, at a little distance below the place where the disciples had
distributed food to the people.

On the same spot upon which the pagan woman
Lais of Naim had knelt yesterday at Jesus' feet praying for her sick daughters, were today those daughters, now both cured, awaiting the coming of Jesus.
They were named Athalia and Sabia, and were accompanied by their maids and men servants. With all
their attendants, they cast themselves down before
Jesus, saying: "Lord, we esteemed ourselves unworthy to listen to Thy instructions, therefore we waited
here to thank Thee for freeing us from the power of
the evil one." Jesus commanded them to rise. He commended their mother's patience, humility, and faith,
for as a stranger she had waited until He had broken bread to His own household. But now, He continued, she too belonged to His household, for she
had recognized the God of Israel in His mercy. The
Heavenly Father had sent Him to break bread to all
that believed in His mission and brought forth fruits
of penance. Then He ordered the disciples to bring
food, which He gave to the maidens and all their
attendants—to each a piece of bread and a piece of

fish—delivering to them at the same time an instruction thereon full of deep significance. After that He went on with the disciples to the inn. One of the maidens was twenty, the other five and twenty years old. Their sickness and the confinement in which they lived had made them pale and wan.

7. Jesus in Iscariot and Dothan. Cure of Issachar

Next morning Jesus left the inn with the disciples and journeyed eastward to Iscariot, distant not quite an hour. On the swampy ground of a deep ravine stood a row of houses, about twenty-five, near a stream of water black and full of reeds. Here and there it was dammed so as to form pools for tanning. Very frequently this water failed, and then they had to let in other sources. The cattle for slaughter belonging to Meroz were pastured around these parts. When needed in Meroz, they were slaughtered here, then flayed, and the hide handed over to the tanners of Iscariot. The ravine in which the little place lay was directly to the north of Machmethat. The tanner's trade, on account of the odors attending it, was held in detestation by the Jews. Although for tanning the hides of the slaughtered cattle pagan slaves and others of the most despised races were needed, yet in Meroz they dwelt apart from the other inhabitants. In Iscariot no calling was carried on but tanning, and it seemed to me that most of the houses of this place belonged to old Simeon, the uncle of Judas.

Judas was very dear and quite useful to his old uncle in his leather trade. Sometimes he dispatched him with asses to purchase raw hides, sometimes with prepared leather to the seaport towns, for he was a clever and cunning broker and commission merchant. Still he was not at this time a villain, and had he overcome himself in little things, he would not have fallen so low. The Blessed Virgin very often warned him, but he was extremely vacillating. He was susceptible of very vehement, though not lasting repentance. His head was always running on the establishment of an earthly kingdom, and when he found that not likely to be fulfilled, he began to appropriate the money entrusted to his care. He was therefore greatly vexed that the worth of Magdalen's ointment had not passed as alms through his hands. It was at the last Feast of Tabernacles in Jesus' lifetime that Judas began to go to the bad. When he betrayed Jesus for money, he never dreamed of His being put to death. He thought his Master would soon be released; his only desire was to make a little money.

Judas was, here in Iscariot, very obliging and ready to serve; he was perfectly at home. His uncle, the tanner Simeon, a very busy and active man, received Jesus and the disciples at some distance from the place, washed their feet, and offered the customary refreshments. Jesus and the disciples visited his house where were his family, consisting of his wife, his children, and his servants.

Jesus paid a visit to the opposite side of the place where, in the midst of a field, was a kind of pleasure garden in which the tabernacles were still standing. All the inhabitants of the place were here assembled. Jesus taught upon the parable of the sower and the different kinds of soil. He exhorted the people to let the instructions they had heard from Him on the mountain near Meroz find good soil in their hearts.

Jesus afterward, with the disciples and Simeon's family, took a little repast standing. During it old Simeon begged Him to admit Judas his nephew, whom he praised in many ways, to a participation in His teachings and His Kingdom. Jesus responded in pretty much the same terms as He had used toward Judas himself: "Everyone may have a share therein, provided he is resolved not to relinquish his portion to another." Jesus performed no cures here, for the sick had already been healed on the mountain.

Jesus and the disciples went from Iscariot back toward the west almost as far as the inn. Then turning to the north, they traversed the valley having the mountain upon which Jesus had taught to the left, turned somewhat northwestwardly, then again to the north, and journeyed along a low mountain terrace toward Dothan, which could be seen lying low in the eastern vale of the plain of Esdrelon. To the east rose the mountains above, and to the west lay the valley below it.

Jesus was accompanied by three troops of men who, having been present at His instructions on the mountain, were now returning in bands to their homes for the Sabbath. When one party left Him, another came up to bear Him company. It was almost three hours from the inn to Dothan, a place as large as Münster. I had a vision in which I saw that it was here that the soldiers sent by Jeroboam to seize Eliseus were struck blind. Dothan had five gates and as many principal streets; it was traversed likewise by two highways. One of the latter led from Galilee down to Samaria and Judea; the other came from the opposite side of the Jordan and ran through the valley of Apheca and Ptolomais on the sea. Trade in wood was carried on in Dothan. On the mountain chain around here and near Samaria there was still much wood; but across the Jordan near Hebron, and at the Dead Sea, the mountains are quite bare. I saw in the neighborhood of Dothan much work going on under tents in the preparation of wood. All sorts of beams for the different parts of ships were put into shape, and long, thin slats were prepared for wicker partitions. Outside the gates on the highways that crossed each other in Dothan were several inns.

Jesus went with the disciples to the synagogue, where a crowd was already assembled, among them many Pharisees and Doctors. They must have had some intimation of Jesus' coming, for they were so polite as to receive Him in the court outside the synagogue, wash His feet, and present to Him the customary refection. Then they conducted Him in and handed Him the roll of the Law. The sermon was on the death of Sara, Abraham's second marriage with Ketura, and the Dedication of Solomon's Temple.

The Sabbath instructions over, Jesus went to an inn outside the city. There He found Nathanael the bridegroom, two sons of Cleophas and His Mother's eldest sister, and a couple of the other disciples who had come hither for the Sabbath. There were now about seventeen disciples with Him. The people from the house on Lazarus' estate near Ginaea, where Jesus stopped recently when He went to Ataroth, were also here to celebrate the Sabbath.

Dothan was a beautiful, well-built old city, very agreeably situated. In the rear, though at a considerable distance, arose a mountain chain, and in front it looked out upon the delightful plain of Esdrelon. The mountains of this region are not so steep and rugged. Peak rises above peak, and the roads are better. The houses were of the old style, like those in David's time. Many had little turrets on the corners of the flat roofs capped by large domes, or cupolas, in which an observer could sit and view the surrounding locality. It was from such a cupola that David saw Bethsabee. There were also on the roofs galleries of roses and even of trees.

Jesus entered many of the forecourts of the dwellings, where He found sick whom He cured. The occupants standing at their doors implored Him to come in, which He did accompanied by two of the disciples. They also in different places begged the disciples to intercede for them, which they accordingly did. Jesus went likewise to the place in which the lepers abode, separated from all others, and there He healed the sufferers. There were many lepers in this city. It may have been on account of their frequent communication with strangers for trading purposes, for besides the trade in wood, the inhabitants of Dothan carried on other branches of industry. They imported carpets, raw silk, and similar goods which they unpacked and again exported.

I saw goods like the above at the house of the sick man whom Jesus was entreated by Nathanael to visit. Nathanael lived at his house. It was a very elegant looking dwelling surrounded by courtyards and open colonnades, and situated not far from the synagogue. The occupant was a wealthy man of about fifty years named Issachar, who was suffering from dropsy. Notwithstanding his miserable condition, Issachar had a few days previously to the coming of Jesus espoused a young woman named Salome, aged twenty-five years. This union was according to legal prescription analogous to that of Ruth and Booz—it gave Salome the right to inherit Issachar's property. The evil tongues of the city, especially the Pharisees, found great fault with this marriage, which at once became the general talk. But Issachar and Salome put their trust in Jesus, for at His last visit to this part of the country, they had recommended their affairs to Him.

The family had been long acquainted with Jesus, even during the lifetime of Salome's parents, for Mary and Joseph when journeying from Nazareth to visit Elizabeth had found hospitality with them. This happened shortly before the Paschal solemnity. Joseph went with Zachary from Hebron to Jerusalem for the feast, after which he returned to Hebron and then went home leaving Mary there. Thus had Jesus, while still in His Mother's womb, received hospitality in this house, to which He now came thirty-one years later as the Saviour of mankind, to discharge in the person of their sick son the debt of gratitude He owed to the goodness of the parents.

Salome was the child of this house and the widow of Issachar's brother, Issachar himself being the wid-

ower of Salome's sister. The house and all the property were to revert to Salome, for neither she nor
Issachar had had children by the previous union.
They were childless and the only descendants of an
illustrious race. They had espoused each other trusting to the merciful healing power of Jesus. Salome
was allied to Joseph's family. She was originally from
Bethlehem, and Joseph's father was accustomed to
call her grandfather by the title of brother, although
he was not really his brother. They had a descendant of the family of David among their forefathers who, I think, was also a king. His name sounds
like Ela. It was through respect to this ancient friendship that Mary and Joseph were there entertained.
Issachar was of the tribe of Levi.

Upon His entrance into the house Jesus was met
by Salome, her maids, and the other servants of the
household. Salome cast herself at Jesus' feet and
begged her husband's cure. Jesus went with her into
the chamber of the sick man, who lay covered up on
his couch, for he was dropsical as well as paralyzed
on one side. Jesus saluted him and spoke to him
words full of kindness. The sick man was very much
touched and gratefully acknowledged the salutation,
though he could not rise. Then Jesus prayed, touched
the sufferer, and gave him His hand. Instantly the
sick man arose, threw another garment around him,
and left his bed, when he and his wife cast themselves at Jesus' feet. The Lord addressed them a few
words of exhortation, blessed them, promised them
posterity, and then led them out of the chamber to
their assembled household, who were all filled with
joy. The miraculous cure was kept a secret all that
day.

Issachar invited Jesus and all His followers to stay
that night at his house and, after the exercises of
the synagogue, to dine with him. Jesus accepted the
invitation, and then went to preach in the synagogue.
Toward the end of His discourse the Pharisees and

Sadducees began to strive against Him. From the explanation of Abraham's marriage with Ketura, He had come to speak of marriage itself. The Pharisees broached that of Issachar and Salome. They declared it insane in a man so sick and old to marry a young woman. Jesus replied that the couple had married in obedience to the Law, and He asked how could they, who held so strictly to the same, blame them. They answered by asking how He could look upon such a union as prescribed by the Law, since so old and sick a man could hope for no blessing on his marriage, consequently such an affair was no other than a scandal. Jesus responded: "His faith has preserved to him the fruit of wedlock. Do ye set limits to the almighty power of God? Has not the sick man married in obedience to the Law? In trusting in God and believing that He will help him, he has done excellently well. But this is not the cause of your indignation. Ye hoped that this family would die out for want of heirs, and then ye would get their property into your own hands." Then He cited the example of many devout old people whose faith had been rewarded with posterity, and said many other things upon the subject of matrimony. The Pharisees were furious, but had not a word in reply.

The Sabbath over, Jesus left the synagogue and, accompanied by the disciples, went to Issachar's, where a grand banquet had been prepared for Him. Jesus, the disciples related to Him, and Issachar himself sat at one table, while Salome, the wife, came and went doing the honors of the same. The other disciples ate in a side hall. Previously to sitting down Jesus had healed several sick. It was dusk, and the miracles were performed by torchlight outside the synagogue and near Issachar's dwelling, where the sick had gathered. I saw among the disciples Judas Iscariot, Bartholomew, and Thomas, also an own brother and a stepbrother of the last named. Thomas had two stepbrothers. They had come thither for the

Sabbath from Apheca, seven hours distant, and they put up at Issachar's, Thomas being well-known to him on account of his commercial pursuits. Though he had acquaintances among the disciples, he had never yet spoken to Jesus, for he was anything but obtrusive. James the Less also had come from Capharnaum for the Sabbath, likewise Nathanael, the son of the widow Anna, eldest daughter of Cleophas, who was now living with Martha. Nathanael was the youngest of her sons engaged at Zebedee's fishery. He was about twenty years old, gentle and amiable, with something of the appearance of John. He had been reared in the house of his grandfather, and was nicknamed "Little Cleophas," in order to distinguish him from the other Nathanaels. I learned that on this Sabbath when I heard Jesus say: "Call little Cleophas to Me!"

The entertainment consisted of birds, fish, honey, and bread. There were in this city numbers of pigeons, turtledoves, and colored birds which ran like hens around the houses, and often took flight to the beautiful plain of Jezrael. During the meal, Issachar spoke of Mary. He recalled the fact of her having been in that house in her youth, and said that his wife's parents had often related the circumstance, telling how young and beautiful and pious she was. He expressed the hope that God, who had cured him through Joseph's Son (he guessed not his Saviour's origin), would likewise give him posterity. All the disciples found hospitality at this house. There were large, open porticos around it on which beds were prepared for them, separated from one another by movable partitions. Of the Dothanites, some were very good, and some very bad. On account of the antique style of its houses, Dothain compared with the other cities in its neighborhood as Cologne with our other German towns.

Next morning when Jesus and the disciples went to walk outside the city, Thomas approached and begged Jesus to admit him to the number of His disciples. He promised to follow Him and fulfill all His commands for, as he said, by His preaching and by the miracles he had witnessed, he was convinced of the truth of what John and all the disciples of his acquaintance had said about Him. He begged, also, to be allowed a part in His Kingdom. Jesus replied that he was no stranger to Him and that He knew that he, Thomas, would come to Him. But Thomas would not subscribe to that, He asserted that he had never before thought of taking such a step, for he was no friend of novelty, and had only now determined upon it since he was convinced of His truth by His miracles. Jesus responded: "Thou speakest like Nathanael. Thou dost esteem thyself wise, and yet thou talkest foolishly. Shall not the gardener know the trees of his garden? The vinedresser, his vines? Shall he set out a vineyard, and not know the servants whom he sends into it?" Then He related a similitude of the cultivation of figs upon thorns.

Two of John's disciples who had been sent to Jesus by the Baptist had an interview here with Jesus and then returned to Machaerus. They had been present at the sermon on the mountain near Meroz and had witnessed the miracles there performed. They belonged to the disciples that had followed their master to the place of his imprisonment and had received his instructions outside his prison. They were warmly attached to him. As they had never witnessed any of Jesus' actions, John had sent them to Him that they might be convinced of the truth of what he himself had told them of Him. He commissioned them to beg Jesus in his name to declare openly and precisely who He was and to establish His Kingdom on earth. These disciples told Jesus that they were now convinced of all that John had announced of Him, and they inquired whether He would not soon go to free John from prison. John, they said, hoped to be released through Him, and they themselves were

longing for Him to establish His Kingdom and set
their master at liberty. They thought that would be
a more profitable miracle than even His curing the
sick. Jesus replied that He knew that John was longing and hoping soon to be freed from imprisonment,
and that he should indeed be released, but that He
should go to Machaerus and deliver John who had
prepared His ways, John himself never even dreamed.
Jesus ended by commanding them to announce to
John all that they had seen and say to him that He
would fulfill His mission.

I do not know whether John was aware that Jesus
was to be crucified and that His Kingdom was not
to be an earthly one. I think that he thought Jesus,
after converting and freeing the people, would establish a holy Kingdom upon earth.

Toward noon Jesus and the disciples returned to
the city and to Issachar's, where many people were
already assembled. The mistress and domestics were
busy preparing the noonday meal. Back of the house
was a charming spot in the center of which was a
beautiful fountain surrounded by summerhouses.
The fountain was regarded as sacred, for it had been
blessed by Eliseus. There was a handsome chair
nearby for the preacher's use and around it an
enclosed space with shade trees, in which quite a
number might assemble for instructions. Several
times in the year, especially at Pentecost, public
instructions were given here. There were besides, in
the region of the fountain, places with long, stone
stalls or narrow terraces, where caravans and the
crowds going to Jerusalem at the Paschal time could
rest and take refreshments. Issachar's house stood
near enough to command a view of the fountain and
its surroundings. The arrangements of the resting
place and the customs observed there were also superintended from Issachar's, where a kind of freight
business was carried on. The caravans unloaded and
unpacked their goods here for Issachar to forward

to other places, and very frequently the merchants
and their servants received hospitality at his house,
although it was not a public inn. Issachar's business
was like that of the father of the bride of Cana in
Galilee. The beautiful fountain had one inconvenience.
It was so deep that the water could be pumped only
with great fatigue. When pumped up, it ran into
basins standing around.

There were crowds assembled around the fountain
on the invitation of Jesus and Issachar. Jesus, from
the teacher's chair, delivered a discourse to the people on the fulfillment of the Promise, the nearness
of the Kingdom, on penance and conversion, and of
the way to implore the mercy of God and to receive
His graces and miracles. He alluded to Eliseus, who
had formerly taught in this same place. The Syrians
sent to take him prisoner were struck with blindness. Then Eliseus conducted them to Samaria into
the hands of their enemies, but far from allowing
them to be put to death, he entertained them hospitably, restored their sight, and sent them back to
their king. Jesus applied this to the Son of Man and
the persecution He endured from the Pharisees. He
spoke also for a long time of prayer and good works,
related the parable of the Pharisee and the Publican, and told His hearers that they ought to adorn
and perfume themselves on their fast days instead
of parading their piety before the people. The inhabitants of this place, who were very much oppressed
by the Pharisees and Sadducees, were greatly encouraged by Jesus' teaching. But the Pharisees and Sadducees, on the contrary, were enraged upon seeing
the joyous multitude and hearing the words of Jesus.
Their rage increased when they beheld Issachar in
perfect health going around among the people, joyfully helping the disciples and his own servants to
distribute food to them as they seated themselves
along the stone benches. This sight so exasperated
them that they stormed violently against Jesus. It

looked as if they were about to take Him into custody. They began again to rail at His curing on the
Sabbath. Jesus bade them listen to Him calmly. He
placed them in a circle around Him and, making use
of His customary argument, said to the chief among
them: "If on the Sabbath you should happen to fall
into the well here, would you not wish to be drawn
out at once?" And so He continued to speak until
they slunk back, covered with confusion. After this
Jesus left the city with several of His disciples, and
descended into the valley that runs from south to
northwest of Dothan.

Issachar had distributed large alms in Dothan,
and sent also to the inn of the little community asses
with various necessaries. The provisions and beverages provided by the disciples and which had become
somewhat stale, he caused to be exchanged for better. He gave to each of them a cup like those used
at Cana, and a flat jug, or pitcher, made of white
material with a ring by which it could hang. The
stoppers were a kind of sponge tightly compressed.
The jugs contained a refreshing drink made of balm.
He gave likewise to each disciple a sum of money
for alms and other necessities.

Judas Iscariot and many other disciples returned
from Dothan to their own homes. Jesus kept with
Him only nine, among whom were Thomas, James
the Less, Jude Barsabas, Simon Thaddeus, little
Cleophas (Nathanael), Manahem, and Saturnin.

After Jesus' departure, the Pharisees recommenced
their mockery and insults. They said to the people:
"One can easily see who He is. He has allowed Himself to be sumptuously entertained by Issachar. His
disciples are a set of lazy vagrants whom He supports and feasts at the expense of others. If He did
right, He would stay at home and support His poor
Mother. His father was a poor carpenter. But that
respectable calling does not suit Him, and so He goes
wandering around disturbing the whole country."

While Issachar was distributing his alms, he constantly repeated: "Help yourselves freely! Take freely! It is not mine. It belongs to the Father in Heaven. Thank Him, for it is only lent to me!"

8. Jesus Goes From Dothan to Endor. Cure of a Pagan Boy

After a journey of about five hours, and night having set in, Jesus and the disciples arrived at a lonely inn where only sleeping accommodations were to be found. Nearby was a well that owed its origin to Jacob. The disciples gathered wood and made a fire. On the way Jesus had had a long conversation with them, intended principally for the instruction of Thomas, Simon, Manahem, "Little Cleophas," and the others newly received. He spoke of their following Him, and through the deep conviction of the worthlessness of earthly goods, of their leaving their relatives without regret and without looking back. He promised that what they had left should be restored to them in His Kingdom a thousandfold. But they should reflect maturely whether or not they could break their earthly ties.

To some of the disciples, and especially to Thomas, Judas Iscariot was not particularly pleasing. He did not hesitate to say plainly to Jesus that he did not like Judas Simonis, because he was too ready to say *yes* and *no*. Why, he asked, had He admitted that man among His disciples, since He had been so difficult to please in others. Jesus answered evasively that from eternity it was decreed by God for Judas, like all the others, to be of the number of His disciples.

When the disciples had retired to rest, Jesus went alone into the mountains to pray.

Early the next morning some inhabitants of Sunem came to Jesus at the inn earnestly begging Him to go with them, for they had some children seriously sick whom they wished Him to cure. Sunem was a

couple of hours to the east of where Jesus then was.
The poor people had long been vainly expecting Jesus'
coming. But Jesus replied that He could not go then,
because others were awaiting Him, but that He would
send His disciples to them. They rejoined that they
had already had some of them in their town, but the
cure of their children had not followed. They insisted
upon His coming Himself. Jesus exhorted them to
patience, and they left Him.

He now went with His disciples to Endor. On the
road from Dothan to Endor were two wells of Jacob,
to which his herds used to be led, and for which he
often had to struggle with the Amorrhites.

Lazarus owned a field near Jezrael at some distance from Endor. Joachim and Anne owned another
two hours to the northeast of Endor, and it was to
it that the latter accompanied Mary on her journey
to Bethlehem. It was from this field that the little
she-ass, that ran on so gaily before the holy travellers, had been taken to be presented to Joseph.
Joachim owned another field on the opposite side of
the Jordan on the confines of the desert and forest
of Ephraim, and not far from Gaser. Thither had he
retired to pray when he returned sad from the Temple, and there, too, had he received the command to
go to Jerusalem, where Anne would meet him under
the Golden Gate.

Jesus paused at a row of houses outside of Endor
and taught. At the earnest request of the people, He
entered some of them and cured the sick, several of
whom had been carried thither from Endor. Among
the sufferers were some pagans, but they remained
at a distance. One pagan however, a citizen of Endor,
approached Jesus. He had with him a boy of seven
years possessed of a dumb devil, and he was often
so violent that he could not be restrained. As the
man drew near Jesus, the boy became quite unman-
ageable, broke loose from his father, and crept into
a hole in the mountain. The father cast himself at

Jesus' feet, bewailing his misery. Jesus went to the
hole and commanded the boy to come forth before
his Master. At these words, the boy came out meekly
and fell on his knees before Jesus, who laid His hands
upon him and commanded Satan to withdraw. The
boy became unconscious for a few moments, while a
dark vapor issued from him. Then he arose and ran
full of talk to his father, who embraced him, and both
went and fell on their knees before Jesus, giving
thanks. Jesus addressed some words of admonition
to the father, and commanded him to go to Ennon
to be baptized. Jesus did not enter Endor. The suburb in which He was, possessed more beautiful edifices than the city itself. There was something about
Endor that spoke of death. Part of the city was a
waste, its walls in ruins, its streets overgrown with
grass. Many of the inhabitants were heathens under
the power of the Jews, and were obliged to labor at
all kinds of public works. The few rich Jews found
in Endor used to peep timidly out of their doors and
quickly draw in their heads, as if they feared that
someone was stealing their money behind their back.

From here Jesus went two hours to the northeast
into a valley that ran from the Plain of Esdrelon to
the Jordan, north of Mount Gilboa. In this valley lay
on a hill, like an island, the city of Abez, a place of
moderate grandeur surrounded by gardens and
groves. A little river flowed before it, and eastward
in the valley was a beautiful fountain, called Saul's
Fountain because Saul was once wounded there. Jesus
did not go into the city, but to a row of houses on
the northern declivity of Mount Gelboe between the
gardens and fields, on the latter of which were high
heaps of grain. Here He went into an inn in which
a crowd of old men and women, His own relatives,
were awaiting Him. They washed His feet and showed
Him every mark of genuine confidence and reverence. They were in number about fifteen, nine men
and six women, who had sent Him word that they

would meet Him here. Several of them were accompanied by their servants and children. They were mostly very aged persons, relatives of Anne, Joachim, and Joseph. One was a young half-brother of Joseph, who dwelt in the valley of Zabulon. Another was the father of the bride of Cana. Anne's relatives from the region of Sephoris, where at His last visit to Nazareth, Jesus had restored sight to the blind boy, were among them. All had journeyed hither in a body and on asses in order to see and speak with Jesus. Their desire was that He would fix His abode somewhere and cease wandering about. They wanted Him to seek a place where He could teach in peace and where there were no Pharisees. They set before Him the great danger He ran, since the Pharisees and other sects were so embittered against Him. "We are well aware," they said, "of the miracles and graces that proceed from Thee. But we beg Thee to have some settled home where Thou canst quietly teach, that we may not be in constant anxiety on Thy account." They even began to propose to Him different places which they thought suitable.

These pious, simple-hearted people made this proposal to Jesus out of their great love for Him. The bitter taunts uttered in their hearing against Him by the evil-minded gave them pain. Jesus replied in affectionate, but vigorous terms, very different from those He was accustomed to use when addressing the multitude or the disciples. He spoke in plain words, explained the Promise, and showed them that it was His part to fulfill the will of His Father in Heaven. He told them moreover that He had not come for rest, not for any particular persons, nor for His own relatives, but for all mankind. All indiscriminately were His brethren, all were His relatives. Love rests not. Whoever dreams of succoring misery, must seek out the poor. After the comforts of this life He did not aim, for His Kingdom was not of this world. Jesus took a great deal of trouble with these

good old people, who listened with ever increasing
astonishment to His words, whose deep significance
gradually unfolded to their understanding. Their
earnestness and their love for Jesus grew at each
moment. He took them separately for a walk on the
shady part of the mountain, where He instructed and
comforted them, each according to his or her special
needs, and after that He spoke to them again all
together. And so the day closed, and they took together
a simple repast of bread, honey, and dried fruits which
they had brought with them.

That evening the disciples presented to Jesus a
young man from the environs of Endor, the son of a
schoolmaster. He was a student preparing to hold a
position similar to that of his father. He begged Jesus
to receive him among His disciples. He had been
informed, he said, that Jesus might perhaps have
some need of him, that He might possibly give him
some office. Jesus replied that He had no need of
him, that the knowledge He came to bring upon earth
was different from that which he had acquired, that
he was too attached to material things, and so He
sent him away.

About noon on the following day, Jesus' relatives
started for Mount Thabor, where they separated and
returned to their homes in different directions. Jesus
had quite consoled and enlightened the good, old people, had infused new life into them. Although they
may not have understood all that He told them, yet
they felt a great calm fall upon their soul, and they
journeyed home with the firm conviction that He had
spoken divine words and that He knew better what
to do and how to shape His course than they could
tell Him. Still more touching than their meeting was
their departure when, with tears and smiles and gracious nods, their demeanor expressive of confidence
mingled with respectful reserve, they took their way
down through the valley. Some rode on asses, others
went on foot leaning on their long staves, and all

with their garments girded for travelling. Jesus and
the disciples, after helping them to mount their asses
and arrange their bundles, accompanied them a part
of the way.

9. Jesus in Abez and Dabereth on Thabor

Jesus and the disciples now went through the valley to a beautiful well, about a quarter of an hour
east of Abez. Several women were standing by it,
having come out of the city to draw water. When
they saw Jesus coming, some of them hurried into
the neighboring houses and soon came back accompanied by several men and women. They brought
basins and towels, bread and small fruits in baskets; they washed His feet, and gave Him and the
disciples to eat. Many others had joined the little
group, and Jesus delivered to them an instruction.
Then they conducted Him into the city where He
was met at the gate by children, little girls and boys,
bearing wreaths and festoons of flowers. They surrounded Him in triumph, and at every step, at every
street corner their numbers increased. The disciples,
thinking the throng too great, wanted to send the
children away. But Jesus exclaimed: "Do ye fall back,
and let the little ones come forward!" At these words
the children pressed around Him more closely than
before. He embraced them, pressed them to His
Heart, and blessed them. The mothers and fathers
were looking on from the doors and vestibules of
their courtyards. At last He reached the synagogue,
where He preached to a crowded assembly. That
evening He cured some invalids at their own homes.
A repast was laid under an arbor still standing from
the Feast of Tabernacles, and of it many people of
the city partook.

Thomas had gone back from Endor to Apheca, I saw
here in Abez some women afflicted with an issue of

blood. They mingled with the crowd, slipped behind Jesus, kissed the hem of His robe, and were cured. In large cities such women would have remained at a distance; in smaller places they were not so punctilious.

A messenger from Cana came to Jesus in Abez. The chief magistrate of the city implored Him to come to see his son, who was seriously sick. Jesus tranquilized him and told him to wait yet a little while. Then two Jewish messengers arrived from Capharnaum. They had been dispatched to Him by a pagan who had already, through the disciples, implored Jesus' aid in behalf of his sick servant. They begged Him earnestly to return at once with them to Capharnaum, for the servant was nigh unto death. Jesus replied that He would go in His own good time, that the man was not dying. The messengers, hearing this, remained for the instruction.

The inhabitants of Abez were chiefly Galaadites of Jabes. They had settled here in the time of the High Priest Heli in consequence of a struggle that had arisen among the people of Galaad. The Judge ruling at that time was consulted in the affair, and he decided that some of the Galaadites should remove to Abez. Saul was wounded near the well of Abez and, on one of the heights to the south, breathed his last. From this circumstance the well was called Saul's Well. The people of Abez belonged to the middle class of society. They made baskets and mats of reeds that grew abundantly in the neighboring morasses formed by the streams running down from the mountains. They prepared also wicker work for putting light huts together, and gave some attention to agriculture and grazing.

Saul and the Witch of Endor

The Israelites were drawn up before Endor near Jezrael, and the Philistines were marching against them from Sunem. The struggle had already begun

when Saul, with two companions—all three in the
garb of prophets—went in the darkness of evening
to the witch of Endor, who dwelt in some old ruins
outside the city. She was a poor, despised creature
still somewhat young. Her husband went around the
country with a puppet show upon his back, practicing sorcery and exhibiting his wonders to the soldiers of the garrisons and other idlers. When Saul
resolved to consult the witch, he was already half-
desperate. The witch at first was unwilling to satisfy his desire. She was afraid of its coming to the
ears of King Saul, who had strictly prohibited all
dealing in witchcraft. But Saul assured her with a
solemn oath that that should not happen. Then she
led him from the room in which they were, and which
had nothing extraordinary in its appearance, to an
obscure cellar. Saul demanded that Samuel's spirit
should be evoked. The witch drew a circle around
Saul and his companions, traced signs around the
circle, and spun threads of colored wool in all sorts
of figures before and around Saul. She stood at some
distance in front of him, a basin of water on the
ground before her, and plates like metallic mirrors
in her hands. These latter she waved toward each
other and over the water, muttering some words and
at times calling something aloud. She had previously
directed Saul through which part of the crossed
threads he was to gaze. By her diabolical skill, she
was able to bring up before the eyes of her inter-
rogators scenes of whole campaigns, battles, and the
figures of those engaged in them. Such a delusion
she was now preparing to evoke for Saul, when suddenly she beheld near her an apparition. Out of herself with astonishment and dread, she let the mirror
fall into the basin and cried out: "Thou hast deceived
me! Thou art Saul!" Saul bade her fear nothing, but
say to him what she then saw. She replied: "I see a
saint rising out of the earth." Saul beheld nothing,
and again he questioned: "What does he look like?"

The woman, trembling with fear, answered: "An old man in priestly robes!" and with these words she rushed past Saul and out of the cave. When Saul beheld Samuel, he fell prostrate on his face. Samuel spoke: "Why hast thou troubled my repose? The chastisement of God will soon fall upon thee! Tomorrow thou wilt be with me among the dead, the Philistines shall conquer Israel, and David will be king." At these words Saul, overcome by grief and horror, lay on the ground like one dead. His companions raised him and placed him leaning against the wall. They tried to rouse him, the woman brought bread and meat, but he refused to eat. The witch advised him not to engage in the battle, but to retire to Abez where the inhabitants, being Galaadites, would give him a good reception. Saul went thither next morning at dawn. The Israelites were routed beyond Mount Gelboe. Saul was attacked not by the whole army of Philistines, but only by a roving party. He was at the moment seated in his chariot, with an officer standing behind him. The Philistines, rushing by, shot spears and arrows at him, though not dreaming that it was Saul himself. He was grievously wounded, and his attendants led the chariot to the plain south of the valley and out of the road upon which Jesus had yesterday been with His relatives. When Saul felt himself mortally wounded, he requested his officer to kill him at once, but the latter refused. Then Saul, supporting himself in the chariot, which had a railing in front, tried to fall on the point of his own sword, but he could not succeed. The officer, seeing his determination, opened that swinging railing in front of the chariot, thus enabling Saul to fall on his sword, while at the same instant he pierced himself with his own. An Amalecite passing at the moment recognized Saul, possessed himself of his regal ornament, and carried it to David. After the battle, Saul's body was laid beside his sons, who had fallen to the east of the scene of slaughter. They had been killed before their father's death. The Philistines used to hack the bodies of their enemies to pieces.

The brook flowing through this valley was called Kadumin. (*Jgs.* 5:21). It is mentioned in Deborah's Canticle. The Prophet Malachias once sojourned here for a time and prophesied. Abez was about three hours from the pagan city Scythopolis.

On leaving the well, Jesus and the disciples proceeded some distance to the east, then turning, pursued their journey northward. He crossed the height that closed in the valley on the north and, after about three hours, reached another at the foot of Mount Thabor to the east. The brook Cison, which rises to the north of the mountain, here flowed around it and off to the Plain of Esdrelon. Here lay the city Dabereth in an angle of the first plateau of Thabor. The view from the city takes in the high plain of Saron and extends to the region in which the Jordan flows from the lake of Genesareth. The brook Cison ran through the whole of this quarter.

Jesus remained at an inn outside the city until the following day, when He went into Dabereth. A crowd instantly pressed around Him. He cured some sick, of whom, however, there were not many, as the air of this place was very pure.

The city of Dabereth was very beautifully built. I still remember one of the houses. It was surrounded by a large courtyard and porticos, from which two flights of steps led up to the roof. Behind the city rose an eminence projecting from the foot of Thabor, and around it wound serpentine paths. It took about two hours to reach the top. All along inside the city walls dwelt Roman soldiers. Dabereth was one of the cities named for the collection of taxes. It had five large streets, each of which was occupied by the workmen belonging to one trade. It was not exactly on the highroad, for the nearest was at a distance of half an hour; nevertheless, all kinds of business were carried on in it. It was a Levitical city, and the imposts raised in it were devoted to the support of sacred worship. The boundary posts that marked the limits of the tribe of Issachar were scarcely a quarter of an hour distant. The synagogue stood upon an open space, also that house mentioned above. Jesus went into the latter, for its occupant was a nephew of His foster father, Joseph.

Joseph's brother, the father of this nephew, was called Elia. He had had five sons—of whom one named Jesse, now an old man, dwelt in that house. His wife was still living, and they had a family of six children, three sons and three daughters. Two of the sons were already between eighteen and twenty years old. Their names were Kaleb and Aaron. Their father begged Jesus to receive them as disciples, which He did. They were to join the band when He should again pass through that part of the country. Jesse collected the taxes destined for the support of the Levites. He superintended also a cloth factory in which the wool that he purchased was cleansed, spun, and woven. Fine cloth was manufactured there, and a whole street was in Jesse's employ. He had also, in a long building, a machine for expressing the juice from various herbs, some of which were found on Thabor, and others were brought hither from a distance. The juice of some was used in dyeing; others, for beverages; and others, again, were made into perfumery. I saw hollow cylinders standing in troughs, in which by means of a heavy pounder the herbs were pressed. The pipes through which the expressed juice flowed ran outside of the building and were provided with spigots. When the pounders were not in use, they were kept in place by means of wedges. They prepared also the oil of myrrh. Jesse and his whole family were very pious. His children went daily, and he often accompanied them, to pray on Thabor, Jesus and the disciples made their home with them while at Dabereth.

There were both Pharisees and Sadducees in this city. They formed a kind of consistory, and held council together as to how they could contradict Jesus. That evening Jesus went with the disciples to Mount Thabor, whither a multitude had preceded Him. There He taught by moonlight until far into the night.

On the southeastern side of Thabor lay a cave with a little garden in front. There the Prophet Malachias had often sojourned. Farther up the mountain were another cave and garden where Elias and his disciples sometimes lived retired, as upon Carmel. These caves were now held as shrines by pious Jews, and thither they used to go to pray. To the north of Mount Thabor was situated the city of Thabor, whence the mountain derived its name, and about an hour westward in the direction of Sephoris was another fortified place. Casaloth was in the valley on the south side of the mountain, northward from Naim, and in the direction of Apheca. The tribe of Zabulon extends farthest to the north on this side. I have heard a more modern name given to this place, and I saw that relatives of Jesus once dwelt there, namely, a sister of Elizabeth, who, like the maid servant of Mary Marcus, bore the name of Rhoda. She had three daughters and two sons. One of the daughters was one of the three widows, friends of Mary, and her two sons were among the disciples. One of Rhoda's sons married Maroni, and died without issue. His widow, in obedience to the Law, entered into a second marriage with one of her first husband's family named Eliud, a nephew of Mother Anne. She lived at Naim and by her second husband had one son, who was called Martial. She was now a widow for the second time, and she is the so-called widow of Naim whose son Martial was raised from the dead by the Lord.

Jesus taught on the open space in front of the synagogue. Numerous sick had collected there from the neighborhood around, and the Pharisees were greatly irritated. There was a rich woman in Dabereth named Noemi. She had been unfaithful to her husband, and he had died of grief. For a long time she had promised to marry the agent that attended to her business, but he, too, was being deceived by her. Noemi had heard Jesus' instructions in Dothain and had been, in consequence, very much changed. She was full of repentance and desired only to beg of Him pardon and penance. She attended Jesus' teaching here in Dabereth, was present at the cures He wrought, and tried by every means to approach Him, but He always turned away from her. She was a person of distinction and well-known in the city, and as her disorders were not public, she had not fallen into general disesteem. While she was trying to approach Jesus, she encountered the Pharisees, who asked her whether she was not ashamed of herself and bade her return to her home. Their words, however, did not restrain her; she was as if out of herself in her eager desire for pardon. At last she succeeded in breaking through the crowd. She threw herself down on the ground before Jesus, crying out: "Lord, is there grace, is there pardon still for me? Lord, I can no longer live so! I sinned grievously against my husband, and I have deceived the man that now has charge of my affairs!" And thus she confessed her sins before all. All, however, did not hear her, for Jesus had stepped aside, and the Pharisees pressing forward had made a great uproar. Jesus said to Noemi: "Arise! Thy sins are forgiven thee!" She obeyed, begging at the same time for a penance, but Jesus put her off till another time. Then she divested herself of her rich ornaments: the strings of pearls around her headdress, her rings, her bracelets, and the golden cords around her arms and neck. She handed them all over to the Pharisees with the request that they should be given to the poor, and then she drew her veil closely around her.

Jesus now went into the synagogue, for the Sabbath had begun. The infuriated Pharisees and Sadducees followed Him. The reading for the day was about Jacob and Esau. (*Gen.* 25:19-34 and *Mal.*). Jesus applied the details connected with the birth of the two brothers to His own time. Esau and Jacob struggled in their mother's womb, thus did the synagogue struggle against the piously disposed. The Law was harsh and severe, the firstborn like Esau, but it had sold its birthright to Jacob for a mess of pottage, for the redolent odors arising from all kinds of unimportant usages and exterior ceremonies. Jacob, who had now received the Blessing, would become a great nation whom Esau would have to serve. The whole explanation was very beautiful, and the Pharisees could bring nothing forward against it, although they disputed long with Jesus. They reproached Him upon several heads: that He attached to Himself followers, that He established private inns throughout the country, employing for the same the money and property of rich widows which should have been given for the use of the synagogue and the Doctors. And so, they said, would it now be with Noemi; besides, how could He forgive her her sins?

Next morning Jesus did not go to the synagogue, but to the school for the boys and girls. The children followed Him even into Jesse's court while He was taking dinner there, and Jesus instructed and blessed them again. The woman lately converted was likewise there with her steward. Jesus spoke with each alone and then to both together. On account of her present sentiments, Jesus advised the woman not to marry again, especially as her suitor was of low origin. She was to deliver to him a part of her fortune and, after reserving sufficient for her own support, distribute the rest to the poor.

After the Sabbath day repast, when the Jews were taking their customary promenade, some Jewish women came to visit Jesse's wife. There, in Jesus' presence, they engaged in an instructive game such

as was usual on the Sabbath. The converted Noemi
was present. The game consisted of a combination of
parables, enigmas, or questions, calculated to instruct
and edify. For example, such questions as the following were proposed: Where had each one her treasure? Did she put it out at high interest? Did she
hide it? Did she share it with her husband? Did she
leave it to her domestics? Did she carry it with her
to the synagogue? Was her heart attached to it? Many
of these questions turned upon the care of children
and servants, etc. Jesus spoke also of oil and the
lamp, of the burning of a well-filled lamp, of the
spilling of the oil, applying all these things in a spiritual sense. One of the women was questioned on
one of these points. She answered promptly and graciously: "Yes, Master! I take great care that the Sabbath lamp is always of the best." Her neighbors were
very much amused at her words. They laughed at
her, for she had not caught Jesus' meaning. He always
gave a very striking explanation, and whoever made
a wrong answer was obliged to give a present to the
poor as a fine. The woman of whom I have spoken
gave a piece of cloth.

Jesus wrote also, before each one, an enigma in
the sand with a reed, the answer to which had likewise to be written in the same way by the one to
whom it was addressed. In this manner He revealed
to each her evil inclinations and defects, so that she
trembled with fear, though without the necessity of
blushing before her neighbor. He advised them especially of the faults of which they were guilty at the
last Feast of Tabernacles, for in the greater liberty
they enjoyed at that time and the merrymaking then
customary, they may easily have sinned. Several of
these women afterward spoke in private to Jesus,
confessed their transgressions, and begged for
penance and forgiveness. Jesus consoled them and
reconciled them to God. During this instruction the
women were ranged in a semicircle under the por-

tico of the courtyard. They sat on rugs and cushions, their backs resting against the stone benches. The disciples and friends of the family were standing on either side at some distance. There was no loud speaking, since the loiterers on the street could, by climbing the wall, have created disturbance, for they were all out in the open air. The women had brought with them as presents for Jesus all kinds of spices, comfits, and perfumes. He gave them to the disciples with directions to distribute them to the sick poor who never could get such luxuries.

Before Jesus returned to the synagogue for the closing services of the Sabbath, the Herodians sent messengers to request Him to meet them at a certain place in the city, since they wanted to speak with Him. Jesus replied to the messengers with a severe expression: "Say to those hypocrites that they may open their double-tongued mouths against Me in the synagogue, for there shall I answer them and others." He added other hard names, and then went to the school.

The Sabbath reading again treated of Jacob and Esau, of grace and the Law, and of the children and servants of the Father. Jesus inveighed so vehemently against the Pharisees, the Sadducees, and the Herodians, that their fury increased at each moment. The necessity in which Isaac had been of removing from place to place and the filling up of the wells by the Philistines, Jesus applied to His own teaching mission and the persecution He endured from the Pharisees. Passing then to Malachias, He announced the fulfillment of his Prophecy: "My Name shall be magnified upon the border of Israel. From the rising of the sun even to the going down, My Name is great among the Gentiles." (*Mal.* 1:5, 6, 11). Then He made known to them all the ways He had traversed on either side of the Jordan, in order to glorify the Name of the Lord. He declared that He would continue His course to the end, and in severe language He quoted against them these other words of the Prophet: "The son shall honor the father, and the servant his master." (*Mal.* 1:5, 6, 11). His enemies were confounded, and had nothing to reply.

When the crowd had left the synagogue and Jesus likewise had withdrawn with the disciples, He suddenly found His way blockaded in one of the courts by the Pharisees. They surrounded Him in one of the halls and demanded that He should answer some questions. It was not necessary, they said, for the people to hear all that they had to say. And then they proposed to Him all kinds of captious questions, especially upon their relations to the Romans who were here stationed. Jesus' answer reduced them to silence. When at last, with flattery and menaces, they demanded that He should give up travelling around with disciples, desist from preaching and curing, else they would denounce and punish Him as a disturber of the peace, as a seditious character, He replied: "Until the end shall ye find upon My footsteps the ignorant, the sinful, the poor, the sick, and My own disciples—those whom ye have abandoned to their ignorance and sinfulness, whom ye have left in their poverty and misery." Seeing that they could gain nothing by their artful words, they left the synagogue with Him. Outwardly they assumed a courteous demeanor, but inwardly they were full of rage, though not unmixed with admiration.

The Pagan Cyrinus of Cyprus

From the school Jesus went in the evening twilight, accompanied by the disciples and the people who had awaited Him outside the synagogue, up to Thabor. A multitude of others and some of His own relatives were already there assembled. Jesus sat down on the mountain, His hearers reclining or sitting below at His feet. The stars were twinkling in the sky, and the moon was shedding around her gen-

tle radiance. Jesus taught until late into the night.
He often did this even after a toilsome day's work
when in the midst of a little band of pious souls. The
peace was then more profound, His audience less dis-
tracted; the heavens, the stars, the wide expanse of
nature, the pleasant coolness of the air, the stillness
reigning around, fell like soothing balm upon men's
souls. They heard their Teacher's voice more distinctly,
comprehended His words more easily, were less confused at hearing their own faults laid bare, carried
His instructions home with them, and pondered them
with fewer distractions. This was especially the case
in the magnificent region in which Jesus now was,
in the wide prospect that unfolded from the heights
of Thabor. The mount itself, on account of the sojourn
of Elias and Malachias upon it for a time, was held
in special veneration.

When Jesus was returning home late in the night,
followed by the crowd, there approached Him on the
way a pagan from Cyprus who had been present at
the instructions. He was one of the occupants of Jesse's
house and had something to do connected with the
manufacture of the essential oils. Up to this time,
however, he had kept aloof through a spirit of humility. But now Jesus took him into a room of the house
where He sat with him alone, as He had done with
Nicodemus, instructing him and answering the questions that he put so humbly, yet with so eager a
desire of learning the truth.

This pagan, a man most noble and wise, was named
Cyrinus. His remarks were most profound, and he
received Jesus' instructions with indescribable humility and joy. Jesus, on His side, was very loving and
confidential toward him. Cyrinus said that for a long
time past he had been sensible of the emptiness of
idolatry and had longed to become a Jew, but that
there was one thing which presented an in-
superable objection, namely, circumcision. He asked
whether it was not possible to attain salvation with-

out it. Jesus answered him in words both familiar
and significant regarding that mystery. He might,
said Jesus, circumcise his senses, his heart, and his
tongue from carnal desires and pleasures, and then
go to Capharnaum for Baptism. At these words, Cyrinus asked why He did not preach that openly, for he
thought that if Jesus did so, many pagans who were
longing for it would be converted. Jesus answered
that if He should say such a thing to the multitude,
blinded as they were by their prejudices, they would
certainly put Him to death, and one must not scandalize the weak. Again, abolishing circumcision might
give rise to multiplied sects; besides, the law was
necessary for some of the pagans as a means of trial
and sacrifice. But now that the Kingdom of God was
drawing near, the covenant of circumcision in the
flesh was fulfilled and the circumcision of the heart
and the spirit must take its place. Cyrinus inquired
also as to the sufficiency of John's baptism, and Jesus
spoke with him upon that point. He told Jesus about
many people who were sighing after Him in Cyprus,
and complained to Him of his two sons who, though
otherwise very virtuous, were fierce enemies of
Judaism. Jesus consoled him and promised that, after
He had fulfilled His mission, his sons would yet
become zealous workers in His vineyard. These sons
were, I think, called Aristarchus and Trophimus. They
afterward became disciples of the Apostles. This most
touching nocturnal interview lasted till morning.

On the sunny side of the mountain were large
reservoirs hewn out of the rocky wall, and in them
were vessels belonging to Jesse, in which were prepared perfumes from herbs and other substances.
The oil dropped from one vessel into another, making many a turn in its course.

10. Jesus Goes to Giskala, The Birthplace of St. Paul

From Dabereth Jesus went in the forenoon with the disciples three hours northward to the plain and city of Giskala, almost an hour from Bethulia. Just at the outset of His journey lay a place to the east, I think Japhia, and another directly opposite toward the west and northward from Thabor. Giskala was situated upon a height, but one not so elevated as that of Bethulia. It was a stronghold garrisoned by pagan soldiers in Herod's pay. The Jews dwelt in a little quarter apart, about fifteen minutes distant from the fortress. Giskala was very different from other cities. There were open squares and large buildings surrounded with palisades, as if to afford space for hitching horses, and all around the city ran a wall with towers, from whose stories troops of soldiers could defend it. All this gave Giskala a very remarkable appearance. Near one of the towers stood the idolatrous temple. The Jews of the little city lived on good terms with the pagan soldiers, for whom they manufactured articles of leather, harness for the horses and military equipment for the men. They were likewise partly the owners and partly the overseers and stewards of the fertile region lying around the city. Far from it, off to Capharnaum, stretched the magnificent country of Genesareth. The citadel stood upon a height up to which led a paved road from terrace to terrace. The little Jewish quarter lay outstretched on the declivity of that same height. Before it was a well, or rather a cistern, for drinking water, which was conducted from distant sources by means of pipes. It was by this cistern that Jesus and the disciples sat down on their arrival.

The residents of the Jewish quarter were just then celebrating a feast and all the inhabitants, young and old, were out in the gardens and fields. The pagan children from the city were present also, but they kept to themselves somewhat apart from the others. When the people spied Jesus going to the cistern, the chief men of the city, with their learned schoolmaster, approached Him. They welcomed Him and the disciples, washed their feet, and presented them fruit, Jesus, still at the cistern, gave an instruction in which He alluded to the harvest in a parable, for in this region at that moment they were busy gathering in their second harvest of grapes and all kinds of fruit. He next went over to where the pagan children were, spoke to the mothers, blessed them, and cured several who were sick.

The Jews of Giskala were on that day celebrating a feast commemorative of their deliverance from the yoke of a tyrant, the first founder of the Sadducees. He lived over two hundred years before Christ, but I have forgotten his name. He was one of the officers of the Sanhedrin in Jerusalem, and was charged to watch over the points of faith not found set down in the written Law. He had tormented the people horribly with his rigorous ideas, one of which was that no reward could be hoped from God, but that He was to be served by them as slaves serve their master. Giskala was his birthplace, but his townsmen held his memory in horror. Today's festival was a memorial rejoicing at his death. One of his disciples was from Samaria. Sadoch, who denied the dogma of the resurrection of the body, continued to promulgate the founder's doctrine. He was a pupil of Antigonus. Sadoch also had a Samaritan accomplice helping to propagate his errors.

Jesus and His disciples lodged with the Elder of the synagogue, and taught in the forecourt of the same. They brought some sick to Him, whom He healed, among them a dropsical old woman. This Elder of the synagogue was a very good and learned man. The people abhorred the Pharisees and Sadducees, and had taken great care to provide themselves with such a teacher. That he might acquire more knowledge, they had sent him travelling far away, even down to Egypt. Jesus conversed a long time with him. As usual, the Elder turned the conversation upon John, whom he praised very highly. He asked Jesus why, powerful and enlightened as He was said to be and as He was in reality, He did not make some effort to free that man so truly grand and admirable.

During His instruction in the forecourt of the synagogue Jesus uttered prophetic words to the disciples concerning Giskala. They were as follows: Three zealots had arisen in Giskala. The first was that one in whose memory the Jews were then celebrating a feast; the second was a great villain, John of Giskala, who had raised a terrible insurrection in Galilee and at the siege of Jerusalem had committed frightful excesses; the third was living at the very time He was speaking. He would pass from hatred to love, would be zealous for the truth, and would convert many to God. This third was Paul, who was born at Giskala, but whose parents afterward removed to Tarsus.

After his conversion and when journeying to Jerusalem, Paul very zealously preached the Gospel at Giskala. His parents' house was still standing, and rented to strangers. It was situated at the extremity of the suburb of Giskala, and at some distance were squares surrounded with palisades and little buildings, like bleaching huts, that reached almost to the city itself. Paul's parents must have carried on the manufacture of linen, or perhaps they had a weaver's establishment. A pagan officer named Achias now rented and lived in the dwelling house.

Cure of the Son of a Pagan Officer

It would be difficult to describe the fruitfulness of the region around Giskala. The people were now gathering the second crop of grapes, different kinds of fruits, aromatic shrubs, and cotton. A kind of reed grew in these parts, the lower leaves of which were

large, the upper ones small. From it distilled a sweet
juice like resin. Here, too, were seen those trees whose
fruit was used for the decoration of the tabernacles.
The fruit was called the apples of the Patriarchs,
from the fact of their having been brought hither
from the warm eastern countries by the Patriarchs.
These trees were trained against walls forming an
espalier, although their trunk was often more than
a foot in diameter. Here also were found many plants
producing cotton, whole fields of sweet-scented shrubs,
and the aromatic herb from which nard is made.
Figs, olives, and grapes were in abundance, while
magnificent melons lay in countless numbers in the
fields, the roads to which were lined with palms and
date trees. In the midst of this luxuriance of nature
were great herds of cattle grazing in the most beautiful meadows covered with grass and herbs. I saw
likewise large trees with great, thick nuts, the wood
of which was exceedingly tough and solid.

As Jesus was walking through the fields and gardens into which the people were fast gathering, groups
collected around Him here and there. He instructed
them in parables taken from their ordinary circumstances and occupations. The pagan children mingled familiarly with those of their Jewish neighbors
in harvest time, but they were somewhat differently
clothed.

In the house in which Paul was born there lived
at this period an officer in command of the pagan
soldiers of the citadel. He was called Achias. He had
a sick son seven years old, to whom he had given
the name of Jephte after the Jewish hero. Achias
was a good man. He sighed for help from Jesus, but
none of the inhabitants of Giskala would intercede
for him with the Lord. The disciples were all engaged:
some busy around their Master, others scattered
among the harvesters to whom they were telling of
Jesus and repeating His instructions, while some others had already been dispatched as messengers to

Capharnaum and into the neighboring districts. The townspeople had no liking for the officer, whom they did not care to have so near them. They would have been glad had he fixed his abode elsewhere. They were, besides, not very friendly in disposition, and even showed very little enthusiasm over Jesus Himself. They went carelessly on with their work, listening to His words, but taking no lively, active interest. The anxious father therefore made bold to follow Jesus, but at a distance. At last he approached Him, stepped before Him, bowing, and said: "Master, reject not Thy servant! Have pity on my little son lying sick at home!" Jesus replied: "It behooveth to break bread to the children of the household before giving it to the stranger who stands without." Achias responded: "Lord, I believe the Promise. I believe that Thou hast said that such as believe in Thee are not strangers but Thy children. Lord, have pity on my son!" Then said Jesus: "Thy faith hath saved thee!" and followed by some of the disciples, He went into the house in which Paul was born and in which Achias now resided.

It was rather more elegant than the generality of Jewish dwellings, though its arrangements were pretty much of the same style. There was a court-yard in front, from which one entered a broad hall, on either side of which were sleeping apartments, or spaces, cut off from the main portion by movable screens. In the center of the house arose the fire-place. Around it lay large rooms and halls, provided with broad stone benches near the walls, upon which lay rugs and cushions. The windows were high up in the building. Achias conducted Jesus into the interior of the house, and some of the servants carried to Him the boy in his bed. The wife of Achias followed veiled. She bowed timidly, and stood somewhat behind the rest in anxious expectation. Achias was radiant with joy. He called in all his domestics who, full of curiosity, were standing at a distance. The boy

was a beautiful child of about six years. He had on
a long woolen gown and a striped fur around his
neck and crossed on the breast. He was dumb and
paralyzed, wholly unable to move. But he looked intelligent and affectionate, and cast upon Jesus a most
touching glance.

Jesus addressed to the parents and all present
some words on the vocation of the Gentiles, the nearness of the Kingdom, of penance, and of the entrance
into the Father's house by Baptism. Then He prayed,
took the boy from his little bed up in His arms, laid
him on His breast, bowed low over him, put His fingers under his tongue, set him down on the floor,
and led him to the officer who, with the mother trembling for joy, rushed forward with heartfelt tears to
meet and embrace their child. The little fellow, likewise stretching out his arms toward his parents, cried:
"O father! O mother! I can walk, I can again speak!"
Then Jesus said: "Take the boy! Ye know not what
a treasure has been given to you in him. He is now
restored to you, but he will one day be redemanded
of you!" The parents led the child again to Jesus and
in tears threw themselves with him at His feet, uttering thanks. Jesus blessed the boy and spoke to him
most kindly. The officer begged Jesus to step with
him into an adjoining apartment and take some
refreshment. This He did along with the disciples.
They partook, standing, of bread, honey, small fruits,
and some kind of beverage. Jesus again spoke with
Achias, telling him that he should go to Capharnaum
and there receive Baptism, and that he might join
Zorobabel. Achias and his domestics did this later
on. The boy Jephte afterward became a very zealous
disciple of St. Thomas.

The soldiers of Giskala, in quality of guards, assisted
at the Crucifixion of Christ. They were on similar occasions employed as police.

Jesus bade farewell to the home of the happy Achias.
He spoke with His disciples of the child and of the

fruits of salvation he was destined to reap. He told
them also that from that same house one had already
gone out who would accomplish great things in His
Kingdom.

11. Jesus Teaches in Gabara.
Magdalen's First Conversion

On leaving Giskala, Jesus did not go to Bethulia,
which was near, but leaving it on the left, He traversed the valley and the plain to the somewhat
important city of Gabara. It lay at the western foot
of the mountain on whose south-eastern slope was
perched the Herodian eyrie Jetebatha. The distance
between the city and the fortress, that is, if one went
around the mountain, was one hour. This mountain,
in which steps were hewn, arose like a steep wall
behind Gabara, whose inhabitants were engaged in
the manufacture of cotton fine as silk, which they
wove into cloth and covers. They made of it also a
kind of mattress, which they stretched and fastened
on hooks. This formed the whole bed. Some others
were engaged in salting and exporting fish.

While still in Giskala, Jesus had sent some of the
disciples around to the neighboring places to say that
He would deliver a great instruction on the mountain beyond Gabara. There came in consequence, from
a circuit of several hours, large crowds of people, who
encamped around the mountain. On the summit was
an enclosed space in which was a teacher's chair long
out of use.

Peter, Andrew, James, John, Nathanael Chased,
and all the rest of the disciples had come, besides
most of John's disciples and the sons of the Blessed
Virgin's eldest sister. There were altogether about
sixty disciples, friends, and relatives of Jesus here
assembled. The more intimate of the disciples were
greeted by Jesus with clasping of both hands and
pressing cheek to cheek.

Crowds of heathens came from Cydessa, one hour westward of the neighboring city of Damna, from Adama and the country around Lake Merom. The people crowding hither brought with them provisions and sick of all kinds. Cydessa was a heathen city in the heart of Zabulon. It was in ruins in the time of Alexander the Great, who bestowed it upon a man from Tyre called Livias. The latter restored it, and led thither many of his pagan countrymen from Tyre. The first pagans that came to John's baptism were from Cydessa, which was very beautifully situated and commanded a view of the luxuriantly fruitful country around.

Magdalen

Magdalen also wended her way to the mount of instruction near Gabara. Martha and Anna Cleophas had left Damna, where the holy women had an inn, and gone to Magdalum with the view of persuading Magdalen to attend the sermon that Jesus was about to deliver on the mountain beyond Gabara. Veronica, Johanna Chusa, Dina, and the Suphanite had meanwhile remained at Damna, distant three hours from Capharnaum and over one hour from Magdalum. Magdalen received her sister in a manner rather kind and showed her into an apartment not far from her room of state, but into this latter she did not take her. There was in Magdalen a mixture of true and false shame. She was partly ashamed of her simple, pious, and plainly dressed sister who went around with Jesus' followers so despised by her visitors and associates, and she was partly ashamed of herself before Martha. It was this feeling that prevented her taking the latter into the apartments that were the scenes of her follies and vices. Magdalen was somewhat broken in spirits, but she lacked the courage to disengage herself from her surroundings. She looked pale and languid. The man with whom she lived, on account of his low and vulgar sentiments, was utterly distasteful to her.

Martha treated her very prudently and affectionately. She said to her: "Dina and Mary, the Suphanite, whom you know, two amiable and clever women, invite you to be present with them at the instruction that Jesus is going to give on the mountain. It is so near, and they are so anxious for your company. You need not be ashamed of them before the people, for they are respectable, they dress with taste, and they have distinguished manners. You will behold a very wonderful spectacle: the crowds of people, the marvelous eloquence of the Prophet, the sick, the cures that He effects, the hardihood with which He addresses the Pharisees! Veronica, Mary Chusa, and Jesus' Mother, who wishes you so well—we all are convinced that you will thank us for the invitation. I think it will cheer you up a little. You appear to be quite forlorn here, you have no one around you who can appreciate your heart and your talents. Oh, if you would only pass some time with us in Bethania! We hear so many wonderful things, and we have so much good to do, and you have always been so full of compassion and kindness. You must at least come to Damna with me tomorrow morning. There you will find all the women of our party at the inn. You can have a private apartment and meet only those that you know," etc. In this strain Martha spoke to her sister, carefully avoiding anything that might wound her. Magdalen's sadness predisposed her to listen favorably to Martha's proposals. She did indeed raise a few difficulties, but at last yielded and promised Martha to accompany her to Damna. She took a repast with her and went several times during the evening from her own apartments to see her. Martha and Anna Cleophas prayed together that night that God would render the coming journey fruitful in good for Magdalen.

A few days previously James the Greater, impelled

by a feeling of intense compassion for Magdalen, had come to invite her to the preaching soon to take place at Gabara. She had received him at a neighboring house. James was in appearance very imposing. His speech was grave and full of wisdom, though at the same time most pleasing. He made a most favorable impression upon Magdalen, and she received him graciously whenever he was in that part of the country. James did not address to her words of reproof; on the contrary, his manner toward her was marked by esteem and kindliness, and he invited her to be present at least once at Jesus' preaching. It would be impossible, he said, to see or hear one superior to Him. She had no need to trouble herself about the other auditors, and she might appear among them in her ordinary dress. Magdalen had received his invitation favorably, but she was still undecided as to whether she should or should not accept it, when Martha and Anna Cleophas arrived.

On the eve of the day appointed for the instruction, Magdalen with Martha and Anna Cleophas started from Magdalum to join the holy women at Damna. Magdalen rode on an ass, for she was not accustomed to walking. She was dressed elegantly, though not to such excess nor so extravagantly as at a later period when she was converted for the second time. She took a private apartment in the inn and spoke only with Dina and the Suphanite, who visited her by turns. I saw them together, an affable and well-bred confidence marking their intercourse. There was, however, on the part of the converted sinners, a shade of embarrassment similar to what might be experienced on a military officer's meeting a former comrade who had become a priest. This feeling soon gave way to tears and womanly expressions of mutual sympathy, and they went together to the inn at the foot of the mountain. The other holy women did not go to the instruction, in order not to annoy Magdalen by their presence. They had come to Damna with the intention of prevailing upon Jesus to remain there and not go to Capharnaum where Pharisees from various localities were again assembled. They, the Pharisees, had taken up their abode together, determined to make Capharnaum their headquarters for awhile, since it was the central point of all Jesus' journeyings. The young Pharisee from Samaria who was present the last time was not among this set; another had taken his place. At Nazareth also and in other places the Pharisees had formed similar unions against Jesus.

The holy women, and especially Mary, were very much troubled, for the Pharisees had uttered loud threats. They sent a messenger to Jesus imploring Him not to go to Capharnaum after this instruction, but to join them in Damna; or He might turn to the right or to the left as seemed good to Him; or better perhaps would it be for Him to cross the lake and preach among the pagan cities where He would run no risk. Jesus replied by sending them word not to worry about Him, that He knew what was best for Him to do, and that He would see them again in Capharnaum.

The Mount of Instruction near Gabara. Magdalen

Magdalen and her companions reached the mountain in good time, and found crowds of people already encamped around it. The sick of all kinds were, according to the nature of their maladies, ranged together in different places under light canopies and arbors. High upon the mountain were the disciples, kindly ranging the people in order and rendering them every assistance. Around the teacher's chair was a low, semicircular wall, and over it an awning. The audience had here and there similar awnings erected. At a short distance from the teacher's chair, Magdalen and the other women had found a comfortable seat upon a little eminence.

About ten o'clock, Jesus ascended the mountain with His disciples, followed by the Pharisees, the Herodians, and the Sadducees, and took the teacher's chair. The disciples were on one side, the Pharisees on the other, forming a circle around Him. Several times during His discourse, Jesus made a pause to allow His hearers to exchange places, the more distant coming forward, the nearest falling back, and He likewise repeated the same instructions several times. His auditors partook of refreshments in the intervals, and Jesus Himself once took a mouthful to eat and a little drink. This discourse of Jesus was one of the most powerful that He had yet delivered. He prayed before He began, and then told His hearers that they should not be scandalized at Him if He called God His Father, for whosoever does the will of the Father in Heaven, he is His son, and that He really accomplished the Father's will, He clearly proved. Hereupon He prayed aloud to His Father and then commenced His austere preaching of penance after the manner of the ancient Prophets. All that had happened from the time of the first Promise, all the figures and all the menaces, He introduced into His discourse and showed how, in the present and in the near future, they would be accomplished. He proved the coming of the Messiah from the fulfillment of the Prophecies. He spoke of John, the precursor and preparer of the ways, who had honestly fulfilled his mission, but whose hearers had remained obdurate. Then He enumerated their vices, their hypocrisy, their idolatry of sinful flesh; painted in strong colors the Pharisees, Sadducees, and Herodians; and spoke with great warmth of the anger of God and the approaching judgment, of the destruction of Jerusalem and the Temple, and of the diverse woes that hung over their country. He quoted many passages from the prophet Malachias, explaining and applying them to the Precursor, to the Messiah, to the pure oblation of bread and wine of the New Law (which I plainly understood to signify the Holy Sacrifice of the Mass), to the judgment awaiting the godless, to the second coming of the Messiah on the last day, and spoke of the confidence and consolation those that feared God would then experience. He added, moreover, that the grace taken from them would be given to the heathens.

Then turning to the disciples, Jesus exhorted them to confidence and perseverance, and told them that He would send them to preach salvation to all nations. He warned them to hold neither to the Pharisees, the Sadducees, nor the Herodians, whom He painted in lively colors by comparisons as just as they were striking. This was peculiarly vexatious to the last named, since no one wanted to be publicly known as an Herodian. They who adhered to this sect did so mostly in secret.

When in the course of His instruction Jesus observed that if His hearers would not accept the salvation offered them, it would be worse for them than for Sodom and Gomorrha, some of the Pharisees, taking advantage of a pause, stepped up to Him with the question: "Then, will this mountain, this city, yes, even the whole country, be swallowed up along with us all? And could there happen something still worse?" Jesus answered: "The stones of Sodom were swallowed up, but not all the souls, for these latter knew not of the Promise, nor had they the Law and the prophets." He added some words that I understood of His own future descent into Limbo, and from which I gathered that many of those souls were saved. Then coming back to the Jews of His own time, He reminded them that they were a chosen race whom God had formed into one nation, that they had received instruction and warnings, the Promises and their realization, that if they rejected them and persevered in their incredulity, not the rocks, the mountains (for they obeyed the Lord), but

their own stony hearts, their own souls, would be
hurled into the abyss. And thus would their lot be
more grievous than that of Sodom.

When Jesus had thus vehemently urged the guilty
to penance, when He had so severely pronounced
judgment upon the obdurate, He became once more
all love, invited all sinners to come to Him, and even
shed over them tears of compassion. Then He implored
His Father to touch their hearts that some, a few,
yes, even one, though burdened with all kinds of
guilt, might return to Him. Could He gain but one
soul, He would share all with it, He would give all
that He possessed, yes, He would even sacrifice His
life to purchase it. He stretched out His arms toward
them, exclaiming: "Come! Come to Me, ye who are
weary and laden with guilt! Come to Me, ye sinners!
Do penance, believe, and share the Kingdom with
Me!" Then turning to the Pharisees, to His enemies,
He opened His arms to them also, beseeching all, at
least one of them, to come to Him.

Magdalen had taken her seat among the other
women with the self-confident air of a lady of the
world, but her manner was assumed. She was
inwardly confused and a prey to interior struggle.
At first she gazed around upon the crowd, but when
Jesus appeared and began to speak, her eyes and
soul were riveted upon Him alone. His exhortations
to penance, His lively pictures of vice, His threats of
chastisement, affected her powerfully, and unable to
suppress her emotions, she trembled and wept
beneath her veil. When Jesus, Himself shedding tears
full of loving compassion, cried out for sinners to
come to Him, many of His hearers were transported
with emotion. There was a movement in the circle
and the crowd pressed around Him. Magdalen also,
and following her example the other women likewise,
took a step nearer. But when Jesus exclaimed: "Ah!
If even *one* soul would come to Me!" Magdalen was
so moved that she wanted to fly to Him at once. She

stepped forward; but her companions, fearing some disturbance, held her back, whispering: "Wait! Wait!" This movement of Magdalen attracted scarcely any notice among the bystanders, since the attention of all was riveted upon Jesus' words. Jesus, aware of Magdalen's agitation, uttered words of consolation meant only for her. He said: "If even one germ of penance, of contrition, of love, of faith, of hope has, in consequence of My words, fallen upon some poor, erring heart, it will bear fruit, it will be set down in favor of that poor sinner, it will live and increase. I Myself shall nourish it, shall cultivate it, shall present it to My Father." These words consoled Magdalen while they pierced her inmost soul, and she stepped back again among her companions.

It was now about six o'clock, and the sun had already sunk low behind the mountain. During His discourse Jesus was turned to the west, the point toward which the teacher's chair faced, and there was no one behind Him. And now He prayed, dismissed the multitude with His blessing, and commanded the disciples to buy food and distribute it to the poor and needy. Whoever had more than enough for himself was to give it or sell it for the benefit of the poor, who were to take home with them whatever they received over and above. Some of the disciples went immediately to execute their Master's commission. Most of those present gave willingly what they could spare, while others just as willingly took some indemnification for it. The disciples were well-known in this part of the country, so the poor were well cared for, and they thanked the great charity of the Lord.

Meanwhile the other disciples accompanied Jesus to the sick, numbers of whom had been brought thither. The Pharisees, scandalized, impressed, astonished, enraged, went back to Gabara. Simon Zabulon, the chief of the synagogue, reminded Jesus of the invitation to sup in his house. Jesus replied that

He would be there. The Pharisees murmured against Jesus and criticized Him the whole way down the mountain, finding fault with His doctrine and His manners. Each was ashamed to allow his neighbor to remark the favorable impression that had been made upon him, and so by the time they reached the city, they had again entrenched themselves in their own self-righteousness.

Magdalen and her companions followed Jesus. The former went among the people and took her place near the sick women as if to render them assistance. She was very much impressed, and the misery that she witnessed moved her still more. Jesus turned first to the men, among whom for a long time He healed diseases of all kinds. The hymns of thanksgiving from the cured and their attendants as they moved away, rang on the breeze. When He approached the sick females, the crowd that pressed around Him and the need that He and His disciples had of space forced Magdalen and the holy women to fall back a little. Nevertheless, Magdalen sought by every opportunity, by every break in the crowd, to draw near to Him, but Jesus constantly turned away from her.

He healed some women afflicted with a flow of blood. But how express the feelings of Magdalen, so delicate, so effeminate, whose eyes were quite unused to the sight of human suffering! What memories, what gratitude swelled the heart of Mary Suphan when six women, bound three and three, were forcibly led to Jesus by strong servant maids who dragged them along with cords, or long linen bands! They were possessed in the most frightful manner by unclean spirits, and they were the first possessed women that I saw brought publicly to Jesus. Some were from beyond the Lake of Genesareth, some from Samaria, and among them were several pagans. They had been bound together only upon reaching this place. Ordinarily they were perfectly quiet and gentle, they offered no violence to one another. But anon, they became quite furious, screaming and hurling themselves here and there. Their custodians bound them and kept them at a distance during Jesus' discourse, and now when all was nearly over, they brought them forward. As the afflicted creatures drew near to Jesus and the disciples, they began to offer vehement resistance. Satan was tormenting them horribly. They uttered the most awful cries and fell into violent contortions. Jesus turned toward them and commanded them to be silent, to be at peace. They instantly stood still and motionless; then He went up to them, ordered them to be unbound, commanded them to kneel down, prayed, and laid His hands upon them. Under the touch of His hand they sank into a few moments' unconsciousness, during which the wicked spirits went out of them in the form of a dark vapor. Then their attendants lifted them up, and veiled and in tears, they stood before Jesus, inclining low and giving thanks. He warned them to amend their lives, to purify themselves and do penance, lest their misfortune might come upon them more frightfully than before.

It was dusk before Jesus and the disciples, preceded and followed by crowds of people, started at last down the mountain for Gabara. Magdalen, obeying only her impulse without regard to appearances, followed close after Jesus in the crowd of disciples, and her four companions, unwilling to separate from her, did the same. She tried to keep as close to Jesus as she possibly could, though such conduct was quite unusual in females. Some of the disciples called Jesus' attention to the fact, remarking at the same time what I have just observed. But Jesus, turning around to them, replied: "Let them alone! It is not your affair!" And so He entered the city. When He reached the hall in which Simon Zabulon had prepared the feast, He found the forecourt filled with the sick and the poor who had crowded thither on His approach, and who were loudly calling upon Him for help. Jesus at

once turned to them, exhorting, consoling, and healing them. Meanwhile Simon Zabulon, with some other
Pharisees, made his appearance. He begged Jesus to
come in to the feast, for they were awaiting Him.
"Thou hast," he continued, "already done enough for
today. Let these people wait till another time, and let
the poor go off at once." But Jesus replied: "These are
My guests. I have invited them, and I must first see
to their entertainment. When thou didst invite Me to
thy feast, thou didst invite them also. I shall not go
into thy feast until they are helped, and then even I
will go in only with them." Then the Pharisees had
to go and prepare tables around the court for the
cured and the poor. Jesus cured all, and the disciples
led those that wished to remain to the tables prepared for them, and lamps were lighted in the court.

Magdalen and the women had followed Jesus hither.
They stood in one of the halls of the court adjoining
the entertainment hall. Jesus, followed by some of
the disciples, went to the table in the latter and from
its sumptuous dishes sent various meats to the tables
of the poor. The disciples were the bearers of these
gifts; they likewise served and ate with the poor. Jesus
continued His instructions during the entertainment.
The Pharisees were in animated discussion with Him
when Magdalen, who with her companions had
approached the entrance, all on a sudden darted into
the hall. Inclining humbly, her head veiled, in her
hand a little white flask closed with a tiny bunch of
aromatic herbs instead of a stopper, she glided quickly
into the center of the apartment, went behind Jesus,
and poured the contents of her little flask over His
head. Then catching up the long end of her veil, she
folded it, and with both hands passed it lightly once
over Jesus' head, as if wishing to smooth His hair
and to arrest the overflow of the ointment. The whole
affair occupied but a few instants, and after it Magdalen retired some steps. The discussion carried on
so hotly at the moment suddenly ceased. A hush fell

upon the company, and they gazed upon Jesus and the woman. The air was redolent with the fragrance of the ointment. Jesus was silent. Some of the guests put their heads together, glanced indignantly at Magdalen, and exchanged whispers. Simon Zabulon especially appeared scandalized. At last Jesus said to him: "Simon, I know well of what thou art thinking! Thou thinkest it improper that I should allow this woman to anoint My head. Thou art thinking that she is a sinner, but thou art wrong. She, out of love, has fulfilled what thou didst leave undone. Thou hast not shown Me the honor due to guests." Then He turned to Magdalen, who was still standing there, and said: "Go in peace! Much has been forgiven thee." At these words Magdalen rejoined her companions, and they left the house together. Then Jesus spoke of her to the guests. He called her a good woman full of compassion. He censured the criticizing of others, public accusations, and remarks upon the exterior fault of others while the speakers often hid in their own hearts much greater, though secret evils. Jesus continued speaking and teaching for a considerable time, and then returned with His followers to the inn.

Magdalen was deeply touched and impressed by all she had seen and heard. She was interiorly vanquished. And because she was possessed of a certain impetuous spirit of self-sacrifice, a certain greatness of soul, she longed to do something to honor Jesus and to testify to Him her emotion. She had noticed with chagrin that neither before nor during the meal had He, the most wonderful, the holiest of teachers, He, the most compassionate, the most miraculous Helper of mankind, received from these Pharisees any mark of honor, any of those polite attentions usually extended to guests, and therefore she felt herself impelled to do what she had done. The words of Jesus, "If even one would be moved to come to Me!" still lingered in her memory. The little flask, which was about a hand in height, she generally

carried with her as do the grand ladies of our own
day. Magdalen's dress was white, embroidered with
large red flowers and tiny green leaves. The sleeves
were wide, gathered in and fastened by bracelets.
The robe was cut wide and hung loose in the back.
It was open in front to just above the knee, where it
was caught by straps, or cords. The bodice, both back
and front, was ornamented with cords and jewels. It
passed over the shoulders like a scapular and was
fastened at the sides; under it was another colored
tunic. The veil that she usually wound about her neck
she had, on entering the banquet hall, opened wide
and thrown over her whole person. Magdalen was
taller than all the other women, robust, but yet graceful. She had very beautiful, tapering fingers, a small,
delicate foot, a wealth of beautiful long hair, and
there was something imposing in all her movements.

When Magdalen returned to the inn with her companions, Martha took her to another about an hour
distant and near the baths of Bethulia. There she
found Mary and the holy women awaiting her coming, Mary conversed with her. Magdalen gave an
account of Jesus' discourse, while the two other women
related the circumstances of Magdalen's anointing
and Jesus' words to her. All insisted on Magdalen's
remaining and going back with them, at least for
awhile, to Bethania. But she replied that she must
return to Magdalum to make some arrangements
in her household, a resolution very distasteful to her
pious friends. She could not, however, cease talking
of the impressions she had received and of the majesty,
force, sweetness, and miracles of Jesus. She felt that
she must follow Him, that her own life was an unworthy one, and that she ought to join her sister and
friends. She became very thoughtful, she wept from
time to time, and her heart grew lighter. Nevertheless, she could not be induced to remain, so she
returned to Magdalum with her maid. Martha accompanied her a part of the way, and then joined the

holy women who were going back to Capharnaum.

Magdalen was taller and more beautiful than the other women. Dina, however, was much more active and dexterous, very cheerful, ever ready to oblige, like a lively, affectionate girl, and she was moreover very humble. But the Blessed Virgin surpassed them all in her marvelous beauty. Although in external loveliness she may have had her equal, and may have even been excelled by Magdalen in certain striking features, yet she far outshone them all in her indescribable air of simplicity, modesty, earnestness, sweetness, and gentleness. She was so very pure, so free from all earthly impressions that in her one saw only the reflex image of God in His creature. No one's bearing resembled hers, except that of her Son. Her countenance surpassed that of all women in its unspeakable purity, innocence, gravity, wisdom, peace, and sweet, devout loveliness. Her whole appearance was noble, and yet she was like a simple, innocent child. She was very grave, very quiet, and often pensive, but never did her sadness destroy the beauty of her countenance, for her tears flowed softly down her placid face.

Magdalen was soon again in her old track. She received the visits of men who spoke in the usual disparaging way of Jesus, His journeys, His doctrine, and of all who followed Him. They ridiculed what they heard of Magdalen's visit to Gabara, and looked upon it as a very unlikely story. As for the rest, they declared that they found Magdalen more beautiful and charming than ever. It was by such speeches that Magdalen allowed herself to be infatuated and her good impressions dissipated. She soon sank deeper than before, and her relapse into sin gave the devil greater power over her. He attacked her more vigorously when he saw that he might possibly lose her. She became possessed, and often fell into cramps and convulsions.

TAN·BOOKS

TAN Books was founded in 1967 to preserve the spiritual, intellectual and liturgical traditions of the Catholic Church. At a critical moment in history TAN kept alive the great classics of the Faith and drew many to the Church. In 2008 TAN was acquired by Saint Benedict Press. Today TAN continues its mission to a new generation of readers.

From its earliest days TAN has published a range of booklets that teach and defend the Faith. Through partnerships with organizations, apostolates, and mission-minded individuals, well over 10 million TAN booklets have been distributed.

More recently, TAN has expanded its publishing with the launch of Catholic calendars and daily planners—as well as Bibles, fiction, and multimedia products through its sister imprints Catholic Courses (CatholicCourses.com) and Saint Benedict Press (SaintBenedictPress.com).

Today TAN publishes over 500 titles in the areas of theology, prayer, devotions, doctrine, Church history, and the lives of the saints. TAN books are published in multiple languages and found throughout the world in schools, parishes, bookstores and homes.

For a free catalog, visit us online at
TANBooks.com

Or call us toll-free at
(800) 437-5876